D1563876

AUGUSTINE'S PREACHED THEOLOGY

Augustine's Preached Theology

Living as the Body of Christ

J. Patout Burns Jr.

William B. Eerdmans Publishing Company

Grand Rapids, Michigan

Wm. B. Eerdmans Publishing Co.
4035 Park East Court SE, Grand Rapids, Michigan 49546
www.eerdmans.com

28 27 26 25 24 23 22   1 2 3 4 5 6 7

ISBN 978-0-8028-8022-2

Library of Congress Cataloging-in-Publication Data

A catalog record for this book is available from the Library of Congress.

For
Robin Margaret Jensen,
who discussed generously
all that this volume contains—
and much that it does not—
in hundreds of dinner conversations

CONTENTS

CONTENTS

FOREWORD

W HEN I ASSIGN MY FIRST-YEAR DIVINITY STUDENTS Gregory of Nazianzus's *Theological Orations*, the first point of shock for them comes with the realization that these orations were *actual* Christian sermons, preached in an actual church and to a real congregation. The initial cause for their incredulity centers on the length of sermons that are so theologically dense. How could a preacher commit such a long text to memory? And how could a congregation listen to such a lengthy message? In a culture so dominated by the visual media, it is hard to imagine the aural experience of listening to orations that were crafted as works of verbal artistry. Moreover, the sermons of the patristic era generally lack illustrative stories that are standard features of contemporary preaching. Rather, the stories used were often vivid word pictures taken from diverse but, to the church father's thinking, interconnected portions of scripture. Often their points were moral or sought to arouse holy emotions of contrition or compassion. Whereas contemporary sermons have a moral or therapeutic focus—a point of overlap with patristic preaching—the thrust of patristic homilies often was simply the depiction of the wonder and mystery of the triune God.

Precisely here in the differences between ancient and modern preaching lies the value of studying sermons of a bygone era. The differences lift us out of our present context with all its cultural norms and social expectations and provide us an opportunity to be reflective about those norms and expectations precisely by showing us alternative ways of living and worshipping under vastly different norms. The recently published translations of patristic sermons, not the least of which being The Works of Saint Augustine: A Translation for the 21st Century by New City Press, is of tremendous value for the modern church, giving pastors and students access to more sermons than ever before, translated into a contemporary literary style that is more easily understood.

Sometimes the content of the sermons reflects values and beliefs drastically different from modern commonplace assumptions. One example might be how Augustine, in his homilies on marriage, argues that the intention behind all holy acts of sexual intimacy must be procreation (see p. 135, below). Even when the sermons, like the Bible itself, seem strange—we're not in Kansas anymore—they have the value of reminding us that we cannot read these texts through the lens of our twenty-first-century Western assumptions. Even familiar terms such as "grace" or "faith" or "reason" do not carry meanings that directly correlate with our modern understandings. Often we need a guide to chart our way through this alien intellectual and spiritual landscape. But with such a guide, we can discover the value of listening patiently to familiar words clothed with different meanings. Paying attention to these sermons delivers us from confining our reading to the echo chamber of our particular form of the Christian faith and in so doing allows us to see the richness that lies in the theological breadth of the Christian tradition across the generations.

Though the differences may be astonishing at times, more often these ancient sermons address perennial pastoral matters with a boldness whose honesty, if shocking, is also refreshing. Such is the case when, in discussing his congregation's questions about giving to the church, Augustine answers in an imagined dialogue. Question: "How much should we give?" Answer: The Law specifies a tenth; this is what the Scribes and Pharisees gave. But then Augustine quotes Jesus's words to his disciples, "Unless your righteousness exceeds that of the Scribes and the Pharisees, you shall not enter the Kingdom of heaven" (Matt. 5:20). Augustine leaves hanging in the air the question, "What does that imply?" (see p. 35, below). Such is the forthrightness of which many a contemporary preacher is envious.

But Augustine was no show orator playing the provocateur simply for the sake of demonstrating his craft. Rather, he deployed such rhetorical frankness because of a deep-seated conviction: God speaks. God spoke through Ambrose's sermons even when Augustine sought nothing more than to assess Ambrose's oratorical gifts. And Augustine's heart was convicted as God's word for him came to him in a certain garden in Milan through Paul's letter to the Romans. For, as John's prologue declares, "In the beginning was the Word and the Word was with God and the Word was God." God's actions in the world are, for Augustine, his mode of speaking to and through creation. In his homilies on Jesus's bread of life discourse in

John 6, Augustine begins by observing that both the barley grains and the barley loaves had the same maker. The seeds were fashioned by the Word, "through whom all things were made," and the loaves were multiplied by that very same Word now incarnate in Jesus of Nazareth. Therefore, they both have the same purpose; they are signs (*sacramenta*) designed to arouse wonder. In the seed, there is the wonder of germination and transformation; and with the loaves, there is the miracle of multiplication. But in both, Augustine says, "Something was brought to the attention of the senses whereby the mind would be alerted, something displayed before the eyes whereby the understanding could be exercised so that we might marvel at the invisible God through his visible works . . . [and thus be] raised up to faith and purified by faith" (*Tractates on the Gospel of John* 24.1; trans. Hill, 423–24). Thus he exhorts his congregants to "*read* the miracle," for it is the deed through which the Word speaks (24.2; trans. Hill, 424). Out of this conviction, Augustine employed all his considerable rhetorical skill to give his people the sense that Christ was speaking *to them*. Thus when he would renarrate an event from the gospel, Augustine would often quote Jesus's exact words in which he addresses his disciples with the second-person plural pronoun. Immediately, Augustine would then rephrase or elaborate on Jesus's words, still using the second-person plural pronoun (e.g., 25.3; trans. Hill, 432). Here Augustine is intentionally ambiguous. Is this simply a paraphrase of Jesus's words? Is the "you" the disciples in the gospel? Or are Augustine's congregants the antecedent? Augustine's answer would be, "Both." For the incarnate Word who spoke to his disciples in first-century Judea now speaks to the church at Hippo through those same ancient words glossed in the words of the modern preacher. The preacher's tasks of reading scripture and proclaiming the Word are, for Augustine, a living speech act, which, like the miracles of the barley seed and the loaves and fishes, raises the congregations' minds through these signs to the God who spoke the signs and whose indwelling luminous Spirit gives understanding.

One of the deep, though rarely spoken, fears of all young preachers is whether he or she will have something new and interesting to say each Sunday for fifty Sundays out of the year for a lifelong ministry of forty or fifty years: "How will I make the resurrection story fresh and interesting to my people for the next fifty Easters?" Augustine, who preached two to three times a week (see p. 2, below), does not seem to have been troubled by that question, in part at least because of his view of the sacramental nature of scripture. When he comes to the end of the feeding of the five thousand, Augustine explains that the twelve baskets of scraps of bread signify the meanings of Christ's teachings that we are not able to consume. This may be because we lack the maturity to grasp certain spiritual nuances in the text. But it also may lie in the surplus meaning Augustine sees as inherent in all scripture. Since Christ, who is the Father's expression of his infinite love for the world, is the content of all scripture, then scripture possesses a surplus meaning that is infinite and inexhaustible. Augustine affirms this when he describes the believers' communion with God in "a vast inner shrine" (*Tractates on the Gospel of John* 25.14; trans. Hill, 442), where, quoting Psalm 35:8–9, "they will get drunk on the abundance of your house" (25.17; trans. Hill, 445). The superabundance of God's goodness, wisdom, and power revealed in scripture means that there will always be new insights to be gleaned and proclaimed.

Augustine's sacramental and christological view of scripture as always having a surplus meaning offers a fuller and more expansive view of scripture. He does not see one passage of scripture as having a single, historical meaning that is confined to the author's intent. Rather, Augustine recognizes that when the Holy Spirit speaks in and through us, whether an ancient prophet or a modern preacher, our words carry more meanings than we intend at that moment. Thus, as at Pentecost, the gospel can be heard and understood as having many meanings, all of which cohere in a message of love.

One of the ironies of Augustinian studies is how little attention, comparatively speaking, has been given to his sermons. Though Augustine speaks at length in *Confessions* about his training in and teaching of rhetoric, the fruit of that early formation has been overlooked. It is as if we have decided that the writings of Augustine the Christian philosopher and theologian—e.g., *Confessions, City of God, On the Trinity*—are the works of enduring value that reveal his true genius, as if preaching were merely one of those duties the bishop of Hippo had to perform in between writing profound theological treatises. Such a view, however, loses sight of an important point. Augustine the convert to Christianity never stopped being Augustine the orator. As critical as he was of the vane aspirations of his teachers and parents who saw oratory as the way to rise socially, nevertheless Augustine, reflecting on the relationship between his early education and his present work as a bishop, prayed, "Turn to your service whatever may be of use in what I learned as in boyhood. May I dedicate to your service my power to speak and write and read and count; for when I learnt vanities, you imposed discipline on me and have forgiven me the sin of desiring pleasure for these vanities" (*Confessions* 1.15.24 [CCSL 27:13; trans. Chadwick, 18]). Augustine the bishop remained the orator whose prodigious skills were now devoted to serving God by fulfilling Jesus's command to Peter, "Feed my sheep."

In the volume before you, Patout Burns offers a corrective to this omission. He has laid out a systematic treatment of the major themes, pastoral and theological, that occur in Augustine's various homilies. As someone who has spent years working through Augustine's corpus, treatises as well as sermons, particularly surrounding Augustine's doctrine of grace, Burns has gained a familiarity with these texts as well as with Augustine's complex North African context to see the overlap and the differences between the treatises and the homilies. His decades of experience reading Augustine make him a perfect guide into these rich sermons. Through his analysis of their theological content and rhetorical artistry, Burns gives us insight into these sermons as examples of pastoral theology, that is, adaptations of themes from his treatises in a homiletical form that would inform, edify, and delight his congregants. Inasmuch as a bishop's sermons in late antiquity were recorded and preserved to be models of exposition for their priests, this volume and Augustine's sermons themselves are not for academics alone. They are also for women and men who know the weekly challenge and the pleasure of preaching the word by which God speaks to his people. *Tolle lege.*

J. Warren Smith

Abbreviations

CCSL	Corpus Christianorum: Series Latina
CSEL	Corpus Scriptorum Ecclesiasticorum Latinorum
MA	*Miscellanea Agostiniana*, ed. G. Morin and A. Casamassa
PL	Patrologiae Cursus Completus: Series Latina, ed. J.-P. Migne
PLS	Patrologiae Cursus Completus: Series Latina, Supplementum
RBén	*Revue bénédictine*
SC	Sources chrétiennes
WSA	The Works of Saint Augustine: A Translation for the 21st Century, ed. John E. Rotelle
Aug.	**Augustinus Hipponensis**
Adu. Iud.	*Aduersus Iudaeos* (PL 42:51–64)
Bapt.	*De baptismo contra Donatistas* (CSEL 51:145–375)
Beat.	*De beata uita* (CCSL 29:65–85)
Ciu.	*De ciuitate Dei* (CCSL 47–48)
Conf.	*Confessionum libri XIII* (CCSL 27:1–273)
Cons.	*De consensu euangelistarum* (CSEL 43)
Corrept.	*De correptione et gratia* (CSEL 92:219–80)
Cresc.	*Contra Cresconium Donatistam* (CSEL 52:325–582)
Doct. Chr.	*De doctrina christiana* (CCSL 32:1–167)
Ep.	*Epistulae* (CCSL 31–31B; CSEL 34, 44, 57, 58)
Ep. Divj.	*Epistulae a Divjak editae* (CSEL 88)
Ep. Io.	*In epistulam Iohannis ad Parthos Tractatus* (PL 35:1977–2062)
Eu. Io.	*In euangelium Iohannis tractatus* (CCSL 36)
Faust.	*Contra Faustum Manichaeum* (CSEL 25.1:251–797)
Fid. et op.	*De fide et operibus* (CSEL 41:35–97)

Gal.	*Expositio in epistulam ad Galatas* (CSEL 84:55–141)
Gaud.	*Contra Gaudentium Donatistarum episcopum* (CSEL 53:201–74)
Gen. litt.	*De Genesi ad litteram* (CSEL 28.1:3–435)
Gen. Man.	*De Genesi contra Manichaeos* (CSEL 91:67–172)
Gest. Pel.	*De gestis Pelagii* (CSEL 42:51–122)
Grat. Chr.	*De gratia Christi* (CSEL 42:125–66)
Hept.	*Quaestiones in Heptateuchum* (CCSL 33:1–377)
Iul. op. imp.	*Contra secundam Iuliani responsionem imperfectum opus* (CSEL 85.1:3–506; PL 45:1337–1608)
Leg.	*Contra adversarium legis et prophetarum* (CCSL 49:35–131)
Lib.	*De libero arbitrio* (CSEL 74:3–154)
Maxim.	*Contra Maximinum Arianum* (PL 42:743–814)
Mor. eccl.	*De moribus ecclesiae catholicae* (CSEL 90:3–156)
Nat. et grat.	*De natura et gratia* (CSEL 60:233–99)
Op. Mon.	*De opere monachorum* (CSEL 41:531–96)
Parm.	*Contra epistulam Parmeniani* (CSEL 51:19–141)
Pecc. merit.	*De peccatorum meritis* (CSEL 60:3–151)
Pelag.	*Contra duas epistulas Pelagianorum* (CSEL 60:423–570)
Perf.	*De perfectione iustitiae hominis* (CSEL 42:3–48)
Petil.	*Contra litteras Petiliani* (CSEL 52:3–227)
Psal.	*Enarrationes in Psalmos* (CCSL 38–40; CSEL 93.1A–95.5)
Quaest.	*De diuersis quaestionibus* (CCSL 44A:11–249)
Rom. inc.	*Epistulae ad Romanos inchoata expositio* (CSEL 84:55–141)
Rom. prop.	*Expositio quarundam propositionum ex epistula ad Romanos* (CSEL 84:3–52)
Serm.	*Sermones* (PL 38–39; CCSL 41, 41Aa, 41Ba)
Serm. Cail.	*Sermones a Caillau editi* (*MA* 1:243–64)
Serm. Casin.	*Sermones in bibliotheca Casinensi* (*MA* 1:413–19)
Serm. Denis	*Sermones a Denis editi* (*MA* 1:11–164)
Serm. Dolb.	*Sermones a Dolbeau editi* (Dolbeau, *Vingt-six Sermons*)
Serm. Dom.	*De sermone Domini in monte* (CCSL 35:1–188)
Serm. Etaix	*Sermones ab Etaix editi* (*RBén* 86 [1976]: 41–48)
Serm. Frang.	*Sermones a Frangipane editi* (*MA* 1:212–37)
Serm. frg. Lamb.	*Sermonum fragmenta a C. Lambot edita* (*RBén* 79 [1969]: 208–14)
Serm. frg. Verbr.	*Sermonum fragmenta a Verbraken edita* (*RBén* 84 [1974]: 253, 265–66)

Serm. Guelf.	*Sermones Moriniani ex collectione Guelferbytana* (*MA* 1:450–585)
Serm. Haffner	*Sermo a F. Haffner editus* (*RBén* 77 [1967]: 326–28)
Serm. Lamb.	*Sermones a Lambot editi* (PLS 2:744–840)
Serm. Liver.	*Sermo a Liverani editus* (*MA* 1:391–95)
Serm. Mai	*Sermones a Mai editi* (*MA* 1:285–386)
Serm. Morin	*Sermones a Morin editi* (*MA* 1:289–664)
Serm. Wilm.	*Sermones a Wilmart editi* (*MA* 1:673–719)
Simpl.	*De diuersis quaestionibus ad Simplicianum* (CCSL 44:7–91)
Spec.	*Speculum* (CSEL 12:3–285)
Trin.	*De Trinitate* (CCSL 50–50A)
C. Th.	**Codex Theodosianus, ed. T. Mommsen**
Cypr.	**Cyprianus Carthaginensis**
Eleem.	*De opere et eleemosynis* (CCSL 3A:55–72)
Ep.	*Epistulae* (CCSL 3B–3D)
Laps.	*De lapsis* (CCSL 3:221–42)
Unit. eccl.	*De catholicae ecclesiae unitate* (CCSL 3:249–68)
Didache	**Didache** (SC 248)
De diuitiis	**De diuitiis** (PLS 1:1380–1418)
Irenaeus	**Irenaeus Lugdunensis**
Haer.	*Adversus haereses* (SC 263–64, 293–94, 210–11, 100, 152–53)
Reg. Carth.	**Registri ecclesiae Carthaginensis excerpta** (CCSL 149:182–228)
Tert.	**Tertullianus**
Bapt.	*De baptismo* (CCSL 1:277–95)
Paen.	*De paenitentia* (CCSL 1:321–40)
Pud.	*De pudicitia* (CCSL 2:1281–1330)
Tyc.	**Tyconius Afer**
Reg.	*Liber regularum*, Texts and Studies, 3.1, 1894 (SC 488)

INTRODUCTION

I N MY FINAL TEACHING POSITION, at Vanderbilt University Divinity School, I was responsible for an introductory course, "The Formation of the Christian Tradition," that provided a survey of the development of Christian doctrine and practice from the period following the formation of the New Testament through the European Middle Ages to the eve of the Reformation. Most of the students in the course were preparing for some form of church ministry and many were already engaged in it. I came to realize that the level of their attention and interest rose when the topic of my lecture was presented in a way that they could imagine themselves using in a sermon. "That'll preach" was the highest form of approval of an early Christian doctrine or interpretation of the Bible. What would *not* preach, what they were certain was sure to be rejected or ignored by the congregations they served or in which they worshiped was met with general resistance. They liked Augustine's doctrine of the gratuity of divine initiative and effective support but not his (thereby entailed) doctrine on the unmerited predestination of the saved. One extended exchange ended with the exasperated student's "I'm not buying it," and my "It's not for sale; I just need you to understand what he wrote and why." Augustine, as will be noted in this study, carefully avoided preaching on predestination and even avoided the topic in his treatises for decades.

The subtitle of this volume was inspired by the Gospel of Luke, "Forgive and you will be forgiven; give and it will be given to you" (Luke 6:37–38), a text that Augustine cited more than twenty times in his preaching and to which he alluded regularly. As the second and third chapters of this volume show, sharing wealth and pardon with one's neighbor were closely linked practices. As the remaining chapters explain, both were deeply rooted in his understanding of the Christian life as manifestations of the presence of charity, the love of God and neighbor, that was the work of the Holy Spirit in the members of the body of Christ.

The Henry Luce Fellowship in Theology through the Association of Theological Schools supported a broad range of research projects. All of them were linked to current practice of religion in the modern world. The grant that supported this study of Augustine's preached theology, despite its historical focus, was thereby directed toward its modern relevance. This study of the relation between Augustine of Hippo's preaching and the development of his theology is one of the reports of that research.

AUGUSTINE AS PREACHER

Aurelius Augustine was bishop of the church in Hippo Regius, in the Roman civil province of Proconsular Africa from 396 through 428.* He had a good literary and rhetorical education in Africa. He was a successful public orator attached to the imperial government in Milan, then the capital of the Roman Empire. In his early thirties, he turned away from that career, received baptism from Ambrose, the bishop of Milan, and returned to Africa, planning a life dedicated to the intellectual exploration of the Christianity in which his mother had raised him. Instead, he was drafted into the clergy as a presbyter (elder) in the port city of Hippo Regius in 391. He was immediately given preaching assignments usually reserved for the more advanced; he preached *On the Faith and the Creed* to the bishops of Africa assembled at the Council of Hippo in October 393. Made bishop and given full responsibility for the church in the city and in many villages in the agrarian area surrounding it, he would continue preaching regularly—two or three times a week—for more than thirty years to the congregation in Hippo. As Augustine traveled extensively in Roman Africa on church business, he was expected to preach in the towns he visited, particularly in Carthage.

Immediately after his first ordination to clerical office, Augustine asked for and received time to study the scriptures on which he would be preaching and writing. He became familiar with them, first in Latin translation of the Greek text of both the Old Testament and the New Testament. Later, he moved to the Vulgate translation that the Roman presbyter Jerome produced from the Hebrew Old Testament and a revision of prior Latin

---

* Hippo, along with much of western Proconsular Africa, remained in the ecclesiastical province of Numidia when Constantine realigned the boundary between the two civil provinces in 314 CE.

2

translations of that Greek text. Augustine occasionally checked other Latin translations and even the Greek version of difficult or disputed passages, though he seldom mentioned such research in his sermons. He eventually acquired a detailed knowledge of the scriptures but admitted that he still needed the written text; unlike some of his congregants, he could not recite long passages of scripture from memory.[1]

Although Augustine prepared his sermons, he did not write them in advance. He had been trained in the common practice of composing by dictating to a secretary; he used it even for his complex treatises. He was reliant on a written text of the scripture as he preached but the plan for a sermon and the supporting materials—mostly related scriptural passages—were probably in his memory. This method allowed him to adapt his presentation to inspirations of the moment and the responses of the congregation. Thus, he was able to provide an exposition of a psalm that the lector proclaimed by mistake. The resulting sermon may not have been as smooth as others, but it did cover the text well. The surviving texts of Augustine's sermons were produced by notaries who made shorthand transcripts during the sermons and turned them into full texts, which were then stored in the episcopal library in Hippo. The same must have been done for the many sermons that Augustine preached in Carthage.

As he approached the end of his career, Augustine began reviewing and editing all his literary production, intending to provide information—date and circumstances of composition and delivery—along with corrections he deemed necessary. His *Reconsiderations* covers all his treatises, in chronological order. Fortunately, most of the treatises he surveyed survived. Unfortunately for historians of his work and times, he never found time to review his correspondence and sermons. Still, many letters and sermons were passed down in various collections, some of which must have been made in Hippo during the years following his death. The texts survived, like much of ancient literature, through the copies and distribution networks of monastic and cathedral libraries. Some are still being discovered in the remnants of those great institutions that were taken over by municipalities and universities.

EDITIONS OF AUGUSTINE'S PREACHED WORKS

The foundational collection of Augustine's sermons was edited by the French Benedictine congregation of St. Maur in the late seventeenth century. That edition introduced a system of numbering the sermons, based on the books of the Bible and the sequence of the liturgical year. That system took hold and became normative. Subsequent discoveries were integrated by adding a letter of the alphabet to the number identifying sermons on the same or similar topic or scriptural passage in the Maurist sequence. These more recent discoveries are signaled in this volume by providing both the name of the post-Maurist collection or editor and both numbers identifying the sermon. Thus, for example, *Serm. Dolb.* 21(159B).3 refers to the third paragraph of Sermon 21 in the collection discovered and edited by Francois Dolbeau and its place (159B) in the Maurist numbering sequence. Some, but not all, sermons in the Maurist collection have both chapter and paragraph numbers. Thus, *Serm.* 71.2.4 refers to Sermon 71, chapter 2, paragraph 4. Since each of the two sets of numbered divisions is continuous through the sermon, the chapter number is sometimes omitted in modern editions and translations. In the *Expositions of the Psalms*, in contrast, some texts required multiple sermons. In these cases, the first number indicates the psalm; the second may refer to the sermon or the paragraph; the final number refers to the paragraph. In some systems, the expositions of Psalms 19–33 are given an additional initial number (1 or 2) to distinguish the longer sermons from the earlier brief commentaries. Thus, *Psal.* 32.1.22 refers to a brief commentary on Psalm 33 and *Psal.* 32.2.2.8 to the longer exposition of Psalm 33, Sermon 2, paragraph 8. Augustine's *Expositions of the Psalms* are numbered according to the Septuagint (Greek) translation of the Psalter. References to the Psalms in the text of the essays use the Hebrew numbering that is common in most modern translations.

This volume has been designed as a resource for identifying and studying Augustine's theology as it was developed in his preaching. References are generally limited to the texts of the various sermons of Augustine, following the standard divisions of Augustine's works into books, chapters, and paragraphs. Where the text of Augustine is translated in the exposition, a reference to the contemporary critical edition of the Latin is also included. Little attempt has been made to coordinate the sermons with parallel treatments in Augustine's treatises and letters. When such connections are considered, the discussion is in the notes rather than the text.

The Chronology of Augustine's Preached Works

As has been noted above, the chronological sequence of Augustine's treatises is indicated in the order of their treatment in his *Reconsiderations*. He provided no such general sequence for either his correspondence or his preached works. The editors attempted a relative chronological sequence of his correspondence, like that of his treatises, by using internal references to persons or topics treated in similar ways in his treatises. In addition, some few external references such as datable events or the names of office holders in the church or empire are found. Sometimes the city in which the sermon was delivered can be coordinated with Augustine's reconstructed travel schedule.

Establishing the chronology of Augustine's *Sermons to the People*, *Expositions of the Psalms*, and *Tractates on the Gospel and First Letter of John* has been a sustained and challenging enterprise. It has been pursued with ingenuity by tenacious scholars of more than ordinary erudition, using the smallest of clues. Perhaps the most significant success has been achieved dating materials to the first decade of the fifth century. This is anchored by correlating the early *Tractates on the Gospel and First Letter of John* with the *Expositions of the Psalms* 119–33, the Psalms of Ascent. Subsequent work on the *Tractates on the Gospel of John* by Marie-François Berrouard and others has extended that success.[2] To these sermons were added another set of *Expositions of the Psalms* and a good number of the *Sermons to the People* discovered in Mayence and edited by François Dolbeau.[3] Pierre-Marie Hombert and Hubertus Drobner have continued and systematized that work.

The present study attempts to exploit these advances in dating primarily to assist in distinguishing the different ways that Augustine spoke about a particular topic. In this sense, in its methods—but not the grand sweep of its erudition—it parallels the work of Anthony Dupont's study of grace in Augustine's sermons.[4] The chronological tables accompanying the *Sermones* and *Enarrationes in Psalmos* in the *Sant' Agostino* website (www.augustinus.it) provide a readily accessible summary of the judgments of specialists on individual texts. The scriptural indices in the *Corpus Augustinianum Gissense* database were then used to identify citations of the relevant scriptural texts in these sermons and detect changes in Augustine's use and interpretation of these passages. The result was a grouping of texts that often suggested chronological development but not without some significant outliers. These results allowed different types of studies that are reported in the following chapters.

In some instances, Augustine's treatment of a topic is concentrated in a small number of well-dated sermons. The most substantial discussion of the eucharist, for example, is to be found in two sets of sermons. In sequential sermons belonging to the *Tractates on the Gospel of John*, and dealing with the latter part of the Bread of Life discourse in the sixth chapter of the Gospel of John, Augustine explained and established his doctrine on the identification of the eucharistic body of Christ.[5] The other discussions are found in short sermons preached to the newly baptized on Easter Day, during the ritual itself rather than immediately following the readings so that only the baptized Christians were present.[6] These presentations manifest no significant change in his thought but different emphasis in presentation.

The forgiveness of sins, in contrast, was explained and urged by Augustine in many sermons, and his presentations exhibit some variety. Moreover, the sermons in which the topic is treated have not been so successfully dated that they can be studied in a chronological order that manifests a development in Augustine's thinking and speaking about the practice. So, the presentation in this volume attempts to catalog the different ways he addressed the topic and the elements they have in common.

The study of baptism shows the influence of the conflict of the controversy with the Donatist party. Adherents of this Christian movement in Africa attempted to separate themselves from the corrupting influence of the idolatry of the Roman Empire and the failures of their fellow believers. They refused to recognize the baptism and holiness of the Catholic communion, with whom they competed for members and social influence. Some elements of Augustine's instruction on baptism seem designed to prepare his hearers for debates with these neighbors—in the streets, shops, and homes of their common city. The discussions of the church's power to forgive sins in the sermons, however, bear the imprint of his engagement in his treatise *On Baptism* with the writings of Cyprian, the bishop of Carthage in the mid-third century, rather than the significantly different approach he took in his polemical treatises responding to Donatist adversaries: the recent bishop Parmenian of Carthage and the emerging leader, Petilian of Constantine, as well as a layman of that city, Cresconius.

Unlike these topics, Augustine's treatment of the heritage of Adam and Eve that defined the condition of their offspring changed, sometimes dramatically. Augustine's early treatments focused on inherited mortality and the consequent development of habits of personal sin. Four sermons preached in Carthage in the summer of 413 CE asserted a doctrine of inherited sin, guilt, and punishment with a clarity and force that is hard to identify in sermons or treatises that preceded the outbreak of the Pelagian controversy in that city a couple of years earlier. The chapter treating this material not only will identify different approaches that Augustine took to the issues but will suggest a chronological development of his thought, albeit one not without unexpected lurches forward or backward.

Using This Book

Each of the following chapters is intended to stand on its own, so that they may be used independently of one another. References are made, however, to parallel or supplementary materials in the other chapters. Occasional explanatory notes will be found at the bottom of the page; references to secondary studies are gathered at the end of the volume. The studies of Christian practices are placed before the four essays on doctrinal issues.

All of the sermons and scriptural expositions studied in this volume are to be found in recent English translation in section III of the collection *The Works of Augustine for the 21st Century,* that was initially edited by John E. Rotelle, OSA. The *Sermons to the People* are in volumes III/1–11, were translated by Edmund Hill, OP, and are preceded by the introduction of Cardinal Michele Pellegrino. The *Tractates on the Gospel of John* are in volumes III/12–13, also translated by Edmund Hill, OP, and introduced by Allan D. Fitzgerald, OSA. The *Tractates on the First Epistle of John* are in volume III/14, translated and introduced by Boniface Ramsey. The *Expositions on the Psalms* are in volumes III/15–20, translated by Maria Boulding, OSB, and introduced by Michael Fiedrowicz.[7] This edition is also available on the *Past Masters* database through many academic libraries. More concise essays under the titles *Enarrationes in Psalmos, In Johannis euangelium tractatus,* and *Sermones* are in the encyclopedia, *Augustine through the Ages,* edited by Allan Fitzgerald, OSA.[8]

The Latin Maurist edition of these works was republished in the *Patrologia Latina* volumes 35–38. That edition, along with the materials discovered more recently is available online through the www.augustinus.it website, along with older translations of many texts in modern European languages. The Maurist editions of the *Tractates of the Gospel of John* and the *Expositions of the Psalms* were reprinted in the *Corpus Christiano-rum, Series Latina*, volumes 36, 38–40. Critical editions of the *Sermons to the People*, beginning in volume 41 of that series, remain incomplete. A critical edition of the *Expositions on the Psalms* is nearing completion in the *Corpus Scriptorum Ecclesiasticorum Latinorum* series, beginning with volume 93/1A.

Readers are encouraged to use the essays in this volume as an introduction and guide to the reading of the transcripts of Augustine's own preaching.

Unless otherwise noted, scripture quotations are translated from the Latin version appearing in the edition of Augustine's text being cited or interpreted.

Chapter One

INTERPRETING THE SCRIPTURE

AUGUSTINE'S PREACHING WAS FOCUSED on the interaction of the message of scripture with the practice and meaning of Christian life. Most of the surviving records of this ministry are concerned with a particular text of scripture rather than on a topic or question: all of his expositions of Psalms, more than half of his treatments of the Gospel of John, all of those on the First Letter of John, and many of his sermons to the people of Hippo, Carthage, and other African churches. In all his preaching, moreover, Augustine constantly cited a wide range of scriptural texts and images to instruct and exhort his hearers. His objective in preaching was seldom limited to the discovery and communication of the meaning of the text, as it was, for example, in his successive commentaries on Genesis and his early treatises on Romans and Galatians. Instead, he sought to articulate how scriptural truths should be lived by Christians. Thus, his constant interpretative guides were both the rule of faith and the law of love.[1]

Augustine never abandoned his interest in the literal and historical meaning of the scriptural text that he articulated in the second book of his treatise *On Christian Teaching*. There he called upon learned Christians to produce dictionaries of the places, animals, and plants mentioned in the Bible, so that the full import of the text might be better understood and appreciated.[2] In written commentary, though seldom in live preaching, he occasionally attended to the Septuagint Greek version of the Psalms and to the variations within and between the Latin and Greek texts of the New Testament to which he had access.[3] When a doctrinal point was at issue, he could rival Origen as a close reader of the biblical text. His developing interpretation of Romans 7:15–25 advanced through an ever-closer reading of that text until he identified inbred lust as a sinful but unavoidable evil.[4]

In dealing with Adam and Christ, he preferred to interpret the whole of Romans 5:12–21 rather than isolate its first sentence.[5]

In his preaching, moreover, Augustine heard the scripture as directed to himself and his congregation. He understood that God could address and move individuals by presenting a particular scriptural text or guiding a speaker to offer considerations adapted to a chosen individual's dispositions—most famously illustrated in the conversion narratives of his *Confessions*.[6] That theory bore fruit consistently in Augustine's sermons: he not only prayed that God would guide his preaching but also sought analogies in the daily lives of his hearers, which they might appreciate and act upon.[7]

Both the words recorded and the actions narrated in the scriptural text carried revelatory meaning for the Christian, Augustine insisted. Christ himself spoke, as shall be seen, not only in the gospels but elsewhere in the Bible. Were Christ to appear before the congregation, Augustine suggested, the vision alone would bring little profit to the gathering unless he spoke. In fact, the gospels showed that Christ's bodily presence had been of little advantage to most of the people who encountered him.[8] Once absent in body, Christ addressed the community in the scripture read aloud, the psalms they sung, and even the sermon they heard.[9] While most events of people's lives were beyond their control, Christ had chosen deliberately the encounters and actions of his birth, ministry, and death. As a result, the details of these events as reported in the gospels could carry his message as fully and meaningfully as his words. As the Gospel of John showed, Augustine noted, Jesus's miracles had to be meditated upon to grasp their full import. Examples were multiplied: Jesus's flight from the crowd that sought to make him king demonstrated the objective of his mission; his prayer on the mountain as the disciples struggled on the stormy sea foreshadowed the earthly church's relation to her heavenly Lord. Similarly, because Jesus suffered voluntarily rather than under coercion, each of the actions of his passion was a revelation of his interior dispositions.[10] The task of the preacher, Augustine explained, was to draw out these meanings of both Christ's words and his actions for his hearers.

PROPHECY AND FORESHADOWING

In practice, Augustine treated the whole of the scripture as intended by God and therefore meaningful. The Bible was the exposition of a single divine plan and operation for the salvation of humanity. Any event or statement within the narrative, therefore, might be relevant to the understanding and appreciation of any other. More particularly, as shall become apparent, the scripture should be read back-to-front, from the perspective of its culmination in the mission of Christ and the life of the church. All the blessed, beginning with Abel and continuing through the last child baptized before the return of Jesus, belonged to the same City of God established in Christ.[11] The Old Testament could be used to interpret the New Testament, since its events not only prepared for but foretold and foreshadowed those that were to follow. In a similar way, the New Testament narratives and letters clarified the meaning and import of the events, laws, and prayers that formed the preceding history of Israel. The religious rituals of Israel found their full meaning—as well as their salvific efficacy—in the death and resurrection of Jesus. Those preceding interpreted and were interpreted by those following.[12] Thus, Augustine affirmed the historicity of both the foreshadowing and the foreshadowed persons and actions.[13] Each had its own place in the narrative, but its significance was not limited to or exhausted by its role in that one place or time. Some of the actors in the ancient drama, moreover, were privileged to understand the fuller meaning of the events in which they participated. Augustine explained that Abraham had grasped that the promise made to him would be fulfilled in Christ; Moses foresaw the New Covenant even as he codified the old; some of the Israelites perceived the reality symbolized by the manna falling from heaven. Christ's work was not only foreshadowed but recognized as his, by at least some in Israel.[14]

The life of the Christian church could be used in this same dialogic way as the Old Testament both to interpret the New Testament scripture and to be clarified by it. The gospel writers had been able to discern the biblical foreshadowing and prophecies of the events they narrated but only later Christians, who knew the worldwide spread of the church, could grasp the fuller import of some actions narrated in the New Testament. Jesus's resurrection clarified his passion predictions about his death that had so confused his disciples. Fourth-century Christians could witness in the spread of the church the fulfillment of the promise of a numerous progeny made to Abraham.[15] As the Letter to the Hebrews had used the Israelite ritual of atonement to understand the saving power of the death and resurrection of Jesus, so would Augustine use that letter to explain the structure of the community's celebration of the eucharistic ritual and its eschatological fulfillment.[16]

Augustine was, of course, on solid and traditional ground in using this interactive interpretation not only of the two testaments but of the life of the church. He found it employed, for example, in Paul's interpretation of the initiations of Israel in the crossing of the sea and of the church in baptism (1 Cor. 10:1–6, 11).[17] The events were so interrelated that the tense of the verbs being used in the text—past, present, or future—did not always determine the sequence of the events. Events could be spoken of as either past or present while the true referent remained in the future.[18] Thus, Christ told his disciples that he had already made everything known to them, though his teaching would be completed by the Holy Spirit only after his return to heaven.[19] Narratives of events as past could be prophecies of what would be accomplished in the future. Thus, the description of completed events in Psalm 22 was actually a foretelling of the future death of Jesus and the prayer he prayed in the midst of his execution.[20] What appeared to be curses pronounced by the prophets were not pleas for divine vengeance but predictions and warnings of what God intended to accomplish.[21] Augustine even found one instance, in Psalm 104:6, in which a past event was spoken of as still in the future.[22] All this clearly showed, Augustine believed, that the scripture reported a complex web of interrelated events, practices, and pronouncements that could be used to interpret one another, even independently of the chronological sequence of the narratives.

In many instances, the application of the interpretative method of foreshadowing and fulfillment was authorized and even required by the scripture itself. The Pauline contrast of Christ and Adam in Romans 5:12–21 and the Johannine linking of the serpent lifted up in the wilderness to the crucified Christ in John 3:14–15 were explicit instances of such practice. The intercessory role of the Israelite high priest was more ambiguous. Augustine applied it to Christ alone while the Donatist bishop Parmenian insisted that it referred to the faithful Christian bishops as well.[23] Thus, these interpretations sometimes did not stand alone; they required more direct support from the scriptures or church practice.

FIGURATIVE INTERPRETATION

Allegorical or figurative interpretation was assigned a distinctive role in Augustine's preaching. Discussing its techniques in *On Christian Teaching*, he enunciated a rule that had been followed by his predecessors, particularly by Ambrose. Whenever a literal interpretation could not be identified that was both compatible with true faith and good morals and would promote charity among the hearers, then a figurative explanation was to be used to find a meaning that was both true and applicable.[24] For example, anthropomorphic expressions applied to God in scripture must be given an allegorical interpretation because true faith affirmed that the divine was incorporeal.[25] Scripture sometimes used obscure language in order to force its readers and hearers to search for these deeper, spiritual meanings. The translators of the Septuagint Greek Bible shared by Christians and Jews, Augustine believed, had intentionally made the meaning of the Hebrew text more obscure in Greek in order to promote this nonliteral interpretation.[26] Multiple figurative meanings might sometimes be discovered for a single text—many of which were compatible with divine truth and might even have been intended by the authors of the sacred text.[27]

To provide some control on the development and use of figurative interpretations, Augustine argued that the exegete must have an independent basis for affirming the truth of any interpretation constructed by allegory. Usually, the truth discovered by figurative exegesis of one passage must be the literal meaning of some other biblical passage.[28] Thus, he explained that these obscure passages that required figurative interpretation were present in the scripture for the appreciation of truths rather than their discovery. They exercised the preacher's ingenuity and prevented the private reader from becoming bored or finding the message insipid. A challenging text was intended to keep a person at the task of searching for God's meaning and to reward the effort expended in finding it.[29]

Such were Augustine's reflections on transferred meaning in the first three books of *On Christian Teaching*, written at the outset of his episcopal service. When reviewing all his works for his *Reconsiderations* after some thirty years dedicated to preaching and writing, he found the treatise incomplete and decided to finish it. In the fourth book, he discussed the employment of allegorical interpretation in preaching; there he focused on its usefulness in delighting the hearers and thereby facilitating communication. Preachers, however, did not share the privilege enjoyed by the sacred writers of making their discourse obscure and difficult to understand.[30] Their objective must always include both instructing their hearers in what ought to be done and moving them toward accomplishing what had been recognized as right.[31] Thus, the use of allegorical interpretation—or indeed any rhetorical techniques—in a sermon must always serve these goals and must never distract from them by calling attention to the eloquence or ingenuity of the speaker. Interpretative tools should stimulate the attention of the hearers, help them to remember and to appreciate—and thus to act on—the truths they learned.[32]

These judgments enunciated at the end of Augustine's career were based on long experience as a preacher. His surviving sermons show that he did not use allegorical interpretation primarily to deal with obscurities in the text of scripture. In most instances, though not in all, the text allowed and even required a literal meaning that was quite plain. Instead, figurative interpretation was used to identify and connect additional meanings rather than to replace that literal one.[33] His objective was to keep the truth of the text alive and fresh in the minds of his hearers.[34]

A few examples will illustrate Augustine's practice. In the second book of *On Christian Teaching*, he had reflected on the application of the praise of the beloved's beautiful teeth in Song of Songs 4:2 to the ritual of baptism. He admitted that this figure delighted him. The beloved's teeth were like shorn ewes, coming up from the washing, each of which bore twins. He used the allegory for his congregation in just this way. The sheep represented Christians cleansed in baptism, who had thrown off their worldly concerns, had given their goods to the poor, and were bringing forth good works in love of God and neighbor. With such teeth, the church, represented by the hungry Peter on Simon the Tanner's roof (Acts 10:13), was invited to eat and assimilate the nations into the body of Christ.[35] Similarly, an allegory Augustine used multiple times to exhort a congregation to repentance and forgiveness compared the three dead persons whom Christ had resuscitated (the young girl, the widow's son, and Lazarus) to penitents submerged in different depths of deadly sin. The first had just died within a house (Mark 5:40–42), the second was being carried out publicly for burial (Luke 7:11–15), the third had been entombed for four days (John 11:38–44). The girl represented those who quickly repented of a sinful intention that had not issued in action; the young man, those who had sinned in action that was perceived by others; Lazarus, those hardened sinners buried and pressed down by the weight of evil habits. A different form of divine action and church ministry was required of the repentance of each.[36] Another type of interpretation was offered each year during the week following Easter when Augustine preached on the appearances of the risen Christ. His congregation came to anticipate and greet with applause his various explanations of the number of fish (153) caught by the disciples in John 21:11. This exchange had apparently become one of the rituals of the Easter season, and he repeated it even in a written exposition of that text.[37] Finally, Augustine and his congregation continued to delight in the application of the parable of the Samaritan and the beaten traveler to the Savior coming to the rescue of fallen humanity. Already traditional, the interpretation recurred more than a dozen times in his surviving sermons.[38]

MULTIPLE REFERENCES TO A SINGLE PERSON

Augustine found one form of typological interpretation particularly important: the Christian practice of reading the Psalms not only as referring to Christ but as the same Christ speaking or being spoken about in different roles. The New Testament writers presented psalm texts as addressed to Christ, such as the divine voice at his baptism and transfiguration (Matt. 3:17; 17:5; Mark 1:11; 9:7; Luke 3:22; 9:35; Ps. 2:7). A collection of such texts identified the Savior in the opening chapter of the Letter to the Hebrews (Heb. 1:5–13). Christ prayed Psalm 22 in his own human reality and as the whole of humanity on the cross with him (Matt. 27:46; Mark 15:34). This form of interpretation was already widely used when Augustine came to reading and interpreting the Psalms early in his presbyterate.[39]

Although the technique of distinguishing multiple roles of a single speaker was pursued more fully with texts of the Psalms because of their regular use in liturgical prayer and preaching, Augustine followed the general interpretative principle that the whole of the scripture referred to Christ and his work. In order to bring this principle into practice, he had to distinguish not only different modes of reference—particularly the historical and prophetic or typological—but also three different senses in which Christ was the subject or object of the biblical speech or narrative.

First, Christ could speak and be spoken of as the Word of God, eternally begotten from and equal to the Father. The prologue of the Gospel of John, the hymn in Philippians 2:6–11, and the formula in Colossians 1:15–20 each begin with reference to Christ in his divine or heavenly state, prior to and independent of the incarnation. Similarly, the Letter to the Hebrews applies Psalm 2:7 ("You are my son, this day I have begotten you") and 2 Samuel 7:14a ("I will be a father to him and he a son to me") to the eternal generation of the Son (Heb. 1:5).[40]

Second, the scripture refers to Christ as the Word of God incarnate: the prologue and hymn texts just mentioned all include such a reference. Psalm 2:7 also was used this way.[41]

Third, scripture can refer to "the whole Christ in the fullness of the church," in the identification of the head with his members.[42] Christ was named as the head who had the church as his body in Ephesians 1:22–23 and 4:13, as well as Colossians 1:18.[43] One of Augustine's favorite examples of this form of interpretation was Christ's challenge to Saul in Acts 9:4: "Why do you persecute me?" Christ, as the Word of God, could not be injured; as a resurrected and ascended human, he was safely in heaven. Christ, therefore, must have spoken as identified with his body, in which he was still under attack on earth.[44] Augustine provided a summary of the three modes in which Christ was engaged with his body in the Psalter: Christ was prayed to as God by Christians; he prayed for Christians as their priest; he prayed with and in them as their head. The faithful should recognize their own voices in Christ's and Christ's voice in their own, as he spoke for, with, and in his members.[45]

The threefold application of this principle of personal interpretation was guided by the import of the statements made in the scripture: how a statement was applied to Christ depended on what it asserted or described.[46] In the chapters dealing with Jesus's miracles and teaching in the Gospel of John, for example, Augustine identified the two "I am" statements (John 8:24, 58) as referring to the Word in his role as the God of Abraham, Isaac, and Jacob.[47] A parallel interpretation was applied to many of the psalms that Christian apologists had used to demonstrate the divinity of Christ in the period prior to the Council of Nicaea in 325.[48] Texts that spoke of Christ as descending or coming to humanity should be understood usually as referring to him in his divine reality. The bread of angels descended and became milk for humans; God came to humans who could not themselves reach up to God.[49] Humanity did not earn the privilege of being taken on by God in Christ; nor did the Godhead die when Christ, who was also God, died in his human reality.[50] Although he clearly affirmed the personal unity that justified the attribution of both divine and human qualifiers to the same individual, Augustine carefully distinguished those properties that belonged to the Savior because of his divine reality from those that were his through his humanity.[51] In commenting on John 3:13, he distinguished the divine Son of God and the human Son of Man as Christ born from the Father and born from Mary. He then argued, however, that Christ's personal unity allowed him to refer to himself as Son of Man in both his original, solitary descent from heaven to earth and his subsequent ascent, accompanied by the members of his body.[52]

Christ was represented as speaking and acting in divine and human ways throughout the gospels. He referred to himself as fulfilling humanly the promises and predictions that he had made divinely through the prophets.[53] When he completed his mission with, "It is finished," (John 19:30), Jesus signaled his human fulfillment of all he divinely had intended to accomplish.[54]

This type of interpretation could be sensitive to the full context of a statement. In the Gospel of John, Augustine explained that Jesus learned to perform marvelous works in his divine generation by the Father. In explaining the expertise that the adolescent Jesus demonstrated to the teachers in the temple (Luke 2:47), he also referred his learning from and being taught by the Father to gifts that were divinely bestowed on his humanity.[55]

In applying this method of interpretation to the Savior's work, Augustine was most interested in the ways that Christ voluntarily assumed human weakness into himself and thereby destroyed human sin. Because the body he received from Mary truly carried the weakness and mortality that were, in others, the consequences and the signs of Adam's sin, he bore the sin symbolically.[56] Although he was courageous, he became truly sad at his approaching rejection and death.[57] He voluntarily accepted the weakness of his fellow humans; he prayed for deliverance and submitted to the divine will in the mortal vulnerability he shared with them.[58]

As an individual who was both divine and human, Christ was also the head of the church and the sole mediator between God and humanity.[59] The differences among the members of his body required further distinctions when scripture texts were applied to Christ in the psalm commentaries and the exegetical sermons.[60] Sometimes Christ spoke together with those of his members who were at rest after death and at other times with those who still labored on earth.[61] More importantly, Augustine recognized instances in which Christ was speaking only for his bodily members and not for himself as their head. Since Christ was without sin, he prayed the penitential psalms as the voice of his churchly body.[62] As was just noted, the expressions of sadness and fear found in the gospels at the approach of the passion belonged properly to Christ as an individual and also to some of the members with whom the head identified himself and for whom he provided the model of submission to the divine will (Matt. 26:39; Mark 14:35–36; Luke 22:41–44). Since Paul and other martyrs had approached death without fear, these texts could be applied to Christ as identified with only some of his members.[63] When Christ cried out as forsaken and overcome by sin on the cross, he spoke for sinful humanity, and even for Adam, existing among his members, rather than for himself as Son of God who could not, or as Son of Man who would not, be separated from the Father.[64] Yet Augustine illustrated and justified the reference of these texts to Christ by the observation that a person claims and protests harm done to any bodily members as done to the whole: a person cries out in pain at an injury to the foot.[65] Thus Augustine assigned statements to Christ as Word, as incarnate, as the church, or as identified with different groups of Christians, depending on the meaning of the text.

THE WHOLE CHRIST

Augustine insisted that the Whole Christ could speak and pray in a single voice, so that the scripture in general and the Psalms in particular used the singular rather than the plural form when referring to the fullness of Christ's person. He taught that the charity given by the Holy Spirit united faithful Christians to one another and to Christ, so that they prayed as a unity rather than a multitude. When they used the scriptural texts attributed to Christ, his members prayed as one speaker united to their head as his body, not as distinct individuals.[66]

Augustine justified this third form of predication, to Christ as identified with his church, by appeal to the implications of statements in the New Testament. As has been noted above, he regularly cited Christ's challenge to Saul when he identified himself with the persecuted faithful (Acts 9:4–5).[67] He added that in the depiction of the judgment that was to follow the resurrection of all the dead (Matt. 25:31–46), Christ identified himself with his followers, so that services granted or refused to them were provided or denied to Christ.[68] He also appealed to Paul's explanation that Christians become children of Abraham by incorporation into Christ (Gal. 3:29).[69]

This identification of Christ with his church was different from the interpretation of an individual, such as Peter, serving as a symbol of the whole or a part of the church. Augustine had refused to follow Cyprian in identifying Peter as representative of the episcopal officers as a body, upon which Christ had conferred special powers and responsibilities.[70] Instead, Augustine argued that Peter served as a symbol of the whole church, whose faith and love he professed. Every Christian was expected to make that profession, to accept the duty of mutual care, and to exercise the power to forgive that they received as directly from Christ as Peter did.[71] Similarly, the scene of the disciples fighting the storm at sea while Christ prayed on the mountain was symbolic of the present condition of the Christian people, struggling on earth while their head interceded in heaven.[72] Peter and the other disciples were symbolic of all but acted only as individuals, succeeding and failing only for themselves.[73] Only Christ was personally identified with his members, acting with and on behalf of his body.

Augustine made extensive use of the personal union between Christ and the church, as will be demonstrated in several of the following chapters in this volume. Its final chapter will review these in an attempt to specify Augustine's understanding of the reality indicated by that personal union through an analysis of the operations attributed to Christ and the church together.

AUGUSTINE AND TYCONIUS'S *BOOK OF RULES*

This distinction of the different forms of predication to a grammatical subject was clearly stated in the *Book of Rules* of the Donatist exegete Tyconius, which Augustine was following in the last book of his treatise *On Christian Doctrine*. The first rule, "The Lord and his Body," states that a given passage of scripture can apply to Christ as divine, as a human individual, or as the church, depending upon its meaning. Even within a single paragraph, the subject of attribution could move from one mode to another. Tyconius used the scriptural description of "one flesh" to identify the personal unity achieved in Christ: the Word of God and the human Son of Man were one flesh in the Savior, according to John 1:13; Christ and the church were one flesh, according to Ephesians 5:31–32. In a voluntary—rather than a fleshly—union, such as that between the divine Father (or Holy Spirit) and the human joined to the Word, such a personal union was not achieved.[74]

In contrast, Tyconius's fourth rule deals with "species and genus" which is translated as the particular and the general.[75] This distinction was to be used when discord arose between a subject and an attribute applied to it. Tyconius illustrated rather than defined this conflict and the proper procedure for resolving it. Some of the promises God made to David in 2 Samuel 7:12–16, for example, applied partially to his son Solomon but others were fulfilled only in Christ and his church. Solomon would build the temple and God would punish him for his iniquities; the secure throne and kingdom, however, were given to David through Christ rather than in Solomon. In Solomon, then, a whole body was signified but not realized; in the Whole Christ it was both signified and realized.[76] Similarly, in both his successes and his failures, Peter could be said to signify or represent but not to be the mixed body—including the good and the evil—that is the church of Christ.[77]

Tyconius's purpose was to develop methods of distinguishing the proper subjects of attribution for scriptural statements. In certain instances, however, his procedures had consequences for church doctrine and practice that Parmenian, the Donatist bishop of Carthage (362/63–391/92 CE), judged unacceptable. Augustine, whose ministry overlapped with that of Parmenian, reported that Parmenian and his fellow bishops condemned Tyconius's judgments that the church was spread throughout the world and that the evil in it should be tolerated until the final judgment.[78] Although Augustine did not report a specific rejection of Tyconius's rule on Christ and the church, Parmenian and later his colleague Petilian of Constantine, who was Augustine's contemporary and opponent, seem to have avoided the identification of Christ with the church. They may have realized, as Augustine argued, that identifying the whole church with Christ precluded assigning to the bishop the role of mediating between God and the Christian people.[79]

As shall become clear in the individual studies that follow in this volume, Augustine not only used the techniques that led Tyconius to these judgments but adopted the first rule as the foundation of his understanding of the church and its sharing in the powers that were proper to Christ himself. Occasionally, Augustine also followed Tyconius's lead in distinguishing the Son of God from the one joined to him and in speaking of the gratuity of the uniting that made a particular man, who had no prior merits, the Christ.[80]

AUGUSTINE'S PRACTICE

Before proceeding to the review of Augustine's practical and theological interpretation of the scriptures in his preaching to congregations, two observations are in order.

First, in a sermon preached in about 403 CE, Augustine apologized to the congregation for his dependence on a book for reading the text of the scripture. He explained that he had not studied scripture from his youth and, as a result, he could rattle off plenty of now useless texts (from Roman literature) but could not recite long sections of the Bible.[81] Perhaps a decade later, he remarked that some people had the whole of the Psalter committed to memory, but he did not.[82] Indeed, many in Augustine's congregation had large sections of the scriptures firmly fixed in their memories. In a letter to his closest friend and collaborator, Alypius, the bishop of Thagaste, Augustine described the Hippo congregation extending the customary evening prayers by singing many hymns in the gathering dark, presumably completely from memory.[83]

Thus, Augustine did not display an exhaustive recall of the scriptural text. Yet, he does pull together sets of texts, even quite disparate ones, that can be shaped into a coherent exposition of a doctrinal thesis, such as the destruction of sin and death in the flesh of the Savior. In the discussion of the redemption, for example, Romans 8:3 and 2 Corinthians 5:12 are joined together to illuminate one another. To these, Leviticus 4:3–4 and Ephesians 5:2 were added to complete an explanation of the efficacy of the sacrificial death of Christ.[84] Identifying and tracking these constellations of mutually interpreting texts proved to be an important tool in identifying sermons that might have been preached in close temporal proximity.[85]

Second, Augustine regularly focused on the exact wording and grammar of a scriptural passage to establish its meaning. He usually trusts the Latin translation he was using but, as was noted above, he occasionally checked alternative Latin versions that he had to hand and, in rare instances, checked the Greek version or referred to what he had learned about the Hebrew when dealing with the Psalms.[86] Rarely, however, did Augustine's interpretation directly attack the literal meaning of a text. Yet such an undermining is clearly evident in his interpretation of the eucharistic body of Christ in the *Tractates on the Gospel of John*. In this instance, he may have grasped the irony operative in the language of the Bread of Life discourse and worked to justify the evangelist's implied meaning by appeal to the Pauline texts that identify the eucharistic and ecclesial bodies of Christ.[87] In a similar way, he used John 1:31–33 as a narrow but solid foundation for multiple aspects of his teaching on the relation between Christ and his ministers in baptizing. This, however, he accomplished only by importing the Matthean narrative of Jesus's encounter with John the Baptist into his analysis of the Johannine one.[88]

If pressed, Augustine might have appealed to the inspiration of the Holy Spirit, responding to the prayers of his congregation that their preacher be guided in what he said to them, so that it was both true and useful for their salvation. [89]

Conclusion

The interpretation of scripture in Augustine's preaching was governed by the twin principles of the rule of faith and the law of charity: his objective was always both to instruct in the truth and to persuade the faithful to live well. Doctrinal exposition, such as the relation of the Trinitarian persons, was rare, though it did occur.[90] Sermons on the issues of the Donatist controversy were occasionally preached in Hippo, but those against the Pelagians were more likely to be delivered in Carthage,[91] where the problem had arisen and was being debated among more educated Christians—some of Roman origin. Moreover, the expositions of the psalms and the Gospel of John that were written but not preached show greater use of the Greek text to control the Latin translation.[92] Augustine's objective in preaching was to move his hearers as much as to instruct them.

In his preaching, Augustine assumed that the events had happened as narrated, and he built both prophetic and allegorical interpretations on this basis. He used these events to tie together not only the Old and New Testaments but also both of these to the life of the church. Christians could find their own struggles and triumphs foreshadowed (and explained) in the biblical events.

Allegorical exegesis was employed in preaching primarily as a means of enlivening the sermons rather than of dealing with historical problems or moral incongruities in the biblical text. Figures could delight the hearers, sharpen their attention, plant the truth more firmly in their memories and imaginations, and thus more effectively move them to action. Even when he was not engaged in allegorical interpretation, Augustine used strong images to represent the meaning and import of the actions to which he was urging his congregation.

All of these interpretative techniques came together in that christological interpretation that included the Christians as members of the ecclesial body of Christ. Augustine brought himself and his hearers into the text by identifying them not only with the disciples but with the Savior.

In the chapters that follow, these techniques of scriptural interpretation will be shown in operation as Augustine developed and supported his teaching on living the Christian life.

Chapter Two

RICHES AND POVERTY

I N HIS PREACHING on the use and sharing of material goods, and on income-producing property in particular, Augustine attempted to guide his congregation in facing the complex challenges of living within a social system some of whose inequities and injustices were evident to him. Though he and the clergy who served with him had accepted Christ's challenge to abandon their property, he recognized that they depended for food, clothing, and shelter on the generosity of other Christians who attempted to serve Christ through the use of private property.[1] As a bishop, he was charged with the care not only of the buildings used for worship and pastoral service but the many income-producing properties the church had received as gifts to support its care of the poor. In discharging this responsibility, he faced many of the same conflicts and challenges as the Christian householders to whom he preached.

In the first decade of his episcopal career, Augustine's teaching about private wealth may have been guided by opposition to the Manicheans, whose "elect" adherents rejected both generation of children and control of property. After the arrival in Africa of refugees from the sack of Rome, however, he became aware of an ascetic teaching that only those who renounced their wealth would gain admission to the kingdom of heaven.[2] A surviving treatise, *On Riches*,[3] supporting this doctrine may have been the work of a disciple of Pelagius. Although its arguments rely on biblical sources—such as Christ's call to renunciation and the comparison of the rich entering heaven to the camel passing through the needle's eye— neither Augustine's preaching nor his letters indicate that he had access to the treatise.[4]

Instead of urging the laity to commit to the alienation of all their property, Augustine attempted to develop and to convince his hearers to implement practices of managing wealth that were guided by the scriptures and responsive to the social realities of their culture. As shall be evident, his efforts usually focused on exhortation to generosity and humility rather than an economic analysis of the generation and distribution of wealth in Roman imperial society.

This study proceeds in five parts. (1) Augustine attempted to break the presumed connection between wealth and righteousness, insisting that neither abundance nor poverty indicated divine favor. (2) He defined three forms of Christian life, distinguished as the renunciation, communal sharing, and private management of property. (3) He taught that dealing with material goods required an asceticism of spirit to counter the influence of Roman culture that defined social status by wealth. (4) The essential Christian practice, necessary in all forms of life, was the sharing of the resources that supported bodily life. Finally, (5) the incorporation of Christians into the body of Christ gave sharing wealth among them—as distinguished from gifts to outsiders—an exceptional religious value. Some overlap and repetition will be noticed in these five sections, as the considerations of wealth and poverty are approached from different perspectives.

WEALTH, POVERTY, AND RIGHTEOUSNESS

Augustine observed that some people's actions betrayed a belief that God provided everlasting life and the heavenly blessings associated with it but that the goods specific to earthly, temporal life either were in the control of the demons or were produced and controlled by human labor and ingenuity alone. Some practiced the cult of the demons and others used whatever strategies were at their disposal—just or unjust—to secure temporal goods. These people, he explained, had failed to grasp the unity and difference of the Old and New Covenants. God had promised and delivered earthly benefits to the Jews so that everyone would understand that these goods were created and distributed by God. Indeed, the account of Job's trials clearly showed that demons and humans could affect a person's bodily health and earthly possessions only with God's permission.[5] So, Augustine concluded, acknowledging God as the giver and governor of earthly goods was appropriate; seeking them from the demons was wrong.[6] Desiring and seeking earthly goods even from God, however, could indicate a failure to appreciate the better and more lasting gifts of the spiritual realm. In developing a figurative interpretation of the two hands of the bridegroom in Song of Songs 2:6, Augustine explained why the left hand was placed under the head of the bride, where Christian faith resides, and the right hand over it. That left hand represented the temporal goods that provide consolation during earthly life but were themselves neither the foundation of happiness nor even a protection for faith. The right hand represented the goods of eternal life that ought to be preferred and sought.[7]

A Sign of Divine Favor or Cause of Divine Disfavor

Preaching on the scriptures, especially the Psalms, gave Augustine many opportunities to teach about wealth and poverty. When the parable of the beggar Lazarus and the rich man who ignored his misery (Luke 16:19–31) was read out, he observed that the indigent and beggars in the congregation nodded in satisfaction at the reversal of roles: they identified with Lazarus and claimed the promise of a glorious future for themselves. The benefits they were enjoying on earth, in contrast, made the wealthy congregants fear future condemnation. Augustine challenged both the anxiety and the false assurance such interpretations aroused. The parable, he insisted, was not a judgment for the poor and against the rich. He asked how Christ could have been favoring the poor and condemning the rich by recounting the lifting up of the beggar into the bosom of Abraham, whom the scripture described as a very wealthy man. Indeed, they should worry that Abraham might take offense and reject the resentful poor. The parable clearly showed, Augustine explained, that the beggar was rewarded for the humility, piety, trust, and obedience to God that he shared with Abraham; the rich man was condemned for trusting in his wealth and refusing to care for the beggar at his gate. The judgment of Christ, he concluded, was based not on the wealth and indigence of the two neighbors but on the justice and humility of the beggar and on the injustice and self-assurance of the rich man.[8] Augustine buttressed this interpretation by appealing to the story of Job: owning earthly goods and enjoying temporal happiness had not transformed him into an evil man. Though his true goodness was hidden from both demons and humans, God knew it and allowed him to be stripped of his family and property so that his piety might be manifest.[9] Abraham demonstrated a similar devotion when he obediently offered to God the son whom he had desired and received as the heir of his property.[10] By declining to take wealth for himself, Augustine elsewhere observed, Christ displayed its irrelevance, not that it was an evil and an obstacle to righteousness that must be rejected.[11]

The Psalms required special attention because they seemed both to show a divine preference for the poor and to present riches as a reward for upright living. Augustine developed strategies for assimilating such texts into his teaching on riches and poverty. Some troublesome passages could be supplemented or even contradicted by others. The psalmist (Ps. 86:1) pleaded for God's help on the grounds of being poor and needy. This did not mean, Augustine contended, that God would not heed the prayer of wealthy persons who had gold and silver, large households and plantations, either by inheritance or through success in business. Their wealth was not held against them as long as they followed the directive of Paul (to whom he attributed the letters to Timothy and Titus) not to think too highly of themselves or to trust in earthly goods. God distinguished people on the basis of pride and humility, he concluded, not riches and poverty.[12] In contrast, Augustine challenged the psalmist's claim never to have seen, during a long life, the righteous in need or their children begging for bread (Ps. 37:25). This scriptural statement should be accepted as true, he allowed, but as testimony to the speaker's limited experience or elderly forgetfulness. In contrast, the Old Testament narrated Abraham and Isaac's migrations to avoid famine (Gen. 12:10, 26:1); in the New Testament, Paul recounted the hunger and deprivation experienced in his apostolic work (2 Cor. 11:27).[13]

Passages that promised earthly blessings—e.g., a fruitful wife and many children around an abundant table—to all who feared God and walked the right way (Ps. 128:1–4) proved a greater interpretative challenge. These texts often did not include exemptions or heavenly alternatives for those who renounced family and property in order to remain faithful to the Mosaic law or to follow Christ. If the statements were taken literally and universally, then most poor Christians, not to mention the martyrs, would have to think that they had somehow gone astray: they either did not receive or had been required to abandon such goods to continue to follow Christ. Moreover, because Augustine preached on this psalm on the day his community was celebrating the feast of Felix of Nola, a renunciant and martyr, he could not overlook the conflict between this scriptural text and the counsels of Christ. Although it did not deny rewards in the future life, this text promised wealth and fertility before death as a sign and reward of piety. Augustine attempted to rescue its meaning by exploiting a grammatical shift in the text—from the plural form in the introductory "blessed are all" to the singular form in what followed, "you will eat" and "your wife," that continued through that whole list of blessings. He was thus able to refer the promises made in the singular to the Whole Christ—the entire church taken as one—rather than continuing the plural reference, which would have assigned the full set of specific rewards to each and every individual Christian (or Jew). By referring them to Christ as head and the faithful as bodily members, he interpreted the blessings as spiritual rather than corporeal, as belonging to the heavenly rather than the earthly Jerusalem.[14] Augustine used this grammatical device in steadfastly refusing to credit any correlation between wealth or poverty and righteousness or unrighteousness. He affirmed that God bestowed and withheld earthly blessings but insisted that these signified neither divine approval nor disapproval, their reception anticipated neither reward nor punishment in the resurrected life.

Augustine taught, then, that God was the source of all the resources and enjoyments necessary and useful for temporal, earthly life; God gave them, and God allowed them to be taken away—by humans or demons. Sometimes God granted the faithful's petitions for these "left-hand" supports and sometimes denied them. In contrast, God always called Christians to the spiritual and lasting benefits that were represented by the right hand of the bridegroom in Song of Songs 2:6.[15]

This understanding of the significance of wealth and poverty was well suited to the experience of Christians in Augustine's time, since they would have found difficulty in correlating the divine distribution of earthly blessings with the manifest goodness or justice of their recipients. Prior to the religious toleration initiated by Constantine, Roman traditionalists had exercised power over the assets and the lives of Christians.[16] Even in the Christian empire initiated by Theodosius and his successors, the traditionalists continued to prosper; some did become Christians in order to gain or retain the privileged access to imperial power through which they might protect and increase their wealth.

Augustine observed that God not only allowed evil people to prosper but regularly either invited or required Christians to renounce or suffer the loss of the earthly benefits of wealth and children. The divine governance, he explained, clearly demonstrated that such things were less valuable and should be subordinated to the spiritual goods that God reserved for the just alone.[17] As Christ had pointed out, God provided sun and rain to both the good and the evil (Matt. 5:45). Augustine amplified Christ's observation by calling attention to all the benefits following from the sun and rain that also were given indiscriminately.[18] This divine liberality, he argued, was intended to discourage people from either accepting or rejecting the gospel for the sake of earthly treasure. If God gave benefits only to the good, then the evil would be drawn to Christianity for the sake of attaining them; if God gave riches only to the evil, then the weak would be discouraged from converting and persevering in Christian faith. By granting and denying bodily things without regard to piety and impiety, God taught that such goods were consolations that supported the earthly journey; Christians must prefer the eternal goods proper to the journey's end that the evil would never share.[19]

Earthly and Heavenly Riches

More generally, Augustine argued that appraising earthly goods as rewards or signs of divine approval could place Christians in danger of falling away from their faith. Seeing the evil prosper could lead to the judgment that God unjustly rewarded the evil and punished the good. It would raise questions about divine governance, especially for those who suffered loss as a consequence of obeying God.[20] The promises of earthly rewards that God made to Israel seem to have led to just these sorts of problems. When they disobeyed God, the Israelites suffered losses that the idolaters of the nations escaped. Although some realized that they should seek higher goods from God, others identified the preservation of earthly goods as a means (rather than a sign) of serving God properly. In a futile attempt to preserve their nation, for example, the Jewish leaders repudiated Christ and gave him up to death.[21] Christians could be subject to the same temptation: when deprived of temporal goods they believed God had promised them, they might judge that God had deserted them and abandon their faith.[22] Thus, Christ discouraged his followers from desiring and seeking temporary goods, even from God. Prosperity during earthly life was not promised to Christians, Augustine concluded. Their rest and happiness belonged to life at the end of the age. They should use well and with gratitude the earthly goods made available to them; their hope, however, should be set on the secure and permanent happiness promised in the resurrection.[23]

The understanding Augustine was urging upon his congregation was illustrated in his exposition of Psalm 73, where he tracked the progress of the psalmist from envy at the prosperity of the wicked toward hope and desire for God alone. The evil claimed that God did not care how they lived and acted; the good feared that their fidelity and obedience had been foolish and futile. Further reflection brought the psalmist to the insight that evil people were deceivers and that God responded in kind, beguiling them with riches. At the end of their lives they would awake, like a beggar from dreams of abundance, to find themselves empty and abandoned. The obedient, in contrast, should recognize that to desire and seek earthly blessings, even as rewards from God, was irrational and unworthy of humans. To love and honor God for any other reward was, in fact, to fail in loving God truly.

> In the name of Christ and in fear of him, I exhort you: whoever among you does not have riches should not lust for them; whoever has them must not trust in them. Attend to what I just said to you. I do not say, "You are condemned because of your wealth." What I say is, "If you trust these things, if you are puffed up by these things, if you consider yourself great because of these things, if you ignore the poor because of these things, if you forget the common condition of the human race because of overweening vanity, then you are condemned." God will have to repay you on the last day by destroying the illusory presumption that you would enjoy such things in God's city. Let those who are rich conform themselves to the Apostle's teaching: *Command,* he said, *the rich of this world neither to feel proud nor to place their hope on the uncertainty of their riches. They should trust in the living God, who gives us the enjoyment of everything in abundance.* (1 Tim. 6:17)[24]

True fidelity, in Augustine's judgment, was to desire and hope for God alone as one's happiness. One might receive and enjoy earthly goods as gifts from God but must place neither trust nor hope in their possession.

In his sermons and oral expositions of scripture, then, Augustine taught that earthly blessings were good but dangerous. Riches could lead to pride and self-satisfaction, to ignoring the human condition, and to neglecting one's responsibilities toward others. Avarice, the love and desire for riches, was a fundamental danger that afflicted rich and poor alike (1 Tim. 6:9–10).[25]

Often, Augustine contrasted earthly goods as temporary or insecure to heavenly goods as safe and lasting. Earthly possessions were like an inn at which a traveler stayed but soon left to the use of another traveler; they were not like the house in which a person made a permanent dwelling.[26] As the poor who dreamed of wealth but awoke to their habitual deprivation, the rich would find themselves awakening at death to destitution; all their property would have been left behind on earth.[27] The Pauline text of 1 Timothy 6:17 described riches as uncertain—which Augustine illustrated by noting that coins were appropriately round because money would not stand up on its own.[28] Only a foolish person would love and trust things that could not endure and were easily lost.

In other instances, Augustine distinguished bodily goods from mental or spiritual ones by the difficulty of sharing them. Only one person at a time could own a field or a house. More generally, he assumed that human beings could not increase the total wealth available. As a result, one person gained only by another's loss. The full purse one found on the street by accident had been lost when another dropped it. Every buyer required a seller, often one pressed by poverty or debt and reluctant to give up possession. One person inherited only on the death of another; one rose in wealth and honor only through another's decline. To desire earthly riches and status, then, was to seek goods that could be acquired only by depriving others of them. How, then, could a Christian pray for the gift of wealth that God could bestow only by impoverishing another? Thus, Augustine compared the economic system to a bitter sea in which fish grew only by eating other fish. Being caught in the net of Christ—and then brought to shore—was first a protection and then a deliverance from this savage competition.[29]

THE CHRISTIAN FORMS OF LIFE

In affirming that God had promised and given earthly goods as rewards for the fidelity of the Israelites and thereby demonstrated that such things were under divine control, Augustine was forced to deal with the New Testament passages that specified different ways that Christians should receive, hold, and use property. In Matthew 19:16–30, Christ invited a rich young man desiring to secure eternal life to distribute his property to the poor and become his disciple. When he declined, Christ advised his followers that those attached to their wealth would experience great difficulty in attaining salvation. In Acts 4:32–35, members of the Jerusalem community were described as pooling their goods and living from a common fund that was under the supervision of the apostles. In 1 Timothy 6:6–10, 17–19, the Pauline writer advised both rich and poor Christians on appropriate attitudes toward wealth. Augustine accepted and encouraged different ways of dealing with personal property based on each of these three texts. In his preaching to the people, as might have been expected, most of his attention focused on those who held and used possessions and on the application of the general principles articulated in the Pauline text.

Renunciation of Wealth

Augustine clearly affirmed renunciation of wealth as a way of perfection
to which Christ invited his disciples. Some Christians did sell their goods
and gave the money to the poor, he reported, accepting, with Christ's help,
the invitation that the rich young man had declined.[30] For the nobility, this
could mean abandoning social status and political aspirations in order to
live in a simpler way, gradually disposing of their fortunes.[31] Paulinus, a
regular correspondent and collaborator of Augustine, had abandoned his
high station to devote his energies and resources to the shrine of Felix in
Nola, where he was made bishop.[32] Melania the Younger and her husband
Pinian dedicated their fortune to the service of the church. They took refuge, after the sack of Rome, on one of their properties in Numidia. During
a visit to Hippo Regius, Augustine's congregation attempted to force Pinian
to accept ordination as a presbyter of their church. The bishop managed
to block the ordination and the wealthy couple found a way to extricate
themselves. Augustine had to defend his congregation against the charge
of being more interested in the couple's benefactions than their service
of Christ.[33]

In receiving donations from wealthy people, either during their lives
or as legacies, Augustine was careful to protect the rights of their children
to the inheritance of property that was necessary to maintain their social
status and its lifestyle.[34]

Jesus's promise that his followers who had abandoned their property
would sit on thrones with him to judge the nations (Matt. 19:27–28) was
intended, Augustine asserted, for Paul and all who had done the same. The
angels joining them in judgment (Matt. 16:27) symbolized those who had
announced the gospel, beginning with John the Baptist.[35] Occasionally,
however, he challenged the assumption that renunciation of possessions
alone brought a person to the fullness of Christian perfection. Christ had
promised heavenly treasure and eternal life, he argued, only to those who
actually followed him in his humility and suffering; giving up one's property was not enough. He reminded the congregation that after abandoning
their personal possessions, one of the disciples had betrayed Jesus and
another had denied him. To this, he added Paul's assertion that distributing
his goods to the poor—even handing his body over to burning—would
profit nothing in the absence of charity (1 Cor. 13:3).[36] Other Christians
had left all for Christ and (perhaps) assumed that this renunciation would
guarantee their salvation; they then failed in time of persecution because

they had trusted in themselves.[37] Abandoning property, then, was a significant step toward a closer following of Christ but did not ensure final perseverance in love of God and neighbor.

Sharing Resources

A second form of renunciation of goods was based on the practice of the Jerusalem church: selling property and pooling the proceeds into a common fund, from which the needs of all members were supplied. The report in Acts 4:32–35 became, among other things, the foundation for the communal monastic life. Provoked by the example of Anthony of Egypt and following models he discovered in Milan, Augustine and his friends had attempted such a form of common life first in Italy and again upon return to his home in Africa.[38] After his ordination as presbyter and with the support of Bishop Valerius, he succeeded in establishing a monastery on the grounds of the church in Hippo. This community became a seedbed for the growth of the monastic movement in Africa, as well as the preparation of candidates for clerical office.[39] Augustine himself wrote rules for the governance of both male and female communities whose members lived from a common fund. Upon becoming bishop, he also established such a community for his clergy in the bishop's house.[40]

Augustine explained to his congregation that the goal of this system of common life adopted by their clergy and the communities of monks and nuns was to eliminate the conflict and competition to which private property could give rise. Those who held goods in common each had a claim on the whole, not unlike the way that every person had access to the light of the sun and the use of the air.[41] The participants were called monks (singles) not because they lived alone—they did not—but because they all formed one *persona*, having one heart and one soul in their many bodies.[42] Their clerical community was a manifestation of the power of charity—the gift and operation of the Holy Spirit—to unite Christians into the body of Christ.[43] When the poor joined such communities, their virtue was not to be discounted and despised because they had so little to abandon. Instead, they were to be praised for renouncing the desire for wealth that afflicted even those deprived of it.[44]

Augustine apparently trusted that his clergy had understood and fulfilled their agreement to give up control of their property, unless they had made arrangements with him to fulfill other responsibilities with it. When one of his presbyters died, Augustine discovered that he had not kept that promise: he had left funds as a legacy to the church that he claimed earlier to have given away but had kept under his own control. Augustine explained the whole problem to the congregation and apologized for the failure to maintain the commitment the clergy had made.[45] A week later, he provided to the congregation a full accounting of the financial affairs of each of its clergy who were living in the bishop's house. This report detailed the arrangements that he had made for some to administer their own property under his supervision. His nephew Patricius, for example, had obligations for the care of his mother that were still being discharged. Others, still too young to alienate their inheritances, used the income for the benefit of the church.[46] Augustine also asked the congregants to support their sharing arrangements by making only such gifts—such as food and clothing—as could be used by any member of the clerical community. Many seem to have preferred making gifts that only the bishop could use.[47] Elsewhere, he commended the laity for their generosity in supporting monastic foundations by gifts of buildings and of farmland.[48]

Two of the clergy of Hippo on whom Augustine reported, the subdeacon Valens and the deacon Faustinus, had held property in common with their siblings.[49] It was to be divided and their portions either given away or dedicated to the needs of the church, so that they would be free of responsibility for it. Among the laity, however, he encouraged heirs to hold an estate in common rather than dividing it into individually owned portions. He explained that Christ's refusal to force the division of an inheritance between two brothers (Luke 12:13–15) indicated his opposition to the avarice that preferred private to shared property.[50] In another sermon on the same text, he explained that in opposing the division, Christ had urged the petitioner to avoid all avarice, even the desire for what was rightfully his own.[51]

Augustine found significant value in the renunciation of private ownership and the communal sharing of property. The practice directly attacked the avarice and desire for the social status that wealth provided and that he found condemned in 1 Timothy 6. Sharing property also fostered the love of God and neighbor that built up the unity of Christians in heart and soul. Even when they retained control over their property, therefore, he urged his people to share the income it produced.

Managing Private Property

Most Christians to whom Augustine preached retained their wealth and maintained their social status while attempting to follow the commandments of Christ.[52] He urged these to follow the guidance of 1 Timothy

6:18 by using their resources to fund good works rather than for personal aggrandizement.[53] Some of them practiced virtue only by being content with their own goods, refraining from stealing, and not impoverishing their neighbors.[54] Some supported the renunciants by endowing their communities with churches, houses, gardens, and fields.[55] Most gave at least some of their income to the poor. They should presume, he warned, that avoiding serious sin would require some of them to suffer the loss of property or to miss opportunities for increasing it. During past periods of persecution, he recalled, many had faced this choice and accepted the confiscation of their wealth. Even in the course of doing business, Augustine reminded his congregation, the practice of justice would often require Christians to tolerate financial loss. In extreme cases, their very lives might be in danger.[56] Some, he lamented, were so attached to their property or desirous of acquiring wealth and its status that they preferred to sin rather than suffer any financial setback.[57]

Those with little property and security were no less in danger from their desire for wealth than the rich were from protecting and increasing its possession, Augustine warned. After the rich young man had refused the invitation to abandon his property (Matt. 19:22), Christ turned to his disciples and noted that it would be very difficult for the wealthy to enter the kingdom of heaven—comparing their passage into beatitude to that of a camel through "the eye of a needle." The disciples responded in astonishment: Would anyone be saved (Matt. 19:24-25)? With some care, Augustine drew out the implications of this exchange. In Christ's time, as in their own, the rich were a small part of the total population and poor people were far more numerous. If Christ had been referring to those who actually held a lot of property, then, the large pool of poor people would have remained available for salvation and the disciples should not have been alarmed at the prospect of an empty kingdom. Being themselves far from rich, he explained, the disciples had understood correctly that Christ's warning was directed not only at those actually wealthy but at all who were filled with avarice and longing for what the rich alone had. Grasping this point, the disciples had reacted to a danger they correctly recognized as universal: "How could anyone be saved?" When Christ and the psalmist blessed and appreciated the poor, Augustine concluded, they intended not the avaricious and resentful who possessed little or nothing but, instead, the poor in spirit who were filled with humility and placed their trust in God. Thus, neither the wealthy who oppressed the poor nor the deprived who hungered for wealth would enter the kingdom. The poor,

Augustine insisted, must not trust in their indigence any more than the rich in their abundance.[58] The Pauline teaching (1 Tim. 6:6–10, 17–19) was even more specific: the poor must place their trust in God and be satisfied with adequate food and clothing. To desire and labor to become rich, powerful, and admired was already to be numbered among the rich.[59]

Enjoying Wealth and Enduring Poverty

Both rich and poor Christians were in danger of believing that wealth guaranteed or at least facilitated a good and happy life. Those who actually enjoyed possessions might trust in them and thereby not only neglect the divine giver but accept the cultural bias that considered the wealthy more important and valuable than the poor.[60] Augustine objected to the saying, popular even among Christians, "Only the rich really live."[61] He pointed to the uncertainty and instability of earthly possessions: people could neither fully secure them for their own use nor guarantee their passage to their intended heirs. In contrast, he urged that God alone could not be lost unwillingly and was the only source of sure happiness.[62]

Detachment from Riches

All earthly goods had "worms" hidden within them that could spoil their enjoyment and value, Augustine observed. Apples, pears, beans, and wheat each had its own pest; the "worm" of riches was pride. Wealth was like a nest in which excessive self-regard was not only nurtured but from which it would never fly away.[63] Wealth was, of course, relative; the poor also might think too well of themselves. A beggar with a few coins to jingle could be more puffed up than the richest senator.[64] Clients with no funds of their own might boast of a powerful patron.[65] In general, however, people mocked these pretensions and quickly cut the puffed-up poor down to size; the rich, in contrast, they admired and flattered.[66] The greater the possessions and social status, then, the more a person was in danger of becoming and remaining proud. Though they appeared great and imposing, Augustine insisted, these people were actually hollow and, consequently, easily toppled into sin.[67]

Thus, Augustine followed the beatitude (Matt. 5:3) in valuing poverty of spirit, based upon humility and trust in God, rather than modesty of financial resources and social status. He insisted that the rich should recognize that their possessions were both uncertain and, potentially, an obstacle to their salvation. The poor should let their indigence prevent them from being inflated by some small advantage over their fellows. Both should place all their trust in God.[68] Thus, to be among God's poor and to be promised the kingdom, both the wealthy and the deprived had to set their hope on God and to avoid pride.[69] Such poor people would enter the kingdom of heaven through the eye of the needle.[70]

Augustine offered many considerations to help the wealthy overcome the temptation to consider themselves better than the disadvantaged. They should acknowledge the poor as fellow humans and even treat them as members of their households.[71] They must never forget that, as children of Adam and Eve, they too shared the human condition. When stripped of their ornaments and finery, they were indistinguishable from anyone else. They possessed nothing in the womb and had brought nothing into the world. They would die and leave behind all their property. Their bodies would rot into the common dust, though perhaps a little more decorously because of the spices in which they had been wrapped. Even the few set above the many in society, those who ruled a household with coercive force, could be protected from pride by remembering that they shared the human situation of their subjects.[72]

By using the Pauline exhortations of 1 Timothy 6, Augustine developed a teaching that focused on the interior disposition of detachment from wealth and could be applied to all Christians: renunciants, monks, and householders, both rich and poor. He then challenged those who maintained property to use it in ways that demonstrated their humility and their trust in God. Both rich and poor could accept earthly blessings as resources for use; God was for enjoyment.[73] The Pauline texts Augustine was following (1 Tim. 6:8, 18), advised the poor to be content with food and clothing.[74] It commanded the rich to do good deeds liberally and generously, exploiting the power and freedom of action that the poor did not enjoy.[75]

Sharing Wealth

If the wealthy were not required to sell all their property and give the proceeds to the poor, then how much should they distribute? For Augustine, the actual amount was not as important as the recognition that the sharing of wealth was a duty. All earthly goods had been received from God, to whom the whole creation belonged, as the property of a slave belonged to the master.[76] People should retain what they needed, Augustine conceded, indeed they might keep more than they actually needed.[77] He considered various standards.

> Let us give a part, but how big a part? A tenth, perhaps, as the scribes and Pharisees were accustomed to give? We should be ashamed. A tenth was given by people for whom Christ had not yet shed his blood. A tenth was given by the scribes and Pharisees. You must not think you are doing something wonderful when you share your bread with the poor (Isa. 58:7)—a gift that expends perhaps a thousandth of your resources. Still, I am not complaining; just do that much! I am so hungry and thirsty that I would be happy with even such crumbs. But I will not fail to repeat the saying of the one who died for us and now lives: *Unless your righteousness surpasses that of the scribes and Pharisees, you will not enter the Kingdom of Heaven* (Matt. 5:20). He is not gently cajoling us; he is a surgeon who cuts into the living flesh. *Unless your righteousness surpasses that of the scribes and Pharisees, you will not enter the Kingdom of Heaven.* The scribes and Pharisees gave a tenth. What does that imply? Ask yourselves. Think about it. How much do you have available; what should you do? What could you give; what would you have left afterward? How much should you spend on works of mercy and how much should you hold back for your enjoyments?[78]

In a tone that might have been slightly mocking, Augustine elsewhere suggested that the poor should not be harsh in judging the wealthy. The rich were not as strong as the poor; they had to eat finer and more expensive food. Because of their delicate constitutions, they would become sick on a rough diet that was the best that the poor could afford. Let the rich eat as they were accustomed, he conceded, as long as they also provided food for the poor. Everyone did not have to eat the same kind of food—at least not until famine forced it upon them. If the rich were not allowed to despise the destitute because they had to beg, neither should the poor despise the rich because they were frail and had to eat fine foods.[79]

The rich, Augustine recognized in a more practical vein, were the ones responsible for storing supplies against the calamities and failures that could come in the future. The actual need for reserves, however, could be difficult to estimate, and the level of a person's trust in God inevitably entered the calculation. Still, if all else were lost, a person would want to be sure that God too had not been alienated by distrust.[80] The issue in making this decision was really the kind of life a person was striving to attain and maintain.[81] The mortal life supported by earthly goods was unstable, ever changing, and quickly over. Happiness was to be found only in a future, truer life.[82] An appreciation of that future life, then, was necessary for setting the proper value on earthly life and the goods that maintained and amplified it.[83]

Transforming Earthly into Heavenly Wealth

In evaluating their present needs, Augustine cautioned, people should make provision not only for their children but for themselves as well. By holding back from the needy, the rich could deprive themselves of the future benefits of their present wealth.[84] The only way to secure the goods of earthly life and be sure that they would be available when they were needed most was to give them away, in hope of receiving them back after death.[85] When people died, they would certainly lose control of all the goods that they had struggled to acquire and retain. Both Christ, in his invitation to distribute wealth to the poor, and Paul, in his exhortation to use it for good works, promised treasure in a future, unending life. Augustine contended that the rich were being offered the opportunity to secure their resources for heavenly life by giving them to the poor. By being shared, the earthly goods that people could hold only temporarily would be transformed into permanent endowments.[86] In heaven, their wealth would be safe from rot and thieves (Luke 12:33).[87]

In his exhortations to almsgiving, Augustine elaborated two analogies for this exchange of earthly for heavenly goods. Merchants often used a contract that allowed them to pay money in one location and have wheat, oil, or some other commodity delivered in another part of the world.[88] Closer to home, he observed that during the winter the sower tossed out grain that had been harvested and stored with great labor only months earlier. In hope of harvesting much more grain during the following summer, the farmer entrusted to the earth what he might have eaten or sold at once. Should not the Christians entrust passing goods to God who would return them later in a lasting form?[89] Placing their wealth in heaven by giving it to Christ who was begging in the poor would also fix the hearts of the rich on the future life and protect them from the attractions of honor and status in earthly society.[90]

Householders might impose a kind of tax on themselves, Augustine suggested, as a way of setting aside funds for distribution to the poor.

These should be separated from those budgeted for the needs of the household, so that parents did not feel they were depriving their own dependents in caring for others.[91] Tensions between providing for one's children and caring for the poor will be explored in greater depth in the chapter on marriage.[92]

Although Augustine insisted that riches were not themselves evil, he preached against the love of wealth and the desire to acquire it. A person might have been wealthy before becoming Christian or might have acquired riches by inheritance, gift, or business once Christian. None of these forms of acquisition violated the conscience, as long as the property had been freely given or sold, righteousness had not been bartered away in the exchange, and the riches did not incite pride or inspire a false security.[93] The poor, of course, were subject to the same temptation to love and desire wealth, as Paul warned (1 Tim. 6:6–10). The truly poor, those free of avarice whom Christ named poor in spirit, were to be found among both the wealthy and the destitute.[94] Hair, Augustine concluded, was a good symbol for earthly goods because it could be cut off without harming the body. As the woman did in wiping the feet of Christ (Luke 7:38), Christians could use their money to wipe away the tears that they shed in sympathy for the suffering of others.[95]

Augustine's teaching on holding wealth paralleled that on marriage. Restraint in the acquisition and use of money was like faithful sexual practice within marriage; it was a proper and laudatory use of a good whose renunciation was better and deserving of greater reward.[96]

ALMSGIVING WITHIN THE BODY OF CHRIST

The principal form of good work performed on the basis of property and wealth was identified as almsgiving. Augustine extended the practice to the poor as well as the rich and identified values it served and functions it performed within the church and civil communities.

As has been seen already, in his expositions of the scriptures, Augustine developed a doctrine of the church as the social body of Christ, of Christ as head, and of Christians as the members of that body. He used a broad range of texts from the New Testament to support the doctrine and applied it as an interpretative principle to both the New and Old Testaments, particularly the Psalms. Two of the texts he used, the account of the final judgment in Matthew 25:31–46 and the risen Christ's confrontation of Paul in Acts 9:3–8, were directly and immediately applicable to the giving of alms and other services. Because in these passages Christ had clearly identified himself with Christians, in being both supported and persecuted, Augustine assigned a religious value to these actions that could not be applied to similar engagements with non-Christians.

Giving to Christians

Augustine explained that although Christ was now risen and safely in heaven, his identification with the members of his ecclesial body meant that he continued to need assistance on earth. Christ made himself available to be served in the Christian poor and thus offered those who responded the opportunity to gain salvation.[97] The heavenly Christ could have cared for his poor members directly, he explained, but preferred that they be served by his other members, who also benefited from the exchange. The point was illustrated by the feeding of Elijah first by a crow and then by the widow, whose entire household was preserved from famine by her service (1 Kings 17:1–16). When recognized as a Christian, therefore, the recipient of an alms was a minister bestowing a greater blessing on the giver.[98] Christ, Augustine suggested, had freely taken poverty upon himself and identified with the poor so that Christians might exercise generosity toward God. Those who recognized and kept faith with him, who were not ashamed of his poverty and his identification with the deprived, would enjoy the heavenly goods that were his by nature.[99]

Using the union of Christ with his members as a foundation for the giving of alms made the recipient's relationship to Christ determine the value of a gift. Augustine found a clarifying parallel between Matthew 25:40—doing for the least of Christ's brothers—and Matthew 10:41–42, on responding to Christian missionaries. In the latter, Jesus promised rewards to those who assisted his disciples when they were sent to preach the gospel. There Christ specified that receiving a prophet or righteous person because of that role or status would bring to the benefactor a share in the reward due the recipient. Similarly, the cup of cold water given because of discipleship would not go unrewarded. To these texts, Augustine added one first found in the *Didache* (1.6) that he regarded as authoritative, "Let your alms sweat in your hand until you find a just person to whom you can give it."[100] Christians had a special responsibility to seek out and care for the just and the servants of Christ. Beggars usually asked for help, but Christ's disciples often preferred to suffer deprivation in silence. Discovering and supporting them was a special service to Christ and made the donor a participant in their good works and holy lives.[101]

Giving to Sinners and Opponents

In contrast, giving to a sinner because of the sin would gain no reward at all. This did not mean that alms should be provided only to those who could be identified as righteous. As one could support a prophet without recognizing the prophecy and thereby fail to share the prophet's reward (Matt. 10:41), so a Christian could and should give to a sinner on the basis of need, without thereby approving and sharing the recipient's guilt. The beggar was regarded first as a human being rather than a sinner and on that basis recognized as an appropriate object of mercy. Augustine suggested that no donation be made if its recipient was employed or proficient in some immoral art. A Christian should hesitate to make gifts to gladiators, actors, fortune-tellers, and prostitutes. Those who received a sinner as a sinner earned no reward. In fact, donors had some obligation to rebuke the sin itself, particularly if the recipient was under their authority or influence.[102]

One might object, Augustine acknowledged, that giving to sinners was opposing God's will by alleviating the very punishment being visited upon them. Not so, he replied. Christ commanded his disciples to love their enemies and do good to those who hated them (Matt. 5:44). He willingly accepted vinegar to quench his thirst from someone who had been mocking him as he suffered; Christians should not hold back from helping their enemies.[103] In addition, the text of Proverbs 25:21-22 advised that God would reward the person who gave food and drink to an enemy. Paul, in Galatians 6:9-10, recommended special generosity to fellow Christians but insisted that alms should be given not only to the just but to sinners and persecutors as well. The sin should be rebuked to make clear that the Christian donor was not approving it.[104]

Thus, although Augustine urged Christians to exercise a special responsibility toward those striving to follow Christ, he taught that they should be generous to anyone in need. Since human hearts were so difficult to judge, being too careful with alms might mean depriving the worthy in order to avoid the unworthy. If Christians had an obligation to known enemies, moreover, then why not to those of whose enmity they were uncertain? If the sower was too careful with his seed in the winter, trying to make sure that none of it was wasted on the road or on rocky soil, he was likely to go hungry at the summer harvest.[105]

In practice, the congregation at Hippo seems to have extended its gifts of financial and material support to Roman traditionalists, Jews, and Christian heretics, all of whom were ready to accept their gifts though they had no intention of sharing their faith.[106] A collection for the poor seems to have been a regular part of Sunday worship. On one occasion, at the end of a sermon and thus before the dismissal of catechumens, candidates, penitents, and the curious others, Augustine announced that the collection was short. The needs of the poor could not be met with what had been given that day. He urged those present to make up the difference to the beggars outside as they left the basilica.[107] On another occasion, when preaching on the wedding garment necessary for participating in the heavenly banquet, he reminded his hearers that this robe was a gift of God. He then suggested that the poor would need heavier garments to get through the winter that was just beginning. If they clothed the poor, he promised, God would clothe them in the charity symbolized by that wedding garment.[108]

Because almsgiving gave Christians access to Christ himself, Augustine concluded that the Christian poor must be givers as well as recipients of alms. He used two instances of Christ's teaching to justify his assertion that even the indigent were expected to care for others in need. When Jesus sent out his disciples, he promised that not even a cup of cold water given to one of his followers would go unrewarded (Matt. 10:42). The specification of cold water, he argued, indicated that the donor did not have the resources to heat the water, perhaps to make it more palatable.[109] The widow contributing her two small coins to the upkeep of the temple provided another model (Luke 21:1–4).[110] He also suggested that the poor could offer services even when they had no goods to share: to help the lame and the blind, to care for the sick, and to bury the dead. The listing of services that could be offered allowed Augustine to include among the almsgivers both the clergy and those living from a common fund: some offered instruction, advice, or sympathy in place of funds, food, clothing, or shelter.[111] He concluded that the love exercised in giving determined the value of the gift and the reward it deserved.[112]

THE RELIGIOUS POWER OF ALMSGIVING

Augustine identified many roles that almsgiving played within the Christian life and the process of salvation. It was not only a means of dealing with the temptation to pride and self-sufficiency on the part of the rich, but a practice of generosity in which the poor also should engage, on an appropriate scale.

Petition and Penitence

As has just been noted, Augustine identified caring for the poor as one of the means of receiving and exercising the charity that was a constitutive element of salvation. In his commentaries on the First Letter of John, Augustine recalled that the Gospel of John had identified the greatest work of love as dying for one's fellows (John 15:13). He then specified delivering them from temporal distress as the first step toward that goal, as a means of nourishing charity. He observed that a Christian unwilling to expend surplus income for the rescue of another was hardly loving at all.[113]

In other contexts, almsgiving was described as lending efficacy to prayer both for a Christian's needs and for the forgiveness of sins. The rich knock on God's door asking for help even as the poor are banging on their own doors. The rich ask for the greatest of goods, God alone, who can be received only as a gift, while the poor ask only for sustenance. As the emaciated flesh of the poor was a plea for alms, the giving of alms was a prayer for oneself, made with hands and life rather than with the voice alone. For the rich to refuse their excess resources to the needy while seeking God's mercy for themselves, Augustine explained, would be like trying to reap without first having sown. Generosity toward the poor, then, was essential to any appeal to God for supplying one's own needs. In this sense, Augustine interpreted caring for the poor as the Christian replacement for the animal sacrifices of Israelite practice.[114]

Almsgiving as a plea for the forgiveness of sins was an established practice for Jews and Christians. Augustine regularly cited Christ's exhortation to "giving and forgiving" in Luke 6:37–38 to indicate these as inseparable forms of generosity extended and received. Almsgiving was the Christian form of the sin offering. It was the regular means of cleansing from the nearly inevitable failures of living and a daily prayer for Christ's help to improve one's life.[115] For more serious sin, however, it could never serve as a substitute for repentance and reform.[116] For some reason, Augustine judged that he had to explain to his congregation that support could be given only from wealth honestly acquired. Alms given from the profits of fraud, theft, or usury could not offset that sin, particularly since the sinner was usually willing to give away only a small portion of the ill-gotten gains. Was Christ to hear the prayers of the beneficiary of the alms for the criminal and ignore the groans of the victim whose money was being dispensed?[117] If the victim was a Christian and thereby a member of Christ, how was the judgment scenario described in Matthew 25 expected to play out? As Christ proceeded to reward those who had clothed him and condemn those who ignored his nakedness, he would come upon the person who first stripped him and then handed back a few scraps of his own clothing.[118] Such a pillager could hardly expect a heavenly reward; even the flames of hell would be a merciful response to such conduct. The graphic images of these sermons suggest that Augustine was dealing with a significant problem: the congregation—or at least the nonbaptized attending the first part of the service—might have contained some known to be rapacious, as well as others who were their victims.[119]

Providing for Eternal Life

On the more positive side, Augustine recommended almsgiving as a means of winning salvation by turning earthly into heavenly goods. Because of Christ's identification with Christians, Augustine could assert that although Christ was rich in heaven, he continued to be poor and needy on earth. He received the gifts—or loans—in his members and he would repay them in heaven.[120] Augustine compared the process to the mercantile transaction through which funds and goods were exchanged between parts of the empire. What was paid for in one port could be delivered in another.[121] Alms, then, were like a loan made to Christ in earthly goods that would then be repaid in heavenly ones. The poor in this schema were like agents for Christ who received advances that he would return.[122] Augustine also compared the system to a complex storage facility for liquids—not unlike the multichambered cisterns of a Roman city—in which something poured into one could pass through a system of pipes and be drawn from another.[123] Christ had designed the system and his promise that it worked could be trusted. The Christian poor, then, had a special role in the economy of salvation: through them temporal and earthly goods could be transformed into lasting and heavenly ones. Their bellies were secure storehouses; they were porters who carried things from earth to heaven.[124]

In response to an objection, Augustine asserted that transfers between earth and heaven could be made either for the donor or another designated beneficiary. Householders argued that they had a responsibility to preserve their goods and pass them to their children; they should not disperse their property as alms to the poor, who were not part of their families. Augustine pointed out that this kind of excuse could be repeated endlessly from generation to generation: no one would ever heed the command of Christ. He complicated the discussion by asking what should be done for a child who died. Might the parents distribute to the poor that part of the inheritance that they had been preserving to support their heir on earth? Or was it to be divided among the surviving children, each of whom would then be enriched through the early death of their sibling? Should not the departed sibling receive a rightful share? The deceased heir had need of the patrimony, and it could be sent along to follow that soul, now awaiting the final judgment of Christ. Let the parent, then, make the contract for transfer of the property and deliver the funds to the child.[125] Augustine suggested another possibility for enriching the entire family: let the father adopt Christ as an additional son, pay out his portion of the inheritance, and thus enrich all his children by making them coheirs of Christ's fortune.[126]

Even a Christian form of usury was suggested by Augustine. Christians judged that demanding more in return than had been advanced in a loan was the exploitation of a debtor's misfortune. When they gave to relieve the misery of another, however, Augustine suggested that they consider this a loan that Christ had signed and certified. The Savior would gladly give back far more than the needy members of his ecclesial body had received. A Christian creditor could count Christ as the most trustworthy of debtors; a hundred times more could be expected in return than had been advanced (Matt. 19:29).[127] This was the one form of usury, Augustine explained, that Christians were allowed to practice.

Almsgiving, as Augustine presented it to his congregation, was a very effective means of dealing with the uncertainty of earthly riches. The person who had temporal property was always anxious about keeping it safe. It had to be hidden away or placed under the supervision of a servant. Even then the wealth was either corruptible—grain, oil, wine, or another commodity—or in danger from thieves. Many masters, he suggested, had been betrayed by servants who fled with their riches or opened the house to a band of plunderers whom they then joined. Much property was immovable—a house or farm—and had to be sold or abandoned. Even if wealth was secure, the owner could enjoy it for only a lifetime and then had to leave it behind.[128] Christ's advice was to move the wealth from earth to heaven where it would be safe under his care and would already be where the owner hoped to follow. Augustine used an analogy: a person knowledgeable about grain noticed that an inexperienced friend had stored wheat underground, where it would get damp. He suggested that it ought to be moved to a higher, dryer place before it began to rot. Everyone in the congregation would have realized that this advice was right and good. Augustine asked: Would it not be wise to follow the advice of Christ—who had built the world—to move wealth to a higher, safer place?[129] He told the story of a man of modest means who exchanged a solid gold coin for a hundred smaller ones and gave a portion to the poor. A thief, at the instigation of the devil, then stole the remainder. Instead of cursing God for allowing the loss, the victim regretted not having given away the whole sum, so that it would still be his in heaven.[130] If Christians really loved their wealth, Augustine concluded, they should be wise about holding onto it. By giving it to Christ's poor, they might enjoy it forever.

CONCLUSION

Augustine's teaching on the limitations imposed on almsgiving by a responsibility for supporting self and family was significantly different from Cyprian's urging that Christians should sell their property and contribute the proceeds to the poor without thinking about the future.[131]

The affirmation of the goodness of wealth itself and the appeal to Abraham and Job as indications that saints could be wealthy might have been motivated by Augustine's concern with Manichean teaching. It might also reveal a division within the community between the rich and the poor, caused by the self-importance of the wealthy and the resentment of the impoverished. Finally, it reflected the bishop's own practice in the management of the productive resources—principally buildings and farmland—given to the church.

In all instances, the sharing of wealth was integral to Augustine's teaching. He insisted that the renunciation of possessions was not required but that their sharing was essential. This paralleled his teaching on fasting: what the person abstaining from food and drink gave up, or its monetary equivalent, had to be donated to the hungry.[132] Although riches were good, the greed that made them private and unavailable to others was evil.

Both the sermons and the discussions of the necessary qualifications for entering the kingdom of God in *The City of God* indicated that Augustine was faced with Christians, even within his own congregation, who defrauded and stole from others. Instead of apologizing and making restitution to their victims, at least some of them attempted to acquire forgiveness from God by giving away a portion of their ill-gotten gains to the poor.[133]

Augustine's attitude toward the possession and use of riches might be parallel to his evaluation of sexual practice among Christians subject to the penal legacy of Adam and Eve. Both were natural goods that God had intended to be part of the human world. Both were misused by humans who had fallen from the love of God into the disordered desire for lower goods. In both cases, proper exercise of the private claims to real property and to the body of a spouse was more difficult to practice than complete renunciation.

Chapter Three

SIN AND FORGIVENESS

T HE FORGIVENESS OF SINS through the rituals of baptism and public
reconciliation was one of the major points of conflict in the North
African church. Tertullian defended the Montanist restriction that denied
a bishop's power to forgive sins such as idolatry and adultery committed
by Christians after baptism. In conflict with schismatics in Carthage who
relied on the intercession of martyrs for the forgiveness of sins and the
Roman church's policy of recognizing baptisms performed by heretics,
Cyprian explained that the college of bishops maintained the unity of the
church and exercised its power to sanctify. He required (a new) baptism for
converts from heretical and schismatic communities but claimed the right
to readmit to communion after appropriate repentance the baptized who
were guilty not only of adultery but even of apostasy. In his controversial
writings, Augustine identified the indwelling of the Holy Spirit in the unity
of the universal church as the basis for its sanctifying power. He argued that
this divine presence in the church enabled even unworthy clergy within the
communion to baptize and to readmit to communion those guilty of serious
post-baptismal sin. This solution achieved a creative integration of the conflicting positions upheld by Tertullian and Cyprian. Unlike their theories,
however, his was guided by attention to the regular, even daily, repentance
and forgiveness practiced by all pious Christians, without the ministry of
the clergy. Especially in his sermons, Augustine reflected on the power to
forgive that Christ had bestowed on all Christians. He directed attention
to Christ's exhortations to exercise that power and Christ's warning that
refusal to forgive others impeded the forgiveness of one's own failures.

This study, like the others in this volume, focuses on the explanations
and exhortations that Augustine offered in his congregational preaching.
The correction and forgiveness of sinners through divine action will be

considered first. The rituals of the church and the ministry of the bishops as mediators of the forgiveness of major sins will follow. Then attention will turn to the more common practice of mutual forgiveness among the people. Finally, the interplay of divine initiative and human ministry in the correction, repentance, and forgiveness of sins will be detailed.

God's Dealing with Sins

Excusing Sins

Some people, Augustine pointed out, took no responsibility for their sins. They kept quiet unless their transgressions came to light; then, they were ready with excuses for their behavior. They appealed to fate and the stars as agents controlling people's decisions and actions: Venus was responsible for adultery, Mars for murder and plunder, Saturn for avarice. Some of these people only repeated popular slogans but others claimed to be adept at reading the influence of the celestial bodies on human activity. Even those posing as experts in such determinism, Augustine observed, usually refused to accept such excuses for the misdeeds of their own spouses, children, and servants. By drawing out the implications of this appeal to fate, moreover, Augustine identified it as blasphemous. Because proponents of celestial determinism admitted that God created and controlled the very stars that they used to explain the operation of fate, they pinned responsibility for their sins on God. Others excused themselves by appeal not to the stars but to their inborn tendencies to sin. These implied that God created them bereft of the strength adequate to resist evil. Such sinners all played a very risky game, Augustine warned, by daring to call God into judgment to defend themselves.[1]

Other sinners were not so impious as to shift full responsibility to God in exonerating themselves; instead, they blamed evil agents in the creation for tempting and persuading them. They suggested that Satan pressured or even coerced them to sin; they complained that God did not help them to resist. Actually, Augustine retorted, God opposed Satan's temptations by warning against evil and urging toward good. What was the point, he asked, of accusing Satan, who would hardly accept the blame and thereby help his alleged victims secure pardon for their sins? Evildoers should accuse themselves, spurn Satan, and seek God's mercy. Forgiveness could be received only by those who took the blame upon themselves.[2]

People—and especially Christians—who made excuses for their sinfulness by accusing God were in the greatest danger. God, Augustine warned, used the sufferings that fill earthly life to correct sinners and prevent them falling into eternal punishment. Failure, inability, or refusal to recognize and heed that warning might indicate that God had already turned hardened sinners over to the lusts of their hearts, pronouncing judgment on them even before their deaths (Rom. 1:24–32).[3] Obstinate self-defense could place a person in danger of being abandoned by God.

In contrast to all of the above, some sinners freely admitted their failings; they did not try to blame God or Satan. They claimed, however, that God was not concerned about the kinds of transgressions they committed. Since everyone failed as they did, God would tolerate common sins rather than having to condemn and punish everybody.[4] If God were really upset with their sinning, they asked, why were they allowed to go on living?[5] In particular, they claimed, God did not care about sins of the flesh, since scripture recognized that all flesh was grass (Isa. 40:6; 1 Pet. 1:24) and, contrary to Paul's claim, the body was not the temple of God (1 Cor. 3:16–17).[6] They might also discount the significance of sins against fellow humans. Supposing that only offenses against God were really dangerous, they failed to notice that the harm they caused might be against a member of Christ's body.[7] To excuse themselves, Augustine pointed out, these sinners denied unwittingly that God practiced the virtue of justice in governing the world. In this sense, they played the fool by saying in their hearts that God—at least a true and just God—did not exist.[8] Being unwilling or unable to imagine God as a just avenger of sin, they corrupted the divine judgment and made God an accomplice in their own evil.[9]

Since all of these points were made in sermons, Augustine must have judged them relevant to at least some persons in his audience, which included not only baptized Christians but long-term catechumens and even traditional polytheists who showed some interest in his teaching (or rhetoric). This observation need not mean, however, that he thought every position he attacked was being espoused by someone attending the sermons. When he suggested, for example, that certain sinners had been abandoned by God because of their hardened hearts, he might have intended his hearers to apply this warning to others who dismissed or ignored Christian moral teaching. His hearers may have encountered and tolerated such deterministic and dismissive attitudes among their traditionalist friends and even been tempted to adopt them. In addressing these excuses, therefore, Augustine warned of the blasphemy involved and offered defenses against it. Still, many teachings that he attacked, such as those excusing particular kinds of sins as so universal that they would have to be tolerated by God, might have found adherents among the Christians—the baptized and the catechumens—who were under his care.*

Presuming on Divine Mercy

Those believers in Christ as Savior who failed to appreciate the need for repentance usually presumed on the divine mercy. Augustine described many forms of this attitude, not all of which were compatible with one another. Elaborating an allegorical interpretation of Christ's walking on the water, for example, he observed that some Christians might be so impressed by the expansion of the church in their time, when the whole world seemed to be converting to Christ, that they might dismiss the warning of Christ coming to judge as an empty threat. They might have believed that he would condemn no one and would save all who had professed Christian faith. Augustine challenged this belief with Christ's warning that not everyone who called him Lord would be saved (Matt. 7:21).[10] Other Christians could have reached the same conclusion from the opposite experience. Few people appeared to observe the commandments carefully; most seemed to be sinners. When Christ arrived for judgment, then, was he really going to condemn the vast multitude gathered on his left and save only the few who deserved to be placed on his right? In the end, would the Savior refuse to take pity on the sinners, or would he relent and welcome everyone into his kingdom? This discounting of a divine warning, Augustine replied, was exactly what Satan had urged in seducing Eve: "Certainly not! You will not die!" (Gen 3:4). He insisted that the threat was real. He also questioned the judgment that few Christians lived faithfully. While God's threshing continued, the chaff was always more evident than the grain. When the wind of judgment finally blew, the true and faithful Christians would be

* The argument that God did not care what humans did to one another turns up regularly in Ambrosiaster's commentary on Romans. See, for example, the comments on Rom. 2:2 and 5:13 in *Ambrosiaster's Commentary on the Pauline Epistles: Romans*, trans. Theodore S. de Bruyn, Writings from the Greco-Roman World 41 (Atlanta: SBL Press, 2017), 37–39, 98–100. See also the introduction to the same volume by Theodore S. de Bruyn, Stephen A. Cooper, and David G. Hunter, xxiii–cxxx.

revealed. Sinners must not presume that the saints would be so few as they could recognize now.[11]

Augustine's congregants also based a presumption of divine mercy on their interpretations of certain scripture passages. In preaching, he considered such appeals and showed that the texts did not provide any basis for trusting that God would save sinners who had not repented. Certain narratives seemed to temper the teaching that Christ would judge the living and the dead. In the Gospel of John, for example, Christ declined to judge the woman taken in adultery (John 8:11); he said, "I judge no one," and later, "I came not to judge the world, but to save the world" (John 8:15; 12:47). Augustine countered this argument in various ways. Christ was contrasting his own judging to the judicial process used to condemn him "according to the flesh," that is, by appearances; he would judge in truth. He had come not for judgment alone but also to seek and save the lost. Had he exercised judgment from the outset, when all were still sinners, then he would have condemned all to death and saved no one. During his first appearance, then, Christ had worked to save sinners; when he returned, he most certainly would judge them.[12] Although Jesus refused to condemn the adulteress, he warned her to avoid sin in the future and thus did not encourage her to rely on a repetition of his mercy if she ignored his command. The punitive function of the law would be fulfilled, but by Christ himself as a just judge rather than by those eager executioners who were no less guilty than their intended victim.[13] Thus, he concluded that Christians who recognized their sinfulness must not be deceived by an unwarranted presumption of the mercy of God.[14]

Christian sinners seem to have used a text of Paul in a more complex way to gain security. Galatians 5:19–21 categorizes a set of sins as works of the flesh and asserts that those who engage in such practices would not possess the reign of God. Apparently, Christians unwilling to repent of and avoid these sins made a distinction between rulers and subjects in the kingdom of God. They professed themselves content to be saved as citizens, rather than undergoing the rigors of repentance in order to qualify for more honorable appointments as God's governing officials.[15] Augustine prefaced his response to this dodge by citing Christ's warning that only those who persevered in charity—not in iniquity and sin—would be saved (Matt. 24:12–13). He then undertook an extended analysis of the proposed interpretation, appealing to both grammatical usage in the text and parallels elsewhere in the scriptures. Even if a distinction could be made between rulers and subjects, he observed, all had to be in the same kingdom or reign. All Romans shared the empire, for example, though few of them ruled it.[16] Yet Paul had not said, "such people will not reign with God," but "they will not possess the kingdom." A parallel could be found in 1 Corinthians 15:50, "flesh and blood will not inhabit the kingdom of God," which Paul then explained by a contrast of mortal and immortal, corruptible and incorruptible realities. That text concluded with the assertion that only those who merited transformation of their animal body into a spiritual body and nature would inhabit the kingdom (1 Cor. 15:50–53). Clearly, then, Paul intended no distinction between holy rulers and sinful subjects within the kingdom of God.

The confusion over status within the kingdom, Augustine suggested, might have been caused by certain narratives in the gospels in which Christ apparently singled out the apostles by promising that they would sit on twelve thrones and judge the twelve tribes of Israel (Matt. 19:28). In this context, he argued, the number twelve actually indicated the much larger group that had left all to follow Christ and serve the gospel (Matt. 19:27), as well as the angels who would assist Christ in the judgment itself (Matt. 16:27). To clinch his argument, Augustine cited the words of Christ inviting those on his right hand to take possession of the kingdom prepared for them (Matt. 25:31–41). Everyone else, including those to whom Paul referred in Galatians 5:19–21, would be sent away into the fire prepared for the devil and his angels.[17] Fruitless to argue that Christ was addressing a small group of rulers who had acted generously toward him in his bodily members but that, in addition to these, he would allow a multitude of unrepentant sinners into the kingdom to serve as subjects presided over by these saints.[18] The detailed refutation to which Augustine subjected this interpretation may have indicated the attraction such proposals exercised over the imaginations of his (church-going) hearers.

A major task of Augustine's preaching was to convince Christians that they must acknowledge and repent their sins, seek divine mercy, and attempt to reform their lives. They must not blame God for their failures or rely on some purported loophole that would privilege Christians or exempt them from the demands of divine justice and the warnings God had provided. The proposals he considered and rejected may have indicated not only the hardness of heart that he suggested in one instance but a belief that the resources Christians had at their disposal were inadequate to fulfill the divine law. Augustine, of course, shared such a judgment, as he amply demonstrated in his writings against the Pelagians. In his preaching, he focused on confession of sin as the appropriate means of approaching the divine judgment. Such repentance was also a necessary step toward receiving divine assistance for fulfilling the law. He explained to his congregation how God was already dealing with their sins and urged them to cooperate in this process.

God's Correcting and Punishing Sin

Against the arguments that God would not actually condemn and punish sinners, Augustine insisted that God was already chastising and correcting sinners. The scriptures taught that death was the consequence and punishment of sin. All the sufferings that flowed from mortality and made earthly life bitter—the difficulties of satisfying bodily and social needs—were a disciplinary scourge of God. These painful experiences of human life should give credibility to the threats of greater penalties still to be visited upon the unrepentant. Nor were bodily sufferings the only torments to fear. Anyone who had experienced the delight of truth and the joy of wisdom already had an inkling of the pain that would result from failing to attain an intellectual vision of the creator—even without any bodily pains being added.[19] The biblical accounts of the retributions that God had visited both on particular sinners and on all the wicked could confirm the evidence of the faithful's own experience of suffering for sin.[20] No one, then, need wait for Christ's sentence of condemnation to the torments of hell to be convinced that God punished and would punish sin.

Augustine generalized from these particular observations: sin could not go unrebuked, either sinners must punish themselves or God would punish them.[21] God intended the sufferings of earthly life to move sinners to correct themselves; those who failed or refused to attack their own sin would be punished by God in the afterlife as well.[22] To discipline oneself during earthly life, however, was very different from being punished by God after bodily death. God visited bodily sufferings and spiritual deprivations on sinners during earthly life in order to move them to repentance. Sinners punished themselves by correcting their sins: they repented the actions, destroyed the evil intentions, and changed the behaviors. By repudiating evil willing and practice, sinners brought themselves into voluntary agreement and practice with the divine will. God would set such penitents free from the bonds of guilt.

Augustine elaborated this explanation of the destruction of sin by self-punishment and correction. Unlike the evil deeds with which human courts dealt, sin was primarily in the intention; God could judge desire and decision as humans would a deed. Created beings could will or act contrary to the command of God, but not with impunity. As long as their intention continued to oppose that of God, they suffered punishments that vindicated the divine sovereignty.[23] When sinners repented, they repudiated their evil intentions and the deeds that followed from them; they turned against and attempted to destroy their own sinful desires and voluntary opposition to the divine command. The symbol of this repentance, Augustine pointed out, was beating one's breast—striking and punishing one's own perverse heart.[24] By repenting, then, sinners attacked their own evil willing and aligned their own intentions with God's punishing "anger." By confessing their sins and engaging in penitential actions—prayer, fasting, almsgiving—they worked to bring their desires, decisions, and actions into conformity with the command of God and thus to destroy the sinfulness in their own intentions.

Augustine found a scriptural witness to this process of self-punishment or correction in Jonah's mission to Nineveh. The prophet warned the people that their city would be destroyed; he announced a delay but gave no hope that the place might be spared. The citizens heeded the threat by using that three-day period to destroy the sinful "city" of their shared evil willing. By prostrations, tears, fasting, sackcloth, and ashes, they changed their communal orientation from evil to good willing; they destroyed the old city and built a new one. They thereby accomplished the work God had threatened and averted any further punishment or loss.[25]

Thus, Augustine interpreted the scriptural language of repentance to make it fit a change in voluntary commitment. In correcting and humbling themselves, repentant sinners punished their evil hearts or offered a sacrifice to God. They admitted their guilt so that God could remit it; they confessed, and God acquitted.[26] During this transition, they were both still sinful and becoming just, as Paul described himself in the seventh chapter of Romans.[27] Their penitential works symbolized both a rejection of evil willing and the labor of building a new orientation. Merciful deeds cooperated in the divine correction; they cooperated with and manifested the effect of the divine mercy at work in the transformation of the penitent's heart.[28]

Using this understanding of the destruction of sin and building of righteousness, Augustine described the different ways that God encouraged and facilitated repentance and self-correction. The disease in the human heart could be allowed to grow, so that it would become manifest and recognized by the sinner.[29] God had embedded a law in nature that could display failures and weakness; God added explicit commands that turned sin into transgression, making it not only worse but manifest and undeniable.[30] The laws requiring and governing sacrifice were used to move the Israelites to acknowledge their sin and to dispel their self-satisfaction.[31] As has been noted, God regularly used the sufferings and troubles of mortal life to correct sinners. The child of David's adultery, for example, was allowed to die as a means of turning his father away from the sin that God was already forgiving.[32] God tolerated evil people in the world not only to allow them the opportunity to repent but to test and confirm others in good.[33] The condemnation of sinners by divine judgment was delayed so that by these rebukes and sufferings they might be moved gradually to repentance and then strengthened in good willing.

Yet, Augustine noted, the very means that God employed to provoke repentance could have the opposite effect and make a person worse. Some refused to acknowledge their sin; they asserted their innocence, complained that their sufferings were unjust, and insisted that God was perverse.[34] Others acknowledged their sin but were distracted by the apparent prosperity of people they considered worse than themselves. Their outrage at the unequal treatment blinded them to the mercy that God was extending to them and others; as a result, they continued in sin.[35]

More often, if Augustine's regular invoking of this theme can be used as an indicator, sinners delayed. They presumed that God would allow them plenty of time to prepare for a reckoning and would even provide ample warnings that their deaths were drawing near. God promised forgiveness to the penitent, Augustine warned, but did not promise a tomorrow for repentance.[36] Foolish people combined God's secure promise of forgiveness with an astrologer's deceitful assurances of the remaining length of their lives.[37] Drawing on the biblical narratives, Augustine compared Noah building the ark and Jonah preaching in Nineveh to Christ expanding the church: each provided time and reason for conversion.[38] When the allotted time ran out and judgment finally came, he warned, repentance would be useless.[39]

The Divine Gift of Conversion

Observation of the different results brought about by divine correction eventually brought Augustine to the judgment that God moved the elect to conversion and repentance rather than only providing the assistance necessary for a proper human response. He had long recognized that God took the initiative in saving individuals. Gradually he came to acknowledge and preach that even the sinner's response to God's offer of grace was a divine operation.[40] A bishop could correct, exhort, and punish by excommunication, but only God's operation within the heart would make the appeals effective and move sinners to confession and correction.[41] He described Christ as himself groaning within the sinners who accused themselves of returning to evil after baptism.[42] This divine intervention was most evident, he explained, in the conversion of those hardened sinners who had habituated themselves to evil and grown deaf to the word of truth. Such people were symbolized by Lazarus dead, bound, sealed in a tomb, and weighed down by the mass of earth covering him. These sinners were trapped, were beyond the reach of human appeals and threats; they could be awakened only by the voice of God speaking in their hearts, calling them forth from the tomb, and placing them in the open to confess their sins. Only then could the voices of their fellow Christians reach them and the hands of the church's ministers untie the bindings that had held them captive in sin and guilt.[43]

This emphasis on divine operation in the correction and conversion of sinners seemed to limit recognition of human initiative; the recovering sinner must give thanks for the divine graciousness that had induced and even produced a change of heart. In Augustine's explanations, however, that divine operation utilized human agents and was mediated by the church in returning sinners to life and health.

Repenting and Forgiving
within the Christian Community

The question of the church's participation in the divine power to forgive sins had a long history in the African church. Tertullian and Cyprian presented opposing solutions in the late second and mid-third centuries by locating that power in the saints following the moral guidance of the Holy Spirit or in the college of bishops as successors of the twelve apostles. In each case, the focus of the debate was on sins committed after baptism that excluded a Christian from the church's communion. In his preaching, Augustine did exhort such sinners to undertake and persevere in the public penance through which they could be reconciled to the church and to God. More regularly, however, he exhorted his congregants to repent the minor sins of daily living. To win God's forgiveness for these, they were to offer and seek pardon from one another for the offenses that they committed in the course of their interactions. In taking this approach, Augustine relied on the promise to forgive in the Lord's Prayer and the power to pardon that Christ extended to the whole community in Matthew 18:18. Taking this approach to the question, Augustine offered a radically different explanation of the power to forgive that Christ conferred upon the church.

Repenting the Sins of Daily Living

The most common form of sinning among Christians were the faults that arose in daily life, as either inattentiveness or disregard for one's responsibilities toward others, as failures to love self and others in relation to God. Using graphic images of destruction through flood and shipwreck, Augustine insisted that these small failings must be recognized and repented in order to prevent them from gradually but eventually overwhelming the sinner. These were repented as they were committed, privately or by personal interaction, rather than through the formal ritual of penance that involved the congregation and its episcopal leader.

In a sermon considering the various forms of repentance, Augustine suggested that Christians should lament their temporal and mortal condition: it was rooted in the original sin; it made humans corruptible and fragile; it disposed them toward personal sin. Mortal life was a temptation, as Job proclaimed; it must be managed by cultivating the desire for that immortal, heavenly life toward which Christians were journeying. Developing this travel theme, Augustine noted that the dust of the road leading to immortality stuck to the feet of the pilgrims and must be washed away daily. Nay, the innumerable sins involved in conducting the necessary business of a family or even a church congregation so splattered the travelers with mud that they were nearly unrecognizable. He briefly reviewed the failures that occurred in seeing, hearing, speaking, eating, drinking, and sleeping—all of which he had elaborated in the reflections on his own life as a bishop in the *Confessions*.[44] He observed that the sexual union of married couples, even when focused on the generation of children, necessarily involved lustful desires that violated the natural order.[45] Although Christians might not practice iniquity and fraud in their business dealings, most were unable or unwilling to follow Paul's exhortation to tolerate and forgive their fellows who did (1 Cor. 6:7). Each daily sin was like a small sore on the skin; taken together, however, they were a rash that covered the body and threatened its life.[46]

58

Although these daily sins could not be avoided completely, Augustine insisted that their deleterious effect on a person must not be ignored. Individually they might be insignificant but cumulatively they could choke and suffocate the Christian life. These sins must be repented daily, with the same regularity and persistence with which they were committed. Augustine offered a variety of illustrations. Water seeped through the joints of a ship and waves lapped over its sides; unless bailed out, it would swamp the vessel and result in the same loss as a sudden shipwreck in a dramatic storm. Grains of wheat were each small, but when multiplied they filled silos and weighed down ships. A heap of sand could be a heavier burden than a chunk of lead. Raindrops turned rivers into floods that carried off houses and farms. Lightning killed with one strike, but rain could slowly overwhelm; a large animal killed with one bite, but the stings of hundreds of insects could be just as deadly.[47] In these examples, Augustine seems to have intended to warn against becoming inured to sinning rather than the piling up of a huge debt of guilt. Repenting of these sins of daily living as they occurred protected the Christian against the major sins that complacency and self-satisfaction would occasion. Thus, Augustine urged that repentance be as regular as sinning. He drew attention to the common action of striking the breast at the plea for forgiveness when reciting the Lord's Prayer. Every Christian—including the clergy—did this during the communal eucharistic ritual, and no one was embarrassed to participate.[48]

Like major sins, daily failings must be countered and resisted not only by recognition and repentance but by penitential works. Augustine recalled the standard practices: weeping, fasting, almsgiving, prayer, and forgiving others. These could be remembered, he suggested, by using the words of Luke 6:37–38: give and forgive.[49] Forgiving enemies, even if they did not seek pardon, was the only way that a Christian could pray the Lord's Prayer sincerely. In it, God's forgiveness was requested according to the measure that one offered forgiveness to others. In addition, Augustine recommended fasting as a means of stopping, or at least slowing, one's sinning.[50]

Augustine's exhortations to repent of the minor sins involved in daily living indicated his belief that the mortal and sinful human condition itself was as much the object of repentance as the specific desires, acts, or habits by which a Christian ignored the exhortations and transgressed the commands of Christ.[51] The process of repentance for this condition usually did not involve the clergy directly as ministers of forgiveness, nor did it always require apology to fellow Christians. Confession for this sinful state of life could be made and forgiveness sought before God, primarily and regularly in attentively praying the Lord's Prayer. He urged the works of penitence—prayer, fasting, almsgiving, and forgiveness of others—as habitual practices rather than temporary intensifications of activity focused on the destruction of a particular sin.

Augustine judged that regular acknowledgment of daily sins and the dispositions that they manifested, along with their repudiation through penitential works, was necessary not only to prevent a gradual decline in Christian living but to forestall the complacency that led to self-righteousness and to cultivate the humility that protected against self-satisfaction. Acknowledging these sins before God was, in this way, even more important than the unending labor to eliminate them.

Repenting and Forgiving Sins against other Christians

Offenses that pitted one member of a local Christian congregation against another sometimes had to be treated differently than either the minor failures that were practically unavoidable in daily life or the major sins that jeopardized one's baptismal commitment to Christ and required temporary or permanent exclusion from the eucharistic fellowship. The former might be forgiven—especially if they never broke out into action—by confession to God alone without involving any other person. The latter required the intervention of the bishop and a ritual of reconciliation, normally but not always before the entire congregation. Sins that divided one Christian from another were usually more serious than the failures of daily life, particularly because they could occasion a lasting division between the parties directly involved and spread to the supporters each drew into the conflict. Reconciliation had to be accomplished in order to avoid damage to the community, but it was best achieved in private or small groups, without amplifying the conflict or using formal, public rituals. Augustine regularly drew his hearers' attention to this form of repentance and reconciliation.

In treating disputes—great or small—that involved another person, Augustine insisted that Christians must not seek vengeance on their fellows: vindication fed on the suffering of another person.[52] Victims who demanded the satisfaction due them in justice, moreover, could expect to be held to that same standard; they renounced an appeal to mercy—from God or their fellows—for their own offenses. Sinners were better advised, Augustine warned, to imitate God, who never took vengeance, even though God sinned against no one and thus never would need to ask another's forgiveness.[53] Christ had made just this point in his judgment on the proposed execution of the woman taken in adultery (John 8:2–11). Her accusers might have followed the rules of justice articulated in the Mosaic law but would do so at their own peril; apparently, they were all subject to a condemnation like that which they were so eager to impose upon her. Christians, then, should always reflect on their own sinfulness before they acted against that of another.[54] Nor should Christians who lacked the resources to enforce a claim of just retribution pray that God satisfy their desire for vengeance. With Christ and the martyrs not (yet) avenged, Augustine asked, would God satisfy the outraged petitioner by abandoning the divine patience that allowed sinners time for repentance?[55] The offended Christian should petition God to kill the animosity rather than the offender.[56] Only by renouncing vengeance, Augustine argued, could a Christian participate in the Savior's mission to correct and reform the offender, to convert an enemy into a friend.[57]

Although Augustine recognized that not every attempt at reconciliation would be successful, he insisted that sinners must be tolerated within the church community in hope of their repentance. He developed this teaching in response to the schismatic bishops who refused to maintain or restore fellowship with the successors of bishops whom they charged with having tolerated apostates among their colleagues and clergy, even a century earlier.[58] The principles and many of the arguments that had been elaborated to deal with apostasy and other crimes against God could be applied to the sinners who were guilty of offenses that injured their fellow Christians.[59] Patience and persistence, he insisted, was necessary for the salvation of both the offender and the injured party.

The Church as a Mixed Body of Saints and Sinners

The church, Augustine insisted, was a mixture of good and evil people in the era before the general resurrection and return of Jesus. The better were burdened by the more sinful but were forbidden to separate from them in an attempt to establish on earth a community of the morally upright. Living in a pure church must remain an eschatological objective: a divine promise and a Christian hope. Augustine used many images, most of them scriptural, both to illustrate the relationship between the earthly and the heavenly church and to encourage his congregation to practice forbearance. The two sons of Isaac, the ugly Esau and the handsome Jacob, were symbolic of the two types of people in the church.[60] Even within Jacob's own body, moreover, the withered thigh that made him limp signified the evil within the church (Gen. 32:24–32).[61] The parable of the wheat and weeds (Matt. 13:24–30) demonstrated that the devil had his own disciples within the church and that they were to be tolerated until God sent the angels to segregate them at the end of time. Unlike the weeds, sinners could repent; unlike the harvesting angels, humans could not distinguish with certainty those who had. The mix, moreover, was not found in a particular segment of the church: it was in the apse and the nave (clergy and people), and in both extended families and monasteries (among the married and the celibate). The presence of a sinner need not stain the assembly or ruin its gathering place: Satan fell while still in heaven; Adam and Eve sinned in paradise; Noah had a sinful son on the ark; and Judas was among the apostles chosen by Christ.[62]

Augustine regularly elaborated the gospel accounts of the disciples' two catches of fish into symbols of the contrast between the heavenly and earthly church. At the outset of their calling (Luke 5:4–11), the disciples were in two boats, representing the circumcised and the uncircumcised; at Christ's command, they lowered their nets without regard for the left or right side of the boat; their catch strained the nets; the boats groaned under the load but did not sink; the quality of the fish was mixed. The second catch, after the resurrection (John 21:4–8), was made from one boat, with the nets lowered on the right side where the good fish were gathered; despite their load, the nets did not tear; all the fish were brought to shore. The earthly church, Augustine explained, was represented by the first catch of fish. The good must remain in the church and tolerate the wicked, though they might be confused and distressed by the combination of moral failure and economic success among their fellow Christians.[63] Similarly, in the parable of the wedding feast, the servants were sent to gather everyone into the banquet hall and only the master sorted them out (Matt. 22:1–14).[64] On the threshing floor that represented the church on earth, the grain and chaff were heaped up together and the heavier grain was hidden by the greater volume of the chaff. Upon his return, Christ would blow away the chaff with his winnowing fan; only the grain that remained on the threshing floor would be gathered into his barn.[65] Augustine added a parallel reflection on the olive press. The sludge went running down the gutter into the public drain for all to see, while the oil flowed unseen into underground vats for safekeeping.[66] Finally, he suggested that in staggering over the waves and through the wind toward Christ, Peter had symbolized the mixture of fidelity and weakness in both individual Christians and the church as a whole.[67]

All these images were used to persuade Augustine's congregants that Christians must tolerate the presence of the sinful and even the unrepentant among the baptized members of their congregation: they had not been assigned the task of judging and separating. God was patiently giving the sinful—with whom every Christian should identify—time to repent and amend their lives before the judgment. Only those who remained within the unity of the church could be saved.[68] Moses was a model for both clergy and people: he remained committed to the idolatrous Israelites, for whom he sought forgiveness, rather than accepting God's proposal to destroy the sinners and raise up a new people through him.[69] Toleration of sinners, then, was necessary. But Augustine insisted that patience was not enough: Christians had to work for the correction and conversion of their sinful fellows.

Beyond Patience toward Forgiveness

In a sermon at the beginning of the Lenten preparation for Easter, Augustine exhorted his congregants to focus on resolving conflicts with and between fellow Christians. No one could sustain a quarrel, however justified, without some kind of sin occurring. The longer the disagreement endured, moreover, the more anger and annoyance were fed by suspicion, grew into hatred, and imprisoned the hearts of the opponents.[70]

Augustine relied on Christ's instructions in Matthew 18:15–18 and the following parable of the two debtor servants (Matt. 18:23–35) to guide his exhortations on resolving conflicts among Christians.[71] To sin against a fellow Christian was to attack a member of the body of Christ and thus to sin against Christ himself. Thus, these sins could not be effectively distinguished from those against God; they had to be repented and removed.[72] Sinners who recognized their failures should humble themselves and seek forgiveness from the persons whom they had harmed.[73] When pardon was either sought and granted or offered and accepted, the sin was forgiven, and the parties reconciled. Offended Christians dared not refuse the pardon sought: according to the teaching of the parable, that would result not only in their forfeiting any appeal to divine mercy for themselves,[74] but also in the return of the guilt for all their prior sins.[75] Their refusal could not, moreover, bind in sin before God a fellow Christian who had sought their pardon sincerely.[76]

When the sinner failed to acknowledge the offense committed or to ask pardon for it, responsibility for initiating the reconciliation fell on the Christian who had been harmed, as was required by the teaching in Matthew 18:15–18. The offense suffered should have been forgiven by the victim, even before the sinner had acknowledged and repented it. In Augustine's view, the self-inflicted wound that bound the sinner in guilt should have been of even greater concern to the victim than the injury— not itself sinful—that had been suffered. Acting under the influence of the same charity that prompted the gratuitous forgiveness of an acknowledged sin, the victim must attempt to heal the aggressor. If the sinful action was known only to these two, the offended party alone should attempt correction in order to facilitate repentance and reconciliation by avoiding further embarrassment of the sinner. If the sinner resisted the admonition and claimed that the offending action had been justified, then the injured Christian should seek the assistance of a few others in resolving the conflict. Only if reconciliation could not be achieved by these informal negotiations should an appeal be made to the congregation and its officers. Even if the procedure resulted in the excommunication of a sinner who refused to confess and repent (Matt. 18:18), the offended party must continue to forgive and to pray for the repentance of the sinner rather than being satisfied with public vindication.[77]

Augustine modified the process laid out in Matthew 18:15–18 in one particular: the text specified that the initial approach to the sinner was to be made in private while the text of 1 Timothy 5:20 required a public reproach. Augustine reconciled these two provisions by explaining that the latter was appropriate when the sin had been committed before witnesses, because that circumstance multiplied the number of victims. The offender had presumed that the witnesses would approve the unjust action and thus had sinned against them as well. As additional victims, they shared responsibility for correcting and healing that sinner, as well as for supporting and joining the efforts of the primary victim to have the evil action acknowledged and forgiven. As witnesses to one sin and victims of another, Augustine suggested that they must be involved in the process from the beginning, rather than waiting to be invited to join after the offender had been approached in private and had refused to acknowledge and apologize for the primary injury.[78]

In other sermons, Augustine elaborated different aspects of the procedure described in Matthew 18:15–18. Mutual love and care were foundational to the entire process. The sin must not be glossed over or dismissed.[79] Christians were called both to tolerate and to care actively for those who had sinned against them. Not only were they to forgive but to correct and even to punish the offenders—if they had authority over them—in an attempt to destroy the sins persisting in their evil willing. To practice a "toleration" that allowed a fellow Christian to remain unchallenged in sin could even be identified as an act of hatred. In clarifying this point, Augustine extended to the entire community those responsibilities generally recognized in families and households.[80] A father who silently tolerated the reckless behavior of his son not only neglected his responsibilities, but he might signal his approval of the sin and suggest that his own abstaining from such behavior resulted not from virtue or the absence of sinful desire but from the passing of the youthful vigor that once had enabled his performance. He might appear to approve his son's taking up where he had left off.[81] Thus, to follow Christ in the practice of love was not only to bear another's burden grudgingly, but generously to work at making the sinner healthy and loveable.[82] This responsibility was greater toward sinners within the unity of the church than those outside it and more pressing for those who held supervisory positions over offenders than among equals.[83]

In this understanding of Christian practice, forgiveness was a prerequisite for correction of the sinner, especially when punishment became necessary. The corrector's heart must be fixed on the recovery of the sinner and not on the injury suffered, just as a physician steeled himself against the pain he was about to inflict in an amputation (performed without anesthetic) and God visited misfortune on sinners for whom Christ had died generously.[84] Thus, Augustine carefully distinguished the anger that often accompanied a reprimand or punishment from the hatred that made a person unable to act for the good of an enemy. Hatred was like the beam in one's eye that prevented seeing and evaluating the splinter in another's. In contrast, the annoyance suffered by a person correcting another in love was easily repented and resolved. A parent's giving voice to frustration with a child did less harm than suppressing that anger and allowing it to grow into hatred.[85] This observation was not unlike the advice Augustine gave to married couples whose mutual love and whose desire to generate children was burdened by the lust consequent upon their mortal condition. The love operative in their fidelity to one another and in their desire to procreate easily won forgiveness for the lust and excesses that accompanied their well-intentioned sexual intercourse.[86] While Christian spouses might agree to contain lust by refraining from sexual practice, even within marriage, they must not escape outbreaks of annoyance or anger by disengaging from one another and renouncing their obligation to help free one another from sin. Christians were responsible to and for one another in struggling against the divisive effects of sin within the community.

Augustine recognized that a Christian might be prevented from or hampered in correcting a sinner. Social structures might limit a person's freedom to confront a superior; an individual's own weakness might make an intervention impractical or ineffectual. In such cases, an unspoken forgiveness and a prayer for divine operation of the necessary conversion might be the only actions available.[87] A corrector also had to be on guard against a temptation to pride and the danger of dealing severely with a sinner.[88] When a rebuke was rejected and the sinner refused to apologize, the offended person might withdraw and seek an intermediary to act in his or her place, rather than taking two or three witnesses to support the renewed rebuke.[89] On the other side, a social superior might find an indirect means of apologizing to an abused inferior, who might be even tempted to pride by an unveiled request for pardon. Kind words or gentle treatment might convey the sinner's regret without disrupting the structured relationship. Still the sinful superior should be careful to humble his or her self before God.[90] Augustine also considered the situation of the accused. A false accusation should be rejected but forgiveness should be extended to the accuser. An accusation should be accepted and recognized as divine mercy when it was true and with regret for the sin of the accuser when false.[91]

Augustine's discussion of the practice of mutual forgiveness highlighted the goods it was to achieve: a quarrel between Christians resulted in injuries to all the parties involved, and consequently to the whole body of Christ. His concern was focused on healing the division rather than on reparations for the injury, which the victim was expected to have forgiven or to be ready to forgive. His analysis also displayed the power of charity to overcome both the evil intention operative in sin and the resentment it could cause among Christians. The detailed considerations by which he elaborated Christ's instructions in Matthew 18:15-18 clearly indicated that he expected Christians to undertake and become adept in the practice of mutual correction and forgiveness.

As a bishop, Augustine also served as a civil magistrate, judging disputes that the parties agreed to submit to his court. He claimed that his objective in this work was to reconcile the contending parties without violating the just claim of either. In order to attain peace, he could not find in favor of the poor person who was in the wrong, but he could urge the rich to benevolence for the poor and the honest to generosity toward the dishonest. Still, he acknowledged that the parties were often dissatisfied. The rich thought him partial to the poor, and the losers were seldom satisfied by the judgment.[92]

Running through Augustine's treatment of mutual forgiveness and the overcoming of divisions between Christians was an understanding of the relation of mercy to justice. He urged that divine judgment must be faced neither with trust in one's observance of the commandments nor reliance on one's generous deeds. Hope and security could be found only in the divine mercy. According to the Lord's Prayer and the parable of the debtor servants, that mercy was neither capricious nor irrational; it followed the standard of a person's own practice. God would continue to be merciful to those sinners who had themselves extended mercy to their fellows. Thus, divine mercy followed its own perfect justice, in which Christians were called to participate.[93]

Forgiveness by the Church through the Bishop

Preaching on the anniversary of his ordination for service to the congregation of Hippo, Augustine reflected on his office and its burdens. Using Ezekiel 33:2–11, he explained that he had been set as a watchman to warn others of the dangers that faced them. He compared himself to a son whom a physician had warned that his elderly father would survive an illness only by staying awake. If the old man went to sleep, he would slip away. The son stood faithfully at the bed, talking to his father, shaking him, pleading with him to stay awake. Like the son carrying out the physician's orders, the bishop served as God's agent for his people. He must warn sinners of danger as they continued unrepentant. He might have preferred to assure them of their salvation, but his promise would carry no weight in the face of God's warnings. So, he pleaded insistently with sinners in his congregation to amend their lives, to turn away from evil while God still gave them time and opportunity to repent.[94] In another context, Augustine reflected on the disciples described in John 6:66 as parting company with Jesus after his discourse on the bread of life. Christ's own experience of losing his followers provided some small consolation to bishops, who regularly found people turning away when they spoke the truth to their congregations about their sins.[95]

Distinguishing Sins

The church's role in correcting and forgiving three types of serious sinners was distinguished by an allegorical interpretation of the three narratives of Jesus raising persons from death. The daughter of the synagogue leader died but was revived almost immediately within the same room; her death was never witnessed in public (Matt. 9:18–26; Mark 5:21–43; Luke 8:40–56). She represented those who sinned in intention but not by action; they then heard the word of God as though it were spoken by the Lord directly and in their own hearts, immediately arose, condemned their sin, and returned to normal Christian life. Both sin and repentance took place within the secrecy of thought and intention, without attracting anyone else's attention.[96] The divine mercy specifically directed the admonition that moved the person to repentance and life. Because neither the clergy nor any member of the church knew the sin, none of them admonished or exhorted the person to repentance. God, however, could use some word or work of theirs to move the sinner.[97] In this case, the sin, correction, repentance, and forgiveness took place between the sinner and God, without the conscious and intentional intervention of a human minister.

In contrast to the daughter of this ruler, the son of the widow of Nain was raised by Jesus as he was being carried out for burial (Luke 7:11–17). His death symbolized a sinful decision that had been acted upon and had come to the attention of others. Such a sinner could be openly reprimanded and warned to repent the sinful action. Other Christians might act as intentional mediators of the divine grace that moved the sinner to repentance; the ministers of the church might supervise the penitential actions through which the sin was removed and ritually readmit the forgiven sinner to the church's communion. In the sermon, Augustine treated this case only briefly, moving on to the third one.[98]

The raising of Lazarus after four days among the dead (John 11:1–44) represented the correction of a Christian burdened by habitual sin. Such persons were blinded to their own evil; they defended their actions as right and just when they were challenged; they rejected correction and allowed malice to rule their lives. Though regularly admonished, they were deaf and unresponsive to the word of truth.[99] The shout by which Christ called Lazarus forth from the tomb symbolized the divine operation that alone could reach and change the heart and mind of such sinners. It shattered the grip of death and raised them to life. Only then did they begin to perceive the evil of their lives, to turn from their actions in disgust, and to resolve to change for the better. Unlike the girl and the young man, Lazarus could not move himself even after he was returned to life. Still bound by the grave clothes representing the guilt of sin, he was lifted and carried from the tomb by the divine power. This action symbolized the public confession in which the divine mercy drew sinners out into the light. Only then were they turned over to the ministry of the church, to be released from the chains of guilt and enabled to walk. Such sinners were subjected to long, public penance, until they no longer stank of sin.[100]

The Bishop as Overseer

The three types of correction illustrated by these allegories distinguished different roles for the church. The bishop might exhort the congregation as a whole without addressing specific sinners or particular sins. The preacher or another Christian in authority might reproach an individual, a group, or the congregation as a whole for a particular sin that had come to light. A sinner who had long ignored or rejected warnings and exhortations might unexpectedly confess and seek the bishop's guidance in repenting habits of sin. The bishop then used the church's rituals of confession, repentance, and forgiveness to reconcile and return the sinner to the eucharistic communion. The bishop's exhortations to repentance may have had some role in all three forms of repentance. He mediated forgiveness sometimes in the second and always in the third form, as minister of the church's ritual of reconciliation.

Augustine's reflections on the role of the bishop in warning the congregation have been illustrated already in the section on the danger of sin, presumption of the divine mercy, and failure to repent before death. Some sins were regularly denounced, such as habitual adultery with a slave or concubine.[101] Sometimes, this general public censure was effective in moving individuals to reject their sin and begin the process of repentance under the bishop's supervision.[102] Occasionally, Augustine had to remonstrate with the congregation about a particular event. On one occasion, they drove away a convert from schism whose motives for seeking entrance into their communion they considered unworthy.[103] Another time, some participated in the lynching of an imperial official and took refuge in the church building.[104]

In other instances, the bishop took the initiative in admonishing a particular individual. Augustine claimed that bishops usually practiced this ministry in private and records of such admonitions probably never existed. The bishop may have learned, perhaps through individuals in the congregation, of sins that were not generally known. Augustine encouraged wives, for example, to confront their husbands about adultery; if their admonition was rejected, the concerned spouses should report the offender to the bishop.[105] He promised to try to speak with the accused, to learn the truth, and to persuade a sinner to repent. He assured the accusers that the objective was correction rather than punishment. If the individual denied the charge, the bishop could do nothing more: he would not make himself both prosecutor and judge.[106] In the absence of a confession or of a judgment by either an imperial or ecclesiastical court, he could not exclude the accused person from participating in the eucharistic communion. In particular, when an action that could be prosecuted as a crime in imperial courts was still not generally known, the bishop could not expose the sinner to judicial attack by someone seeking revenge.[107] Augustine explained that he might advise the sinner to acknowledge the sin in private and to refrain voluntarily from communion during a period of repentance but he could not force the issue or require any action that might publicize the sin and reveal the sinner.[108]

The bishop's ministries of public rebuke and private correction sometimes meet resistance. Many Christians resented being accused of sin.[109] Some tried to silence their episcopal critics by offering or making gifts to the church. Some bishops, like hireling shepherds, avoided the risk of confronting a powerful sinner.[110] Congregations might suspect that their bishops had failed to reproach reputed sinners whom they observed continuing to receive the eucharist. Augustine tried to explain the complexity of the bishop's position: he did not always know what people assumed he knew; even when he knew, generally he would avoid accusing a sinner in the presence of the congregation. His objective was to cure, not to condemn.[111] Yet some members of his congregation could testify, from personal experience, that he did rebuke and correct.[112]

Augustine's efforts to encourage repentance seem to have been motivated not only by concern for the salvation of the sinners but also by the need to curb their negative influence within the congregation. In his sermons to the neophytes following their baptism, he warned that they would find many examples of evil living among their fellow Christians.[113] Some people would invite them to the races when they should be going to the church. Others would mock them for turning away from drunkenness, debauchery, astrology, spells and charms, shows and fights.[114] Others still might praise the ascetic life, but warn converts that it was too difficult and caution that giving away one's property to the poor was imprudent.[115] These bad Christians were doing the devil's own work within the church, Augustine complained, setting up obstacles to the aspirations of the good, impeding the conversion of traditional polytheists, and generally doing more damage to the church than its enemies among the Jews, heretics, and schismatics ever did.[116] In these ways, Augustine was attentive to the social effects of personal sin and his inability to bring known sinners to public repentance.

The Ritual of Repentance

In his appeal to sinners, Augustine focused on their standing both before God and in the community. Christians who recognized that they had committed serious sin after baptism, Augustine explained, must not only turn away from the evil behavior and improve their lives; they must deal with the guilt they had incurred by disobedience of the divine will. Though the evil intention that constituted sinning and the guilt that resulted from it were sometimes identified in Augustine's preaching, he recognized that guilt remained even when the evil intention had been rejected and the evil behavior brought to an end. In explaining the status of newborn infants, for example, he affirmed a guilt arising from their participation in the sin of Adam, although they were not willing that evil personally at the very early stage of their lives and could not repent it. They were baptized—with the assistance of sponsors who spoke for them—in order to remove the guilt that would prevent their salvation should they die.[117]

Augustine had found an opportunity to distinguish three stages in liberation from serious post-baptismal sin in the allegorical interpretation of the resurrection of Lazarus discussed above. Resuscitation signified the repentance of the sinner: in response to the admonition of Christ and the church, the person willingly turned toward good and away from evil. Exiting the tomb into public view symbolized the confession of sins and the performance of penitential actions in the presence of the church community—that is, when the penitent was sinning no longer but still was bound by guilt. Unbinding of the grave clothes represented the exercise of the church's power to release from guilt—on earth and in heaven—and the sinner's resumption of life in the communion.[118] Penitents, then, must not only accept correction and stop sinning but acknowledge and reject the evil they had done. Only then might they be released, forgiven, and returned to the eucharistic fellowship.[119]

Augustine elaborated each of these stages. The penitents must reject their pride and evil willing by offering God a contrite and humble heart. In seeking the divine mercy, they should exercise mercy toward others by almsgiving.[120] Second, they should not trust in private repentance to overcome their failures and win divine forgiveness; instead, they must have recourse to the power of forgiveness that Christ committed to the church. They must make their sin known, at least to the bishop. The action might have been not only a serious evil for the sinner but a cause of scandal for others in the congregation, hindering their own practice of the Christian life. The bishop, who had to care for the good of the congregation as well as that of the individual, might require the sinner to submit to the full ritual of penance. This public display of repentance and humility would profit the sinner seeking forgiveness and the Christians struggling against similar temptations, as well as promoting reconciliation with those who had been harmed by the sinful action.[121]

Rather than relying on their private resources to win divine forgiveness, Augustine argued, sinners should trust Christ's promise that whatever was loosened on earth by the keys of the church would be loosened in heaven.[122] The power of the keys had been given to Peter not as an individual, he explained, but as representative of the whole church as the body of Christ, whose faith in Christ as savior he had confessed.[123] In this sense, Augustine intimated, the full community's intercessory appeal to God in response to the public acknowledgment of sin was more effective than the individual's private petition.[124] Some sinners undertook public penance voluntarily but others had to be excluded from communion by the bishop until they confessed before the congregation and performed these rituals of repentance.

A number of the penitents were present for the sermon that was integral to the eucharistic ritual on Sunday. At least some of them then were dismissed after the sermon by an imposition of hands and an exhortation to pray. Augustine occasionally expressed disappointment with their enactment of repentance and improvement of their lives. The humiliation they had suffered in accepting the status of penitent would count for nothing, he warned, unless they changed their behavior. He pleaded with them to cast off delight in sin and conform themselves to the commands of God. They seemed to presume both a long life and a warning adequate to arrange for the reconciliation and restoration to communion that were given to any penitent who requested them at the time of death. Their behavior filled the bishop with fear because extended delay could signal an unwillingness to repent that would result in condemnation by Christ. He begged them to have mercy on him, at least, as he worked to fulfill the responsibilities of his office by preparing them for the divine judgment.[125]

Penitential Acts

The practice of requiring penitents to perform activities demonstrating a rejection of sin and a petition for pardon was well established before Augustine's time. He affirmed that prayer, fasting, and almsgiving were integral to the process of turning from sin and gaining divine forgiveness. Scripture as well as church practice clearly showed that a sinner could not simply desist from past behaviors; the burden of those evil deeds had to be removed.[126] Like the prodigal son (Luke 15:11–24), penitents should be angry with themselves and turn that anger toward destroying the evil within their hearts. To pull out their hair, to dress in sackcloth, to roll in ashes, and to beat their breasts all symbolized these attacks on their ill will that penitents were mounting within themselves. They were, Augustine explained, battering their spirits and offering them as a sacrifice that God would not reject.[127] "Grief is the companion of repentance; tears are the witnesses of that grief," he observed.[128] Citing John the Baptist's demand for fruits worthy of repentance (Luke 3:8), Augustine interpreted rooting out and burning a bad fruit tree as a symbol of cleansing the heart of the evil manifest in past sins. That repudiation of sinful behavior also had to be performed by acts of mercy that were the fruits of repentance. Augustine credited penitential actions with eradicating past sins from the heart and the exercise of mercy with both manifesting that change of intention and winning divine forgiveness for one's guilt.[129] These considerations appeared in his preaching on the most important penitential actions—fasting and almsgiving—and in extending forgiveness to others.

Augustine's exhortations to fasting as a penitential practice occurred primarily in his sermons preached at the beginning of the annual Lenten preparation for Easter. Using Psalm 35:13, he reminded his hearers that because fasting could humble the soul, it was an appropriate preparation for the celebration of Christ's humbling himself in death on the cross.[130] It also rendered the soul merciful and forgiving of others, which was essential to winning God's pardon of one's own sins.[131] Christ's example, in the desert after his baptism, indicated that fasting strengthened the soul in time of temptation.[132] Because it symbolized the soul's withdrawal from the love of temporal goods,[133] it both strengthened against temptation and

73

fostered prayer.[134] Fasting intensified almsgiving when penitents gave to others what they took away from themselves.[135]

Scripture testified that almsgiving could erase prior sins (Sir. 3:30; Dan. 4:24). Augustine developed this point in two ways: directly from the words of Christ and by connecting almsgiving to receiving divine mercy. For the first, he referred to the description of the judgment in Matthew 25:31-46. Christ warned that he would condemn the sinners who had refused to wipe out their evil deeds by practicing mercy toward others in almsgiving. Augustine concluded that turning away from sin would bring salvation only if a person added works of mercy toward others. John the Baptist had warned the Pharisees to show actions worthy of repentance: to avoid sins in the future was not sufficient; they must eradicate the evil that had been done in the past, must cut down the evil tree and throw it into the fire. John specified feeding and clothing the poor as the works that would wipe out sins (Luke 3:7-11).[136] For many Christians, Augustine concluded, the giving of alms, along with the forgiving of offenses, was the only hope for salvation.[137]

Augustine also made a direct link between extending mercy to others by almsgiving and receiving mercy from God in forgiveness. Sinners had to show mercy so that mercy might be shown to them (Matt. 5:7), and they needed to give in order that they might receive (Luke 6:37).[138] Mercy both healed and washed away sin,[139] as scriptural precedents illustrated. Giving alms had made Cornelius and his household worthy of receiving the gospel.[140] The refusal to care for the beggar at his gate had brought condemnation upon the wealthy man dining in splendor (Luke 16:19-31).[141] His wealth itself was not the problem, since the beggar had found rest in the bosom of a very rich man—Abraham.[142]

Finally, Augustine exhorted sinners to forgive those who had sinned against them. Although traditionally it had not been treated as a penitential act, Augustine linked forgiveness to almsgiving through the text of Luke 6:37-38: "Forgive, and you will be forgiven; give, and it will be given to you."[143] He exhorted penitents to appeal for divine mercy by extending pardon to those who had sinned against them, reminding them of the promise made in the petition for forgiveness in the Lord's Prayer.[144] The importance of offering forgiveness was emphasized even more, as has been seen, in Augustine's exhortations to repentance for the small failures of daily living and especially in his teaching on mutual reconciliation.

Delaying Repentance to Escape the Ritual

In a sermon dedicated to repentance, Augustine issued a clear warning to baptized sinners who were apparently planning to delay public penance and take advantage of the promised deathbed forgiveness and communion.

The most secure way to prepare for the divine judgment was to accept baptism, to live its commitment without falling into sins against the Decalogue (since living free of all sin was impossible), and to continue so until the end of life. Those who delayed baptism until the approach of death ran a risk of dying without it.[145] Had they waited to be baptized until they approached the end of their lives, then died before they sinned again, however, they could expect to enjoy the peace of the Lord.

Baptized Christians who had violated their baptismal renunciation of evil by some major sin could win forgiveness and restoration to the eucharistic fellowship by sincere repentance and changed behavior. By living the rest of life well, they could face the divine judgment with security.

The status of Christians who accepted baptism, violated it by serious sin, and then delayed repentance and reconciliation until their last hour was, in Augustine's judgment, most dangerous. Unlike the lifelong catechumens baptized as death approached, these sinners had violated their earlier baptismal commitment. Unlike the sinners who repented and were reconciled, they had not turned away from sin while they were still alive and healthy; nor did they attempt to live well after repenting. Instead, like the lifelong catechumens, they delayed until their health failed and their opportunities for the sinning they found delightful had been exhausted. They did not renounce sinful practice so much as suffer abandonment by it. Only with alternatives disappearing did they finally turn to God for forgiveness and salvation. Augustine stated that he could not be sure that God would accept such half-hearted repentance, whether such penitents would be forgiven or condemned. In practice, he exploited this uncertainty. Because he did not know that a change of heart for fear of punishment rather than love of goodness was useless, he pleaded with sinners and tried to frighten them into repentance. Because he did not know whether the reconciliation ritual was effective or useless for the frightened, he agreed to perform it. But he professed not to judge its efficacy; he could assure no one. In that uncertainty, he did what he could for the reluctant penitents: he performed the ritual of restoration to communion for dying sinners who requested it. To remove that uncertainty, he begged penitents long separated from the eucharistic fellowship to change their lives and regain the communion of the church while they were still healthy. Then, they would make a good end to their lives and could look forward to peace with Christ.[146]

THE POWER OF FORGIVENESS

The sins of daily living that were privately repented and those committed against other Christians that were forgiven through reconciliation of the two parties were the only types of offenses that most Christians in Augustine's time had to repent. The sins that required the intervention of the bishop were expected to be rare. In particular, the ritual of public confession, excommunication, and reconciliation could be used only once in the lifetime of a Christian.[147] Augustine's attention in his preaching was, therefore, directed primarily to those sins in whose repentance and forgiveness he, as bishop, had no necessary role. He constantly exhorted his congregation to the practices of correction, apology, and reconciliation through which such sins were forgiven. He may often have intervened to urge opposing parties to settle a quarrel, but that ministry required great discretion. Like the private rebuke of sinners, its successes and failures were neither recorded nor reported.

Attention must now be directed to the relationship between the power of forgiveness that was exercised by the bishop in the public ritual used for major sins and that operative when Christians corrected or apologized for offenses against one another or repented for their daily minor failures.

Divine and Human Interaction

The foregoing distinction of three practices of forgiveness is based on the types of sins and the processes of removing them. Two stages in that transition can be distinguished: repentance and reconciliation. Repentance was focused on the rejection of sin; it involved an acknowledgment of the disordered intention and actions; it required the performance of actions directed against that defect. A change of heart or intention had to occur: the sinner had to reject a defective desire and attempt to have it become a right intention leading to good actions. Often, but not always, this was initiated by an admonition that confronted the sinner about an evil action and then was supported by punishment designed to change the sinful disposition. Reconciliation, in contrast to repentance, restored the sinner's relationships with God and with other humans that had been damaged by the sinful willing and action. These relationships with God and with other humans were related but not identical. From the parable of the two debtor servants that followed the command to forgive an offender (Matt. 18:23–35), Augustine drew the lesson that a refusal to forgive and be reconciled to an offender impeded a person's being reconciled to and forgiven by God. This connection was illustrated in his description of the interaction that resolved a conflict between Christians. The forgiveness given and received by the reconciling parties not only restored their relationship but mediated the divine forgiveness of sin committed by one against the other and facilitated the divine forgiveness of the sins of daily living committed by both.

Correction

The mediation of divine correction through the admonitions of the local bishop and aggrieved Christians was most fully discussed in Augustine's allegorical interpretation of the three revivals of a dead person recounted in the gospels, which has already been examined. The three resuscitations were first introduced by Augustine in his commentary on the Sermon on the Mount as allegories for the degrees of sinning: in the heart, in deed, and in established custom. In his preaching, the allegories were more fully elaborated and he was more attentive to the series of actions, both divine and human, particularly in the case of habitual sin.[148] The three individuals, it will be recalled, were the daughter of a synagogue leader (Matt. 9:18–26; Mark 5:21–43; Luke 8:40–56), the son of a widow (Luke 7:11–17), and Lazarus of Bethany (John 11:1–44). He distinguished the three by the depth of their engagement in the bodily and social reality of death and, allegorically, of sin. His analysis could also be used, however, to illustrate different roles for the church in the mediation of the divine operation of repentance for serious sin.

The young girl was revived almost immediately and in the same room in which she had died. Even though the sin was serious enough to cause death, it did not fall under the church's requirement of excommunication and supervised repentance because it was never manifest in action. Because the widow's son appeared dead in public, his death symbolized a sinful decision that had been acted upon and had come to the attention of others. The ministry of the church could mediate the divine correction that moved the sinner to repentance and could supervise the penitential actions through which the sin was destroyed.[149] Lazarus had not only died and been publicly buried but was under the earth for four days. God worked directly in moving sinners symbolized by this situation to recognize, repent, and confess their sin; only then could the ministers of the church supervise their penitential actions and loosen the bonds that separated them from the community and from God.[150]

In developing this allegory, Augustine was attentive to the distinction between the secret work of God within the sinner and the more manifest ministry of the church. In the first instance, the sin was secret, and God alone worked: admonishing and moving the sinner to repentance. In the second, both clergy and laity could admonish their fellows who acted on a sinful intention; their correction might mediate a divine gift of repentance. Then, the ministry of the bishop guided, and the exhortations of the faithful sustained the sinner through the penitential actions that attacked the sinful intention. In the third case, Christians could pray for the hardened sinner but only the voice of Christ could penetrate to the heart and renew its life. The rejection of sin and decision to acknowledge it before the congregation took place within the heart of the sinner, unobserved by others. The ministry of the church began in receiving the confession; it continued through the penitential actions that gradually destroyed the habitual orientation toward evil and nourished new patterns of willing and acting; it culminated in restoring the penitent to communion.[151] Each of these revivals from death to life was a symbol of recovery from a deadly sin, though only the two that issued in action allowed or required the intervention of the bishop and congregation as ministers of divine operations.

In discussing the conflicts between Christians that did not involve deadly sin, Augustine's attention was focused primarily on the ministry of the human agents rather than on the divine operation that made their interventions effective. The responsibility for initiating the reconciliation rested upon both the parties: the offended by admonition and the offender by apology; neither was exempt from the responsibility to begin the process. The response was also specified and rested on each party: the admonished offender must seek pardon or explain the challenged action; the petitioned victim must offer and grant forgiveness. When this interchange failed to bring repentance—for a sin or a false accusation—other Christians were obliged to come to the assistance of the aggrieved parties. Their objective was to contain the damage, prevent a division within the community, and move toward a restoration of peaceful relations between the parties. In these cases, the mediation of the church was primarily carried out by the involved members of the congregation or even the family, without the intervention of the clergy. Only when this process failed and the congregation itself was damaged was the ministry of its agent, the bishop, required. Augustine insisted that these human actions—of admonition or accusation, apology or explanation—mediated divine grace.

Repentance for the sins of daily living might have been mediated by admonition of a harmed person or a witness to the offense. More regularly, however, it was fostered through the practices of prayer—particularly the regular recitation of the Lord's Prayer, with its petition for and promise of forgiveness.

Citing 1 Corinthians 3:7, in which Paul insisted that only divine operation made preaching and exhortation effective, Augustine identified a divine operation moving the sinner to repentance as necessary for the success of human admonition and correction. Christians who labored for the conversion of their sinful fellows were ministers in the service of this divine action.[152] He found exemplary instances of prayer for the divine conversion of a sinner in the petition of Christ that brought the witnesses to his crucifixion to repentance and faith and in the dying prayer of Stephen that was answered by the conversion of Paul.[153]

Reconciliation

"Loosening on earth and in heaven" was a way of talking about the forgiveness of manifest sins through the ministry of the church.[154] Specifically, it was accomplished by welcoming penitents to the congregation's eucharistic communion from which they had voluntarily withdrawn or been involuntarily excluded.[155] The power to bind and loosen from guilt was associated with the gift of the Holy Spirit and God's dwelling in the living temple formed by the union of holy Christians. The body of the faithful, to which Augustine referred as "the dove," was endowed with divine power that enabled it to act on behalf of sinners.[156] By themselves forgiving the sinner, by praying to God for the repentance and forgiveness of the sinner, and finally by welcoming the penitent sinner back into their eucharistic communion, the faithful were cooperating with a divine movement within themselves and mediating God's own forgiveness to the sinner.[157]

In Augustine's interpretation of the New Testament, Peter generally bears the person of the church,[158] or more specifically of the good and faithful within the church, in contrast to Judas who represented the evil.[159]

Peter confessed the belief upon which the whole church was built. The faith blessed in him was what God revealed rather than what a human achieved, as was shown by Peter's failure of faith, as he immediately rejected Christ's prediction of his passion and his subsequent denial of Christ during it.[160] In his repentance and profession of love after Christ's resurrection, he again represented all the faithful. In response, Christ commended his sheep to the faithful represented by Peter.[161] Later, in Acts 10, the whole church was instructed to receive the nations in the person of Peter dreaming on the roof in Joppa.[162] In Augustine's understanding, then, the power of releasing from the guilt of sin had been given to Peter not as an individual but as representative of the church as a whole, which Augustine identified as Christ's body.[163]

Augustine also used this explanation of the role of Peter as acting in the person of the church in order to justify—against the Donatist schismatics—the effective ministry of sinful bishops, who were not endowed with the Holy Spirit and, thus, could not hold or exercise the divine power to sanctify. He supported that interpretation by a close reading of the passages in the New Testament dealing with the forgiveness of sins. The very words Christ spoke to Peter in Matthew 16:19 were repeated in Matthew 18:18 when he addressed all the disciples.[164] This same power to forgive bestowed on Peter in Matthew 16:19 and on the disciples in Matthew 18:18 was identified in John 20:22–23 as the gift of the Holy Spirit, where it was given again to the whole company of disciples hiding in fear after Jesus's execution and reported resurrection.[165] Finally, Augustine noted that if Christ had intended the power for Peter as an individual, the church would have been able to use it only when he was present and would have lost his authority to forgive upon his death.[166] He repeatedly avoided the interpretation offered by Cyprian that identified Peter and the apostles, as predecessors of the church's bishops, as the recipients and holders of the power to forgive sins.[167]

The gospel texts dealing with the power to sanctify had been the subject of controversy in African Christianity for two hundred years, as many of Augustine's hearers might have known. At the beginning of the third century, Tertullian had insisted that Matthew 16:18–19 referred to a special privilege of Peter as the founding leader of the church, who had exercised it to open the gates of heaven through baptism and to free Israel from the domination of the Mosaic law (Acts 2:22–42; 15:10–11). The church's power to forgive was distinct from the episcopal office; it had not been transmitted to any successor in office. That gift was identified with the Holy Spirit and was lodged in and exercised by the holy members of the church who followed the discipline of Spirit—rather than only in its bishops, as Tertullian's episcopal adversary contended. He noted the giving of the power to forgive directly to the disciples in Matthew 18:18, but argued that it applied only to sins committed against a fellow human being, not against God.[168] A half-century later, Cyprian had reached a different conclusion, but ignored Matthew 18:18. Peter, he claimed, had represented only the apostles (and not the whole church) in receiving the keys (Matt. 16:19). The same power later had been given to all the apostles (John 20:22–23) as the founders of the episcopal college. Through the college, that power was transmitted to those bishops who were joined in unity as the foundation of the church.[169] Adapting and modifying both positions, Augustine insisted that Peter had represented the whole church and thus that the power of forgiveness was shared by all the faithful, that is, by those endowed with the Holy Spirit's gift of love.

In his writings directed against the Donatist schismatics, Augustine fully developed the explanation of the church's power to forgive sins and its exercise through the prayer of the holy community, rather than by a power or authorization conferred upon the clergy and dependent for its efficacy upon the holiness of the college of bishops.[170] In his sermons, he occasionally alluded to this explanation but elaborated it only rarely. In Sermon 295, for example, he began with the conferral of the power of forgiveness upon Peter as the representative of the whole church, using Matthew 16:19. Thence, following Cyprian's argument, he showed that this same power was conferred upon all the apostles in John 20:22–23, where it was identified with the gift of the Holy Spirit. Finally, he moved to Matthew 18:15–18, where all Christians were commanded to exercise this power in the forgiveness of those who offended against them. He concluded with the allegorical reading of the raising of Lazarus, in which Christ commanded his disciples to loosen the resurrected man from the bonds of sin.[171] Occasionally, he referred to the text of 1 Peter 4:8, "Charity covers a multitude of sins," that he also used to identify the power to destroy sins and to argue that it was operative in the love exercised between Christians.[172]

In his citations of the words of Christ authorizing and empowering Peter, the disciples, and every Christian to forgive sins, Augustine preferred the plural version of the text found in Matthew 18:18 to the singular used in Matthew 16:19. The grammatical forms of the words Jesus used in conferring the power to bind and loosen differ slightly in the Latin versions of Matthew's Gospel that Augustine used. When Christ addressed Peter, the verbs and their objects ("bind," "loosen," "whatever") were in the singular form (Matt. 16:19); when he addressed all the faithful (Matt. 18:18), however, both the verbs and their objects were in the plural. When preaching, Augustine used the singular form (Matt. 16:19) only six times,[173] four of which were in speaking about Peter serving as the sacrament or symbol of the church.[174] Still, even in this type of usage, in two other instances he used the plural form even though the grammatical subject (Peter) was singular.[175] He used the plural form more regularly: when commanding the disciples to release Lazarus,[176] in considering the Holy Spirit as the power of binding and loosening,[177] and when referring to the church's exercise of that power.[178] In one instance, he used the plural form in referring to the scriptural text conferring the power to forgive and the singular in exhorting individuals within the congregation to exercise it.[179] Clearly, Augustine understood the power of binding and loosening as given to the church as a whole, as a gift and responsibility conferred upon every Christian and habitually urged that the exercise of forgiveness was a work imposed upon all.

In other sermons, particularly those preached in the first decade of the fifth century when he was intensely engaged in responding to Donatist writers and in attempting to bring the Donatists back into communion with his own church, Augustine further specified the group within the church who received, maintained, and exercised the power of forgiveness. Those whom God had predestined, whom he foreknew would remain firm in their fidelity and charity made up the inner core of the church and secured its holiness.[180] These Christians were present in every generation; unlike the college of bishops, they were known only to God.[181]

Indeed, Augustine seems to have understood the laity's exercise of the forgiveness of sins in the process of mutual correction, apology, and forgiveness not only as the more frequent but as the standard practice of the church. In this interpretation, the intervention of the bishop and use of the public ritual of confession would have been recognized as unusual, required only when the offense affected not just individuals but the entire congregation or church and was thus beyond the authority of any individual Christian to forgive.[182] Whether the bishop acted in a gathering of the congregation or in the privacy required by the confession of a crime subject to prosecution in imperial court, he served as the agent of the community and using power that he was authorized to exercise as its designated leader. This, as shall be seen, was also the way that Augustine explained the bishop's role in the celebration of the eucharist.[183]

CONCLUSION

Augustine's discussion of the forgiveness of sins in his preaching addressed not the refutation of the Donatist problem but the exercise of the power to forgive that was bestowed upon all Christians by the gift of the Holy Spirit. He directed his hearers' attention to the correction, repentance, and reconciliation to be employed regularly among the faithful, practices that every Christian would have been required to initiate or to join as pardoner, pardoned, or witness. Giving priority to this practice allowed him to interpret the rituals presided over by the episcopal leaders as engaging the full assembly of the faithful in confronting, supporting, and offering forgiveness to the penitent who had offended the church as a body. In this way, he was able to specify that the charity inspired by the Holy Spirit and nourished in the hearts of the faithful was itself a participation in the divine love that forgave and overcame the failure to exercise it adequately. By forgiving one another, Christians exercised not an authority or agency but the divine power of the love the Holy Spirit operated in them.

Thus, Augustine exhorted the faithful to exercise their power by correcting and forgiving one another. He explained that in so doing they were not only following the example but sharing as members in the work of Christ, their head. Individually and corporately, they were not only invited but required to participate in the forgiveness that Christ had performed and now continued to perform, in the power of the Spirit, through them.

In his development of this understanding of forgiving sins, Augustine recognized its place—along with the sharing of goods—at the very heart of Christian holiness. Even under the prompting and guidance of the Holy Spirit, Christians would fail in fulfilling the commands and observing the prohibitions of Christ. Their hope for salvation was based not on the righteousness of their actions and intentions but upon the graciousness of God in moving them to repentance and forgiving their refusals and failures. They would experience that graciousness and share its fruits by offering and receiving it within the church.

Baptism

I N PREACHING, AUGUSTINE ADDRESSED the Christian doctrine and practice of baptism more fully and on more occasions than he did those related to the eucharist. Much of his treatment of the sacrament of initiation was directly pastoral: he explained what the sacrament required of, and accomplished for, the recipient; he urged catechumens to receive it sooner rather than later. He used opportunities provided by the day's scripture readings to expound Catholic teaching, particularly on the relationship between the ritual of baptism and the operation of the Holy Spirit. Some of this exposition was in defense of Catholic doctrine and practice against the Donatists, who normally refused to recognize Catholic baptism on the grounds that those bishops were tainted by a heritage of apostasy and thus incapable of communicating the faith.

This exposition will proceed, with some necessary overlap, from the pastoral to the doctrinal preaching of Augustine on baptism.

PASTORAL CONCERNS

Events and Practices Foreshadowing Christian Baptism

Most, if not all, of Augustine's concerns about the practice of Christian baptism were included in his regular exposition of the two events in the history of Israel that apostolic writers had interpreted as foreshadowing Christian baptism: the flood (1 Pet. 3:20–21) and Israel's crossing of the Red Sea (1 Cor. 10:1–13). His discussion of the baptism of Jesus by John was also oriented toward pastoral considerations, although the exposition of John's baptismal ministry was more often used to score doctrinal points against the Donatists. He made less use of male circumcision as a precedent for baptism, perhaps because Paul had treated this practice as a central mandate of the Mosaic law from which Christians had been freed.

Following 1 Peter 3:20–21, Augustine treated the universal flood that cleansed the earth of sinners as a foreshadowing of the purification of the conscience of the baptized. The ark floating on the water was a symbol of the church and its role in this process of salvation.[1] During the whole of the age before the return of Christ, the church rides on the waters of baptism as the ark had floated on the flood. The incorruptible wood used to build the ark symbolized the faithful saints who were baptized in the unity of the church.[2] Like the ark containing both clean and unclean animals, the church included both good and bad Christians. When the waters receded, however, Noah offered a sacrifice of the clean animals only. At the end of time, corresponding to the ark resting on solid ground, God would accept only those Christians who had been cleansed from sin.[3] In another reflection, Augustine explained that the olive branch returned to Noah by the dove symbolized Christians who had been baptized outside the church but later entered its unity. In his version of the text of Genesis 8:11, the branch that the bird carried back to the ark had both leaves and fruit. The green leaves signified the words used in the baptismal ritual and the oil-bearing fruit symbolized the charity of the Holy Spirit that built the unity of the church. Had the dove found leaves but no fruit on the branch, he explained, it would not have brought it back to the ark.[4] Augustine used this story in his normal fashion, offering symbolic interpretations that would exhort his hearers to make themselves worthy of their received or anticipated baptism by cleansing themselves from sin and adhering by love to the unity of the church.

Paul's comparison of the Corinthian Christians to the Israelites who had been liberated from Egypt by passing through the Red Sea and traveling through the desert toward the promised land (1 Cor. 10:1–13) was elaborated by Augustine into a figurative treatment of the Christian life. While they were in Egypt, the Israelites were burdened with earthly works and oppressed by Pharaoh. Similarly, the catechumens delaying baptism served their sinful habits under the control of the devil.[5] When the Israelites left Egypt, they were hounded by Pharaoh and his army all the way into the sea. So, the petitioners preparing for baptism were pursued by sins, temptations, and their demonic master right up to the baptismal font.[6] The entire force of the Egyptian army was destroyed in the sea. In the same way, all prior sins were forgiven by baptism, and no guilt remained in the baptized.[7] Finally, the red color for which the sea was named symbolized Christ's blood shed on the cross that empowered the water of the font to destroy sin and evil.[8]

Having explained the liberation from the sins committed before baptism that had already been accomplished for a large portion of his congregation, Augustine followed the Pauline exhortation based on the trials of Israel in the desert, as the people traveled toward the promised land. Christians, he observed, should recognize the age in which they lived as a wilderness and themselves as on pilgrimage in hope of attaining the homeland prepared for them.[9] Although the baptized could regret but not undo the sinful actions of their prior lives, they could and should overcome the temptations that they faced after baptism. Freed from slavery, they must struggle against the obstacles and conquer the opponents of the peaceful life toward which they journeyed.[10] They must live in desire and patient hope for what was promised, rather than settling for their earthly life as the best that God could provide.[11]

Following Paul, Augustine pointed out that God had supplied food and drink to Israel in the desert, but that the people had grown weary of it and longed for the tastes they had left behind in Egypt. The manna delivered to Israel foreshadowed the scripture that God offered to Christians. In the water from the rock, the faithful could recognize the drink that Christ provided in the eucharist. Christians, Augustine urged, must cultivate these gifts rather than looking back to the pleasures they had enjoyed before committing themselves to Christ.[12] Baptism was the beginning of a lifetime's journey, he insisted, a process of gradual renewal in which Christ was guiding the church as Moses had led Israel. The people should trust that the God who had delivered them from sin would strengthen them against temptation.[13]

The circumcision of male infants on the eighth day after birth was a third foreshadowing of Christian baptism in the Old Testament. Augustine usually preferred to contrast the circumcision of the flesh to that of the heart, in which evil desires were cut out.[14] He also interpreted the ritual as a foreshadowing of participation in the resurrection of Christ, in which the old life of Christians would be cut away.[15] He did, however, compare the use of circumcision in Israel to Christian baptism as the ritual establishing membership in the church, particularly in questions relating to the baptism of infants.[16] In this context, he linked the ritual to the faith of Abraham rather than the Mosaic law.[17] In one instance, he argued that as the sons of circumcised fathers still required circumcision to be joined into the people of Israel, so the children of baptized parents required baptism to free them from the inherited guilt with which they were born.[18]

Finally, Augustine presented Christ's baptism by John as an example of humility that was to be followed by both recipient and minister. Acceptance of the ritual was a symbol of the self–emptying that Christ had practiced in becoming human.[19] In response to Christ's presenting himself for baptism, John had professed his own lower standing. Their humble submission to one another was the fulfilling of righteousness to which Jesus urged John. Thus, Christ had provided a model for converts who might have considered themselves more learned, disciplined, or even holy than either the ministers through whom they would receive the sacrament or the Christians to whom they would be joined in communion by it.[20] John, for his part, had not claimed the power to transmit his own justice to those he baptized, as Donatist bishops did for themselves.[21]

Augustine argued that the baptism of Jesus by John was not the inauguration or institution of Christian baptism; the two rituals were radically different. Jesus had insisted on receiving the same baptism of repentance that John offered to others, he explained, in order to show that John's baptism was not greater than the baptism that Jesus himself would offer to everyone else.[22] He assigned the efficacy of Christ's baptism to his death and resurrection and to his gift of the Holy Spirit.[23] In discussing the baptism of Jesus by John, then, he focused on the exemplary humility of the minister and recipient in a ritual of repentance.

Although Augustine used many types and exemplars of Christian baptism, he preferred the escape of Israel from Egypt, its baptism in the Red Sea, and its difficult journey through the desert toward the promised land. This narrative provided the opportunity to address not only liberation from guilt and sin but the limited efficacy of baptism that did not deliver Christians from their evil desires and the other temptations that they still had to endure and overcome. Moreover, the exodus narrative could be used to locate segments of Augustine's congregation in different stages of the process and to urge them forward along its path.

Exhortations Arising from Baptism

To a repentant recipient, baptism offered the forgiveness of all the sins that had been committed already, no matter the seriousness of the offense. The form of personally committed sins—thought, word, deed—was irrelevant; all guilt was removed.[24] In Augustine's teaching, baptism also removed the guilt of the sin committed by Adam and Eve to which all of their off-spring were subject.[25] This abolition of sin and guilt was accomplished by the gift of the Holy Spirit that Christ had sent upon the church.[26] Thus, Augustine could compare baptism to the wine and oil that the Samaritan had poured upon the wounds of the unfortunate traveler in the parable of Luke 10:30–35.[27]

To encourage the unbaptized, Augustine detailed some of the sins whose forgiveness was witnessed in the New Testament. From the cross, Christ prayed for the forgiveness of those responsible for his execution and of those jeering as he died. Those sins—like that of a patient murdering the physician who was compounding medicines from his own blood—were forgiven for the Jews who later responded to the preaching of the apostles in Jerusalem and received baptism. The first Christian martyr, Stephen, he conjectured, may have been among those receiving divine mercy through Christ's prayer. Stephen's own prayer for the forgiveness of those stoning him was answered in the conversion and baptism of Paul.[28] Thus, Augustine exhorted catechumens to trust the divine mercy and not to hold back from baptism because of the enormity of the sins of their prior lives.

To receive this liberation from all their guilt, Augustine warned, adults had to repent of their sins rather than presuming that their offenses would be set aside without any penitential engagement. This baptismal renovation was accompanied by the pains of childbirth; it could not begin until the old, sinful life had been rejected and set aside.[29] In preparation, he urged, those seeking baptism must pray for forgiveness and, in particular, should forgive those who had sinned against them.[30]

Although baptism removed all the guilt of prior sins, Augustine explained, the newly baptized would still be burdened with the fragility of their mortal flesh. Their evil desires and the sinful habits they had cultivated would be cured only gradually and through much struggle. They would be completely liberated only through death and resurrection.[31] Even children, who would have developed few if any bad habits by the time of their baptism, would later have to struggle with the concupiscence that affected all the offspring of Adam and Eve.[32] Nor did baptism destroy the bad habits that adults had developed when the guilt of their prior sinful actions was removed: drunkards, for example, would not find themselves cured by the ritual. The baptized, then, should be careful not to allow evil habits to take root and to crowd out good customs.[33] A Christian's battles against the desires of the flesh, the chains of habit, the influence of imperial culture, and the temptations of the devil could be won with God's help or be lost by human negligence. Though even the faithful could be expected to fail regularly in small ways, Augustine insisted that they were capable of meeting the standard Paul had set in Galatians 5:16: not to capitulate to the desires of the flesh and allow them to move into action.[34]

In particular, Christians were expected to keep themselves free of the serious sins that would require their exclusion from the eucharistic communion. For the sins of daily living that would not be completely avoided, they should continue the penitential practices that had preceded their baptism: praying for pardon, exchanging the offering, granting and seeking forgiveness with their fellows, and providing support to the poor.[35] Such repentance, Augustine assured his congregation, was both necessary and effective.[36] In the often difficult practice of granting pardon to others, he suggested that the faithful always remember with gratitude the full and free pardon that God had granted them in baptism. They might recognize themselves in the narrative of the debtor servant (Matt. 18:23–35) and offer to others a forgiveness like the one that God had given freely to them.[37] Augustine taught the faithful that although they had been cleansed of all guilt in baptism, they did not yet live in full righteousness and should continue to seek God's forgiveness.[38]

Some of the baptized, however, failed to live up to the liberation and new life that they had received in baptism. They retained the sacrament of baptism itself, but they abandoned the commitment and the gift of the Holy Spirit that had accompanied its reception. In the words of 2 Timothy 3:5, they had the appearance but not the virtue of piety.[39] Because their evil was now hidden under the Christian name, they were in a worse condition than they had been before being baptized. They were no longer members of the body of Christ; instead, as false brothers within the church, they had lost the gift of the Spirit just as had the heretics and schismatics outside it.[40] False Christians, Augustine warned, could not rely on their baptism alone to secure their salvation; on that foundation they had built a life of sin rather than good works. Nor should they presume that God would provide an opportunity for a deathbed repentance to revive the baptism that they had violated. Although he conceded that God had promised to forgive the sins of those who delayed baptism until the time of death, Augustine refused to provide the same assurance of divine mercy to the baptized sinners who deliberately waited until the end of their lives to attempt repentance.[41]

Flagrant sinners, Christians in name only, proved a danger not only to themselves but to other members of the congregation. Addressing the newly baptized on the day that they were to join the assembly in the nave of the basilica for the first time, Augustine warned them to choose good models for their Christian lives.[42] Some of the baptized regularly participating in the eucharist and falsely presenting themselves as faithful Christians were agents of the devil and ready to lead others astray.[43] Yet he assured the neophytes of his own trust that God had not allowed his ministry in the community to be entirely in vain. Vice was often easier to recognize than virtue, and he believed that the congregation included many faithful Christians leading good lives.[44]

Baptism, in any case, was only a beginning and the newly baptized would have to work hard to fulfill the commitment they just had made.[45] As faithful, they should regularly recall the grace of their baptism, Augustine urged, because returning to it in memory was itself a renewal of the original gift of God's forgiveness.[46] As members of the body of Christ, they should recognize in themselves persons sanctified and freed of their sins. In such a confession of divine mercy, they would exercise not pride but gratitude, claiming their holiness as the gift of God rather than their own achievement.[47]

Augustine regularly took this pastoral approach to preaching about baptism, exhorting and warning the catechumens to accept the sacrament and the faithful to use it well. The points on which he focused on the typological interpretation of the Israelite escape from Egypt, crossing of the Red Sea, and journeying to the promised land were repeated in other sermons. All guilt was removed in baptism when the sacrament was received with repentance. That baptism, however, was only the beginning of a long struggle against the desires and appetites that could lead back into sin. New temptations would arise that the baptized must overcome. The daily toll of small sins meant that baptism inaugurated rather than completed the process of repentance and forgiveness that would accompany a Christian on the pilgrimage to a heavenly reward.

Infant Baptism

The baptism of infants and children had been practiced in the African church for centuries when Augustine began his ministry in Hippo. At the end of the second century, Tertullian had advised against it on the grounds that it was unnecessary because the infants were innocent and were better served by waiting until they could make a personal commitment as young adults.[48] In the middle of the third century, Cyprian argued that the baptism of infants was entirely proper, though he did not challenge Tertullian's argument that they were born innocent of sin.[49] Augustine recognized the practice but did not devote extensive attention to it until its meaning became controversial.

Caelestius, one of Pelagius's disciples, argued in Carthage that baptism was necessary for infants to enter the kingdom of heaven, but that it did not imply any sinfulness on their part that merited punishment in the afterlife. In his judgment, guilt could arise only from sin that involved responsible free choice; all recognized that infants were incapable of such decisions.[50]

Augustine, in response, insisted that the practice of child baptism, particularly the emergency conferral of the sacrament on dying infants, indicated a Christian belief that those who died without baptism would be justly condemned by God. Although they had not sinned personally or individually, he explained that they were bound by a guilt inherited from Adam. He argued that parents brought infants to Christ as their Savior for healing and liberation from sin, to free them from everlasting death, and to secure eternal life for them. If the infants themselves could speak words rather than only cry and weep, they would acknowledge that they were born sinful.[51] In one sermon, he imagined the scene of a disciple of Pelagius disputing with an anxious mother, insisting that her child did not need baptism because the infant was not sinful but only mortal. Like Christ, the child was born in the likeness, not the reality, of sinful flesh.[52] To anchor the argument, Augustine recounted in detail the report of a nursing mother who discovered her infant dead and immediately carried him to the local shrine of St. Stephen. Her prayer that he be revived was answered. Her son was baptized and anointed; he received the imposition of hands and the eucharist. The rituals completed, he immediately relapsed into death. Satisfied, she placed him in a grave, treating it as the lap of the saint who had intervened to save him.[53] This set of miraculous events, Augustine suggested, provided a divine confirmation of the Christian belief in the necessity of baptism even for children who had no power to decide anything for themselves.

Augustine's fullest presentation to a congregation of the necessity and efficacy of infant baptism was in a sermon delivered in Carthage.[54] He devoted extended attention to the proposal that infant baptism provided not eternal life, to which the innocent infants were entitled, but access to the kingdom of heaven. Without baptism, infants, who were incapable and thereby innocent of personal sin, would enjoy some form of eternal life, though not a share in Christ's reign, for which baptism was necessary.[55] In response, Augustine argued on scriptural grounds that a human being could escape damnation only by gaining access to the kingdom of heaven through Christ.[56] He pointed out, for example, that Matthew 25:34–46, 1 Corinthians 6:9–10, and Acts 4:12 offered only heaven and hell as final destinies for human beings.

Then, Augustine turned to the scriptural evidence that both sides would accept as excluding the unbaptized. Beginning with the teaching of John 3:5 that rebirth through water and the Spirit was necessary for entering the kingdom of God, he led the audience through a careful review of Jesus's explanation of the function of baptism.[57] Christ told Nicodemus, "No one can ascend into heaven except the one who descends from heaven, the Son of Man, who is in heaven" (John 3:13).[58] Jesus was on earth but claimed to be in heaven as well, indicating that he, the Son of Man, was one person in both divine and human natures. The one Christ was both Son of God and Son of Man, at once sitting in heaven and walking on earth.[59] The question was how Christians—both born and reborn—could enter the kingdom of God if only those who had descended from heaven could ascend into heaven. The reborn, Augustine explained, could ascend to heaven because baptismal rebirth made them members of the Son of Man. The Christ, as Son of the Father and son of Mary was one person: he was also head of a body composed of the faithful members of the church. He had descended without his individual or ecclesial body but would ascend with both the body given by his mother and that composed of the faithful Christians who had been joined to him in baptism. To ascend into heaven, then, a person must be incorporated into Christ, must become a member of the one Christ who both descends alone and ascends with his faithful members attached to him (1 Cor. 12:12).[60]

How, Augustine then asked, did baptism make a sinner a member of the body of Christ, who is free of all sin? Christ explained the process to Nicodemus by referring to Moses's action of lifting up the serpent in the wilderness so that all who had been bitten by the snakes could be healed. The Son of Man must be lifted up, so that whoever believed in him might have eternal life (John 3:14–15). This meant, Augustine explained, that whoever believed in the crucified Christ would not perish but would have eternal life.[61] An infant, however, was incapable of looking upon and believing in the crucified Christ. Yet, as the infant had been wounded by the act of another—Adam—so it could be healed through the act of another—a baptismal sponsor. A faithful Christian presented the infant for baptism and made the necessary profession of faith in response to the minister's questions. The Spirit of Life in that parent or sponsor regenerated the child in Christ. Augustine constructed a contrasting parallel that linked birth and rebirth: a child generated through human weakness into the life of the present age would be reborn through the strength of Christian love into the life of the age to come.[62]

Infants who had been baptized with the profession of faith made for them by sponsors were recognized as believers. The ancient, approved, constant, and most securely established practice of the church, Augustine reminded his hearers, was to treat baptized infants not as catechumens but as believers, as among the Christian faithful.[63] As believers in Christ, they were neither judged nor condemned but promised eternal life; nonbelievers were already judged and the wrath of God remained upon them (John 3:15–18, 35–36). Eternal life, he concluded, could be promised only to those who had faith in Christ and the baptismal sacrament of that faith.[64]

Augustine's usual objective in arguments built upon the practice of infant baptism was to assert the universality of human sinfulness, whose consequences could be escaped only by adherence to Christ as savior. The Pelagian focus on John 3:5—unless someone has been born again from water and the spirit, that one will not enter into the kingdom of God—as a foundation for a distinction between eternal life and participation in the kingdom of God, however, required a different approach. Membership in the body of Christ was shown to be necessary for ascent into heaven; for an infant, membership in Christ's ascending body could be achieved only through the baptismal commitment of faith. Augustine introduced the inheriting of Adam's guilt into the argument as a contrast that justified the sponsor's performing an infant's declaration of faith: as Adam had harmed, the sponsor helped. That status, in turn, was confirmed by the church's practice—to which the Pelagians agreed—of treating baptized infants as believers among the faithful.[65]

Later in his conflict with the Pelagians, Augustine used the necessity of baptism for the salvation of both children and adults as an indicator of divine election for salvation without any preceding personal merits. God's elective intention was manifested by one child being brought to baptism before death while another died without passing from Adam to Christ.[66]

His treatment of infant baptism and original sin demonstrated the diversity and range of Augustine's controversial preaching. Appeal to the practice of presenting sick infants for baptism would have been, as he knew from personal experience, a convincing argument for his congregation in Hippo.[67] It would also have served as a clear indicator of the mystery of divine election—even when this required miraculous and temporary resuscitation. His careful analysis of John 3:5–15, part of which was used by the Pelagians, would have impressed (and perhaps even convinced) the more educated audiences he addressed in Carthage.[68]

Doctrinal Issues

In his sermons, Augustine treated doctrinal issues at length. Some of these efforts were important for his congregation in Hippo, but others were presented in Carthage, where the treatment of a topic might have been requested by his friend Aurelius, the bishop of that city and, by that office, the leader of the bishops of Africa. In the discussion of the ministry of John the Baptist in his *Tractates on the Gospel of John*, for example, he elaborated the difference between the baptism that John had been sent to offer and the baptism that Christ gave through his disciples. The relation between the sacrament of baptism and the gift of the Holy Spirit was treated on three different occasions. A distinction between the sacrament and its sanctifying effects was applied, in other sermons, to the relationship between the performance of the ritual of washing and the corresponding changes produced by the operation of the Holy Spirit: the unity of the church, the forgiveness of sins, incorporation into the body of Christ. Augustine occasionally distinguished the sacrament from its reality.[69] Usually, however, he contrasted the sacramental ritual to particular spiritual effects that were relevant in the context.[70]

The instruction Augustine provided in discussing these issues supported the congregation's collaboration in the process of integrating converts from the schismatic Donatist church, who were admitted to Catholic communion without being baptized anew. This kind of teaching was fuller and broader in scope than Augustine's more polemical preaching against the Donatists, and later the Pelagians, in which he attempted to equip his parishioners and other hearers for arguments with their friends and neighbors. In his sermons, however, Augustine did not explore the permanent effects of the ritual in the detail found in his treatises.

The Baptisms of John and of Jesus

Augustine was interested in the baptismal ministry of John not as a type or foreshadowing of Christian baptism but as a contrast to it. The difference between these two forms of baptism and their administration was a foundation of his teaching.

The ministries of John and Jesus began in much the same way: preaching repentance in anticipation of the advent of the kingdom of heaven (Matt. 3:2; 4:17).[71] John, however, recognized and proclaimed that Christ, and only Christ, had power to baptize with the Holy Spirit.[72] He presented himself, then, as a subordinate collaborator rather than a competitor to Christ.[73]

In early portions of his *Tractates on the Gospel of John*, Augustine focused on the difference between the ministries of John and Jesus. Both had received the mission to baptize, and each recognized the baptism of the other as different than his own (Matt. 21:25; John 1:26–27). More to the point, Augustine noticed that they exercised their ministries differently: John performed the ritual himself while Jesus assigned it to his disciples (John 3:23; 4:1–2). Jesus could have given his disciples "baptisms" of their own, Augustine explained, but with the result that individual ministers would have offered baptisms of varying types or efficacy—as the Corinthian Christians later thought they had (1 Cor. 1:12–17). Augustine's interpretation of 1 Corinthians 1:13 implied that such baptisms might have varied in the holiness they conferred.[74] Instead, he insisted, Jesus authorized his disciples to confer his own baptism, with the Holy Spirit, so that its effect might be the same in every case.[75] As a result of working through these ministers, Jesus also baptized more disciples than John.[76]

Augustine used this distinction between the baptismal practices of John and Jesus to explain what John had learned through the Holy Spirit's descending upon Jesus (John 1:33). The revelation was not that Jesus was the greater of the two or that John ought to seek baptism from Jesus rather than baptizing him. John, Augustine claimed, already knew that Jesus was Lord and Truth, and that Jesus was practicing humility in presenting himself for baptism.[77] What John learned was the way that Jesus baptized with the Holy Spirit: that the Spirit's power remained upon him as the Christ even when he assigned the performance of the baptismal ritual to his disciples. The efficacy of Christ's baptism, then, depended on the holiness not of its particular minister but on that of Christ, upon whom the Holy Spirit descended and remained.[78]

Augustine's analysis and interpretation were guided, and even forced, by his contention that the Donatists erred in assigning the efficacy of baptism to the holiness or fidelity of the minister performing the ritual, rather than recognizing that the power of the Holy Spirit rested upon Christ and was shared with the church as his body. Even when the baptizer was just and good—as John was and as Peter, Paul, and Apollos would be—human holiness did not produce the effect of the baptism of Christ with the Holy Spirit. The divine power was operative when God's gifts were conferred through the actions of human ministers, even those who did not share the gift of the Spirit.[79]

These arguments had been developed a few years earlier in an extended sermon that Augustine had preached against the contention of the Donatist bishop, Petilian of Constantine in Numidia, that the fidelity of the bishop administering the sacrament was the source of the true faith and holiness of the baptized.[80] He argued that the Donatist bishops were, in practice, attempting to replace Christ as the object of the believer's trust by making the bishop the source of the righteousness received in the sacrament.[81] Since no one could be certain of the dispositions of another human being, he asked, would not the Donatist do better to recognize that all the baptized were reborn through the divine power, as the Gospel of John taught (John 1:12–13)?[82] Augustine made the opposite argument for the Catholic teaching. The scripture showed that faithful Christians need not defend the holiness and uprightness of their ministers; they relied on the power of Christ.[83]

In subsequent sermons in the series on the Gospel of John, Augustine returned to this affirmation that the efficacy of Christian baptism depended on the divine power rather than the holiness of the minister of the ritual. He compared that sacramental ministry to the role of the scribes and Pharisees accurately transmitting the teaching of Moses by their words, even though their actions did not exemplify it.[84] Additional support for this position was found in Paul's claim that the gospel of Christ could be offered even by preachers who were motivated by envy, ambition, or competition (Phil. 1:15–18). The apostle must have recognized, Augustine suggested, that these sinful missionaries would have been baptizing as well as teaching.[85] He illustrated these points by appealing to the transmission of the divine promise to Abraham through procreation. By both his wives and their slaves, Jacob had generated sons who enjoyed the full status of patriarchs. In the same way, the minister of baptism, in the mother's role, did not affect the status of children who had God's word as their paternal seed.[86]

In a sermon preached about a decade later than these initial commentaries on the Gospel of John, Augustine revisited this interpretation of Christ's "baptizing with the Holy Spirit." He explained that it meant that after his resurrection, he would confer the Holy Spirit and its power to forgive sins (and to expel demons) upon the church. Thus, he continued to affirm that the gift of the Holy Spirit and the efficacy of the baptismal ritual were anchored in Christ. In this later period, as shall be seen in the next two sections, Augustine argued that the power of the Spirit was communicated to and exercised first by the disciples of Jesus and then by the church and its ministers.[87]

The baptism of John was preparatory for that of Jesus. Once Christ had been revealed, John's baptism was no longer necessary and his mission ceased.[88] Christ's baptism looked to the future and would fill the world through the ministry of his disciples.[89] Thus, the Acts of the Apostles 19:1–7 portrays Paul as requiring that those who had received only the baptism of John should be given that of Christ as well.[90]

Baptism and the Gift of the Holy Spirit

The distinction between the sacrament of baptism and the gift of the Holy Spirit was addressed by Augustine for two different purposes. He intended it as a support for his teaching—just examined—that the religious status of the minister of the ritual neither guaranteed nor hindered the operation of the Holy Spirit. He also developed the assertion that a person could receive and would retain the sacrament of baptism, with its dedication to Christ, even without continuing to share the gift of the Holy Spirit. This doctrine had a pastoral application that was noted above: a warning that the ritual was salvific only when it was complemented by the repentance and faith of the recipient and the Spirit's gift of charity. It had another practical application, however: the ritual of baptism performed in schism or heresy was not to be repeated when the recipient subsequently entered the communion of the true church.

In support of his point about the irrelevance of the holiness of the minister of baptism, Augustine used the narrative of the initial chapters of the Acts of the Apostles to show that the Spirit could be given with or without human intervention. He contrasted the one case in which a particular kind of minister—one of the Twelve—was required for giving the Holy Spirit to the three instances in which the Spirit was conferred without any human mediation. The deacon Philip baptized the Samaritans who had been converted by his preaching and miracles; they received the Holy Spirit, however, only when Peter and John arrived to lay hands upon them. The coming of the Spirit could be clearly discerned by the gift of languages, Augustine explained, that was still being received at that time (Acts 8:5–17).[91] The contrast between Philip, who could work miracles, and Peter and John, who could give the Spirit, led Simon Magus to judge that these powers belonged to some but not all ministers.[92] To clarify Peter's rejection of Simon's error, Augustine cited three other instances in which the Spirit was conferred and received without any human mediator. The Spirit had descended upon the disciples in the upper room as a direct divine gift.[93] When Philip was sent by the Spirit to aid the Ethiopian eunuch, the Spirit came upon that convert immediately after baptism, according to Augustine's version of the text (Acts 8:39), without any need for the apostolic ministry of Peter and John.[94] The Spirit also descended unexpectedly upon the centurion Cornelius and his household while Peter was preaching to them—in order to convince Peter that these Gentiles should be baptized and welcomed into the community (Acts 10:44–48).[95] God acted when Peter—having misunderstood an earlier dream—was uncertain what should be done. Through these four instances, Augustine demonstrated both that the gift of the Spirit was not dependent upon human mediators and that its granting was not always the effect of the ritual of baptism, though it was associated with it.

In these and other sermons, Augustine amplified his second point: that a person could receive and retain baptism without enjoying the presence of the Holy Spirit.[96] In his own day that gift was no longer manifest in speaking multiple languages. He identified the sign of the Spirit's presence as charity—the love of God and neighbor. Thus, he recognized that some unconverted petitioners could be baptized in his own communion without repenting their sins or truly professing faith in Christ. Simon Magus provided a convenient example of a person who had been baptized but had not received and retained that gift of the Holy Spirit. Peter denounced the self-centered love that Simon manifested in his attempt to acquire spiritual power for his own aggrandizement (Acts 8:9–24).[97] Augustine also offered Ishmael and Isaac as types or precedents demonstrating the distinction between those who had only the sacrament of baptism and those who had both the sacrament and the spiritual gift. By fleshly generation, both were children of Abraham; only Isaac was also son of God's promise to his father.[98] Like King Saul's gift of prophecy, Augustine explained, Christians could receive and exercise some other gifts of the Holy Spirit without sharing the charity that would make them holy and acceptable to Christ.[99] Using still another illustration, Augustine argued that because both good and evil persons could retain baptism, it could not be understood as the wedding garment necessary for sharing the king's marriage feast (Matt. 22:11).[100]

Simon, Ishmael, Saul, and the improperly clad guest could be used to exemplify false Christians who had received baptism through a visible washing and invocation of the Trinity but had not received or had not retained the gift of the Spirit that would make them members of Christ.[101]

Augustine offered other examples that illustrated the situation of heretics and schismatics and helped him explain why they were recognized as already baptized when they asked to be received into the communion of the worldwide church. Extending an image that he had developed in treatises against the Donatists, Augustine explained that the baptism of Christ always marked the baptized as belonging to Christ, whether the ritual was performed by a worthy or unworthy minister within the unity of the church or a renegade in heresy or schism, whether upon a repentant and faith-filled or an insincere and faithless recipient. He compared that consecration given in baptism to the imperial brand or tattoo that identified a soldier of the emperor or an animal of a particular owner.[102] The mark itself seems to have been the cross of Christ on the forehead rather than a letter or number on the hand of a soldier.[103] Although this mark was not visible to others, Christians were conscious of it and retraced it to indicate their allegiance to Christ, particularly in appealing for divine protection when harm was threatened.[104] Augustine asserted that once applied in baptism, the mark was permanent; it was never to be repeated or defaced.[105] Similarly, a finger or other limb cut from a body retained its shape, though it was not alive; so a Christian separated from the church could keep baptism and profess the creed but lack the Holy Spirit.[106] He accused the Donatist bishops of stealing the sheep for which Christ had paid with his blood, even though they could mark them only with the sign of Christ. A baptism that had been conferred and received in opposition to the unity of the church also could be compared to a plate bearing the name of a powerful person that an owner of lower social status might post at his door in order to protect his house from attack. When Christ took over the "property" from its deceitful, demonic occupant, he did not change the name plate that subsequently had become truthful by his acquisition.[107] A schismatic or heretic separated from the church or an unrepentant sinner within its visible unity might have the same baptism, hear the same gospel, celebrate the festivals of the same martyrs, and attend Easter services. In the absence of the gift of the Spirit, however, neither Christ's baptismal mark nor all those pious practices were effective for salvation.[108]

Thus, Augustine demonstrated that the sacrament of baptism could be conferred, received, and retained both inside and outside the unity of the church, from a holy or sinful minister, by a faithful or faithless recipient. The ritual could be performed and would consecrate the recipient to Christ even without the retention of the Holy Spirit's gift of charity. The ritual of baptism itself was never to be repeated. The gift of the Spirit could be conferred or restored by the subsequent repentance of a sinner, by the profession of true faith by a heretic within the true church, or by the reception of a schismatic from outside its unity. Intentional unity with Christ and the church would make the enduring baptism salvific.[109]

The Holy Spirit and the Baptismal Forgiveness of Sins

Augustine distinguished the sacrament of baptism and its indelible mark from the gift of the Holy Spirit that he associated with both the forgiveness of sins and participation in the unity of the church. In a sermon preached almost a decade after those considered just above, he attempted an interpretation of Jesus's warning that a word spoken against the Holy Spirit would not be forgiven. He identified this blasphemy as the refusal to repent and accept the forgiveness of sins provided to the saints through Christ's gift of the Spirit. In the Gospels of Mark (3:28–30) and Matthew (12:31–32), this statement about blasphemy was at the conclusion of a conflict with the Pharisees over the power that Jesus himself exercised in casting out demons. By using the statement that connects the two parts of the Matthean narrative, "One who is not with me is against me, and one who does not gather with me scatters" (Matt. 12:30), Augustine contrasted the unity of Christ's kingdom to the division existing in the realm of Satan. The spirits of greed and luxury, for example, were opposed to one another, though both were abuses of money. Despite their conflict, both were practiced in the demonic realm. Those who did not gather into unity with Christ were scattered, he concluded, in their pursuit of conflicting evil ends. Thus, he contrasted the evil spirit as the instigator of division to the Holy Spirit as the principle of unity.[110]

Augustine then spent considerable effort in demonstrating to the congregation that in Matthew, Christ could not have been referring to just any word spoken against the person and works of the Holy Spirit, since these usually could be repented and forgiven. Christ must have intended some particular type of rejection of the Spirit that could justify an everlasting condemnation.[111] Augustine then compared the narrative in the Gospel of Matthew 12:31–32 to that in Mark 3:29 and Luke 12:10, searching for some clue to the sin that Christ specified.[112] Using his understanding of the Spirit as the Trinitarian bond of union common to the Father and Son, he argued that Christ's gift of the Holy Spirit joined true Christians to the Trinity and gathered them into the unity of the fellowship of the church. Essential to this operation of the Spirit were the twin effects of removing the sin that separated humans from God and empowering Christians to perform the closely related activities of expelling demons and forgiving sins. The forgiveness of sins and liberation from the satanic society of the guilty were the first steps in a process of salvation that would culminate in the perfect unity of charity, the fullest gift of the Spirit.[113]

On the basis of these considerations, Augustine identified the sin to which the three gospel statements referred as the resistance of impenitent hearts. A refusal to repent prevented the Holy Spirit's joining them to God and moving them to accept and exercise the gift of charity, the forgiving love that would initiate, increase, and perfect justice in their lives. Inside or outside the congregation of the one church, these sinners did not gather with Christ; instead, they scattered with the conflicting demonic spirits. Although they might bear the name and share the sacraments of Christ, they were set firmly in opposition to his forgiving Spirit and thereby bound in their sins. Unless they were moved toward repentance—and forgiving others—during their earthly lives, these blasphemers against the Spirit would be forgiven their own sin neither in this age nor the next.[114]

By focusing on the Holy Spirit as the principle of unity within the church, Augustine explained to his congregation why the schismatic person's sins were not forgiven when the sacrament of baptism was received in separation from and opposition to their fellowship. By subsequent conversion to their church and being joined into the communion that the Spirit formed, however, heretics and schismatics were freed from their sins. The earlier baptismal ritual became effective without having to be repeated.[115] Being joined into the unity of the church was both the means and the effect of receiving the Spirit's gift of charity.

In other sermons, Augustine appealed to the text of Matthew 18:18 in which Christ gave his disciples the power and command to forgive sins committed against them.[116] A parallel text, John 20:22–23, associated Christ's bestowal of this power upon them with the gift of the Holy Spirit. Christians could exercise the power to forgive sins, he explained, by the operation of the Spirit dwelling in the holy saints as in a living temple (1 Cor. 3:16; 6:19). God formed and dwelled in that church; God forgave sins through the forgiveness actually practiced by the saints.[117] In his sermon on the unforgivable blasphemy, Augustine concluded that the efficacy of baptism in forgiving sins was dependent upon the recipient's willingly being joined to the faithful within the church, in whose union the Spirit dwelt. God sanctified sinners through the loving communion of all the faithful rather than only through the agency of its minister.[118]

By distinguishing the sacramental ritual from the loving and forgiving operation of the Holy Spirit among the saints, Augustine could explain why heretics, schismatics, and false Catholics received and retained the baptism of Christ even when they lived in opposition—open or hidden—to the unity of the church. They could receive the grace and blessings of the sacrament, however, by converting and being joined through the bond of love into that union.[119] In that unity, they would share the support, forgiveness, and peace that were the work of the Spirit.[120]

These closely related doctrinal issues—the sacrament of baptism, the Holy Spirit's gift of love, the unity of the church, and the forgiveness of sins—were first developed in Augustine's writings against the Donatist schismatics and in contemporary preaching. Although the issues were fully treated in only a few of his surviving sermons, occasional remarks have been noted in sermons that were focused on different topics. Augustine's concern with baptismal validity and efficacy in his ordinary preaching may have reflected the engagement of the faithful in Hippo with the Donatist controversy, which divided the Christians of that city. Augustine's concern with street-level discussion and conflict between Christians belonging to competing churches is evident in sections of other sermons that were aimed directly and openly at those opponents. Even in these doctrinal expositions, however, Augustine's preaching was connected to pastoral considerations, such as the need to cultivate the gift of the Spirit in order to participate in the blessings of the sacramental ritual. His lumping together heretics, schismatics, and false Christians within the Catholic communion and his contrasting them with the faithful who lived and acted by the inspiration of the indwelling Holy Spirit were intended as a warning for his own congregation, as well as an explanation of the danger in which their schismatic opponents lived. Like baptism, belonging to the visible unity of the Holy Spirit in the church was necessary but not in itself salvific. A Christian had to forgive and be forgiven.

CONCLUSION

Augustine made only indirect and veiled references to the ritual of baptism because it was subject to the discipline of secrecy. It was described and explained to the petitioners on the day before their night baptism during the Easter vigil, but these sermons were delivered in sessions from which other nonbaptized persons were excluded and apparently were not recorded by scribes for wider distribution.[121]

Although he dealt with significant doctrinal issues, Augustine's preaching on baptism was primarily pastoral, situating the ritual and its effects in the sequence of events that formed the Christian life. The ritual itself was preceded by repentance for past sins and training for the future life of faith and good works. By using foreshadowing events, such as the Flood and Israel's escape from Egypt through the Red Sea, Augustine described the transition from the service of Satan to a life committed to Christ, one that would require an extended struggle against temptation before receiving the promised eternal life. He discussed the changes that baptism accomplished from those it only began. He warned against a return to former ways of living and the great danger of failing to accept and utilize the gift of the Holy Spirit that was conferred in baptism.

Augustine's discussions of doctrinal questions in his preaching were occasioned by the scriptural text he was following—such as his *Tractates on the Gospel of John* or the texts set for a day when a particular topic was treated, such as the readings preceding Sermons 71 and 99 that required exploration of the operation of the Holy Spirit in baptism and the identification of the unforgivable sin of blasphemy against the Holy Spirit.

Controversy with the Donatists and Pelagians also occasioned doctrinal instruction. A sermon on the feast of the birthday of John the Baptist was turned into an extended discussion of the role of clerical holiness in determining the efficacy of baptism, in rebuttal of the Donatists. The conflict with the Pelagians required Augustine to revisit Jesus's conversation with Nicodemus and treat that section of the Gospel of John in greater detail than he had six years earlier when preaching through the text of that gospel. Usually, however, Augustine did not preach on a topic at the same level of detail that he wrote about it. His exposition of the formation and function of the fellowship of the faithful as the living temple of the Holy Spirit (the "society of saints") that mediated sanctification and forgiveness to the baptized, for example, can be recognized in the sermons but was more fully elaborated in the writings against the Donatists.[122]

Occasionally, however, the sermons provide a more sustained and even a different explanation than is found in Augustine's writings. The argument against the Pelagian use of the third chapter of the Gospel of John to explain infant baptism establishes a connection between that practice, belief in Christ, and inherited guilt that was compatible with but went beyond not only the teaching of the *Tractates on the Gospel of John* but some aspects of Augustine's discussion in his letter to Bishop Boniface.[123] In particular, that sermon appealed to the church's tradition of regarding infants as believers, perhaps because his earlier sacramental explanation would not have been convincing to his audience.[124] The discussion of the unforgivable sin against the Holy Spirit in Sermon 71 provided an answer that had escaped him in an earlier written commentary.[125] In Sermons 99 and 71, Augustine also elaborated the role of the church community as the temple of the Holy Spirit in the forgiving of sins and sanctifying the recipient of the sacrament of baptism that had first been developed in his treatise *On Baptism* in 404.

Augustine's presentation of the practice of infant baptism in Sermon 294 approached the doctrine of inherited guilt as a corollary of belief in Christ as savior and did not attempt to explain the mechanism of its transmission. A careful analysis of his writings on the subject indicates that this understanding of Christ's unique and universal role was the foundation of his teaching on the effects of the sin of the first parents of humans. His avoiding the problem of explaining the transmission of guilt in the sermon supports the interpretative hypothesis that it was a secondary issue on which the truth of the doctrine did not depend. Augustine could then use the availability of baptism to a dying infant as an indicator of merciful but just divine election, as he did in other sermons. Finally, the appeal to the church's practice not only of baptizing infants but of then regarding and treating them as among the faithful suggests his belief that such traditional practice could be trusted as a form of divine revelation.

Chapter Five

EUCHARIST

T HE EUCHARISTIC RITUAL with its sacramental participation in Christ, was the usual context for Augustine's preaching. Yet he seldom spoke about the part of the ritual that followed the sermon: the prayers of petition, the offering, and the sharing of bread and wine. Like baptism, it was protected by the discipline of secrecy; only the baptized could be present and participate; all others were dismissed after the readings and the sermon. In preaching and writing, then, Augustine usually limited himself to what could be explained and understood without providing more information than was available to anyone who had heard the scripture's witness to the practice: the narratives of its institution in 1 Corinthians (11:23–26) and the synoptic gospels (Matt. 26:26–29; Mark 14:22–25; Luke 22:15–20), the discussions of its efficacy in the "Bread of Life" discourse in the Gospel of John (6:35–58), and the Pauline exhortations, also in 1 Corinthians (10:16; 11:27–34). The regular exception to this rule was the sermon delivered to the newly baptized (neophytes) on Easter Day. During the long vigil service the night before, they had participated in the eucharistic ritual immediately following their baptism. In the celebration on Easter morning, Augustine taught the new Christians the responses and actions used in the service, along with the meaning of the sharing of consecrated bread and wine.

Even within these limitations, however, Augustine was able to clarify the religious meaning of the eucharist for catechumens and others who were attentive to his ordinary preaching. He identified the eucharistic food with the flesh and blood that the Word had assumed in the incarnation. With some regularity, he pointed to the efficacy of the prayer of Jesus for the forgiveness of those mocking him during his execution. Many of them responded to the preaching that followed the gift of the Holy Spirit. They believed, were baptized, and then, he asserted, drank in faith the Lord's blood that they had shed in fury.[1] In his preaching on the Gospel of John, he explained the life-giving power toward which Christ drew his hearers in the Bread of Life discourse. In other sermons, he explored the Pauline teaching on the mystery of the unity of Christians with Christ and one another, symbolized by the eucharistic food. Thus, Augustine communicated the religious significance of the ritual without revealing the specific practices of its celebration.[2]

The following review of Augustine's preaching on the eucharist will begin with the sermons presented to the neophytes on Easter day. Three sermons judged authentic will be considered together because they follow the same pattern of exposition and make the same points. Then, his interpretation of the Bread of Life discourse in the Gospel of John will be analyzed over the three sermons dedicated to it. In both expositions, excerpts from the sermons will be used to display Augustine's technique of slanting the scripture texts toward his preferred interpretation. Finally, a more systematic review of this teaching will integrate evidence from the *Sermons to the People* on the texts with the issues that are the focus of the sermons to the neophytes and on the Gospel of John.

INSTRUCTION OF THE NEWLY BAPTIZED

The normal time for the baptism of adults was the night vigil service that opened the community's weeklong celebration of the resurrection of Christ. During the Saturday preceding this night service, the candidates received instruction on the baptismal ritual so that they might participate in it properly. However, they had been given no prior teaching to prepare them for the eucharistic ritual in which they would share for the first time later in that same vigil service. On the following day, Easter Sunday, the bishop provided an instruction to the neophytes about the eucharist they had received the night before. Three such sermons have survived that are judged authentic.[3] These provide a privileged insight into what Augustine considered most important for the newly baptized to know about the eucharist and their participation in it.

The instruction to the neophytes was not given during the sermon that Augustine preached to the people immediately after the readings. The eucharistic ritual was subject to the discipline of secrecy; it should not be described to the unbaptized, even to Christians living as catechumens.

> What is hidden and not public in the church? The sacrament of baptism and the sacrament of the eucharist. The non-Christians can see our

good works, but the sacraments are hidden from them. The things that they can see rise up from those that they cannot, like the whole of the visible cross rises from the base of the cross fixed in the earth.[4]

During some of his *Sermons to the People* on Easter morning, Augustine apologized for the brevity of his presentation to the gathering as a whole, which could have included pagans and Christian catechumens. Not only was he exhausted from the long ritual during the prior night, he explained, but he would give another instruction to the neophytes later. These sermons seem to have been delivered without a reading from scripture[5] and while standing at the altar rather than sitting on the episcopal chair.[6] Augustine referred to the loaf (or loaves) of bread and the chalice as actually present on the altar table.[7] Because the tenses of the verbs referring to the sanctification of the bread and wine vary in these sermons, they do not permit a more precise determination of the place of this unusual sermon in the sequence of the parts of the eucharistic ritual.

The three sermons that were recorded by secretaries and have survived (as well as others that scholars have judged inauthentic) are generally short.* Augustine covered a variety of topics in each of them, without significant elaboration. He taught the neophytes the words and meaning of the celebrant's invitations and the congregation's responses made during the eucharistic prayer and the distribution of the sacramental bread and wine. They had heard these during the ritual on the prior night but may not have been able to make out the words as the congregation spoke them, perhaps quietly or in less than perfect unison. Augustine explained the meaning of the statements and the benefits for which the participants were praying, for example, in the petition that God would lift their hearts to heaven.[8] He also elaborated the implications of the "amen" with which they responded at the end of the eucharistic prayer and in accepting the bread and wine identified with the body and blood of Christ.[9]

Augustine also explained that the words of sanctification spoken over the eucharistic elements identified them with Christ and with the Christians who formed his ecclesial body.

This loaf of bread that you see on the altar, sanctified through the word of God, is the body of Christ. This cup, or rather what the cup contains, sanctified through the word of God, is the blood of Christ. Through

* Each of the three is under eight hundred words, with *Serm.* 272 just over five hundred.

these things, the Lord Christ willed to entrust to you his body and blood, which he shed for you, in the forgiveness of sins. If you receive it worthily, you are what you receive. For the Apostle says, "We many are one loaf, one body" (1 Cor. 10:17), in explaining the sacrament of the Lord's table.[10]

In these sentences, the Pauline orientation of Augustine's teaching is evident. He began by asserting that through the words of institution, the bread and wine were identified with the body and blood that Christ derived from Mary and that had been fixed to the cross and poured out for the forgiveness of sins. Without even signaling the transition, however, he also identified it as the social, churchly body into which baptism had incorporated the neophytes as members, "If you receive it worthily, you are what you receive." He did not assert that this worthy reception effected the incorporation. That effect was attributed to the exercises of the catechumenate, culminating in the baptismal ritual and the gift of the Holy Spirit the night before. In each of these sermons, Augustine made the same transition from the individual, physical flesh and blood of the Savior to the Christians who were formed into his social body.[11]

Directing the neophytes' attention to the bread and wine on the altar, Augustine introduced the distinction between a sign and the reality it signified. He explained the difference between their ordinary appearance and extraordinary meaning.

> What you see here on the table of the Lord looks like what you are accustomed to seeing on your own tables. It appears to be the same, but it has a different power. Consider this: [this morning] you are all the same human beings that you were [yesterday, before being baptized]; you are not presenting different faces to us. Yet you are new. Though old in your bodily appearance, you are new by the gift of holiness. In the same way, what you see here is new. As you see, it remains bread and wine; with the coming of its sanctification, however, this bread will be the body of Christ, and this wine the blood of Christ. The name of Christ and the grace of Christ will have given it a force that it did not have earlier, even though it looks just as it did before. Eaten before, it would fill up your belly; eaten after, it builds up your mind.[12]

Again, Augustine continued by elaborating the similarity between this change in the ceremonial food caused by the sanctification and the change in the neophytes worked by their baptismal process. They had died and had been buried with Christ; as Christ had risen from among the dead, so they walked now in newness of life (Rom. 6:4).[13]

Once again, he turned to the mystery of their unity with and in Christ, citing Paul's statement in 1 Corinthians 10:17.

> "One loaf of bread," he said. No matter how many loaves were put there today, "it is one bread." No matter how many loaves are on all the altars of Christ throughout the world, "it is one bread." What does he mean, "one bread?" He [Paul] says it in a few words: "We many are one body." This bread is the body of Christ, about which the Apostle said in speaking to the church, "You, then, are the body of Christ and his members" (1 Cor. 12:27). You are what you receive, by the grace that redeemed you. You affirm it when you respond, "Amen." What you see is the sacrament of unity.[14]

The loaf of bread was the sacrament of the united body of Christ, into which the faithful were joined at baptism. That one reality made the many loaves that served as its sign into one loaf, a single eucharistic bread. In this assertion, Augustine was following the principle that the reality being signified determined the proper meaning of its sign. Intelligibility and truth flowed from the signified to the signifier.[15] In this case, the unity of the Whole Christ—head and members—determined the meaning of the loaves of bread and the cups of wine, imparting its unity to their multiplicity and giving them a new force and value.

In a similar Easter morning instruction, Augustine distinguished the body of Christ shared in the eucharist from the flesh that the Word had received from Mary.[16] Recalling the creed that the neophytes had memorized and professed in their preparation for baptism, he reminded them of the body in which Christ was born, nourished, grew, worked, was persecuted, died, was buried, rose, ascended, sat in heaven, and would return to judge. How, he then asked, was this bread that body and the contents of the cup that blood?

> These things, my friends, are called sacraments because they are understood as different from what they appear to be. What is seen has a corporeal form; what is understood has a spiritual benefit. If you want to understand the body of Christ, then attend to the Apostle as he spoke to the faithful: "You, then, are the body of Christ and his members"

(1 Cor. 12:27). If, therefore, "You are the body of Christ and his members," then your mystery is placed on the Lord's table; you receive your mystery. You respond, "Amen," to what you are. By so responding you endorse it. You hear, "The body of Christ," and you answer, "Amen." Be members of the body of Christ so that your "amen" may be true.[17]

In this third instruction, like the other two, Augustine affirmed the relationship between the eucharistic sacrament and the human flesh and blood in which Christ had lived mortally and continued to live immortally. Even in answering the question he posed to the congregation, however, he quickly shifted from the flesh and blood derived from his mother to the social body of Christ that the congregation was. The saving reality signified by the bread and wine was the ecclesial body that united the faithful and identified them with Christ.

Augustine did not attribute the incorporating and salvific power to the body received from Mary in which Christ had been raised into heaven. When Christians shared the eucharistic food with an "amen," they affirmed that they belonged to the body they ate and drank in its sacrament. Their faithful lives would verify (or their failure deny) this profession of identity with Christ. Only someone who was living in the body of Christ, he warned his hearers, could truly and worthily receive it sacramentally. Here, again, Augustine signaled that adherence to Christ validated the reception of the eucharist rather than being caused by it.

In these sermons, then, Augustine focused on the Pauline teaching of the unity proper to the body of Christ that his members should maintain and cultivate. In each of these sermons, he compared the process of initiation that had been completed in their reception of baptism to that of making the bread and the wine that would symbolize the reality the neophytes had become. Bread was made from many grains that were ground and mixed together; the flour was moistened so that it would hold the shape of the loaf.

When you were exorcised, that was like being milled. When you were baptized, you were being sprinkled. When you received the fire of the Holy Spirit, you were being baked. Be what you see before you and receive what you are.[18]

Then he extended the analogy to the wine.

Friends, remember how wine is made. Many grapes hang on a branch, but the juice of those grapes is mixed together in unity. In this way, the Lord Christ represents us. He wanted us to belong to himself. He established the mystery of our peace and unity on his table.[19]

Augustine then drew the conclusion from these analogies.

Those who receive the mystery of unity and do not hold to the bond of peace receive this mystery not as a benefit but as a witness against themselves.[20]

The bread and wine symbolized the unity of Christians in the body of Christ. They were, in the words of Acts 4:32, "of one soul and one heart in God."[21] Anyone who did not belong to that unity of heart and soul received its symbol or sacrament unworthily, and thus as a condemnation.

Once again distinguishing the sacramental bread and wine from the reality it signified, Augustine warned that these passing, material things must not be taken lightly.

What you see is transitory; the invisible thing that it signifies is not passing but permanent. The signs are taken, eaten, and consumed. You do not think that you are using up the body of Christ, do you? You do not think you are devouring the church of Christ, do you? You do not think you are eating the members of Christ, do you? Certainly not! Here they are being cleansed; there they will be crowned. Although the things that serve as signs seem to be passing away, the reality they signify continues.[22]

The new Christians were warned not to treat the eucharistic bread and wine as ordinary food that had only temporal significance. They were urged to recognize in them the reality of Christ in his fullness, incorporating the faithful Christians who were in process of being purified and would be glorified. The bread and wine would be consumed, digested, and its power exhausted; the reality they signified would endure forever and included the Christians with Christ.

Throughout these short sermons to the neophytes, Augustine was constantly focused on the same points: the signs were not to be confused with the reality they signified; that reality was the body of Christ into which he joined all faithful Christians. To eat the flesh and drink the blood of Christ in truth, he insisted, meant to adhere to that unity. To take the sacrament while rejecting adherence to that unity was a deceitful gesture: it was to bear false witness against oneself.

Without introducing and explaining the formal distinction of sacrament from reality, Augustine called attention to the effects of the words of consecration in changing the meaning and force of the eucharistic bread and wine. Although he affirmed their symbolic relationship to the human body in which Jesus had lived on earth and continued to live in heaven, he focused the attention of his hearers on the ecclesial body of Christ, in which Christians were joined to one another in Christ. The essential meaning of the eucharistic ritual, with its sanctification and sharing of bread and wine, was the unity of the church, into which the neophytes had been incorporated by baptism, to which they must adhere, and that they must cultivate in their dealings with one another. Augustine presented the eucharistic bread and wine as a mystery uniting individual Christians to one another and celebrating congregations, the whole church, and the Savior whose identity all shared.

The Bread of Life Discourse in the Gospel of John

Augustine completed an exposition of the Gospel of John in 124 tractates. The fifty-four that cover the first twelve chapters, or what is now called the "Book of Signs," were apparently recorded by a secretary as they were preached to the people. The remaining seventy were composed without an audience, though the "sermon" form was retained—as it was in those expositions of the psalms that were not preached.[23]

In the three sermons dedicated to the discourse following the multiplication of food (John 6:25–72), Augustine provided his most sustained surviving consideration of the eucharist. Unlike the instructions that were addressed to the newly baptized on Easter Day, the *Tractates on the Gospel of John* seem to have been presented to an assembly that allowed catechumens and even persons who had no formal identification with the congregation. Because the eucharistic ritual was protected by the discipline of secrecy,[24] Augustine avoided references to the specifics of the rite. The term *panis* (bread) appeared regularly, since it was used extensively in the gospel texts under consideration. *Calix* (drinking cup), which was used in the sermons to the neophytes as a companion to *panis*, appears only twice in these expositions.[25] One of these two uses might have had a eucharistic meaning—in reference to the martyrdom of Lawrence of Rome, which was being celebrated on the day that the third sermon was delivered.[26] Augustine referred to the sacramental or signing function of bread and wine only once, as being apt for signifying the unity among many individuals that he judged essential to proper participation in the eucharist.[27] These expositions, then, stand in sharp contrast to the sermons to the neophytes, in which he constantly referred to and even gestured toward the loaves and cup present for all to see on the table of the Lord.

Unlike the short discourses to the newly baptized, tractates 25–27 on the Gospel of John present a sustained study of Christ's sharing of eternal life with his disciples that addressed tensions between that Gospel's interpretation of the eucharist and the Pauline one that Augustine used more regularly. In them, he had to argue for and justify identifying the social or ecclesial body of the Whole Christ—rather than the individual body in which the Savior had been born, worked, died, and rose—as the reality signified by the sacramental ritual and foods. The absence of a full discussion of the eucharistic presentation of the flesh and blood of the Savior in these expositions might have resulted from an audience that included nonbaptized persons, with whom such knowledge was not to be shared.[28]

The following detailed review of Augustine's exposition of the Bread of Life discourse in John 6:25–72 is divided into analyses of four elements of his eucharistic doctrine: the distinction between a sacramental sign and the reality to which it corresponded; the identification of the reality represented by the eucharistic signs; the efficacy of that reality in conferring eternal life on the participants in the eucharistic ritual; and the disciples' error of identifying that reality as only the individual, fleshly body of Jesus. In this extended analysis, Augustine argued for his identification of the reality shared in the eucharistic ritual as the ecclesial body of Christ, that included his individual human body.

In these sermons on the Gospel of John, Augustine can be observed adapting the Johannine text on Christ as the bread of life to an understanding of the eucharist based upon the Pauline doctrine of the Christians as members of the body of Christ. The exposition displays a preacher working on a text. This set of sermons has few parallels in the surviving record of Augustine's preaching.[29]

A Sacrament and Its Reality

Augustine had already used the paired terms "sacrament" and "reality" (*sacramentum et res*) for interpreting both historical types and allegorical actions in the Gospel of John. Ishmael persecuting Isaac foreshadowed the sufferings of the elect; the bronze serpent was a symbol of the healing death of Christ; Christ's curing the blind symbolized his enlightening the minds of his disciples.[30] In considering the multiplication of food as one of Jesus's signs, Augustine utilized these terms for the eucharistic teaching. The manna given to Israel in the desert and the barley loaves and fish that Christ had distributed to the crowd were both signs referring to the same reality: the heavenly, life-giving bread that Christ identified with his full self.[31] Anticipating his later appeal to the water flowing from the rock that sustained Israel in the desert, Augustine drew an additional parallel to the Samaritan woman's failure to distinguish between fresh well water and the reality that Christ was offering her (John 4:13–15).[32] In each case, the hearers focused on the bodily nourishment but failed to grasp it as the sacrament whose corresponding reality was eternal life. In this sense, Augustine found, once again, Jesus's earthly interlocutors failing to understand his message in the way that Nicodemus had misunderstood the rebirth that Christ offered.[33]

The second part of tractate 25 and the first part of tractate 26 on the Gospel of John were devoted to John 6:35–47, with its questions of belief in Jesus and the divine gift that moved the elect to faith and thence to eternal life. This discussion marked an advance in Augustine's polemic against the Pelagians but was not directly relevant to his thinking on the eucharist.

Beginning with John 6:48, however, the gospel text and Augustine's exposition of it turned back to the promise of bread from heaven and the life that it would provide.[34] From this reality, Augustine distinguished the life provided by the foods that served as signs or symbols of the heavenly bread—both the manna eaten by Israel in the desert and the Christian eucharistic bread. These sacramental foods supported the body's life but were unable to prevent its death: both Israelites and Christians eventually died, even though they had adequate food and drink. The heavenly bread, in contrast, empowered those who fed on it to avoid the eternal death against which Christ warned. To attain this unending life, however, a person had to eat the visible food spiritually—that is, they had to grasp it as the signifier of the higher reality, rather than receive it only as a nourishment for bodily life. Moses, Aaron, and Phineas profited from eating the manna sacramentally; many Israelites did not. In the same way, the morsel of bread that Jesus handed to Judas at the Supper was good as food, since all the others at the meal ate the same food without bodily harm. Satan entered into Judas (John 13:26–27) because he failed to grasp and respond to the fuller meanings of the morsel that Christ offered him. Similarly, Paul warned the Corinthians that they were eating and drinking judgments against themselves precisely because they had not discerned and respected the body of Christ that was signified in sharing the food of the Lord's Supper (1 Cor. 11:17–32).

In order to receive the heavenly bread for eternal life, Augustine explained, the recipients had to distinguish the visible sacrament from the reality and the power it not only represented but made operative. To accomplish this, he suggested, they must cleanse themselves in preparation for receiving it—repenting even their daily sins and offering pardon to those who had offended them. The baptized in the congregation would have recognized this reference to the communal recitation of the Lord's Prayer and the sharing of the kiss of peace that preceded and prepared for the distribution of the eucharistic bread and wine. If Christians neglected the implications of sharing the higher reality signified by the bread and wine, if they took it as ordinary food, they would not only lose its benefit but suffer harm.[35]

Augustine then used Jesus's next statement, "This is the bread that comes down from heaven" (John 6:50), to continue exploring the distinction between a sacrament and its reality. He explained that the two sacraments—Israelite manna and Christian bread—both signified the same reality, the heavenly bread. In support of this identification of the meaning of the different symbols, he cited Paul's warning to the Corinthians that the Israelites had suffered as a result of abusing the sacraments of their time. They had been baptized into Moses in the cloud and the sea; they all ate the same spiritual food (1 Cor. 10:1–3) but most of them had not pleased God and, as a consequence, they had died in the desert (1 Cor. 10:5). In extending this threat to the water that the Israelites drank from the rock following them, Paul identified that rock as Christ (1 Cor. 10:4). Reversing the direction of Paul's argument (from the source to the water itself), Augustine then asserted that the sacramental meaning of the water applied to the manna: both symbolized Christ, who was also the reality corresponding to the sacramental food of the eucharist. All these forms of sacramental food—manna, water, bread, wine—he concluded, signified and carried the eternal life granted by Christ.[36]

In this way, Augustine explained and established a distinction between sacrament and reality in the eucharistic celebration. The sacramental forms—manna and water—had been different for the Israelites than the bread and wine given to the Christians; the reality was the same for both sets of signs—the life of Christ. Because of the reality that they signified, these sacraments resulted in either benefit or harm for the persons using them. To avoid death, the recipients would have to eat and to drink with the heart rather than only with the mouth.[37] They must prepare for and act upon the eating and drinking in ways appropriate to the reality being signified and shared.

The gospel reading was not fully adapted to Augustine's explanatory purpose. It linked the manna provided to Israel to the bread provided to Christians, but it did not specify a Christian drink corresponding to the water flowing from the rock. Perhaps the discipline of secrecy prevented Augustine from introducing a reference, in a sermon accessible by the unbaptized, to the Christian drink (wine) that corresponded to the water provided to the Israelites in the desert. He could not, however, omit the Pauline reference to the symbolism of the water because it provided the authority for identifying the manna with Christ (1 Cor. 10:1–4).

The Reality Signified in the Eucharist

Christ's announcement that the living bread coming from heaven was his own flesh that would confer eternal life on the world (John 6:51) required a full discussion of the reality to which he was referring. Anticipating the confusion that this claim had provoked among Christ's hearers—and any in his own audience who were unfamiliar with the eucharistic ritual—Augustine played on the carnal minds of the hearers: "the flesh was confused by the bread that Christ called flesh, and all the more because he called it flesh."[38] Augustine moved to explain the relationship between the sacramental sign—manna or bread—and the life-giving flesh of Christ. In this process, he would also have to specify the "body" that Christ claimed could confer eternal life upon its recipients.

Augustine began to identify the flesh that Christ called living bread by showing that the Lord could not have intended his individual human body. For this purpose, he stepped outside the gospel context to appeal to the commonly accepted distinction and relation between body and soul within human beings. He asked his hearers to distinguish their invisible souls from their visible bodies and recognize that these two were united to form an individual human. All—or at least all the living—would agree that the soul gave life to the body rather than the body conferring life on the soul. Next, he asked them to acknowledge that a soul could give life only to its own body, the body in which it dwelt, and not to a separated body, one belonging to someone else. One body, he declared, could not live by another body's soul. Returning to the gospel text, he inferred that Christians could receive life from Christ, as the living bread came down from heaven, only through being animated by the soul of Christ. For this to happen, they had to belong to the body of Christ. Yet the individual body of Christ was exclusively his own. When Christ claimed that his flesh was life for the world, then, he must have been referring to the body he shared with Christians. That shared life and body required a distinct and shared soul that gave life to the shared body.* The Savior's individual soul was not extended into the bodies of Christians.[39]

Augustine then recalled Paul's statement: "We many are one loaf of bread, one body" (1 Cor. 10:17) and identified the body of the Whole Christ, living by the Spirit of Christ, as the reality signified by the sacramental bread.

> This is the sacrament of fellowship, the sign of unity, the bond of love. All who desire to live have a place to live and a source of life. Let them approach; let them believe; let them be joined into this body, so that they may be enlivened by it.[40]

The one loaf served as a sign of the one body that Augustine, following Paul, identified as the ecclesial body into which faithful Christians were joined to Christ and to one another, in which they shared the life-giving Holy Spirit. If his hearers failed to follow his argument and grasp his point, if they referred the eucharistic bread to the fleshly body that the Word had assumed from Mary in becoming Christ, then they would have been confused and impeded, as the disciples were described as being in the gospel narrative.

Having distinguished the physical from the social body of Christ, Augustine may have realized that his identification of the church as the living

---

* Augustine was crossing a gap by extending the analysis of a single organism to a social one. In so doing, he used the bridge that Paul had already constructed in 1 Corinthians. Eventually, however, he would have to acknowledge that the ecclesial body of Christ contained many persons and explain how the Holy Spirit functioned as the soul of such a reality.

bread of Christ that brought life to the world could give rise to a very different objection among his hearers. In John's Gospel, the disciples of Christ had been shocked by the proposal that eating his human flesh would bring them eternal life. Augustine's own hearers might have been shocked no less by his proposal that fellowship in the congregation then surrounding them could provide the eternal life for which they hoped. He did not back away from the objection. Instead, he exhorted them not to be embarrassed by their fellow communicants. They should look to themselves and be concerned lest they become rotting limbs that had to be amputated from the body. Let them strive to become worthy members of the assembly; let them not prove a stumbling block to their fellows; let them be healthy, ready, and attractive members who hold firmly to that body of Christ, so that they might live for God and by God.[41]

Augustine then used the challenge presented by unworthy Christians to interpret the dispute that arose among the hearers of Jesus, who were arguing with each other like opponents in a law court. Christians who shared the eucharist must not treat one another in that way; they were one loaf and one body. God made them dwell together in unity. Both among the ancients and in his own congregation, Augustine argued, Christ's requirement of unity challenged his followers. Only by adhering to the fellowship of the church, he taught, could they eat the heavenly bread that gave eternal life.[42]

The Efficacy of the Eucharistic Reality

Having identified the ecclesial body of Christ as the reality signified by both the manna and the eucharistic food, Augustine undertook an extended discussion of the way in which this ecclesial body of Christ conferred eternal life upon its members. In the process, he also established that eternal life was given to humans only through incorporation into this body.

Augustine found further evidence in the text of the gospel that the life promised by Christ was eternal rather than temporal, bodily life. Christ was addressing living persons when he said, "Unless you have eaten the flesh of the Son of Man and have drunk his blood, you will not have life in you" (John 6:53). His hearers were already in actual possession of bodily life, though they did not enjoy it free of mortality. Christ's next statement asserted that those who ate his flesh and drank his blood were not only promised but already were endowed with eternal life, "Those who eat my flesh and drink my blood have eternal life" (John 6:54).[43] He said, "have," rather than "will have," Augustine observed. Christ meant, he explained, that those who did eat and drink him *actually have* eternal life; those who did not eat and drink him would continue their temporal bodily life, but they do not have eternal life.[44] The food that supported temporal life was necessary but not sufficient; humans could die even though they had plenty to eat and drink.* He then elaborated his point.

> The food and drink that is the body and blood of the Lord works differently. Whoever does not receive it does not have life; whoever does receive it has life, and that life is eternal.[45]

This claim that those who received the reality signified by the eucharistic bread and wine already had eternal life required that this reality and the life it gave be not bodily and spatial but spiritual and intentional. Thus, Augustine concluded:

> He wanted them to understand, therefore, that this food and drink was the fellowship of his body and its members.[46]

In explaining carefully and exactly the statements of Christ in the Bread of Life discourse, Augustine elaborated the scriptural foundation for the doctrine he asserted in his sermons to the newly baptized. The life-giving flesh and blood of Christ referred neither to the Savior's individual body nor to the individual bodies of the Christians who shared the bread and cup. Instead, Augustine argued, the reality shared was the body of the Whole Christ, head and members, in which the faithful were already living.

In mid-sentence, Augustine seems to have recognized the implication of his statement: eternal life, once possessed, prevented death. Those who received it would retain it. The implication of his assertion was that every Christian baptized and sharing both the bodily signs and the spiritual reality of Christ's body and blood within the visible unity of the church

---

* Without making an explicit reference to it, he excluded from the eucharist an effect similar to that assigned to the Tree of Life in the Garden of Eden. It had protected Adam and Eve from bodily death, although it had not conferred immortality, a life free of the possibility of death. *Gen. litt.* 6.25.36, 11.32.42; *Ciu.* 13.20, 23.

would actually receive and retain eternal life. That, however, was unsustainable and implausible. His analysis required a more specific and narrow definition of the body of Christ that he credited with giving eternal life to those who belonged to and received it.

> That is the holy church made up of the predestined, called, justified, and glorified saints, who are faithful to him. The first of these, predestination, is already complete. The second and third, calling and justification, have been, are now being, and will be accomplished in the earthly lives of the elect. The fourth, glorification, is present in hope but still future in its reality.[47]

This qualification of the life-giving body and blood as the society of saints—still being called, converted, and sanctified—was necessary to meet Christ's specification that its eating and drinking already conferred eternal life, though not yet in the full and perfect form that it would attain in the still future bodily resurrection and glorification.

Thus, Augustine identified the reality signified by the eucharist sacrament not as the full assembly of the church—that included the evil as well as the good—but as the fellowship of the saints within that assembly, those who actually shared and would continue to share eternal life. The members of that society had been selected by divine predestination.[48] That divine election was being worked out over the course of the ages as the saints were called and justified. It would remain incomplete, however, until all the faithful had been resurrected and glorified. The reality symbolized by the bread and wine was the body of Christ as it grew in time—the blessed among the dead, the faithful still being saved on earth, and those not yet born—all chosen by God for the fullness of immortal glory.

Having specified the ecclesial body of Christ as the reality signified by the eucharistic bread and wine, Augustine turned to its sacramental presentation and participation.

> The sacrament of this reality, that is, of the unity of the body and blood of Christ, is presented on the table of the Lord in some places daily and in others at regular intervals of days. That sacrament is received from the Lord's table, to life for some and to death for others. The reality whose sacrament this is, however, brings life to all and death to none who belong to it.[49]

The entire communicating congregation received the sacrament, but its members could not assume that everyone also participated in the reality it signified.

Augustine was directing his congregation's attention to the ultimate consequence of receiving the eucharist rather than considering each instance of participation in the ritual. This perspective would emerge more clearly as he explored the effects of the two manners of eating and drinking. Even when received alone, without its reality, the sacrament participated in the power of that reality: it would cause harm to those who did not belong to the body of Christ. Like those Israelites who proved unfaithful, some Christians did not please God, failed to share the life of Christ, and finally would fall into eternal death.[50]

Citing John 6:54 with its final phrase, "And I will raise them up on the last day," Augustine again distinguished between the eternal life conferred upon faithful Christians and the immortal bodily life that they would be given in the resurrection. By sacramentally participating in the body of Christ, faithful Christians enjoyed eternal life in their spirits during earthly life, then in the period of rest that followed bodily death, and thereafter fully in heaven. They received the promise of immortal bodily life in baptism and the eucharist; the reality would be given upon the return of Christ on the last day.[51]

Continuing his exploration of the reality signified by the sacrament, Augustine argued that the bread and wine were appropriate signs of the social or ecclesial body of Christ. In a parallel to the instructions given the newly baptized and the only reference to the eucharistic wine in this commentary on the sixth chapter of the Gospel of John, Augustine observed that the bodily food used in the eucharist was prepared by joining together many grains and mixing the juice of many grapes. These could sustain bodily health, but only temporarily. The only food and drink that could confer eternal life, he asserted, was the fellowship of the saints whose peace and unity would become full and complete.[52] This unity of the saints— who would remain faithful—was the body and blood of Christ that was entrusted to Christians in the eucharist.[53]

To confirm his interpretation of the reality corresponding the eucharistic sacrament, Augustine reversed the apparent meaning of John 6:56, "Those who eat my flesh and drink my blood remain in me, and I in them," to turn it into a definition of the eating and drinking rather than an assertion of its effect.

> This, therefore, is the meaning of eating that food and taking that drink: to remain in Christ and to have Christ remaining in oneself. For this reason, the person who does not remain in Christ and in whom Christ does not remain, clearly neither eats his flesh nor drinks his blood. Instead, that person eats and drinks the sacrament of this great reality, and that to condemnation.[54]

To eat and drink Christ, one had to dwell in Christ and have Christ dwelling in oneself. Only those who were pure of heart and would see God, he explained, could properly approach the sacrament of Christ. When the unclean presumed to take the sacrament, they brought down ruin rather than blessings on themselves.[55]

These implications of Augustine's identification of the reality of the sacrament with the ecclesial body of Christ emerged gradually as he guided his congregation through the text of John 6: only those who already belonged to the society of saints, who were part of the reality symbolized (and would remain in it), properly received its sacrament. Participation in the eucharistic ritual, he taught, displayed and celebrated the unity of Christ's body; it did not cause either that body itself or a Christian's participation in it.

Augustine turned briefly from his exposition of the body and blood of Christ entrusted to Christians in order to discuss Christ's next statement describing his relationship to the Father as a model for his giving life to Christians: "As the living Father sent me, and I live because of the Father, so whoever eats me will live because of me" (John 6:57). Distinguishing between the divine and human realities in the Savior, Augustine sorted out the different meanings of Christ's living "because of the Father." He then returned to the meaning of the second part of the sentence, "whoever eats me will live because of me," that had already been clarified. That eating and drinking signified Christian sharing in the Son through the unity of his body and blood; it conferred the eternal life that humans attained only through being joined into Christ's ecclesial body.[56] Augustine began the next sermon with this text of John 6:57, again explaining that remaining in Christ defined the eating and drinking as indwelling and being indwelt, adhering to the body of Christ so that one was not left alone.[57]

Thus, in his exposition of the meaning of the consumption of the body and the blood of Christ, Augustine attended to the conferral of eternal life upon Christians through their union with Christ as members of his ecclesial body. He consistently reversed what appeared as a causal meaning in the Johannine text. The individual body of the Savior, his flesh and blood derived from Mary, could not communicate eternal life to Christians. It was not, therefore, the reality signified by the eucharistic sacrament. That reality was the ecclesial body whose head was Christ and whose members were the chosen, called, and justified saints being led to glory. These faithful Christians were joined into Christ's ecclesial body by the gift of the Holy Spirit that operated as its enlivening soul. The ritual action of sharing the sacramental food in the unity of the church was, then, a sign and affirmation of intentional adherence to Christ and one's fellow saints. That ritual participation in the eucharist would vivify only if the prior ritual actions already were in effect: if through baptism, anointing, and the laying on of hands, the recipient already had been and continued to be identified with the reality that was accepted sacramentally. Anyone who had failed to be joined into and remain in Christ—by hidden or open impurity of heart or separation from the congregation—received only the sacramental food, and that for death and judgment. Belonging to Christ and sharing eternal life was the meaning, the condition, and even the cause of right participation in the sacramental ritual. It was not the consequence or effect of the sacramental food or its eating.

The Sacrament and the Individual Body of Christ

The final section of the Johannine discourse following the multiplication of food provided the opportunity for Augustine to engage misunderstandings of the statements of Christ that emerged both in the gospel narratives and in his own time.

Beginning with John 6:60, the narrative shifts to a conflict among the disciples of Jesus. Augustine judged that they believed that Christ was proposing to slice off and serve to them the flesh in which he, as Word of God, had clothed himself. His "hard saying," about eating his flesh and drinking his blood should have made them attentive to a divine mystery, he suggested. Instead, they turned away, not considering that what they heard as horrifying words might conceal a great gift.[58]

Jesus's initial response showed his disciples that he knew what they were thinking: "What if you see the Son of Man ascending to where he was before?" (John 6:62). Seeing Christ ascend into heaven with his body whole and entire, Augustine explained, would dispel the notion that he had intended to distribute his flesh to them. Then, if not before, they might realize that his gift to them would not be eaten like bits of food. Augustine might have been suggesting that the disciples were thinking of Jesus as a sacrificial animal, through the eating of whose flesh his disciples could enter fellowship with God.[59]

Christ's explanatory response to his disciples' objection provided an opportunity for Augustine to recall the point he had introduced in the prior sermon in the series, commenting on an earlier objection in John 6:52: spirit gives life to flesh; flesh does not enliven spirit.[60] How, Augustine asked, could the disciples be thinking that dead flesh—a carcass or butchered meat from the market—could provide eternal life? In saying, "The spirit is what gives life; the flesh can accomplish nothing" (John 6:63), Christ was not repudiating his own incarnation and the bodily tasks that he would later assign to his disciples. Living flesh and the works performed through it were beneficial. The spirit, however, was the source of such action; it used the flesh as its instrument in good operations. Augustine concluded that the disciples had missed the point and were thinking of dead flesh, deprived of spirit.[61]

Rejecting all explanations that involved swallowing the flesh and blood of Christ, Augustine repeated the explanation provided in the prior sermon: only soul or spirit could give life, and that only by dwelling in the body it vivified.[62] The meaning of eating the flesh and drinking the blood of Christ was the communicant's remaining in Christ and Christ remaining in the communicant (John 6:57). For Christ to dwell in them, Christians had to be members of his body.[63] Augustine continued:

> To be members of Christ's body, Christians have to be bound together in unity. What binds us together in unity if not charity? Whence comes this charity of God? Ask the Apostle: "the charity of God," he says, "is shed abroad in our hearts through the Holy Spirit who was given to us" (Rom. 5:5). Therefore, "the Spirit gives life" (John 6:64). That Spirit makes the members of the body alive, and only those members that belong to the body of Christ that the Spirit enlivens.[64]

The Holy Spirit, like the soul of a human body, could give life only to those members who were joined to the body in which the Spirit dwelt and who acted in unison under the impulse of the Spirit. Christians, Augustine insisted, must love and cling to the unity of the church, that is, to the body of Christ. If they were separated from the church, they were not Christ's members and did not live by his Spirit. In this sense, then, "the spirit is what gives life; the flesh can accomplish nothing" (John 6:63).[65]

Augustine concluded the exposition by insisting that the words of Christ about the bread of life that comes down from heaven and gives life must be interpreted as a reference to the mission of the Holy Spirit that animated the ecclesial body of Christ by the operation of charity in its members. To take his words as an exhortation to eat his human flesh and drink his blood—really or symbolically—was a complete misunderstanding. Over and over, Augustine insisted that the human flesh of Christ—mortally living, dead, or immortally living—was not the medium for transmitting eternal life. The Spirit-filled body—Christ as head, Christians as members—provided access to eternal life.

In this extended analysis, Augustine must have recognized that he was using the terms body and soul in analogous or symbolic ways. The Holy Spirit was indeed sent upon the church but not incarnated in it. He justified this extension by appealing to the Pauline language in 1 Corinthians to interpret John 6.[66]

EUCHARIST AND BAPTISM

Some of Augustine's *Sermons to the People* echo and occasionally amplify points that he made in the sermons to the neophytes on Easter morning and the *Tractates on the Gospel of John*. In the present section, ideas presented in the *Sermons to the People* will be introduced to elucidate particular points.

Sacramental Sign

The distinction of sacrament and reality served a variety of different purposes in Augustine's preaching and writing. The church's eucharistic ritual, for example, was a symbol of the self-offering Christ was making at the heavenly altar.[67] The closest parallels to the use of sacrament and reality for understanding the eucharist, however, are to be found in Augustine's discussion of baptism.

In his conflict with the Donatist schismatics, Augustine had to explain why the ritual of baptism was not to be repeated even though it had been performed originally in schism or heresy, where opposition to the unity of the church prevented the reception or retention of the reality it signified.[68] To accomplish this, he assigned a permanent and irrevocable consecration of the baptized as the effect of the performance of the sacramental ritual of washing and invocation of the divine name. As has been seen in the study of baptism, the sign of this effect—probably the cross traced on the forehead—was compared to the military tattoo that marked a legionary as the emperor's servant.[69] From this ritual action and its effect of a permanent marking of the baptized as belonging to Christ, he distinguished the gift of the Holy Spirit that was received through the imposition of hands and effected a union with the ecclesial body of Christ. The presence of the Spirit could be lost in any of the many ways that a person might fail to maintain the union of love with Christ and his members. Because of the enduring consecration effected in baptism, however, the Spirit's gift of holiness could be regained through subsequent conversion, repentance, and the ritual of reunion (imposition of hands) with the communion of the holy church. The individual could reject or accept the reality symbolized by the baptismal ritual and marked by the character but could not remove or abandon either the consecration or its mark. The baptized bore the sacramental sign forever, as a source of benefit or punishment.[70]

Augustine applied the terms sacrament and reality to the eucharist in both parallel and different ways than he used them in the analysis of the baptismal ritual and its effects. In both instances, the same reality admitted of different sacraments: the crossing of the sea and the church's rituals of washing; the reception of manna and water for Israel in the desert and the sharing of consecrated bread and wine for Christians at the altar. As with baptism, the eucharistic sacrament could be separated from the reality it signified when the mode of its reception contradicted and rejected that reality. In that case, it brought judgment and condemnation upon the recipient. Unlike baptism, however, the sacramental signs of eucharistic celebration and reception were temporary and regularly repeated; the ritual effected no indelible character on the recipient.

The Reality Signified

Augustine taught that the sacraments of baptism and eucharist signified the same religious good, though in different ways. The reality symbolized by each was membership in the body of the Whole Christ, which he also called the society of saints or the dove.[71] Baptism established that incorporation into Christ by cleansing from sin and disposing the baptized to receive and retain the Holy Spirit's gift of charity.[72] Participation in the eucharistic ritual manifested and affirmed that existing union with Christ as a member of his ecclesial body. The two sacraments together were integral to the initiation of a Christian.

The reality—the ecclesial body of Christ—symbolized by the eucharistic food actually conferred eternal life upon its worthy recipients. In Augustine's understanding, that eternal life was realized by the faith in Christ that worked through love of God and neighbor under the influence of the Holy Spirit (Gal. 5:6).[73] That love and life could be received, retained, and exercised only in the visible unity of the church. Within that visible unity and as its core, the Spirit's gift of love formed the fellowship of the saints and shaped them into members of the ecclesial body of Christ, its head. Augustine's specifications excluded the unbaptized, Christians intentionally separated by schism from the visible church, and even the unconverted or unrepentant within the visible unity of the church.[74] In this and the analysis considered earlier of the body of Christ signified by the eucharist,[75] Augustine did not attempt to distinguish from this fellowship of the saints within the visible church those baptized Christians currently living in the love and unity of the communion who would eventually fail, die unrepentant, and be condemned.*

Christ, taken in his fullness as divine and human, individual and corporate, was the reality signified and shared by participation in the sacrament of the eucharist.

Receiving the Sacrament

As Augustine explained in a sermon to the candidates preparing for baptism, the power of the eucharist was in the unity of the faithful with and in Christ. Once having been joined into the body of Christ and made his members, they would become what they received.[76] In another sermon, he specified that the mutual indwelling of Christ and the Christian was the consequence of fidelity to the commands of Christ (1 John 3:24; 1 Cor. 15:5).[77]

Augustine made this same point by considering those who received the eucharist unworthily, eating and drinking judgment against themselves (1 Cor. 11:29). As the narrative of the institution of the eucharist in the Gospel of Luke makes clear (Luke 22:21), Judas was present for and shared the sacrament at the Lord's Supper before going out to betray him. Did

---

*His use of the idea of predestination to describe the ecclesial body of Christ was only positive: that the true members of the church, by divine assistance, would not fail. Their fidelity corresponded to the gift of the power of forgiveness and sanctification they exercised through their prayer within the earthly church. See the discussions on pp. 63–67, 76–79, 163–70, 271–73.

eating the flesh and drinking the blood of Christ make him dwell in Christ and Christ in him? The same might be asked of others who participated in the eucharist within the gathering of the congregation but with a deceitful heart, or of those who later turned apostate. The eating and drinking to which Christ referred, Augustine argued, was an intentional as much as a physical action. He illustrated his point by comparing eucharistic participation to that blasphemy against the Holy Spirit which prevented the forgiveness of sins. This sin had to be understood as a specific type of blasphemy that justified such a terrible punishment. So too, eating the flesh and drinking the blood of Christ was an action that was specified by its manner rather than by the food and drink being consumed.[78] Elsewhere, Augustine made the same point: no Christian must presume that eternal life could be gained by just any type of eucharistic participation.[79] Although he seems not to have made the point in his sermons, this understanding would have allowed the sacrament but not the reality of the eucharist to occur in the Donatist churches, where the ritual was celebrated in opposition to the universal communion.

Augustine taught that the union with Christ's ecclesial body that brought a Christian eternal life was the effect of conversion and baptism and then the cause of eating his flesh and drinking his blood in the eucharistic ritual. The unconverted who approached the altar intentionally opposed to the unity of the church shared not the reality of Christ, but only its sacrament, and that to their punishment.

THE BODY AND BLOOD OF CHRIST

In sermons not addressed to the newly baptized and not explaining the Bread of Life discourse in the sixth chapter of the Gospel of John, Augustine occasionally spoke more freely about the individual human flesh and blood of Christ. Three types of treatment will be considered here.

The Eucharist and the Immortal Bodies of the Saints

The eternal life proper to the body of Christ was received into the souls or spirits of the saints during their earthly lives; it was retained during their peaceful wait between death and resurrection. Only in the resurrection on the last day would their bodies also receive the immortality proper to eternal life.[80] When he explained the heavenly condition of the saved in sermons not focused on the eucharist, Augustine treated immortal and blessed bodily life as a consequence of incorporation into the body of Christ: it was an extension of the grace of the head into his members. Augustine used the text of John 3:13, "No one ascends into heaven except the one who descends from heaven, the Son of Man who is in heaven," to show that Christ alone could enter heavenly life, concluding that humans could enjoy that resurrected life only as members of his body. The Word of God did not bring a body from heaven when he descended to earth, but he did return to heaven in the fullness of the body he had assumed. In the union of head and members symbolized by the eucharistic food and ritual, he joined the faithful intentionally into his social body as members. In the resurrection, he would add their bodies to his own, sharing eternal life with them in his own proper fullness.[81] This understanding of the social or ecclesial body of Christ specified its relation to his individual human body.

The condition of those who died outside the unity of the body of Christ would be very different. All would indeed be raised (John 5:28–29) but those who had not been set free by the grace of Christ and joined into his social body would be returned to a lustful body for the everlasting death of punishment, to an unending bodily life of suffering and regret.[82]

The Flesh and Blood of Christ

In interpreting the Bread of Life discourse in John's Gospel, Augustine explicitly rejected an identification of the individual human body of Christ as the life-giving reality symbolized by the eucharistic food and drink. He judged that flesh and blood—either alive or dead—could not itself confer bodily life, much less eternal life.[83] He made similar points in other sermons: the power signified and shared in the eucharistic ritual was as inexhaustible as life itself. It was to be celebrated sacramentally and visibly but must be understood as spiritual and invisible.[84]

In his analysis of the efficacy of the eucharist, Augustine was particularly interested in the body that the Word had assumed from Mary and brought into heaven. To demonstrate the efficacy of praying for the forgiveness of enemies, he observed regularly that Jewish Christians later drank the blood that Jesus had shed for them on the cross—even as they jeered.[85] Similarly, he underlined the futility of unworthy participation by noting that Judas had received the (eucharistic) bread at the Supper from Christ's own hands.[86] Augustine's interest in the individual human body of Christ in dealing with the eucharist was focused primarily on dispelling the disciples' overly literal understanding of his meaning in John 6:60. His human body would have been quickly used up had it been the medium for transmitting life in the eucharistic ritual. Moreover, its intact assumption into heaven showed that his individual body, even in its resurrected state, was not the object of Christ's promise.[87]

The flesh and blood that the Word received from Mary functioned for Augustine's thinking, much as it had for Paul's, as the foundation and the symbol of the ecclesial body, of which Christ—as an individual human— was head. Had the Son of God not assumed both a human soul and body, he would not have united humans to himself in both their parts.[88] The human body of Christ would be assigned an essential role in his redemptive work, but it was not a medium for the transmission of either sanctifying charity or even bodily immortality from the Savior to the saved.

Eucharist as Memorial

Augustine's observation about the Jews converted through the preaching of the apostles formed a link between the blood actually shed on the cross and that ritually drunk in the eucharistic ritual. In sermons preached in association with the annual commemoration of the death of Jesus, however, he did not exploit this sacramental reality. Instead, he spoke of the celebration as a memorial that recalled the event and renewed its presence in the Christian memory. The service did not repeat or replace the event, which could happen in reality only once. Like tracing the cross on one's forehead that recalled the marking in the baptismal ritual, the celebration kept the reality from fading into the past. In this sense, the eucharist served as the Christian sacrifice commemorating Jesus's death, as the more varied practices of Israel had foreshadowed it.[89]

In the sermons preached to the neophytes, Augustine spoke more openly about the eucharistic ritual than he did when preaching to an audience that might include the unbaptized. There he affirmed the divine operation, associated with the words of consecration, that bestowed sacramental power on the bread and wine. It was to this reality sacramentally presented that the recipient's "amen" was addressed.[90] This sacrament conferred a meaning upon the bread and wine that made the eucharist a celebration of the mystery of the faithful Christians themselves as constituent members united in the body of Christ.[91] The reality of Christ, which included all his members, was still growing toward its fullness; it continued to be both hidden and manifest in that sacramental action; it would be fully revealed in the resurrection of the faithful when the realized body of the Whole Christ—head and all members—would be glorified. During the earthly time following the ascension of Jesus, that body could be discerned in the unity of the church and in the love exercised by Christians. In the eucharistic ritual, the reality of the body of Christ was affirmed and enacted, by the performance of its sacramental sign—the sharing of bread and wine in his memory.

Augustine taught that Jesus Christ was sacramentally present in his full and complete humanity in the bread and wine. In its sharing, he could be affirmed in his divinity and his individual humanity—and recognized in his fuller social or ecclesial reality. Thus, Augustine could affirm that the converted Jews drank in faith the blood they had shed in fury, even while insisting that this blood was life-giving only in its role as symbolic of the Spirit-filled ecclesial body of the Savior.

Conclusion

As in the discussion of baptism, the distinction between the sacrament and the reality it signified was important for understanding the eucharist; moreover, the reality of each sacrament was much the same. The two had to be treated differently: the sacrament of baptism was given only once but the eucharist was received repeatedly. The reality of the eucharist and of baptism was the full body of Christ, formed by the gift of the Holy Spirit. In baptism, the Christian's incorporation was established; in the eucharist, it was manifested and affirmed. As the symbol of the recipients' unity in Christ, participation in the eucharist followed baptism in the process of initiation and the unbinding of a penitent or schismatic in reconciliation.

In explaining the reality symbolized by the eucharistic bread and wine and the ritual of its shared consumption, Augustine focused on the social or ecclesial body of the Whole Christ, rather than the individual human body in which the Savior was born, died, rose, and ascended into heaven. In his individual body, Christ was understood as "head" of the social body whose members were the elect faithful in the process of being saved. In this sense, the eucharistic elements symbolized both the individual and the social bodies of Christ, in relationship to one another.

Augustine explained the life-giving effect of participation in the eucharist as the operation of the Holy Spirit that produced eternal life in the human spirit and, at the resurrection, a blessed immortal life in the body. The Holy Spirit operated in the social body, he explained, like a soul did in an individual human or animal body: it provided life only to the members of that body; any members that were cut off from the body died. Noting that one body could not provide life to another, he argued that the individual flesh of Christ could provide neither immortal bodily nor eternal spiritual life to the Christian. Thus, Augustine did not accept the explanation that new life could be transmitted to Christians through a sacramental (symbolic or realistic) sharing of the "divinized" human flesh and blood of Christ.

To provide the benefits Christ promised for "eating his flesh" and "drinking his blood" in John 6:53–58, those realities had to be understood, Augustine concluded, as the intentional union of Christians to Christ in his ecclesial or social body. Worthy sacramental participation by consuming the eucharistic foods signified and affirmed the Christian's intentional participation—under the influence of the Holy Spirit—in the body of Christ. Those who received the sacrament without intentional incorporation into Christ—either in schism or as aliens within the visible unity of the church—violated the meaning of the ritual; they were harmed rather than helped by that deceitful action.

In this understanding of the eucharist, the great mystery was not what the original disciples of Jesus misunderstood in John 6:60: the sharing of human flesh and blood. The mystery was what Paul rebuked the Corinthian church for failing to discern: the incorporation of Christians into the body of the Whole Christ (1 Cor. 11:17–34). That mystery, in Augustine's perspective, was the identification of Christ with the church community and the mediation of salvation to one another by the faithful who formed—actually still imperfectly and ambiguously—the body of Christ.

As in explaining the distinction between reality and sacrament in baptism, Augustine warned that a person could receive the sacrament without sharing in the reality it symbolized.

The reality of the eucharist, the union of Christ and his members, imparted a symbolic unity to its sacramental elements: all the loaves of bread and the cups of wine on the altar in one church formed one loaf and one cup with those on all the altars throughout the world. In sharing the food and drink each Christian affirmed unity to all the faithful joined into the body of Christ.

Chapter Six

MARRIAGE

A UGUSTINE ENGAGED QUESTIONS of marriage and sexual generation both early and late in his teaching and preaching career. His first treatise on the creation narrative in Genesis, *On Genesis against the Manichees,* countered the belief that sexual intercourse and generation served the forces of darkness by continuing the imprisonment of life-giving light in earthly bodies. A decade later, his *On the Good of Marriage* addressed the relative values of consecrated virginity, continence, and marriage. There he elaborated an explanation of three goods of marriage: sexual fidelity, the generation and education of children, and the bond joining the spouses as long as they both lived. In his major commentary *On Genesis according to the Letter,* and in the consideration of the narrative of humanity's sin and fall in *On the City of God,* Augustine's attention focused on a marital issue that became central to the Pelagian controversy: sexual desire as both a consequence and a cause of sin. After the condemnation of Pelagius in 418, Augustine carried on a debate with Bishop Julian of Eclanum in Italy over the original condition of humanity, the consequences of its fall in Adam and Eve, and the transmission of their guilt through sexual generation.

The debates with the Manichees and the Pelagians over sexual generation and the origin of lust played only a minor role in Augustine's preaching to congregations on Christian marriage. His surviving sermons were focused primarily although not exclusively on practices such as sexual fidelity and the management of lust. A few sermons provided extended treatments of marriage. Three of these were contemporary with the composition of *On the Good of Marriage.* Preaching during the days following the celebration of the birth of Jesus, he argued that Mary and Joseph were true spouses to one another and parents to Jesus, even though they never engaged in sexual intercourse. In another sermon, he considered the responsibilities of spouses toward one another. In explaining the Decalogue in Sermons 8 and 9, Augustine gave extended attention to adultery and sexual practice that was not intended for generation of children.[1] Two other sermons dealing with marriage are more difficult to date. In one he distinguished the sexual practice appropriate for different vocations and stages of life.[2] When exhorting his congregation to forgive offenses suffered, Augustine reminded them that they needed God's forgiveness for their own sins, suggesting that immoderate use of sexual intercourse within marriage was a common failure.[3] Overall, Augustine seems to have preached more often about the sins commonly committed against the ideals of Christian marriage than about the ideals themselves.

This consideration of Augustine's preaching on marriage focuses on its goods and ideals, beginning with sexual fidelity and the generation of children. It will then turn to the use of sexual intercourse in order to preserve marital fidelity. On this foundation, Augustine's discussion of the ideal of sexual continence within marriage and his explanation of the spouses' participation in the union of Christ and the church can be understood.

Sexual Practice in Christian Marriage

Sexual Fidelity

Although Augustine seldom preached primarily about the sin of adultery, the topic appeared more often than any other in his sermons on marriage and was seldom overlooked in any sermon about sin. Roman family practice was directed to protecting the property rights of legitimate children; as a result, the imperial law restricted wives more than husbands.* The spouses of free-born men were legally protected against seduction and rape. In addition, Augustine noted, wives were supervised carefully by their husbands. Many other women, particularly servants over whom a free male had control, were accorded no such protection from sexual exploitation. As a result, Augustine's denunciations of adultery and his exhortations to fidelity regularly dealt with the behavior of those males.

Augustine's surviving sermons indicate that he considered sexual relations outside marriage a major failing of African Christians. He remarked

---

* A child's mother could be identified; its father could not. Male access to Roman matrons had to be restricted to their husbands.

that when he spoke about homicide as an obstacle to entering into heaven, no one showed fear; at the mention of fornication, however, he could hear the sound of people in the church pounding their breasts in a plea for divine mercy.[4] He warned that it was a serious sin that, unlike intercourse with one's spouse for pleasure rather than procreation, could not be repented by almsgiving alone.[5]

Unlike Roman law, Christian teaching required sexual fidelity of both spouses. Christian husbands had to be satisfied with their wives and were allowed neither a concubine nor sexual relations with servants or prostitutes.[6] When the text of 1 Corinthians 7:4 was read out, the men in the congregation cheered Paul's granting them authority over the bodies of their wives. Augustine responded by pointing out that this text gave wives the same authority over the bodies of their husbands. In Paul's judgment, men were under the same Christian law as women: in marrying, the spouses had given over the disposition of their bodies to one another.[7] In other matters, Augustine explained, a wife was subject to the rule of her husband; in the obligation to practice and the right to require sexual fidelity, spouses were equals. A wife should be patient with her husband's failings and errors even in the management of her personal property, for example, but not with his violation of her right to his sexual fidelity.[8] Fulfilling this obligation, he added, deprived her husband not of his honored position within the marriage but of a shameful vice.[9]

The conflict between Roman practice and the law of the church could be a source of confusion. Some Christian women apparently were convinced that God allowed adultery for husbands, though forbidding it for wives. Even those who recognized infidelity as sinful for both sexes were led by Roman custom to regard it as less serious for husbands. In practice, a wife caught with her houseboy could expect to be taken to court, but a husband found with a serving maid had committed no crime. Wives were right to complain of the injustice, Augustine observed. He asserted that husbands had no right to demand the fidelity they refused to give. The best way for a husband to secure the fidelity of his wife, he suggested, was to be satisfied with her, just as he expected her to be satisfied with him.[10]

Augustine accepted and employed the assumption of both biblical teaching and Roman culture that husbands were the superiors of their wives. In discussing the gospel narrative of the birth and early life of Jesus, he pointed out that Mary had accepted her subordination to Joseph. She named him first, for example, in rebuking Jesus for staying behind in the temple without their permission (Luke 2:48). She was, he concluded, more subject to Joseph precisely because she was more chaste.[11] In the gospels, he observed, Jesus's genealogy ran through Joseph because he was prior to Mary in both natural and divine law.[12] Augustine even offered an allegorical interpretation of Pharaoh's killing male and sparing female infants: he was destroying the masculine virtues and nourishing the feminine vices.[13]

Paul had given husbands precedence over wives just as Christ was head of his church (Eph. 5:23). From this, Augustine argued that husbands should rule and guide their wives. What sort of example, he asked, did a husband provide by falling victim to the first hint of temptation? Did he expect his wife to conquer where he had failed? That would be an upside-down household. Indeed, a husband must be careful because his wife might follow his lead and claim the same privilege he exercised.[14] Augustine granted that woman had been created from and for man; she was his flesh, his spouse, and his servant. To rule the one subjected to him, however, the husband must subject himself to his own superior, God.[15]

Yet, Augustine recognized that husbands faced challenges to practicing fidelity that their wives did not. Roman custom did not provide the same social constraints for men that were imposed on their wives. Women experienced the force of both public law and family pressure; men needed only to fear Christ and to respect the rights of their peers. Even their friendships and associations with other men worked against them. Roman traditionalists regarded strong sexual lust as an indicator of virility. Anyone who capitulated at the onset of temptation could expect to be acclaimed brave and strong; anyone who steadfastly resisted and overcame sexual desire would be mocked as timid and weak. Self-respecting men would shun murderers, thieves, perjurers, and schemers, but would gladly welcome into their company the lecherous masters who abused and exploited their servants.[16] The imperial culture, then, ridiculed Christianity's understanding of male virtue.

Augustine worked against those ideals of Roman male culture, but he also adapted them in challenging unfaithful husbands and advising their wives. When a husband's behavior disqualified him as her guide, his wife should look past him to Christ. In this way, she would be unashamed to be faithful to an unworthy husband; she still owed her chastity to God and Christ, even if her husband had forfeited any claim to it.[17] For the sake of Christ, then, she should even ignore the injustice of her situation and in charity try to bring her husband to fidelity.[18] Women, he urged, should not seek the empty honor accorded tolerant Roman matrons or the approval of her husband by ignoring his infidelities. She should be jealous of her husband's fidelity, for the sake of his salvation. Augustine urged wives to invoke the aid of the bishop in confronting and reforming an unfaithful husband, rather than appealing to the imperial courts—which could provide only a divorce.[19]

Augustine applied a parallel standard to the unmarried, both men and women. He urged the young men who had been baptized and were participating in the eucharistic communion to preserve themselves for their future wives, just as they expected young women to do for their husbands. Here too, he recognized that they did not enjoy the legal and social restrictions and supports that protected unmarried women; they had to rely on the fear of God.[20] Since catechumens were committed to receiving baptism in the future and already identified themselves as Christians, they should observe similar restrictions of their sexual activity.[21] While still unmarried, they were not to take concubines, even those they planned to dismiss when they took a wife. If married, they must be satisfied with their wives.[22] Finally, the use of prostitutes was forbidden to all.[23]

Augustine recognized the obstacles to observing approved Christian practice. Still, he exhorted his hearers to fidelity, drawing primarily on Paul's responses to the questions posed by the Corinthian congregation. In particular, he drew upon the guiding principle that Christians were members of the body of Christ and its application to forbidding the use of prostitutes (1 Cor. 6:15). Baptism had made the bodies of Christians members of Christ's body. Sexual intercourse joined two bodies into one flesh, independently of any acceptance or rejection of marriage. Paul's injunction against prostitutes, moreover, applied to anyone who was not one's spouse.[24] The bishop affirmed the harshness of this judgment that reduced the concubines of married men to the level of prostitutes.

> Someone will say, "She is not a prostitute; she is my concubine." I ask: "You who claim this, do you have a wife?" He responds, "I do." I insist, "Then, whether you like it or not, she is a prostitute. So, go and tell her that the bishop has insulted you, because you have a wife and another woman sleeps with you. I don't care who she is, she is a prostitute. You might claim that she is faithful to you, that she sleeps only with you and with no one else. Since you consider her so chaste, why are you committing fornication? If she sleeps with only one, why do you sleep with two?" This is not allowed; it is forbidden; it is wrong. Such people are headed for hell.[25]

In this (imagined) dialogue, Augustine was careful to specify that the disgrace rested on the husband whose marital infidelity turned his concubine into a prostitute and then shamelessly attempted to claim her fidelity as his own. Augustine's outrage was not fueled directly by shame over his own earlier (confessed and well-known) unmarried practice. During their union, he claimed to have been faithful to the mother of his son, just as she had been to him. His dishonor was in failing to commit himself to her as she had to him.[26] In contrast, a husband's infidelity treated a concubine like a prostitute. In another sermon, however, he charged the (sexually faithful) Christian concubine with joining her own body to an adulterous partner. A Christian man should respect the members of Christ not only in his own body but also in that of the woman he would take as his sexual partner. By fornication or adultery, he would dishonor Christ in one or both of them.[27]

In a forceful extension of this exhortation, Augustine accused the Christians of Bulla Regia, where he was visiting, of turning women into prostitutes for their own financial profit, rather than helping them to escape that work. Had these women no souls, he asked; had Christ not poured out his blood to save them too? Indeed, Christ had promised that prostitutes and tax collectors would enter the kingdom of heaven, even ahead of the "righteous" (Matt. 21:31).[28] Christians must treat their bodies, those of their partners, and those of their servants, he concluded, as members of Christ.

Sometimes Augustine appealed to the identity of Christian bodies as temples of the Holy Spirit that God had cleansed (1 Cor. 6:19). Even if they harmed no one else when they abused their bodies, still Christians would dishonor the temple of God.[29] Developing a parallel to add power to Paul's teaching, Augustine asked: Would any husband bring a prostitute into the bedroom where his wife slept?[30] Would he bring a prostitute into his home to live with his wife, or if he were unmarried, with his mother and sister? Why then, would he let love of her live in his heart along with the love of God? If he would not so dishonor the honorable blood of his family, why would he dishonor the blood Christ shed for him?[31] In another sermon, he posed a related question: Having driven God out of the temple of his body by polluting it, could a Christian really expect the ejected God to hear his prayers?[32] In all these instances, he was appealing to a sense of religious reverence that had become distorted by Roman social customs, rather than to a violation of the ritual purity that had protected Israelite sacrificial practice from sexual pollution and was then being applied to the Christian altar.*

Finally, Augustine appealed to the goodness and beauty of chastity, which his congregants recognized in some instances but not in all. Husbands, he suggested, might come to appreciate chastity by attending to the value they placed upon modesty in their wives and, particularly, the daughters whom they intended to become other men's wives. By reflecting on the honor of the women of their own families, they might come to respect fidelity in the wives of others and even in themselves.[33]

Fear of punishment could serve as a guard against evil actions; Christians, however, were called to a fear based on the love of justice and of God. As children dreaded disappointing the parents who loved them, Augustine suggested, so Christians should fear falling short of God's expectations. In this spirit, he claimed, virgins exercised a greater love by taking upon themselves the burden of living in continence. For love of Christ, they gave up marriage and the sexual practice that it would permit them. They even dared, in some instances, to act against their parents' wishes—and plans for their marriages—in order to please Christ.[34]

Augustine's preaching on marital fidelity indicated that he considered it a major challenge, at least for Christian husbands, who were not restricted by Roman legal or cultural barriers. He also seems to have recognized, at least occasionally, that some Christian women had little power to prevent their own sexual exploitation, as wives, servants, concubines, or prostitutes. He urged both husbands and wives to take responsibility for the fidelity of their spouses: the former by controlling their own behavior and the latter by enforcing their exclusive rights. Citing 1 Corinthians 6:12–20, he asserted that the union that Christ established with his members included their bodies. Though he had ignored the bodily union established by the rituals of baptism and eucharist in explaining their life-giving power, he offered it as the primary motive for good sexual practice.[35] He insisted that sexual

---

* In his preaching on marriage, he never endorsed the notion that sexual intercourse made a person unworthy of contact with the divine or sacred. This belief was, however, found in African church legislation, apparently under the influence of the Roman church. A letter written by the Roman bishop Siricius was included in the records of the Council of Thelensis in 418 (CCSL 149:59–63). On its use in African episcopal meetings in 390 and 418, see Charles Munier's observations in his introduction to the record of the Council of Thelensis, CCSL 149:55.

practice outside marriage had a destructive effect on union with Christ and led to condemnation. As shall be seen below, he also would credit sexual union within faithful marriage with a positive, though indirect, contribution to maintaining Christian participation in the body of Christ.[36]

Sexual Practice within Marriage

In his successive commentaries on Genesis and in his treatise *On the Good of Marriage*, Augustine discussed the marriage of Adam and Eve in their original condition and the divine command to increase, multiply, and fill the earth with humans. When preaching, in contrast, his treatment of sexual practice within marriage was based upon the consequences of the mortality and lust that had been imposed on humanity as punishment for the sin of Adam and Eve. The freely controlled, joyful, and even blessed form of generation that God instituted for humanity in its original condition was forever lost. Because each human individual would die, no matter how carefully life had been cultivated and protected, generating children was necessary to preserve the human race. Humanity was like a tree that remained evergreen by constantly replacing the leaves it shed.[37] Mortal humans had to generate in a mortal way; like the animals, they were driven by appetites and desires, were subjected to pain and the futility of decline and death. By God's merciful governance, the power of appetite and desire was not only a punishment but also a means of salvation. It could be used to call humans back from their fallen condition and prod them toward their heavenly destiny. When humanity was finally freed from mortality in the resurrection, the process of generation would also cease.

In his preaching, Augustine dealt with generation and sexual relations as these were practiced by his congregants, with little speculation on what they might have been had Adam and Eve not sinned.[38] The Israelite patriarchs, rather than the first human parents, provided Augustine with the models of marital practice to which he exhorted Christians. His explanations served a double purpose. He defended these Israelite polygamists against attacks by Manichees who condemned sexual generation. He attempted to establish the primacy of intention in evaluating sexual practice. Abraham and Jacob should not be judged slaves of lust who abused their wives and servants for their own satisfaction. The patriarchs and their partners, Augustine claimed, used sexual intercourse in obedience to the divine command to build up the great people that God had promised them—through which the whole world would be blessed and the system of eternal salvation established. The Israelite patriarchs were not addicted to sexual pleasure; they accepted the mortal form of generating children as a duty; they fulfilled it with prudence and even resignation. Had God granted it to them, these holy people would have preferred to procreate without engaging in sexual intercourse, as Joseph and Mary would willingly generate Christ. Abraham's obedience to God in generating his sons was evidenced by his subsequent willingness to sacrifice the son who had been promised and given to him. Because they were so virtuous, God had allowed the patriarchs multiple wives and partners, through whom they could increase the elect people. Had the Lord of Israel intended to indulge a desire for the pleasure of sexual intercourse independently of generation—as the Manichees charged—then the women would have been assigned multiple husbands. That arrangement would have increased pleasurable sexual activity without resulting in a more numerous progeny. Augustine found an illustration of the more abstemious practice in the single small meal that had sustained Elijah through his forty-day walk to Horeb (1 Kings 19:6–8). Like that prophet, the patriarchs would have been happy to maintain their bodies and increase their people without being subjected to the demanding appetites and sensual pleasures of eating, drinking, and copulating.[39]

Augustine taught that sexual relations within marriage should be used exclusively for the purpose of generating: this was the practice of perfect marital chastity.[40] He explained that this was the proper way to preserve oneself as a holy and incorrupt temple of God.[41]

Although Roman practice was different from that of the Hebrew patriarchs, Augustine found the divine intention reflected in the Roman marriage contracts that specified the generation of children as the purpose of the union of husband and wife. He interpreted these documents as setting the proper limit to the use of sexual intercourse within marriage. Indeed, he asked, would any father joyfully give his daughter as bride or her husband accept her as wife for a less honorable purpose? Neither would publicly admit that she was intended for the satisfaction of her husband's lust. In the marriage agreement, the two men became relatives, not procurer and client. Even people who actually married for the satisfaction of lust pretended that they did so for the purpose of generation—in the same way they justified their careful attention to special foods as the necessary means of preserving their health. To exceed the honorable purpose of generation in the practice of sexual intercourse, Augustine contended, was a violation of the marriage contract and of the Christian's body as a temple of God.[42]

Yet Augustine recognized that remaining within the limit he attributed to patriarchal practice, the Mosaic law, and the Roman marriage contract was seldom achieved by Christian spouses.[43] He judged that anyone capable of such restraint was capable of refraining altogether from sexual activity, in the practice of continence.[44] From Pauline teaching, he developed a second understanding of marital holiness that acknowledged and restrained the force of lust.

Concessions to Human Weakness

Although the success of their efforts was always uncertain, Christian spouses must always intend generation as the outcome of their sexual intercourse, Augustine taught. Thus, they should avoid intercourse when they had good reason to judge that conception was unlikely. In any case, they should not act for the purpose of satisfying bodily appetites.* Intention, then, was essential to distinguishing well-governed from excessive sexual practice. Success in restraining sexual desire was virtuous, and failure sinful.[45]

Pauline teaching in 1 Corinthians 7:5–6 provided a resource for dealing with the difficult task of governing sexual practice. Although Christian couples should abstain from sexual relations for the sake of prayer, they should do so only by mutual consent. In addition, Paul warned against extending these periods of restraint lest one or the other be led into adultery by intemperance. Augustine understood Paul as permitting sexual intercourse within marriage to relieve the pressure of bodily appetite without regard for the purpose of generating. This teaching allowed the spouses to transgress the proper limit of sexual practice that was defined by the purpose and probability of generating; however, it required them to maintain the exclusivity proper to marriage itself by restricting their practice to their marriage partners.[46] Although this "immoderate" pattern of sexual intercourse within marriage was sinful because it exceeded the purpose of generating, it was pardonable because it maintained virtuous fidelity.

A concession, Augustine observed, was not an approval of something good but a toleration of something evil and sinful. He used a contrast to illustrate his point. In 1 Corinthians 7:8, Paul counseled the unmar-

* Augustine gave little attention to this dilemma; he noted its components. As a Manichee, Augustine had learned to avoid intercourse during the stage of the menstrual cycle when conception was more probable. See *Mor. eccl.* 2.18.65.

ried and the widowed who could not maintain continence to marry, since this was better than to burn. Since marriage was itself a good, however, this advice recognized and approved the choice of this (lesser) good; Paul had not conceded an evil to the unmarried and widowed. In his advice on limiting periods of abstinence, then, Augustine argued that Paul had not made a concession of marriage and its proper sexual practice for the purpose of generation. Rather he tolerated excessive sexual practice—an evil—between faithful spouses as a means of maintaining the good of fidelity in their marriages.[47] Because the sexual relations being conceded were intended for the satisfaction of desire rather than the generation of children, Paul allowed but did not command the married to return to sexual relations after a period of abstinence for prayer.[48] The better course, as Paul elsewhere exhorted, was for the spouses to possess their bodies not in the sickness of satisfying desires arising from mortality but "in holiness and honor" (1 Thess. 4:4–5), either by abstaining completely or limiting themselves to intercourse for the sake of generation.*

Augustine went beyond this specification of the allowance, however, to interpret Paul's teaching and advice in 1 Corinthians 7:5 as an assertion that spouses owed one another sexual practice, even if it was immoderate, when this was judged necessary to prevent the failure of either party by adultery. In marrying, he taught, each spouse gave the other the exclusive right to sexual intercourse not only for the generation of children but also for the management of the chronic illness of sinful sexual desire. Augustine judged, however, that although Paul required spouses to accept intercourse for the requiting of lust, he had not commanded them to ask for it. When they did seek it, they should regret the weakness that their request manifested.[49] If both were capable, Paul urged them to follow his own, better practice, which Augustine interpreted as mutual agreement to live together in continence.[50]

Even better than marital continence, Augustine insisted, was the love practiced in caring for a spouse driven by lust, in acting mercifully toward

* Augustine offered two interpretations of this statement in his sermons. In *Serm.* 51.13.21 he interpreted "honor and holiness" as continence, linking it to 1 Cor. 7:29, "having wives as not having them." In *Serm.* 278.9.9, he interpreted the phrase as the limitation of intercourse to the intention to procreate. In *Serm.* 278.9.9 and 278.14.14 Augustine read *uas* (vessel) as a reference to the body of the person addressed rather than to that of the spouse and built his interpretation on the cleansing of one's own body as the temple of God.

one's spouse who was in danger of adultery. The spirit of Augustine's interpretation of Paul was displayed in the conclusion to one of the few sermons he dedicated to marriage.

> Love one another. If the husband can abstain and the wife cannot, let him pay but not collect the marital debt. The husband who does not ask acts mercifully in giving what he does not ask. I dare to say without hesitation that this is an act of mercy. If you, the husband, do not pay this debt and your wife is overcome by lust, or if you, the wife, do not pay it and your husband is overcome by lust, then your spouse will become an adulterer. I do not want any of you to attain a greater honor by willing the condemnation of your partner.[51]

So Augustine recommended a different practice that protected fidelity by permitting lustful action justified by loving intention.

> Stop collecting but continue paying the marital debt; that practice will be credited to you as continence. Your intercourse, then, would be not demanded in lust but granted in mercy. Say this to your God: Lord, you recognize in me what you gave to me (the gift of continence), but I have heeded your warning. You created both me and my spouse; you will that neither of us be lost.[52]

In Augustine's judgment, this merciful participation in sexual intercourse was a virtuous act; it was more pleasing to God than exercising the esteemed virtue of continence. In this teaching, Augustine was urging the practice of the Hebrew patriarchs and matriarchs as the example to be followed by Christian spouses. Both engaged in sexual intercourse in fulfillment of the divine will: the former for generating the promised people, the latter for the salvation of their partners. In his exposition of the First Letter of John, Augustine cited 1 Peter 4:8, "charity covers a multitude of sins," to explain a parallel situation.[53]

Spouses sinned by seeking sexual relations for the satisfaction of desire rather than the generation of children, as has already been seen. Augustine explained, however, that this sin was pardonable because the good of marital fidelity, even when preserved through this sexual excess, interceded for and mitigated the guilt of that sin. The spouse being supported by the excessive practice repented and won pardon through prayer, fasting, and almsgiving, in the same way as was done for other sins of daily living, such as the immoderate use of food and drink.[54] As has been noted, Augustine regularly used this pardonable sin as an example to remind his congregants that they needed the divine forgiveness petitioned in the Lord's Prayer—and must fulfill its promise to forgive others.[55]

Continence within Marriage

Augustine's explanation of the concession of immoderate sexual activity within faithful marriage—intercourse that was intended for the satisfaction of desire rather than the generation of children—was complemented by his exposition of the Pauline exhortation of spouses to practice complete abstinence from sexual intercourse. In 1 Corinthians 7:29, Paul advised those who were married to act as though they were not. In his sermon on the marriage of Mary and Joseph as the parents of Jesus, Augustine took the opportunity to promote the ideal of continent marriage.[56] In a contemporary sermon that may have been required because of the attraction of the monastic communities that were being established in Africa, he again considered the practice of continence within marriage.[57]

In the sermon on Mary and Joseph, Augustine claimed that many Christian spouses refrained from sexual relations in order to focus more fully on the conjugal love (charity) that was the foundation of marriage. They sought to serve God together by sharing spiritual goods rather than fulfilling bodily desires through sexual intercourse. This kind of marriage, he explained, heeded Paul's exhortation in 1 Thessalonians 4:4-5 that spouses possess their bodies in holiness and honor. It was the only type of marriage that Augustine compared to that of Christ and the church (Eph. 5:25).[58]

The renunciation of sexual intercourse may have been undertaken after spouses had generated children, as seems to have been the practice of the clergy.[59] Augustine offered a justification for thus limiting the duty of procreation. Before the coming of Christ, the pious Israelites were called to generate abundantly, to build the people through which Christ would come, and in that people to prefigure the later expansion of the church throughout the world. This duty was imposed on the holy fathers and mothers; they served God by propagating, even though they were capable of practicing continence. That virtue was in their hearts but the time proper for its practice—along with virginity—did not arrive until after the birth of Christ. In the union of Mary and Joseph, he argued, a new form of marriage was instituted, proper to the mission of Christ and the life of his church.[60]

The commitments to mutual support made in marriage tempered the value that could be set upon continence. Spouses had exchanged rights to sexual intercourse and agreed to unite in one flesh; they could change that agreement only by acting together in free mutual consent.[61] As has been noted above, neither could put the other in danger of adultery in seeking this more excellent practice. Augustine constructed a dialogue with a spouse preferring continence in order to illustrate his teaching.

> A husband cannot make a decision on his own and say to his wife, "I am able to be continent. Join me in this if you can; but if you cannot, you must not stand in my way. I will accomplish what I am able to do." What is this? You, husband, do you want your partner to perish? If the weaker flesh is not able to be continent, then the weaker will is going to end up in debauchery. By sexual impurity, she will be condemned. Your crown must not be her punishment! You are wrong; this must not be allowed to happen![62]

Augustine moved to a different step in the argument: the goodness of marriage itself, which was not to be rejected.

> You reply, "If someone is going to be condemned for debauchery, better she alone than both of us together." If you say this, you are wrong again! Marriage itself is not condemned. "What God has joined together," does not condemn you but "let no human separate," does (Matt. 19:6). You are only a human. By adopting continence without the agreement of your wife, you—as a human—are trying to separate what God has decided to join together. "But God," you say, "is separating us, since I am doing this for God's sake." You could make that point if you could find it written somewhere that God said, "If you are joined carnally to your wife, I will condemn you." Then you could do as you propose, lest you be condemned together.[63]

Although continence within marriage was a higher good, it was intended to perfect the goodness of the marriage, not to destroy it.

> Instead, you should attend to the Apostle of Christ saying, "A wife does not have authority over her own body; that belongs to her husband. In the same way, the husband does not have authority over his body; that belongs to his wife. Do not defraud one another" (1 Cor. 7:4-5).

When he said "defraud," he was referring to denying what is due to your spouse, not to committing adultery. He was talking about paying what was owed; he was requiring spouses to fulfill their marital obligations to one another.[64]

For this reason, Augustine insisted, Paul had advised Christian spouses to separate only temporarily, as a respite of continence for the sake of prayer. He did not command those capable of continence to return to sexual relations. Instead, he warned those not capable of continence to return to the practice of intercourse, lest they fall into temptation and adultery.[65] Augustine remarked elsewhere, as has been noted above, that anyone who could restrict the practice of sexual intercourse within marriage to the sole purpose of generating children was capable of abstaining from it altogether.[66]

Augustine urged his married congregants to restrict their sexual relations to the purpose of generating children—the practice of marital chastity—and together to work toward continence within their marriage. He recognized that a divine gift was necessary to achieve this ideal, toward which most would be unwilling to strive. Indeed, many would have considered continence a punishment, something which they would never be moved to ask from God. Yet Augustine insisted that it must not be endured as a punishment but only sought as a gift from God.[67] As has been seen, however, Augustine discerned the working of charity and mercy even within the exclusive fidelity that he believed was practiced by the majority of Christians. That fidelity usually fell short of the standard of marital chastity, much less the ideal of continence. Still, God would forgive its excesses for the sake of the faithful love and mutual care of the spouses.

THE BOND OF MARRIAGE

In preaching about marriage, Augustine's attention focused most often on the challenges of sexual exclusivity. He occasionally spoke about the other aspect of marital fidelity, the lifelong commitment by which marriage endured until the death of one spouse. His teaching was consistent and clear.

Once married, a couple was allowed to separate only because of the adultery of one party, according to the teaching of Matthew 5:32 and 19:9. Even then, both parties remained bound to each other for life, and neither was allowed to remarry as long as both lived.[68] This interpretation of Christ's teaching allowed Christian husbands to follow the Roman law that required husbands to divorce an adulterous wife.[69] Augustine justified a Christian husband's dismissal of an unfaithful wife on the grounds that she had demonstrated her unwillingness to fulfill the role of a spouse.[70] He showed some suspicion of husbands who forgave and retained unfaithful wives: the apparent mercy and pardon might cover a more base desire to continue enjoying the woman, rather than living alone as Christian teaching would require after civil divorce.[71] Faithful wives, in contrast, were not legally required to divorce an adulterous husband. Augustine encouraged them to attempt to win their adulterous husbands over to fidelity rather than leaving them.[72]

In one sermon, Augustine offered the example of a husband who planned to divorce a faithful wife in order to marry another who was more wealthy or beautiful. In such cases, he explained, not even separation was allowed. God would certainly hear the protest of the abandoned wife and condemn the husband. Augustine quickly added the caution that has been examined above: that such action was not allowed even for the more noble motive of practicing continence. The husband had accepted responsibilities in marrying that he could not abandon. Augustine even compared those obligations to iron shackles.[73]

In his treatise *On the Good of Marriage*, Augustine developed more fully the religious significance of the bond of marriage. In preaching, however, he focused on its moral requirements.

Marriage and Property

Roman marriage was intended for generating children and transmitting family property from one generation to the next. Its practice brought conflicts with Christian ideals in two areas. Spouses were to be loved for themselves and not sought for the wealth that they might bring to a marriage and pass to its offspring. In addition, both the children and the Christian community had claims on a family's property and the income it produced. Augustine recognized the transmission of property through marriage as closely related to the resources necessary for the generation and care of children in following generations. He also insisted that caring for their children did not dispense parents from their obligations to the poor. In preaching, he suggested practices that met both responsibilities.

Marriage partners often were sought and chosen, Augustine noted, on the basis of wealth and the ensuing social status that their union would confer. He protested that to choose a spouse for the sake of gold, silver, income-producing property, or family status was not to act with a chaste and gracious love. A spouse should be loved as God should be loved, for personal goodness. To love and marry for the sake of gain was a type of adultery or fornication. What, he asked, would happen if the spouse's wealth was confiscated by the government and the social standing was lost—as happened more than occasionally among the Roman nobility? In some cases, the truth and chastity of the partner's love was demonstrated; fidelity and mercy toward a spouse who suffered a reversal would enrich the marriage.[74]

The claims of children upon their parents' property presented similar problems. Much wealth was in the form of agricultural property that produced income. The status and future opportunities of children depended upon sharing in a patrimony that would provide the economic base for their families in the next generation. When Augustine exhorted Christian parents to share their wealth with the poor through almsgiving, they sometimes resisted by asserting their children's rights to the property. They were not hoarding their wealth or squandering their substance on themselves, parents claimed; they were maintaining and expanding the patrimony for the use of their children. This sort of excuse, Augustine countered, would be used by generation after generation, so that no one in the family ever would fulfill the command of Christ to feed and clothe the poor. Had the creator of both parents and children, the God who fed them with the richness of the earth, no claim on that precious patrimony?[75]

To challenge the primacy of family rights, Augustine posed a case in which Christian belief came into direct conflict with the preservation of earthly patrimony. What would parents do when one of their children died? Would they uphold and act on the Christian belief that their child was alive in the presence of Christ? Did they trust Christ's promise and warning that what was given or refused to the poor would be counted as given or refused to himself (Matt. 25:31–46)? Did they believe, then, that donating the deceased's portion of the patrimony to the poor could help win eternal salvation for the dead child? Or would they, instead, hold the patrimony intact so that they could divide that child's portion among the surviving siblings, thereby giving them cause to rejoice in the death? The deceased child, Augustine urged, had urgent need of those funds. In this way, the death of a child was a test of parents' faith: Did they believe their child was simply dead and without hope or did they trust the promise of Christ?[76]

Furthermore, Augustine suggested that parents might look as well to their own true good by contributing some of their wealth to the poor, for the sake of their own salvation. Should they be concerned only with the earthly fortunes of their children?[77] He suggested yet another possibility for enriching the entire family: let the father adopt Christ as an additional son, pay out his portion of the inheritance, and thus enrich all his children by making them coheirs of Christ's fortune.[78]

Yet, Augustine did recognize that children had a claim to their patrimony. On occasion, he had to protect those rights against the imprudent generosity of parents. Januarius, a presbyter serving in Augustine's church at Hippo, claimed to have placed some of his assets in trust for his daughter, who had entered a monastic community. His son also entered a monastic community. The presbyter then changed his mind and left his estate to the church. Augustine refused the father's legacy and insisted that he would accept it only from the son and daughter when they were of age to make the gift themselves.[79] Similarly, he protected the inheritance of his deacon and later successor, Eraclius, who was still a young man.[80] In both cases, Augustine was refusing to allow children to give their patrimony to the church before their life-paths were settled. To justify these actions, he appealed to the precedent set by Bishop Aurelius of Carthage, who had returned the gift of a wealthy man because the children he had not anticipated fathering needed the property for their support.[81]

As has been seen in the chapter on wealth and almsgiving, Augustine proposed that parents who preserved their property for transmission to their children should use its income not only for the maintenance of the households but to support the Christian community and to provide food, shelter, and clothing for the poor.[82]

CHRIST AND THE CHURCH

The Marriage of Christ and the Church

The exhortation to Christian spouses in Ephesians 5:21–33 presented the union of Christ and the church, "in one flesh," as a model to be imitated by Christian spouses. This phrase had been used in Genesis 2:24 as a general characterization of the union of marriage. In Matthew 19:4–6, it was employed in that sense to forbid divorce. In 1 Corinthians 6:15–16, however,

Paul extended it to all sexual unions—even those that were not within a marriage—as a warning against adultery and fornication: the members of Christ must not be made "one body" with a prostitute.[83] The use of the Genesis text is Ephesians 5:31 might have been construed as a further Pauline extension of that idea to Christ and the church. It would then have made a direct connection of faithful and mutual sexual union in marriage to the bodily relation of Christ and the church.

Augustine accepted the text of Genesis 2:24 as a basis for condemning divorce, fornication, and adultery but refused to recognize any connection of the Ephesians text to human sexual union. Instead, he was willing to apply this mystery of the unity of Christ and the church being two in one flesh only to marriages like that of Mary and Joseph that were lived in continence, without sexual intercourse.

As has been seen in the review of Augustine's eucharistic interpretation of John 6, his doctrine was focused not on a fleshly union between Christ and Christians but on the spiritual or intentional union in the charity that was the gift and operation of the Holy Spirit.[84] There, he preferred the assertion in 1 Corinthians 12:27 that Christians were members of Christ. From this, he could argue that Christ as head and Christians as body were one flesh and spoke with one voice. This enabled him to attribute statements and actions of the head to the members and vice versa.[85] Augustine used this understanding of the relationship of Christ and his ecclesial body as a general principle for the interpretation of scripture.[86] In this context, he undertook a careful analysis of the statement about Adam in Genesis 2:24 and its use by Paul in Ephesians 5:31–32 and the parallel use by Christ himself in Matthew 19:4–6.

Augustine's consideration of the Pauline use of "two in one flesh," in Dolbeau Sermon 22 (341 augmented), came in a summary statement of the ways that scripture spoke about Christ. Christ, as Word, was equal to the Father. As mediator, he was Word and flesh, one individual. That same Christ was also joined, as head, to the church as body. In Ephesians 5:31, Paul had described this union as being, "two in one flesh," the term used for Adam and Eve as spouses in Genesis 2:24. To prevent a misinterpretation that would apply their sexual union to that of Christ and the church, Augustine immediately pointed out that Paul had not intended the Genesis text in the sexual sense that might be inferred from Matthew 19:5–6. Instead, he meant the head-body relationship of husband and wife, as it appeared in 1 Corinthians 11:3, to relate Christ as husband and wife as head and body.

Sometimes, so that you might understand the relation between the head and the body [in Christ], the Apostle appealed to what is said about the husband and wife in Genesis: *They will be two in one flesh* (Eph 5:31; Gen 2:24). Pay attention to what the Apostle was saying, so that we do not seem to be speaking rashly on the basis of our own guesswork. *They will be two in one flesh*, he said and then added, *this is a great mystery* (Eph 5:31). To prevent anyone thinking that he meant the natural coupling of the two sexes and bodily intercourse of the husband and wife, he then says, *I am speaking about Christ and the church* (Eph 5:32). What is said in Genesis must be understood as it exists between Christ and the church. *They will be two in one flesh, no longer two but one flesh* (Matt. 19:5–6). As between husband and wife, so between head and body—because *the man is the head of the woman* (1 Cor. 11:3). So, whether I say head and body, or I say husband and wife, understand a single one.[87]

In support of his interpretation, he offered Acts 9:4, where Christ, as heavenly head, protested Saul's assault on himself in the earthly church, his body. He then followed with Colossians 1:24, where Paul assigned his own sufferings to Christ, again in his earthly body. In both cases, the sufferings of the church belonged to Christ because of his unity with the church, as heavenly head and earthly body.[88]

Thus, Augustine interpreted Ephesians 5:31–32, which he believed had been written by Paul himself, as using the intentional union of Christ and the church—which was not sexual—as the culmination of the long exhortation addressed to Christian spouses in Ephesians 5:21–33. The head-body union of Christ and the church, then, determined the meaning of Genesis 2:24, as it applied to the marriage of Christians. The spouses participated in the mystery of Christ and the church by fidelity and love, through care and respect.

Similar arguments are found and amplified in other sermons of Augustine's. In his commentary on Psalm 139, he turned to the creation narrative to show how the formation of Eve from Adam had foreshadowed and illustrated the unity of Christ and the church. They were one flesh because Eve had been formed from Adam, as the church would later be formed from Christ. The woman was made from the man and belonged to the man; thus, their union was characterized by being two in one flesh (Gen. 2:24; Matt. 19:6; Acts 9:4). Once again, however, he specified the meaning of the relationship as that of head to body by appeals to 1 Corinthians 12:27, Matthew 19:6, and Acts 9:4.[89]

In the same way, he recalled that in Romans 5:14, Paul said that Adam was the "figure of the one who was to come." Adam was a foreshadowing of Christ because Eve was made from his side while he was sleeping; the fulfilling reality was the sleeping Lord—dying in his passion and pierced with a lance on the cross—from whose side poured out the water and blood that symbolized the sacraments of baptism and eucharist by which the church was formed. Christ's suffering was prefigured in Adam's sleeping. As Eve came from the side of that sleeping man, the church came from the side of this suffering man. Adam and Eve were two in one flesh because Eve had been drawn from the body of Adam and belonged to him; the church was made by the sacraments of baptism and the eucharist that symbolically flowed from the side of Christ. So, the church was from him and for him.⁹⁰ By using this explanation, Augustine avoided reference to sexual intercourse in explaining the unity in flesh of Christ and the church.

In the exposition of the Gospel of John, Augustine further developed this relationship between Adam and Christ. Paul, he claimed, wanted to prevent the "two in one flesh" being understood through sexual intercourse in marriage. Augustine observed that the usage in Genesis 2:24 included a reference to the husband leaving father and mother to cling to his wife. Christ fulfilled this type by leaving the Father to empty himself in taking the form of a servant and appearing to humans without displaying his equality to the Father. He then left his mother in abandoning the synagogue of the Jews, from which he was born in the flesh, and he clung to the church that he gathered from all the nations.⁹¹

In Augustine's interpretation, the oneness in flesh that was foreshadowed in Adam and accomplished in Christ was focused upon the derivation of the church from Christ and of Eve from Adam, rather than the subsequent sexual union of Adam and Eve. It was accomplished by Christ taking mortal flesh from Mary and through his redemptive death founding the church that became an extension of his Marian body.* Adam had included Eve, first in his body as originally created, and then as one with

* The individual human body that the Word of God received from Mary served, in Augustine's understanding, as both the foundation and the symbol of the ecclesial body whose head he became. This relationship was developed in Augustine's understanding not only of Christian marriage but of Christ's redemptive death and eucharistic presence. For the use of this relationship between the body of the Savior and the church in understanding the eucharist and the redemption, see pp. 112–23 above and pp. 203–6 below.

him in flesh even after she was formed as a distinct human; the Whole Christ included the church—as both his body and his spouse. Augustine might have intended to contrast the perfect unity of Christ and the church speaking "in one voice" throughout the scripture to Adam and Eve, who spoke in different voices as they sinned and were subsequently united in body rather than spirit. The exhortation in Ephesians 5:21–33, then, had not been fulfilled in Adam and Eve. It was fulfilled in the spiritual union of Christ and the church, who spoke with one voice. And it would be fulfilled in the Christian spouses who imitated that union in the church, as members of Christ's body.[92]

Thus, Augustine concluded that the phrase "two in one flesh" applied primarily to Christ and the church when used in Ephesians 5:31 and its citation of Genesis 2:24. It was to be understood not as parallel to the sexual union of husband and wife but to their unity in one person (in Christ), speaking with a single voice.[93] By analogy, the term could be used for a human marriage when the union between the spouses was like the one that united Christ to the church and to the Christians joined together in it, as the Pauline exhortation specified, in loving, caring for, and forgiving one another. In a sermon that may have been contemporary to the one just considered, Augustine applied the text of Ephesians 5:25 to the union of the parents of Jesus. Mary was subject to Joseph; he loved her as a coheir of grace, in honor and holiness (1 Thess. 4:4), as Christ loved the church. On that basis, Augustine argued that sexual relations were not of the essence of Christian marriage.[94]

The use of the marriage of Mary and Joseph had a distinct advantage for Augustine's interpretation: it did not include a sexual union. According to his reading and adamant use of 1 Corinthians 7:3–4, the spouses were equals in their sexual rights, though in little else.[95] The subordination of wife to husband, as expressed in 1 Corinthians 11:3, was essential to the application of the marriage metaphor to the church and Christ,[96] particularly in the text of Ephesians 5:21–33 that culminates in the baptismal washing of the wife by her husband.

Augustine's interpretation of Ephesians 5:21–33 would seem to count against any appreciation of the sexual relations of Christian spouses—either in marital chastity for the generation of children or in mutual support in restraining lust—as a means of participating in that union. The unity in one flesh was more appropriately understood in the Adam-Christ typology through the derivation of woman from man (Gen. 2:21–22) and the church from Christ. Indeed, he might have considered marriage irrelevant to Christian incorporation into the personal union of Christ and the church.

Participation in the Marriage of Christ and the Church

Augustine's rejection of a sexual interpretation of the mystery of the marriage of Christ and the church in one flesh (Eph. 5:31–32) was coordinated with his understanding of the participation of individual Christians in that union. They were joined to Christ as members of the church, of a body that was at once virgin, wife, mother, and widow. The church's relationship to Christ was established by faith, hope, and love; it was independent of an individual member's family affiliation or state of life. The family and sexual status—married or unmarried, virginal or continent, widowed or remarried—of individual Christians was not constitutive of the status of the church: it did not make the church a bride, virgin, or widow. Rather, the faithful participated in the roles belonging to the church through its complex relationship with Christ, its head. In the infancy narratives of the Gospels of Matthew and Luke, Augustine suggested, these roles were symbolized by Mary as virgin, Elizabeth as mother, and Anna as widow.[97]

The virginity of the church, Augustine explained, did not depend on the bodily integrity that few women (or men) possessed.[98] He explained that the bodily integrity of virgins, and of Mary, the mother of Christ, was religiously significant because it symbolized the integrity of spirit that was the virginity proper to all Christians: full faith, firm hope, and sincere charity.[99] In this sense, the church's virginity was itself the work of her spouse. He had found her a prostitute, fornicating by idolatry and serving demons. He had liberated and cleansed her by his death; he had restored her integrity.[100] This church was represented by the virgins awaiting the bridegroom, who abstained from evil deeds and performed the good works symbolized by their brightly burning lamps (Matt. 25:1–13).[101] Augustine noted that in 2 Corinthians 11:2–3 Paul asserted that he had espoused the Corinthian church to Christ as a chaste virgin and warned against the seduction of Satan who had tempted Eve. In writing this, he concluded, Paul must have been referring to the integrity of faith rather than that of body, since Eve had failed by a mental sin rather than by copulation with the serpent.[102] The bodily integrity of the church's consecrated virgins, then, signified the spiritual fidelity of the church as a whole.[103] They were joined to Christ not in some distinct manner but in the same way as other Christians, through the union of the church as a whole to Christ.[104]

Extending an analogy between Mary, the church, and individual Christians, Augustine explained the general sharing of the roles of wife and mother. As Mary bore Christ bodily, the church gave birth to Christ spiritually in Christians by baptism and the sharing of charity. As Mary bore a single individual, the church was the mother of unity in a multitude.[105] Individual Christians also might share in the church's maternity, he suggested, by leading candidates to baptism.[106] In addition, the hearts of Christians could imitate the womb of Mary by conceiving the virtues of truth, peace, and justice—all personified in Christ—and bringing them forth in good works.[107] Christ himself affirmed this analogy by identifying anyone who did the will of his Father as his brother, sister, and even mother (Matt. 12:50).[108]

The church on earth was also a widow. She was separated from her husband in heaven but relied on his aid and looked forward to his return. Each Christian who practiced such dependence upon God as the only source of help was such a widow.[109]

These explanations of Christian participation in the marriage of Christ and the church reflected Augustine's interpretation of "two in one flesh" in Ephesians 5:31. That relationship encompassed all three sexual roles open to Christians: marriage, widowhood, and virginity or continence. In elaborating the ways that the church and individual Christians enacted each of these roles, Augustine addressed marriage only through a spiritualization of its generative office. The only marriage that he compared to that of Christ and the church was the continent, even virginal, union of the parents of Jesus. The sexual fidelity proper to spouses was assigned no symbolic value, no role similar to that of the bodily integrity of virgins.[110] Continence, either within or apart from marriage, was judged the marital state proper to the clergy who served the congregation.

Although adultery could be presented as a violation of the Christian's relationship to Christ, using 1 Corinthians 6:15–16 on union with a prostitute, the text was never reversed to characterize fidelity to a spouse as a form of bodily integrity or purity that symbolized the commitment of the individual and church to Christ.[111] Although Augustine understood the exercise of charity by which faithful spouses supported one another in containing lustful desires, he assigned no Christian symbolism to their faithful sexual union.[112]

Conclusion

Augustine's preaching on marriage was primarily focused on sexual immorality: adultery, marital intercourse for satisfaction of desire rather than procreation, and, to a lesser extent, divorce. His creativity was evident in the ways he found to identify and denounce evil and to exhort to good. The Pauline teaching in 1 Corinthians (6:15–20; 7:4–8, 29; 11:2–3) and Ephesians (5:21–33) was developed beyond its immediate context and purpose, not only to explain the mutual responsibilities of partners in managing lust and protecting each other from adultery, but also to urge abstinence or continence within marriage as the ideal, as a proper participation in the union of Christ to the church. In a similar way, Augustine used the Roman marriage contract as a support for narrowing the purpose of the sexual union to the generation of children.

The influence of his understanding of the personal union of Christ and his ecclesial body, in one flesh and one voice, was most evident in Augustine's interpretation of Ephesians 5:31 in parallel to Genesis 2:24 and of the Christian sharing in the church's relation to Christ as virgin, wife, mother, and widow. This understanding of marriage, however, did not focus on the offices that derived from the mortal condition of humanity: the sexual generation of children operating under the burden of mortality and lust. Although this duty—and the accompanying management of property—were of highest importance in Roman and even Israelite practice of marriage, they would drop away in the resurrection when humanity was freed from bodily death. Moreover, the Christian anticipation of that eternal bodily life through baptism and the eucharist reduced the role of marriage and family in the life of the community.

Augustine identified no positive contribution that sexual relations within marriage made to the spiritual union of the spouses, through which they participated in that of Christ to the church. Virginity rather than sexual fidelity was the bodily symbol of commitment to Christ. Even the assistance that spouses offered one another in dealing with sexual desire—particularly participation in intercourse by a spouse who preferred continence—was not linked to the redeeming and cleansing work of Christ. The members of Christ would be desecrated by being joined to a prostitute (1 Cor. 6:15), but to possess them in holiness and honor (1 Thess. 4:4) was either to practice continence or to limit sexual practice to the generation of children, which Augustine regarded as equally challenging. Continence was the ideal toward which Christian spouses were exhorted.

A tension between the spiritual union of Christ to the church and the sexual unions of husbands and wives is clear in Augustine's understanding of marriage. In individual marriages, he particularly valued the mutual love and care that he considered the essential core of marriage. He interpreted it as a participation in the faith, hope, and love that joined Christians into the church and thereby into a marital union with Christ. The relationship established upon sexual practice, even when directed to its proper end of generation and suffused with mutual support and mercy, was necessarily limited to the couple. Spouses exchanged and respected exclusive rights to one another's sexual activity. The generation and education of children, moreover, justified private rights over property and much of its income. The spiritual union fostered and supported by marital continence, in contrast, was a friendship that could be universally shared, open to the whole of the church. When chosen early in the marriage, it enabled the spouses to place their entire property at the disposal of the church and the poor. In his surviving works, however, Augustine never explicitly interpreted the couple's efforts to contain and subdue their lust through sexual fidelity as a progress toward that universal charity.

In his commentaries on the original state of humans in Genesis and the final condition of the blessed in resurrected glory, Augustine explored the goodness that God may have intended for sexual union and generation, but he never approached them in his preaching.[113] The original capacity for sexual intercourse fully integrated into marital love had been lost through the sin of pride and its punishment before the first humans had a chance to exercise it; it was never to be restored.

Chapter Seven

THE MINISTRY OF THE CLERGY

AUGUSTINE'S PREACHING ABOUT THE CLERGY and its role in the process of salvation was largely related to the issues of the controversy that arose between rival bishops of Carthage, Caecilian and Donatus, in the early fourth century. That conflict had begun over the qualifications of the bishops who ordained Caecilian as bishop and, consequently, the standing of Caecilian himself. The party that coalesced around Donatus made a charge of apostasy during the Diocletian persecution against one of the bishops who had ordained Caecilian. The conflict quickly spread to all the other bishops—even those outside Africa—who accepted Caecilian into their communion at his ordination and rejected the claims of Donatus to be the true bishop of Carthage. Thence, the debate moved to the efficacy of the sacramental ministry, particularly baptism, of Caecilian, his colleagues in Africa, and, finally, the worldwide Catholic communion that supported him.

Like his predecessors on the Caecilianist (Catholic) side of the long conflict, Augustine disputed both the facts over which it began and the theory that supported continuing accusations against the successor bishops in the communion that had accepted Caecilian. Most of his contribution to the debate was in treatises written in the early fifth century, but the controversy spilled over into some of Augustine's sermons. In these, he addressed the understanding of the role of the clergy in the sacramental ministry of baptism and ordination, as well as the religious purity necessary for exercising those roles. Augustine went beyond the focus on these two rituals, however, to address other clerical responsibilities: forgiving sins committed after baptism, preaching the gospel, and presiding at the eucharist.

The Minister of Baptism

In three sermons, Augustine attacked the Donatist notion that the holiness of the bishop was necessary for conferring the Holy Spirit and forgiving sins in administering the sacrament of baptism.

Sermon 266, preached on the vigil of Pentecost, presented a text that immediately evoked the Donatist conflict, "Let not the oil of the sinner stick to my head" (Ps. 140:5).[1] The anointing oil used in baptism symbolized the gift of the Holy Spirit. According to Donatus, the oil consecrated and applied by an unworthy bishop would not confer the Holy Spirit on the newly baptized. Augustine distinguished the anointing oil proper to humans, all of whom were sinners to some degree, from the oil of Christ, which was holy even when it was applied by a sinner.[2] Augustine then reviewed the narratives in the Acts of the Apostles that recounted the giving of the Holy Spirit through various ministers and even without any human mediation. He argued that the gift was independent of the holiness of the ministers.[3] In support of his argument, Augustine pointed to various occasions on which the Holy Spirit was given in a way that showed that this gift was independent of the ministers through whom it was conferred. On the original Pentecost day, the Spirit had descended, without any imposition of hands by a minister, upon one hundred and twenty of Christ's disciples as they were united in prayer.[4] The Spirit also descended, without the imposition of human hands, upon the Ethiopian eunuch whom the deacon Philip evangelized and baptized (Acts 8:26–39).[5] Then, Peter and John were called from Jerusalem to confer the gift of the Holy Spirit, by imposition of hands, upon some Samaritan converts whom the same Philip had evangelized and baptized. This action provoked the error of Simon Magus who attributed the power to give the Spirit to the apostles themselves and attempted to purchase it from them for his own use. This misunderstanding led to a clarification of the independence of the Holy Spirit from the control of the minister (Acts 8:14–24).[6] Finally, the Spirit descended upon Cornelius and his whole family, in the presence of Peter but before he either baptized or imposed hands upon them (Acts 10:23–48). The Spirit, Augustine concluded from this survey, moved independently of the Christian minister. It could descend without any ministerial action or be given by the imposition of a bishop's hands. The fruitfulness of the Spirit's indwelling in the Christian, he argued, remained unaffected by the holiness of the minister when one was involved; the Spirit did, however, afflict an unworthy recipient, such as Simon.[7]

In commenting on the baptism of Jesus in his preached exposition of the Gospel of John, Augustine presented a similar explanation of the relation between Christ and the minister of baptism.[8] In the first sermon on this event, Augustine raised the question of John the Baptist's ability to recognize Jesus. According to Matthew's Gospel, when Jesus presented himself for baptism, John immediately protested that he was unworthy to perform the ritual and should himself be baptized by Jesus. Only after his baptism by John, however, did the Spirit descend upon him (Matt. 3:13–17). Augustine concluded that John did not first identify Jesus through the Spirit's later descent upon him but must have known who he was before Jesus presented himself for baptism. In the Gospel of John, in contrast, the baptism of Jesus plays no part in his recognition by John the Baptist (John 1:24–34). Instead, the Baptizer said that he had been advised to recognize the Lamb of God through the descent of the Spirit upon Jesus—though that vision is not narrated in this Gospel. John also identified Jesus as the one who baptized with the Holy Spirit—and realized that Jesus was greater than he. These differences between the accounts of the encounter between Jesus and John in the Gospels of Matthew and John presented Augustine with a problem and an opportunity.[9]

In the next sermon of the series on the Gospel of John, Augustine began by distinguishing what John the Baptist learned from the vision of the descent of the Holy Spirit upon Jesus: by baptizing with the Holy Spirit, Christ exercised a divine power that made his baptism surpass the one given by John. Christ, Augustine went on to explain, could have given and transferred to his disciples a power to give baptism. Had he done so, however, each of them, like John the Baptist, would have performed a baptism proper to himself, and the recipients of these various baptisms would have received a holiness proportionate to that of the individual baptizer. This interpretation was supported by the error that the Corinthian Christians later made in comparing the different ministers who had baptized them (1 Cor. 1:10–17). Instead of relying on their own holiness, Augustine argued, Christ's disciples functioned as his ministers; they conferred Christ's baptism and, through it, Christ's holiness rather than their own. Even while he was still on earth, Augustine noted, Christ had followed this procedure: he had not performed baptisms; he acted only through his disciples (John 4:2).[10]

Because the Spirit both descended and remained upon him, Christ alone exercised a divine power to baptize, first through his disciples and then through the ministers of his church who performed the ritual.[11]

Christ, rather than the minister, Augustine concluded, always conferred the baptism and guaranteed its holiness.[12] Thus, the minister of the ritual, whether good or bad, always conferred the one, efficacious baptism of Christ.[13] An unworthy minister, then, could be compared to a stone channel in which nothing grew, but through which life-giving water flowed to a garden.[14] Baptism sanctified the recipient because of Christ's power, independently of the holiness or sinfulness of its minister.

In the third sermon on the baptism of Jesus by John in the series on the Gospel of John, Augustine repeated the observation that John the Baptist had learned that the power to baptize with the Holy Spirit, symbolized by the descending dove, had both come to and remained upon Jesus; he alone baptized with the Holy Spirit. Augustine repeated the implications of this observation: when Jesus later commanded his disciples to baptize, he did not transmit that power to them; instead, he made them his ministers who would act by a power that remained properly and exclusively his own. Because Christ retained that power and exercised it himself, the efficacy of Christian baptism was always the same; it did not vary according to the holiness of the particular minister; Peter, Paul, and Judas all provided the one baptism of Christ.[15] Later in the same sermon, Augustine extended the interpretation. When the apostles Peter and John went to Samaria to impose hands upon the converts baptized by Philip, they did not themselves confer the Spirit: they prayed, and the Spirit was given (Acts 8:17).[16]

John the Baptist's statement in John 1:33—that because the Spirit descended and remained upon Jesus, he alone baptized with the Holy Spirit—was cited elsewhere in Augustine's preaching to demonstrate that the power to baptize belonged to Christ alone and was exercised independently of the merits of the minister performing the ritual.[17] Nowhere else, however, did Augustine emphasize the observation made in the commentary on that Gospel: that the Spirit's remaining upon Christ indicated that the power of baptizing was not passed to the disciples who performed the ritual.

As has been noted in the prior chapter dealing with the ritual of baptizing, the power of Christ that was exercised through the ministry initially of his disciples and subsequently of the clergy of the church guaranteed multiple effects of the baptism. The permanent and irreversible dedication of the recipient to Christ was accomplished in all recipients, independently of variations in their personal dispositions and the level of their adhesion to the society of saints within the unity of the church. The communication of the Holy Spirit, through whose indwelling the recipient was freed from the guilt for all past sins and incorporated into the body of Christ, was accomplished and sustained only in the recipients who repented of their prior sins and exercised the gift of love of God and neighbor that bound them to the saints within the church.[18]

In considering other operations of Christ's power through the ministry of the church, Augustine was not required to account for a permanent change in the recipient's religious status similar to the dedication accomplished in baptism. In these other actions—such as the mutual forgiveness of sins among Christians, the offering of and participation in the eucharist, and the communication of divine teaching through preaching—his explanation of the exercise of Christ's power to sanctify was like that offered for the forgiveness of sins in baptism through the mediation of the "society of saints."[19] There he implied that Christ's holiness and power to sanctify were extended to the whole church rather than being exercised exclusively by or through the clergy.[20]

THE MINISTER OF RECONCILIATION

The Clergy and the Community

In Sermon 99, preached within a year after the meeting with the Donatists in Carthage in 411, Augustine addressed the role of the minister in carrying out the work of the Holy Spirit.[21] Considering the gospel text of the sinful woman who washed the feet of Jesus in the home of Simon the Pharisee (Luke 7:36–50), he focused on the question raised in the minds of the guests present at that dinner: How could Jesus, whom they considered only human, forgive sins? Unlike the Donatists, Augustine observed, these Jews understood that forgiving sins was beyond the authority and power of a human being; it belonged to God alone. He then returned to the earlier discussion of the events in Samaria narrated in Acts of the Apostles (8:9–24), comparing the forgiveness of sins to the divine giving of the Holy Spirit both through and without the use of a minister.[22]

In this instance, Augustine attended to the forgiving work of the Holy Spirit through all the believers rather than through the ritual actions of the clergy in baptizing. How he asked, could Christ have promised all his disciples that the sins they loosened on earth would be loosened in heaven? In response, he appealed to Matthew 18:18 where Christ not only authorized but required all his disciples to release and bind sins committed against them. He also cited John 20:22–23 where Christ bestowed the Holy

Spirit upon his disciples to empower them to forgive and retain sins. Taken together, Augustine argued, the two texts clearly showed that the power of forgiveness was divine rather than human because it belonged to the Holy Spirit, and that it was effective because the Holy Spirit dwelt and operated in the faithful saints whom it formed into a living temple, the church.[23] As with the reception of baptism, he asserted, the penitent could trust the divine power to cleanse from sin, independently of the holiness—but not the ministry—of a human agent.[24]

As has been seen above, all Christians were obliged to offer forgiveness to those who sinned against them (Matt. 18:15–18).[25] Unlike the ministry of dedicating people to Christ and conferring the Holy Spirit by baptism and the imposition of hands, the bishop shared this responsibility for forgiving the sins of the baptized with all the faithful.[26] In considering the role peculiar to the bishops, then, Augustine focused not on the regular repentance and pardon of the sins of daily living but on those offenses against God or the church that harmed not particular individuals but the whole congregation. Such sins were beyond the power or authority of any individual to forgive; such sins required the communal rituals of exclusion, repentance, and reconciliation over which the bishop presided as leader of the congregation.*

To explain this formal penitential process, Augustine interpreted Christ's resurrection of Lazarus (John 11:17–44) as an allegory of the restoration of a hardened sinner. He divided that narrative into four stages or actions: the rolling back of the stone closing the tomb, the calling of Lazarus to come forth, the living man appearing in the grave clothes, and the untying of those bindings by the disciples of Jesus. Serious sinners were oppressed and held down by the weight of the law and the established habits of their evil lives, symbolized by the earth and stone of the tomb. The labor of correcting, rebuking, exhorting, and inviting these Christians to repentance was symbolized by the rolling back of the stone that enclosed Lazarus in the tomb. That work was successful only when the voice of the bishop pleading with the sinners was accompanied by that of Christ speaking within their hearts. Only God could move the heart and bring a

---

* According to Matt. 18:17, a Christian sinner who refused to repent when pardon was offered by the offended party alone and before witnesses was to be called before the entire church. If that failed, the sinner was to be permanently excluded from the community. The offense had been raised to a level that disrupted the whole congregation.

Christian dead in sin back to life. Next, Lazarus coming out of the grave represented newly penitent sinners confessing their offenses and praising God for the gift of repentance. Though they had turned away from their former way of life, they were still bound by the guilt of their evil deeds and intentions, represented by the grave clothes. Through the penitential discipline and rituals of the church, they would be set free. This role of the church was indicated in the narrative of the resuscitation by Christ saying to his disciples, in reference to Lazarus' bindings, "Unbind him, and let him go" (John 11:44).[27]

This command to the disciples, Augustine explained, clearly indicated the power given the whole church to bind and loosen.[28] A sinner who had broken with the communion of the church could not be forgiven and restored, as some penitents would have preferred, by private prayer and penitential actions. The sinner had to acknowledge failures before the congregation; the whole church would then intercede with God for forgiveness of the repented sins. After a period of repentance visible to the community, the leader of the church then imposed hands to release these penitents from the bonds of exclusion from communion. Christ himself had specified this procedure in giving the church the power to bind and loosen.[29]

The Power of Peter

Cyprian, the mid-third-century bishop of Carthage, had established the interpretation of Peter as a symbolic person in receiving the power conferred in Matthew 16:19. He specified that Peter represented the apostles as a group and, thus, the college of bishops that succeeded them in the work of sanctifying and governing the church. Cyprian had constructed this interpretation by combining Matthew 16:19 and John 20:22-23. Christ first assigned the authority to an individual, Peter, in order to show that it was a single power that could be shared but not divided. Then, after his resurrection, Christ gave the same power, by breathing out the Holy Spirit directly on all the apostles—who enjoyed the same status as Peter—to show that it was both held in common and based upon a shared gift of the Holy Spirit.[30] In this understanding, Peter functioned as a symbol of the bishop of an individual church and of the community of bishops as a whole.

Augustine interpreted Peter himself as a symbol of the church as a whole, not as the representative of the bishops alone, either as individuals or a collective. This understanding allowed him to harmonize all three instances of Christ's giving the power of binding and loosening sins: in

Matthew 16:16 (to Peter) and 18:15–18 (to every Christian), and in John 20:22–23 (to the assembled disciples). Augustine argued that the power of binding and loosening exercised by the bishops belonged to the whole church; as leaders, the bishops were responsible for exercising that communal power for the types of sin that affected not a single member or small group but the whole community.[31]

In a sermon on the celebration of the martyrdoms of Peter and Paul (June 29), Augustine gave extended attention to the role of Peter in receiving from Christ the authority to forgive sins.[32] Using the first of Cyprian's passages, Matthew 16:19, Augustine asserted that in receiving the power of the keys, Peter had acted neither as an individual nor as a bishop but in the person, or as the representative, of the whole church.

> As you know, before his passion, the Lord Jesus chose the disciples whom he called apostles. Among all of these, Peter alone was worthy to serve as a personification of the whole church. Because of this role as a personification of the whole church, which he alone played, Peter was chosen to hear, "I will give to you [singular] the keys of the kingdom of heaven." These keys were received not by a single individual but by the unity of the whole church. Peter is acknowledged as outstanding because he represented the universality and unity of the church when he was told, "I turn over to you," something that was actually being given to everyone.[33]

Next Augustine turned to the second passage Cyprian had used. In the Gospel of John, Christ conferred the Holy Spirit and the power to forgive sins on all the disciples gathered together on the evening following his resurrection (John 20:22–23). Unlike Cyprian, however, he identified those assembled apostles as representing the church rather than only the college of bishops.

> Now, in order to understand that the church received the keys to the kingdom of heaven, listen to what the Lord said to all his apostles in another place, "Receive [plural] the Holy Spirit," and then, "if you [plural] forgive anyone's sins, they are forgiven; if you [plural] hold them bound, they are bound."[34]

To complete the argument that Peter and the apostles represented the whole church, Augustine then turned back to the Gospel of Matthew. He used the text of Christ conferring the power—and the command—to forgive upon all Christians (Matt. 18:15–18), but he continued to refer the statement to Peter, as personification of the whole church.

> This statement (John 20:22–23) is about the keys, about which it was said, "the things you [plural] loosen on earth will be loosened in heaven; and the things you [plural] will have bound on earth will be bound in heaven." But this he said to Peter.[35]

The exact parallel of the statements in Matthew 16:19 and 18:18—they differ only in the singular and plural forms of the verbs "loosen" and "bind"— allowed Augustine to continue interpreting the text as addressed to Peter as representative of the whole church. He could use both the singular and the plural forms in the same way because he judged that in the first narrative (Matt. 16:19) Peter was representing all the faithful in receiving the power. He applied this same interpretation to the second narrative (Matt. 18:15– 18), arguing that Peter served as a symbol of every Christian.

> To understand that Peter was acting in the person of the entire church, attend to what was said to Peter and what was said to all the faithful. "If your fellow sins against you [singular], rebuke that fellow in private between the two of you alone. If that person will not listen to you [sin- gular], use one or two other persons in addition to yourself. For, it is written, "every testimony shall be confirmed by the mouth of two or three witnesses" (Deut. 19:5, quoted in 2 Cor. 13:1). If the person will not listen to them, bring the matter to the church. If the person will not listen to the church itself, then you [singular] should treat that person like a Gentile or a tax collector (Matt. 18:15–17). Amen, I say to you [plural], what you [plural] bind on earth will be bound in heaven and what you [plural] loosen on earth will be loosened in heaven (Matt. 18:18). The dove binds and the dove releases. What is built on the rock binds and loosens.[36]

"The dove" was a term that Augustine had developed in his treatise *On Baptism* to refer to the entire body of faithful Christians united in love by the gift of the Holy Spirit. This group was the depository of the sanctifying power that Christ conferred on the church. The dove exercised that power by intercessory prayer.[37]

In other sermons, Augustine reversed the order of the argument but made the same point: the daily exercise of this power of forgiving sins by all the faithful (Matt. 18:18) proved that Peter had been representing the church—or the communion of the true Christians within the church—in receiving and exercising this power (Matt. 16:19). The church excommunicates and reconciles; it binds and loosens on earth and in heaven. One person, Peter, represented the holy church—all the good within the visible community—in receiving and exercising this power. In a similar way, Judas represented all the evil in the church, to whom Christ said, "You will not have me with you always."[38] Peter, he observed in another sermon, could not have been addressed as an individual and received a power belonging to himself alone: Paul, James, and John received the same power; indeed, the whole church, as the body of Christ, continued to use these keys every day.[39]

In yet another sermon, Augustine insisted that the authority to forgive sins had been given not to the bishops alone but to the people as well. Distinguishing between the clergy seated in the apse of the church and the people standing in the nave, he explained:

If this (referring to the plural form in Matthew 18:18) was said to Peter alone, then only Peter used the power. Peter has died and gone away. Who binds now; who releases? I dare to say, we too have those keys. What am I saying, that we bind and we loosen? You too bind and you release as well. A person is bound by being separated from your fellowship; in being separated from your company, the person is bound by you. When someone is reconciled, that person is loosened by you because you, too, ask this of God for that person.[40]

The binding of sinners and releasing of penitents was accomplished by excommunication and reconciliation, by their separation from and reunion with the eucharistic fellowship of the faithful. Although the bishop supervised these processes, the sinners were bound and released by their relationship to the body of the faithful. The faithful bound the sinners by exclusion and released them by inclusion. The connection between the earthly and heavenly actions was the prayers of the united faithful for the divine forgiveness of the penitents. Though the rituals of excommunication and reconciliation were performed by the bishop, Augustine insisted that the leader of the community served as a minister of the power of the keys that had been conferred upon the whole body of the faithful. As was noted above in the discussion of baptism, the binding and releasing were properly understood as the sinner's self-exclusion from that union of charity and then being restored to it through the divine operation that responded to the prayers of the saints.[41]

In these explanations, Augustine was drawing out the implications of his teaching on the more informal mutual forgiveness among Christians.[42] The authority to forgive sins had been bestowed on the church itself and on those within the unity of the church who were filled with the charity of the Holy Spirit. They exercised this power on behalf of one another on a daily basis. When, however, one of the Christians refused to participate in this process of mutual forgiveness or was guilty of a sin that attacked and broke the sinner's bond of love with the church as a whole, then the congregation had to act as a body, as Matthew 18:15–18 specified. Serving as the leader of that body, the bishop pronounced the exclusion of the sinner from the eucharistic fellowship; he spoke for all the faithful in urging the sinner to repent; he led the intercessory prayers of all that sought God's forgiveness for the sinner.[43] In circumstances that required secrecy to protect the sinner from penalties imposed by the imperial judiciary, the bishop could also represent the community in receiving the private confession of sins.[44] Augustine's thesis was that the bishop acted in the person of the church as a whole, exercising an authority that had been conferred upon it by Christ. As Peter had borne that person of the whole church in receiving the power to bind and loosen, so the bishop acted in the person of the church in exercising that authority. Augustine contradicted Cyprian's thesis that Christ had conferred the power to sanctify upon the college of bishops, whom Peter had represented in Matthew 16:19. On the basis of the more fully elaborated parallel in Matthew 18:15–18, he argued that Christ had conferred the power to forgive upon all Christians and specified that its successful exercise could require the collaboration of the whole congregation. This solution fit Augustine's general theory of relation between bishop and people.[45]

In other sermons dealing with the relationship of Christ to the church and the sharing of his divine power to forgive with Christians, Augustine further specified the group that he had named as the "dove" or the "society of saints" in his evaluation of Cyprian's writings.[46] The "saints" who were formed into the core of the church were not all those who had received the sacraments of baptism and eucharist, nor even those who lived in the unity of the Catholic communion. The saints who received and exercised the power to forgive and bind were the predestined whom God had chosen, called, sanctified, and foreknown would remain faithful in charity. They could be referred to as the firmament of the heavens, the stars in the sky, the house of God, the footstool of the Lord.[47] Such a group was always being replenished in the church, like the new growth of an evergreen tree, as the preceding generations were gathered into the heavenly and eternal life.[48] This group of Christians, which could be identified only by God, provided the stable holiness that was required of the recipients and exercisers of the church's power to forgive that was conferred in Matthew 16:19 and John 20:22–23.

PRIESTS OFFERING AND INTERCEDING

Because the Donatist controversy focused on the church's power of forgiving sins and its exercise by the clergy, Augustine gave more attention to the rituals of baptism and penance for sins committed after baptism than he did to the celebration of the eucharist. The priesthood of Christ and its participation by the church and its clergy were discussed briefly in his commentaries on the Psalms and the Gospel of John; they were treated more fully in two sermons. Augustine focused on the function of Christ as priest in offering sacrifice and interceding for the people. He used a typological interpretation of the Israelite rituals that seems to have been guided by the text of Hebrews 7–9, although he never cited it in these expositions.

Once each year, Augustine recalled, the Israelite high priest passed alone through the veil setting off the holy of holies to offer the blood of the sacrificed animal.[49] In making that offering, the priest interceded for the assembly of the people that remained standing outside. The priest's role required that he be free of bodily blemish and ritual impurity.[50] He had no one else to intercede on his own behalf.[51] Augustine then explained that Christ had fulfilled the function prefigured in this ritual by making a single offering of himself, not once each year but once for all time. He offered on the cross the human flesh that he had received from the virgin. Then, rising from the dead and passing through the heavenly veil, he entered the sanctuary that had been symbolized by the earthly one. There, as both priest and victim, he offered his restored flesh as the firstfruits of humanity and the necessary expiation for sin.[52] This offering was the perfect and effective one: made not at an earthly altar but at the altar in heaven;[53] made by a perfect priest, free of all sin even in mortal humanity; made by an intercessor who needed no one to intercede for himself;[54] alone of all who had borne flesh, he was worthy to intercede in the heavenly sanctuary.[55] Once established in this heavenly role, Christ continued to offer himself and intercede for his people, the sole mediator between God and humanity (1 Tim. 2:5).

Augustine illustrated the Christian priest's relationship to Christ and to his congregation by directing attention to the arrangement of the clergy and people during the eucharistic celebration. In the Israelite ritual that prefigured the sacrifice of Christ, the priest entered the sanctuary alone while the people stood outside. The role of the Israelite priest had foreshadowed that of Christ rising and entering the heavenly sanctuary to offer himself. The Christian people were not separated from their clergy as the Israelites had been from their high priest, with the clergy alone at the altar inside a veiled space and the people outside it. The Christian people were gathered at the earthly altar with their bishop, Augustine pointed out. As they began the ritual prayer, the bishop reminded all to lift their hearts on high; they responded that their attention was focused there on the Lord.[56] They then joined their bishop in making the offering: they saw what he did, they heard and voiced their assent to the prayer he spoke, and they received the gifts from the altar.[57]

In the church buildings of Augustine's Africa, the altar was placed within the nave—the main body—of the church, so that the clergy stood at it and the faithful surrounded it. The altar area was slightly raised and surrounded by a low railing that segregated but did not separate the clergy from the people.[58] The clergy was not standing within a veiled or otherwise hidden space that symbolized the heavenly sanctuary in the way that the Israelite tabernacle or the temple's holy of holies did. Thus, the leader of the eucharistic ritual was not symbolically identified with Christ in a way that separated and distinguished him from the people. The congregation and its clergy were gathered around the earthly altar in anticipation of joining Christ, as his glorified priestly body, within the heavenly sanctuary, participating in his one continuous offering.[59] The fulfillment of the Israelite ritual foreshadowed in Christian practice showed, he insisted, that even now the entire church shared the priesthood of Christ.*

* Claims have been made, in the last half-century, that the laity were separated from the clergy and the altar in early Christian worship spaces. These assertions are based on ideological grounds and without foundation in archeological or textual witness to ancient Christian practices. For a discussion, see Robin M. Jensen, "Recovering Ancient Ecclesiology: The Place of the Altar and the Orientation of Prayer in the Early Latin Church," *Worship* 89 (March 2015): 99–124, as well as the contrary evidence provided above.

In a polemical thrust at the claim that had been made by the Donatist bishop of Carthage in the last third of the fourth century, Augustine explained the status of the bishop among this priestly people. Parmenian, he recalled, had claimed that the bishop served as mediator between God and the people of his church. Augustine protested that the Donatists thrust the bishop into the place of Christ, who was proclaimed the only such mediator in 1 Timothy 2:5.[60] Christ—but not the Christian bishop—was prefigured by the Israelite priest who interceded for others but had no other to pray for him. The church had prayed for both Peter and Paul (Col. 4:3; Acts 12:5).[61] The bishop, he insisted, was a member of the body of Christ, along with the people he served.

In one of these sermons against the Donatists and in his commentary on the Gospel of John, Augustine also compared the situation of Christ in heaven and the church on earth awaiting his return to that of the narrative in Matthew 14:22–24: Jesus prayed on the mountain as the disciples struggled against a storm, in a night-crossing of the sea.[62]

Christ shared his priesthood with the church, Augustine argued, extending his teaching that the church, as the body of Christ, shared and exercised his power. He focused on the Israelite anointing of priest and king, adding the Petrine affirmation that Christians were a royal priesthood (1 Pet. 2:9). In Israelite practice, both priest and king were anointed; as the Anointed, Christ bore the person of both king and priest.[63] He was the son of David through Mary—Augustine used Romans 1:3 rather than the lineage of Joseph in Matthew 1:1–17—and a descendent of Aaron through the line that Mary shared with her cousin Elizabeth (Luke 1:36). Having established Christ's priestly role, Augustine showed that he exercised the office of king not only in guiding his people but in leading them in the battle against Satan, both in resisting temptations and in conquering death, the final enemy (1 Cor. 15:25).[64] The ritual of baptismal anointing made Christians members of Christ's regal and priestly body, through which they shared his powers.[65] Thus, Augustine concluded that the Israelite anointing of king and priest was fulfilled in Christ and through him extended to the whole body of the faithful. The title was applied to the bishop only as the leader or supervisor of the congregation.[66]

Augustine explained that the title "priest" was used for the bishop, though not for the presbyters or deacons.

> All of us bishops are called priests because we were placed in charge.
> The entire church is the body of that one priest. His body belongs to

the priest. Thus the Apostle Peter applied the title to the church itself: a holy people, a royal priesthood (1 Pet. 2:9).[67]

The priesthood of the bishop derived from that of the universal church as his body, which shared the one priesthood of Christ, its head.

Thus, Augustine understood the church's sharing in the offering and interceding of Christ in the same way as its participation in his sanctifying power in baptism and forgiving sins. The power belonged properly to Christ himself; the faithful Christians who were joined and formed into his body by baptism participated in his priestly power and prayer. The bishop was a member of that body and, if he was perseveringly faithful, shared the priestly power Christ bestowed on his members. The bishop acted as the leader and minister of the church but—contrary to the Donatists—his office did not make him its priest, intercessor, or mediator.

PREACHERS OF THE GOSPEL

Augustine raised a fourth question related to the Donatist controversy, one about the role and efficacy of the bishop as a teacher and moral guide for Christians. He usually framed the question and his response primarily by applying to the Christian clergy Christ's direction in Matthew 23:2–3 regarding the teaching and practice of the scribes and Pharisees: heed the teaching of the bishops and presbyters but do not follow their example when it was sinful.

Yet Augustine seems to have recognized that the problem might not be limited to a conflict between word and deed, to a failure to practice what one preached. Some bishops might be ignorant or misguided in their interpretation of the scriptural texts; others might be intentionally deceptive in seeking their own advantage and attempting to justify their deviant practices. While acknowledging the problems, Augustine assured his hearers that divine operation both through the words of the preachers and within the minds or hearts of the faithful could protect them from harm. Moreover, as he had in treating sacramental ministry, he insisted that only these divine operations actually made the preaching ministry effective by leading its recipients to a fuller understanding and practice of the message of Christ. God would not move their hearts to follow bad teaching and advice.

Augustine often treated the problem of ministerial failure in moral guidance in its simplest form—right teaching accompanied by bad example. He applied Christ's statement about the teaching of the scribes and Pharisees (Matt. 23:2–3) to the Christian clergy. Usually, he simply assumed that bishops spoke the truth;[68] in some instances he affirmed it explicitly.[69] The clergy who taught and preached would never be so audacious as to instruct the Christian people to sin, he suggested. Mercenaries would not urge the people to prefer their own advantage to that of Christ nor would thieves dare to exhort their congregants to steal. The social and religious context—speaking to a congregation from the elevated chair in the apse of a church—and the people's ability to recognize obvious falsehood could be trusted to restrain evil preachers.[70]

Augustine's principal point was that the gospel could be rightly preached even by one who did not follow it.[71] Bishops, both good and evil, were ministers distributing goods taken from the storehouses of Christ.[72] God could offer and the hearer could accept the truth even when it was delivered by an unbelieving preacher.[73] In support, Augustine cited Paul's evaluation of immoral preachers: they pursued their own interests rather than those of Christ; they served their own bellies rather than God; yet they did preach the gospel (Phil. 1:18; 2:19–21).[74] The sinfulness of the bishop, therefore, did not justify a person rejecting the message he preached or breaking away from the unity of the worldwide church in search of a minister who presented himself as more upright.[75] Anyone who ignored the truth an evil bishop proclaimed and preferred the example of his actions would be condemned along with him as a companion in sin whose useful instruction—supplemented by the example of other Christians—had provided a guide to good living.[76]

Augustine applied this teaching to his own work. At the end of a sermon, he recognized that his hearers might be asking themselves whether he fulfilled all that he had been exhorting them to accomplish. In response, he suggested that this was not the right question to ask: even if at the present he could claim to meet the standard he set, he knew himself too well to promise that he always would do so in the future. Let them, then, judge him by Christ's standard and either praise or accuse him. When they appeared before Christ as their judge, however, they must not expect to plead their bishop's failures as an excuse for their own.[77]

In four surviving sermons, however, Augustine recognized—or was forced to acknowledge—that a sinful bishop might not speak the truth of the gospel. The assumption apparently supporting Christ's command to follow the teaching of the occupants of the teacher's chair might not be fulfilled. The objection was posed by Christ's teaching that speech arises from the heart (Matt. 12:34): an evil person cannot speak well. It was illustrated by proverbs: grapes are not gathered from thorns nor are figs picked from thistles; a bad tree cannot bear good fruit; a tree is judged by its fruit (Matt. 7:16–18; 12:33–35; Luke 6:43–45). In response to the challenge of the first text, Augustine once again noted that Christ had attributed the authority of the scribes and Pharisees to the chair of Moses on which they sat. That chair was a symbol of the law of Moses that they had learned and retained in their memories as the basis of their teaching. When they repeated it, they were not speaking from their own evil hearts—from which only false-hood would come—but passing on the truth they had received. He suggested the example of an evil herald or spokesman working for a righteous judge. Speaking from his own heart, the herald would have proclaimed neither the condemnation of his friends nor the exoneration of his enemies. By his position, however, he was bound to announce what the judge had decided. Similarly, a bishop could preach the truth he had learned and retained in his memory even if he did not follow it.[78] The image of the grape among thorns and the other proverbs provided an opportunity to elaborate on the responsibilities of the laity who were served by a sinful bishop. A vine could be intertwined with a thorn bush that supported it; its grapes would then be surrounded by sharp thorns. The vineyard worker or hungry passerby had to be careful to avoid the thorns in reaching for the grapes. By attending to the branch from which the cluster hung and following the vine down to its own root, however, the two plants and their fruits could be distinguished.[79]

In his own preaching, Augustine did not consider explicitly the problems of Christians being led astray by their bishops' lack of learning in interpreting the scripture or of rhetorical skill in explaining it. Instead of criticizing or excusing those who did not share his natural endowments and unusual education, he regularly confessed his own need of divine assistance. He asked his hearers to pray that God would reveal the true and appropriate meaning of the text to him and thereby to them.[80] He was often tentative in offering interpretations of difficult passages.[81] Moreover, he claimed, the laity had resources to protect themselves against the failures of their bishops. The scriptures on which the bishop preached were read out to the congregation before they were explained; that proclamation could be used to avoid confusion about the moral responsibilities arising from the texts. When confused or uncertain, the laity could always persevere in the Christian faith and practice they had attained and adopted, in the hope that the clear understanding they desired would eventually be provided by God. Since faith—and its practice in good works—must always precede understanding (Isa. 7:9), this patient hope was a necessary virtue for Christians to practice.[82]

Occasionally, however, Augustine did recognize that a preacher might intend to lead his congregation astray. Paul's warning against the Judaizers in Galatians 1:9 was not meant for that time alone; later preachers also supported heresy.[83] The Donatists regularly asserted, for example, that their bishops alone could sanctify the faithful; they acted as thieves who led their own people astray and tried to steal Catholics from the flock of Christ.[84] In his extended exposition of Ezekiel 34, Augustine described as mercenaries those bishops who urged their congregations to follow them in seeking the goods of the earthly age, and thus to build their lives on sand. They avoided warning Christians that as coheirs to the kingdom of Christ, they were to expect not only harsh treatment from the traditional culture but correction and testing from God. Such leaders created a false sense of security by assuring their people that God would sustain them and would not permit them to be tested beyond their capacity to resist (1 Cor. 10:13). They failed to draw out the implications of a commitment to the following of Christ.[85] Other bishops might claim that the danger of clerical bad example addressed in Matthew 23:2–3 was limited to the Jewish context in which Christ had spoken originally. Or they might mislead by explaining that in his directive Christ was warning the laity against usurping the teaching office of the clergy by questioning their bishops.[86] Again, Augustine suggested that Christians could protect themselves against such leaders by their acquired understanding of the faith and by attention to the scriptures read out to them. Often, conflicts with what preceded or followed in the biblical passages misinterpreted by these liars would expose their deception.[87] Augustine urged that deceivers be rejected or ignored.[88]

Sinful bishops who did not practice the gospel they preached and deceitful bishops who falsified the gospel to justify their practices, Augustine insisted, would not evade divine condemnation. They could not plead that, despite their sins, they had served God's purposes and provided some benefit to their congregations. Their own failures in practice would have undone any good they might have brought about by preaching the truth—unless their hearers had heeded Christ's warning and disregarded their bad example.[89] He contrasted these evil bishops to the three youths whom King Nebuchadnezzar had promoted to administrative posts in the Babylonian Empire after God had delivered them from the fiery furnace (Dan. 3:30 [Vulgate 3:97]). Like many Christians, those faithful Israelites had been citizens of the heavenly city pressed into the service of an earthly kingdom. Mercenary bishops were actually citizens of the earthly city serving as resident aliens in the heavenly kingdom, to which they did not belong.[90]

In addition to addressing and attempting to resolve these difficulties, Augustine offered a more general understanding of the efficacy of Christian preaching. Only the divine grace made preaching effective in instructing and motivating congregations. The words of the preacher sounded in the ears of his hearers but would bear fruit only as God operated within them to enlighten and inspire understanding and action. Paul had made this point explicit in 1 Corinthians 3:6: "I planted, Apollos watered, but God gave the growth."[91] Christ himself would protect his people from preachers who distorted the meaning of scripture. When a passage was ripped from its context, the Lord would direct the hearers' attention to what preceded and followed in the text, so that they could be preserved from the deception.[92]

In these explanations, Augustine was applying to the preaching ministry an explanation of the providential control and interior teaching that he had developed in his reflections on the working out of divine election in the conversion of the saints.[93] Like his understanding of the role of the minister of baptism, this thesis was applied to all preachers, not only to those who deviated in practice or deceived in word.[94] Augustine argued that God would use their misguided and even their evil intentions and actions to achieve good outcomes for the elect.[95] He justified this interpretation by appealing once again to Paul's evaluation of his rivals who acted out of envy and spite in preaching the gospel (Phil. 1:15–18). Paul had rejoiced that Christ was proclaimed. In this way, Augustine justified the toleration of clergy who preached the truth that they neither understood nor believed nor practiced.[96]

This understanding of God's role in guiding the preacher and enlightening the hearer was reflected in Augustine's practice before the congregation to which he preached regularly. He and his hearers, he insisted, were pupils of the same master teacher, though they had different roles to play in the process of learning.[97] He asked them to pray that God would guide him to what he ought to say to them and then shape his speech so that it fit the dispositions of their hearts and would lead them to good works.[98] He trusted that when his rhetoric fell short, God would enlighten their minds.[99] Finally, he urged his people not to defend his reputation when he was attacked by enemies lest they appear to be placing trust in him rather than in Christ.[100]

Although Augustine recognized his own limitations and those of his fellow bishops not only as models of Christian behavior but as interpreters of the scriptures, he insisted that Christ's promise to care for his flock was fulfilled through their preaching. In commenting on Ezekiel 34:13, "I will feed them on the mountains of Israel," he identified these mountains as the writers of the divine scriptures. These human authors gave Christ's sheep rich pasture on which they could safely feed, through them the sheep could clearly hear the voice of their true pastor.[101] They were the model for every preacher and the proof that the ministry could succeed.

Augustine's teaching on the roles of good, inadequate, and evil ministers in the proclamation of the gospel and instruction in Christian living was similar to that he developed for dealing with their administration of baptism. The sacrament's power was derived from Christ himself; its actual effect depended on the repentance, faith, and subsequent good living of the baptized under the influence of the Spirit's gift of charity that was conferred upon them. In the same way, Christ's truth could be communicated even by a preacher who did not believe or practice it. The doctrine preached could itself expose the ignorance or ill will of the minister and warn the hearers against his example. Despite a minister's infidelity, the Christian could safely receive and follow the gospel through his preaching.

WATCHING OVER THE CONGREGATION

Augustine had argued that the title of priest belonged properly to Christ and to his ecclesial body but only derivatively to the bishop. Christ, he insisted, was the only priest, the only mediator, and the only one who offered sacrifice. As his ecclesial body, the faithful in the unity of the church shared the priestly title and power of Christ. The bishop bore the title of priest as a leader of this priestly people and, if he was among the faithful, shared its power of forgiving and sanctifying through intercession. As minister of the rituals of baptism, eucharist, and reconciliation, the bishop also acted as agent or spokesman of Christ and the church, exercising a power not properly his own. The perseveringly faithful participated in this priestly ministry through the prayers that the Holy Spirit inspired in them. In this way, Augustine protected the efficacy of the sacramental ministry from any deficits in the holiness of the clergy or the laity.

The office that Augustine assigned to the bishop was leader, the one in charge (*praepositus*). In speaking of the ways in which that role was exercised, he used three titles: pastor or shepherd, *episcopus* or watchman, and pilot.

"Pastor" was a preferred descriptive title because Christ had applied it to himself (John 10:11, 14) and used it to name the function that he later assigned to Peter (John 21:15–18). Augustine found two closely related elements in the commissioning of Peter. First, Christ began by questioning Peter's love for him and only then charged him with a task. In so doing, Christ not only provided Peter an opportunity to reverse his triple denial but indicated that caring for the followers of Christ was an office of love. As such, the responsibility belonged not only to the clergy but to every Christian. Augustine elaborated this point by linking Christ's prediction of Peter's voluntary death to the generosity expected of all Christians: following Christ in laying down one's life for his sheep was the calling of both the pastors (John 10:11; 21:18) and the sheep (1 John 3:16).[102] Second, in receiving his pastoral call, Augustine understood Peter as a representative of the entire church rather than, as Cyprian had, of the college of bishops. Christ as the head addressed Peter as his body, in and through whom he would work as pastor.[103] The faithful pastors were members joined to the one good pastor, Christ.[104] They held the sheep in common with Christ, as his rather than their own.[105] In this commissioning, Christ fulfilled the promise God made in Ezekiel 34:15 to shepherd Israel personally rather than finding and assigning trustworthy pastors to that task.[106] The bishops were at once pastors and sheep belonging to his flock.[107] They were called to share the love of Christ and to exercise it by caring for the Christian people, working for Christ's sake rather than their own benefit, like hirelings or thieves.

To explain the responsibility of the pastor, Augustine used the meaning of the Greek term *episcopos*, whose Latin equivalent was *superintentor*, indicating an overseer or watchman.[108] He compared the clerical role to that of a guard in a vineyard ready for harvesting.[109] This office was symbolized by the raised position that the bishop's chair occupied in the basilica, which indicated not his dignity or honor but his responsibility and duty to warn and protect. Indeed, Augustine insisted, this office was to be performed in great fear and humility because the bishop would have to render an account for the flock entrusted to him.[110] He acted as attorney for God: he could neither ignore a warning that God gave nor make a promise that God did not.[111] From his elevated position, the bishop could see the members of the congregation coming into and leaving the church but could not see what they were doing at home or in their work. Moreover, he could observe their actions but not read their thoughts. For this reason, he had to pray and trust that Christ would guard and care for them where he could not.[112]

Using the metaphor of the ship's pilot, Augustine reminded the people that his assignment did not relieve them of all responsibility for the good of the church. Although he was its pilot, they were passengers in the ship of the church and would enjoy its safety or suffer its peril.[113] The requirement that bishops be above reproach (1 Tim. 3:2) did not give Christians license to be reprehensible. If bishops were watchmen, the laity should provide something good for them to guard.[114]

The people were to show appropriate humility and to practice obedience toward the bishops. They should be careful of the warning that Christ gave in sending out the disciples to preach, "whoever rejects you rejects me" (Luke 10:16). If Christ was referring only to those missionaries whom he had sent out during his earthly ministry, then the people could despise their bishop with impunity. If Christ was referring to the bishops as well, however, they had best take heed that an insult to the bishop would be counted as an injury by Christ.[115] Even then, Augustine was careful to limit the authority of the bishop. He was their teacher only as a subordinate and, with the people, a fellow student of Christ. The bishop teaching from his *cathedra* was not the true master, whose seat was in heaven; he was more like an older student who could offer advice and tutoring to the others in the class.[116]

The Bishops as Successors of the Apostles

The relationship between the apostles and the bishops had been at the heart of Cyprian's theology: he understood the Twelve as the original episcopal college; that body of bishops was the recipient and custodian of the power to sanctify conferred by the Holy Spirit. The bishop was God's judge during the earthly life of the church.[117] Following this lead, the Donatist bishop Parmenian had argued that the holiness of the church depended on the fidelity of the bishop and even the purity of the episcopal college as a whole, because a single tolerated sinner would pollute his tolerant colleagues.[118] Augustine responded, as has been seen, that the holiness of the church was realized by the Holy Spirit indwelling and operating in the faithful and incorporating them into the body of Christ; holiness and the power to sanctify was entrusted to the predestined and persevering members of Christ's body who would not fail. He applied Cyprian's argument that Peter stood for the unity of the Twelve, not in their binding and loosening but in their pasturing of Christ's sheep. He clarified Cyprian's position, however, to make clear that Christ had designated Peter not as sole pastor but as the symbol of the unity of all the pastors.[119]

Augustine preferred, again in contrast to Cyprian, to distinguish between the roles of the apostles and the bishops who followed after them. In his preaching, this separation was accomplished by exploiting scriptural passages that allowed him to contrast the selection and roles of the two groups. In his commentary on Psalm 44, for example, he seized on the text, "In place of your fathers, sons are born to you; you set them up as rulers over the whole earth" (Ps. 45:16). The fathers, he explained, were the apostles whom Christ had chosen and sent to preach the gospel. They had eventually died and were no longer leading the church. In place of them, the church—being addressed in the psalm—had generated sons and then established them all over the world to continue the work of the apostles. He explicitly noted the paradox that the church generated the bishops as sons whom it then established as rulers, in the places of the original fathers.[120] Similarly, in the commentary on Psalm 127, he distinguished the builders from the caretakers of the city of God. The custodians were responsible for guarding and protecting the people who formed that city. In this case, however, he did not explicitly distinguish the role of the apostles as builders from the bishops as watchmen, since he noticed and took into account Paul's description of his own role as a guardian in 2 Corinthians 11:3.[121]

Unlike Cyprian, then, Augustine understood the episcopal college not as a self-perpetuating body, succeeding to the Twelve, that guaranteed the faithful preservation of the sanctifying power and right teaching of Christ in the church. The church, as the body of Christ, was established on those faithful who received, cultivated, and preserved the gifts of the Spirit. Thus, as he found himself weakening with age and infirmity, Augustine proposed to the congregation that the deacon Eraclius should be approved to begin sharing his responsibilities and to succeed him as bishop after his death.[122] Augustine argued that the bishops were made and established by the church; they were its sons and servants even as they governed it.

Although Augustine maintained the primacy of the church—and its officers—as members of the body of Christ sharing his power and work, he clearly distinguished the administrative and supervisory functions of the bishop from the sanctifying ones. Had he occasion to do so, he might have placed under this same heading the disciplinary and legislative functions that the bishops exercised in provincial and regional councils.

Conclusion

Augustine interpreted the Donatist leaders as asserting that the sacramental ministry of the Christian clergy required that they hold and exercise the power to sanctify and must, therefore, be free of any sin or impurity that would make them unworthy subjects and exercisers of that power. In response, he taught that the efficacy of the sacramental ministry depended not upon the holiness of the clergy but upon that of Christ himself, to whom the divine power of sanctifying was natural and proper. Through his understanding of the indwelling of the Holy Spirit that formed faithful Christians into the body of Christ, Augustine was able to explain their participation, as a body, in the powers proper to Christ himself. In their sacramental ministry, then, the clergy functioned as authorized agents of Christ in his fullness, both head and members. If they were among the faithful, the ministers also shared the sanctifying power operative in the sacraments; if not, they were only the agents of Christ and of his faithful members who did. The faithful people participated in the sacramental ministry through their intercessory prayer and the exercise of love by which they welcomed and supported converts and penitents into their union. Augustine developed this understanding of clerical ministry and ecclesial power in explaining the efficacy of the conferral of baptism, the celebration of the eucharistic offering, and the forgiveness of post-baptismal sins. He explained the priesthood of the bishop and clergy as derived from that which Christ extended to and exercised in the church as his body. The ritual of ordination, which he treated as the assignment of an office of governance and an authorization to act as minister for Christ and his body, was treated only tangentially in the surviving sermons.[123]

The sacramental theory that recognized the clergy as ministers of Christ alone was developed to explain the efficacy of baptism as a consecration performed outside the true and holy church—in schism or heresy—but was applied to unworthy ministers functioning even with that church. The holiness of Christ guaranteed that the effect of the ritual in marking its recipient as a Christian could be neither reversed nor repeated. Through the ritual, Christ also conferred the gift of the Holy Spirit who purified from sin, indwelt, and incorporated the recipient into his ecclesial body. The union of the faithful within the church, as the body of Christ, made the saints share not only his holiness but his power to sanctify. The recipient of baptism, therefore, could retain and exercise the gift of the Spirit only by intentional unity with the faithful, which was normally manifest by adherence to the visible communion of the universal church and participation in its eucharistic celebration. In this way, Augustine explained the church's participation in the sanctifying operation of Christ in baptism as the exercise of a divinely inspired love for God and neighbor by his faithful members.

In considering the forgiveness of post-baptismal sins, a similar explanation was employed. The power to sanctify had been granted to Peter as the personification of the whole church, rather than as representative of the episcopal college. Binding a sinner was accomplished through exclusion from the communion of the faithful; forgiveness and release from sin was given by God in response to the prayers of the faithful and through their accepting the penitents into their communion. Through the action of the bishop—excluding and including—the power of forgiveness that the faithful shared with Christ as his members was exercised for penitents. In the same way, the priestly powers of offering sacrifice and interceding before God belonged properly to Christ and were shared with his body. The bishop's priestly title was derived from his role as leader of the congregation whose core was the union of the faithful, which Peter called a priestly people. Their own priestly identity, of course, derived from Christ, whose members they became in baptism and remained through charity.

Augustine had to adapt his understanding of the efficacy of sacramental ministry to the preaching and teaching office of the bishop. He argued that the truth of the gospel of Christ was presented in the scripture and in the sermons of bishops and presbyters, even those whose behavior did not illustrate the teaching and exemplify the life of Christ. He relied on the scripture read out in the liturgy to warn the congregation against the bad example, the ignorance, and even the deceit of its bishop. He also found a way for the operation of God, as interior teacher of both speaker and hearer, to make the preaching of all bishops effective in instructing, converting, and exhorting their congregations. In this way, Christ could also use the scriptures and the good example of Christians to correct the errors and falsehoods of the clergy.

Only the office of bishop or pastor was assigned by Augustine to the leader as a commission from Christ to care for his flock. Still, he explained that the authority to govern that was derived from Christ passed through the church, which generated and established bishops, rather than through succession from the Twelve whom Christ initially had appointed to preach the gospel and build up the church.

For the most part, then, Augustine understood the clergy as agents of the church, which was the union of all the faithful as the body of Christ, and as agents of Christ himself through their being established by the church as its leaders. In this, he was radically different from the Donatists in refusing to assign to the office or person of the bishop a holiness that derived from Christ independently of the laity. As a result, he argued that the holiness of the church depended not upon the worthiness of its ministers but upon that of Christ and his members joined in the Holy Spirit.

By defining the body of Christ as the union of those Christians within the visible church who were predestined and foreknown by God as persevering in faith and love and by assigning to that group a participation in the sanctifying power of Christ, Augustine effectively replaced the college of bishops as the center of the church and the seat of its holiness.

THE SAVING WORK OF CHRIST

THE SAVING WORK OF CHRIST was treated extensively in Augustine's sermons. For the most part, the topic arose not in his preaching on the gospel narratives of the passion and death of Jesus but in expositions of the text of the psalms that he interpreted as the speech of Christ in one of his roles or identities—particularly as son of Mary and as head of the church. He also used a selection of Pauline texts, most regularly 1 Corinthians 6:19–20, that described the redemption as the paying of a price. Another significant text described the binding of the strong man and plundering of his goods (Matt. 12:29) that was used to interpret Christ's control over the demons. Perhaps the most creative was the use of 2 Corinthians 5:21 in which God is described as causing Christ "to be sin" in order to effect the condemnation of sin. On the basis of these scriptural materials, Augustine built different but related explanations of the meaning and effect of the death, resurrection, and ascension of Christ.

Because this study is focused on Augustine's preaching, the exposition will begin with his most common way of referring to the death of Christ in his sermons, even though it did not include a fully elaborated explanation. The essay will also attempt to illustrate the variations on his major themes that Augustine used to communicate with the congregations he was addressing, even at the cost of presenting lists of the images that he piled on one another. Two major theories Augustine used—Christ's binding the strong man and condemning sin in his own flesh—provide the foundation of this chapter. The other sections detail Augustine's elaboration of their implications, particularly in the case of his bodily ascension into heaven.

Paying the Price to Purchase Humanity

In his preaching, Augustine most often, indeed normally, referred to the saving work of Christ as the purchase or redemption of humanity from captivity or slavery at the price of his blood. Without further specification, this was hardly an explanation of the death of Jesus, its effect in freeing Christians from sin, and its moving them toward eternal life. Augustine did offer such explanations, one of them directly related to this purchase language, though even in that one the blood could be more accurately described as the expenditure necessary for a complex legal operation rather than the price exchanged for a property or a person. Yet when Augustine wanted to speak only a sentence or two about the redemption, especially in moral exhortation, he usually employed the language of purchase: Christ was the buyer; his blood was the price; the devil was the selling owner; the whole of humanity was the property acquired.[1] By analysis of a large number of such remarks, a description of this work of Christ can be constructed that specifies each of its four elements.

The Price

The text on which Augustine based this use of purchase language was 1 Corinthians 6:20, "You were bought at a price," where it functions as the foundation for a moral exhortation. The passage itself was quoted only three times in his sermons and expositions of the psalms, in each case for that hortatory purpose.[2] The term "price" was used for the blood of Christ, however, some seventy times, fifty of these with no further explanation or elaboration. Paying a price in blood to purchase Christians seems to have been a (or even *the*) standard way of characterizing the meaning and effect of Christ's death among Augustine's people, one that he not only could assume but was willing to affirm and to build upon.

Usually when Augustine referred to the blood that Christ poured out as the price for Christians, he provided no further elaboration.[3] Once, he contrasted it to the gold and silver that other masters paid to acquire their servants.[4] On another occasion, he insisted that Christ spilled true blood, since the price paid by Truth could not be false.[5] Noting that a person could bleed a bit without suffering much harm, he pointed out that the opening of Christ's side by the lance showed that he had given all his blood and had paid with his life.[6]

The price could be treated as ransom for captives from an enemy, identified as the devil.[7] It was sufficient not only for Christians but for the whole world;[8] it covered bodies as well as souls.[9] Though the transaction also was described as a commercial deal,[10] the blood of the only begotten Son was a gift supplied by God to the beneficiaries.[11] The cost expended indicated the value God set on the people that had been acquired;[12] it showed why the deaths of the saints and martyrs were precious in the sight of God (Ps. 116:15).[13] It was, moreover, a price that Christ graciously shared, in the eucharist, with those he had redeemed.[14] Though the price always was identified as the blood of Christ, the ways in which it functioned in the liberation of humans varied. Some of these will now be explored.

The Sale

The devil's sale of sinners to Christ was contrasted to the procedure by which they had earlier sold themselves into captivity through consent to his temptation.[15] In return for their innocence and freedom, they had received only a little pleasure from the forbidden tree.[16] This small compensation stood in sharp contrast to the cost expended in freeing them from that servitude, a price beyond the capacity and resources of the sinners.[17] Only the one who could not sell himself by sinning was capable of buying back all those who had turned themselves over to the devil.[18]

Yet the sale and transfer of ownership was not definitive. Even after they have been purchased by Christ, people could and did sell themselves again into slavery.[19] Augustine warned that Christ would refuse to share the property right for which he had paid so dearly; he might abandon an unfaithful servant to the devil's sole ownership.[20]

The Acquisition

Augustine's attention focused on the action of Christ in purchasing humans through the spilling of his blood. Using the models of buying a servant and ransoming a captive, he emphasized the ownership of humans that Christ had acquired and the consequent limitations of their autonomy in dealing with him. This approach also provided a weapon to be employed against the Donatists, who had restricted Christ's dominion to Africa and then claimed even these possessions for themselves.[21]

In Adam and Eve, the human race had been captured or purchased by the devil and their whole progeny was then born into slavery, working in the service of the demons.[22] Christ then paid a price adequate to the liberation not of Christians alone but of the whole of humanity; he acquired property rights over every human being.[23] Since humans neither contributed to their redemption nor merited in any way the payment that Christ made for them, he enjoyed a sole right over them that he did not share with anyone.[24] This free and generous expenditure on their behalf imposed an obligation of recognition[25] and gratitude that was the basis for Paul's exhortation to faithful service, so regularly repeated by Augustine.[26]

Augustine also adapted a standard accusation that the demons had attempted to compete with God's salvific plan by anticipating many of his prophesied and foreshadowed actions and even of the rituals given to his followers. None of those demons, he remarked, had attempted to mimic this part of Christ's work; their idols never spilled any blood for the redemption and purchase of the human race.[27]

The generosity of Christ's action was also elaborated by Augustine's setting it in the broader context of creation and adoption. Other masters could purchase their servants, and that with their money rather than their blood. As God and Creator, Christ had a more fundamental claim to the service of humans.[28] Once humans had violated that right by fraud in selling themselves into slavery, Christ sought, found, and redeemed them.[29] In doing so, moreover, he had not transferred their servile status from one master to another. Instead, he had liberated them from slavery and made them members of his own family. Christ welcomed siblings rather than acquiring servants.[30]

Christ's generosity intensified obligations of gratitude and service rather than absolving Christians of them. Augustine elaborated this point in a variety of observations. Christian masters and mistresses demanded faithful service from their own servants, whom they had acquired with money; they must recognize an even greater duty to serve Christ who had paid for them in blood and at the cost of his life. In anticipation of a civic festival, he warned his hearers to remember the great price at which they had been bought and to act accordingly, separating themselves from their neighbors who did not acknowledge their debt to Christ. Boasting of the great mercy of God toward them, he cautioned, should be accompanied by a strenuous effort to avoid sin.[31] Christ had not simply purchased humans but had made Christians his home and temples of the Holy Spirit. They must glorify God by keeping their bodies inviolate. In particular, they must not join the members of Christ to prostitutes.[32]

Christ's purchase had also established, Augustine asserted, a fundamental equality among Christians. Each should remember that by paying one and the same price for all, Christ had made every human precious to himself. Augustine drew out the implications of this for the way that Christians treated their fellows. A wife must demand fidelity from her husband for the sake of Christ whom they both were to serve. The learned and experienced must respect the great cost at which the salvation of the weak had been purchased; they should be careful not to confuse or discourage them. The poor were no less valuable to Christ than the wealthy, since Christ had paid the same for both. Christians could not disregard others as beneath their attention and assistance: Christ's payment had set a standard value on each one.[33] In a reflection on the commissioning of Peter in John 21, Augustine illustrated this point. When a master acquired especially valuable sheep, he entrusted their care to a servant whom he deemed responsible, in particular to one whose own private funds (*peculium*) were adequate to compensate for losses the master might suffer from the shepherd's negligence. For this reason, Christ interrogated Peter before charging him with the care of those he had bought with his own blood. Peter proved worthy of that trust, giving his own life not for sheep that he lost but to keep all of them safe for Christ.[34]

Augustine used the price that Christ had paid to interpret the statement in Psalm 116:15, "Precious in the sight of the Lord is the death of his saints."[35] Preaching on the feast of the martyr Vincent of Saragosa, he remarked that the brutal martyrdom showed the lengths to which Christ was willing to go to retain what he had bought. Like a man whose honor and power were at stake in protecting his property from encroachment by others, Christ strengthened his disciples against attack.[36] Since that same price had been paid for every Christian, Augustine elsewhere remarked, each of them should be prepared to follow the martyrs in defending Christ's rights over them.[37]

The redemption of all of humanity at the cost of Christ's blood also provided Augustine with an opportunity to attack the Donatists, who claimed that the contagion of apostasy had reduced the true Christian church to the territory of Africa, so that it no longer spread throughout the world.[38] Psalm 22, which Christ had prayed on the cross, clearly set out not only the cost but the reality Christ had acquired through the piercing of his hands and feet, the laying bare of his bones. All the ends of the earth, it prophesied, would remember and turn to the Lord (Ps. 22:17, 27).[39] In his exposition of this psalm, Augustine elaborated Christ's dominion. In the case of an inheritance, he recalled, a search was made either among the family for the one designated as heir to the deceased's property or for the person outside the relatives who had bought title to it. Christ had gained the entire world by purchase, from the rising of the sun to its setting.[40] The blood price was adequate, and he had acquired the whole.[41] Christ, moreover, had exercised that dominion. Because his price had bought more than a few witnesses in Jerusalem, he sent the disciples to preach in the whole world.[42] For this same reason, Christ would judge the whole of humanity at the end of time.[43]

This purchase price, Augustine insisted, was adequate for the whole world and not just for a portion of the Christians living in Africa. If Christ had paid only for Africa, he speculated with his congregation, then all of them would be Donatists, though they would be called simply Christians. One of the reasons for reading out Psalm 22 in the liturgy celebrating the death of Jesus, he explained, was its clear statement of the terms of that transaction.[44] The Donatists refused to recognize the contract clearly recorded in the scripture because they wanted Christ to be satisfied with Africa. They rejected the implication that both parties to the African conflict were Christians, siblings and fellow servants purchased by Christ for the same price.[45] Augustine made the same point in reflecting on the text of Matthew 24:23, in which Jesus had anticipated the emergence of schisms where parties would claim that Christ was in one place or another but refuse to recognize that his dominion encompassed the whole world.[46] Christ knew his own among those he had purchased and warned them to withdraw from such iniquity.[47] It appeared, Augustine suggested, that those claiming that Christ's blood had won him only African disciples either undervalued the price he had paid or thought entirely too well of themselves. Christ knew what he had paid and what he had purchased.[48]

Finally, Augustine charged that the Donatist bishops claimed the congregations for themselves rather than acknowledging in them the sheep that Christ had purchased for himself—and themselves as among that flock rather than rulers over it. Those bishops, who had not poured out their own blood for it, held the flock of Christ cheap. The Catholic leaders, in contrast, did not refer to the sheep as their own; they recognized that the congregations and their clergy were the property of the one who had bought them all. The gospel itself was his deed of possession, and his blood the price.[49]

The claim that Christ had used his life blood to purchase humanity from the devil proved flexible in Augustine's preaching. From it he drew exhortations to gratitude and fidelity to Christ, to mutual care of others within and outside the congregation, to recognition of the dignity that Christ's price had bestowed upon every human. He also used it to attack the Donatists for attempting to exalt their own virtue at the cost of depriving Christ of full and proper reward of his generosity.

Yet the assertion of Christ's ownership of the sinful humans he had purchased and liberated had to be tempered because Christians were not servants but friends, even family members who had been exalted by the high price paid for their ransom and freedom. The ambiguity of the notion of purchase as a description of Christ's redemptive work was deepened in Augustine's consideration of the transaction between Christ and the devil.

The Transaction

Although Augustine regularly and with little qualification compared Christ's voluntary giving of his life on the cross for the salvation of humanity to the purchase of a servant and the ransom of a captive, more than occasionally he called attention to the ways in which Christ's action was different from such transactions.

Augustine described the way that human beings had sold themselves into slavery or gone into captivity as a this-for-that exchange.[50] More useful for his analysis of Christ's purchase, however, was Judas's sale of Christ to the Jewish authorities. Judas did not keep the money and the Jewish leaders failed to retain control over the person whose betrayal they had purchased. The person whom the one sold and the others bought was made, through their very actions, not a captive to be eliminated but a permanently active savior freely given to Christians.[51] Judas, Augustine observed, deceived himself and threw away the money without recognizing what Christ, in the same transaction, had given to liberate even his betrayer and executioners.[52]

In a similar way, Augustine sometimes treated the blood of Christ not as a price paid but as a cost expended to achieve the breaking of the devil's power and the liberation of humanity. Like the other aspects of the "purchase" theory, this way of describing the transaction was not explained in detail in any one sermon or exposition. Augustine's thinking can be discerned through the qualifications and cautions he occasionally added in discussing Christ's purchase. The devil, as Augustine often said, was holding sinners captive.[53] Unworthy though he was to drink the blood of Christ, the devil had the power of spilling it. That blood, then, was used to bait a trap for the devil. The "price" was hung on the cross in Christ's mortal flesh, where the evil one was delighted to see it.[54] The enraged devil then killed Christ, unjustly spilling the innocent blood on the ground.[55] By attacking Christ in this way, Satan actually bound himself.[56] Augustine described the spilling of the blood as the effacing of a legal document. The blood erased or blotted out the writing on the bond by which human sinners were held as debtors.[57] It deleted the debtor's note and destroyed the oldness of sin.[58] The pouring out of blood invalidated the instrument of captivity.[59] The devil thereby lost his grip on those he had been holding, suffering a deprivation without any commensurate gain.[60] He was forced to pull back from those he had held as guilty; he had to let them go free.[61] Thus, the transaction was not to be understood as an exchange in which one good was given for another received.[62] The blood was not the payment that the enemy acquired and kept for handing over guilty humans to Christ. Instead, Christ deprived the devil, took his possessions for his own, gave nothing in return, and suffered no permanent loss.

This summary of his qualifications of the understanding of the redemption as a sale and purchase clarifies the foundation of Augustine's regular use of the buying and selling of sinful humans, with the price as Christ's blood and the good acquired as the whole human race. His commercial description depended on a forensic explanation of redemption in which Christ provoked the devil into violating the terms on which he had held humanity subject to sin and death. That legal theory was detailed in both Augustine's preaching and his treatises.[63] The abbreviated version he so regularly presented to his congregation was focused on the blood of Christ as the price in a sale, or more properly, the bait in a trap. Although it did not suit his meaning particularly well, Augustine may have preferred the language of price and exchange because Paul had used it in 1 Corinthians 6:19–20. It also served the hortatory purposes of establishing the Christian's debt to Christ reviewed above. He insisted, however, that the devil had been despoiled rather than enriched in the transaction.

Augustine's other interpretations of the efficacy of Christ's death were more fully developed in his *Sermons to the People* and his expositions of the Psalms, the Gospel of John, and the First Letter of John. The consideration of these explanations begins with the theory most closely related to the language of the purchase transaction that was regularly used: the forensic theory of the violation of an innocent human's right to freedom from death, the loss that Satan suffered by the unjust act of killing Christ, and the consequent liberation of humans from sin and death.

PLUNDERING THE STRONG MAN'S GOODS

The Synoptic Gospels share an account of conflict between Jesus and his Jewish opponents concerning the source of the authority he exercised over the demons in casting them out of humans.[64] They accused him of acting in secret collaboration with Satan to deceive the spectators. Jesus first responded that a kingdom divided against itself could not endure, asserting that the kingdom of God, coming in his ministry, was the force more likely to be at work in these exorcisms. In each of the three accounts, Jesus then compared Satan to a powerful householder who must be overcome and bound before his possessions could be taken away. Since Jesus was evicting the demons and liberating their captives, the implication was that he—a stronger one, in Luke's version—was overcoming and binding Satan.[65]

Christian authors developed Jesus's response into an explanation of his redemptive work as a contest in which the demon was defeated and bound so that humans might be set free of his control.[66] Augustine elaborated such an explanation three times in his treatises, with minor variations.[67] In those discussions, Augustine attended to considerations that played no significant role in his preaching about redemption. He noted that Christ had suffered in righteousness before exercising his superior power by rising in glory. He also insisted on the unity of willing between the Father and the Son. This prevented an interpretation of the salvific action as a transaction in which Christ assuaged divine anger or paid a debt that God had to collect from creatures. Instead, he explained that the Son had become human in order to enact a restoration of humanity within the created order. These considerations required that Augustine interpret the conflict between Christ and Satan as employing forces that could be exercised by creatures: fidelity and justice on one side; a rebellious will and coercive power over mortal bodies on the other. In this way, Augustine explained the redemption as God's acting through Christ to remove an obstacle within the created world to humanity's union with the divine. He ruled out an explanation in which the Savior identified with humanity and then satisfied a requirement—be it punishment or satisfaction—arising from divine justice, thereby permitting God to again extend life and love to humans. Salvation, he insisted, was an initiative by the Trinity—Father, Son, and Holy Spirit—to fix a problem among the creatures. Discussion of these sorts of issues found little or no place in Augustine's preaching about the work of Christ. The explanations he offered to his congregation, however, were compatible with and guided by the principles he established and conclusions he reached in these writings on redemption.[68]

Augustine referred to the struggle between Christ and Satan in many sermons, elaborating one or another aspect of it as the occasion presented itself. In five of the surviving sermons, two of them expositions of the Psalms, he joined together the central elements of the theory: the unjust killing of the innocent Christ and the consequent despoiling of the devil.[69] The elaboration of the theory will be considered under four titles.

The Two Mediators

Augustine laid out the foundations of the conflict between Christ and the devil in his long New Year's Day sermon that editors have titled "Against the Pagans."[70] Salvation of human beings required their liberation from both sin and death. Persistence in sin unto bodily death brought eternal death. Mortality was not itself an obstacle to union with God, as was demonstrated by the death of Christ and his martyrs. In humans, however, bodily death was the consequence and punishment of sin; it should be abolished once sin was overcome and its guilt removed.

Two mediators of salvation proposed themselves to humans. The devil presented himself as immune to bodily death, though he was unable to share this immortality with humans. Instead, he proposed himself as a guide in iniquity; he was preparing humans who subjected themselves to him to share his eternal death in alienation from God. Christ, in contrast, offered himself as accepting bodily mortality but free of the sin that entailed death for other humans. Christ proposed to lead humans back to a condition like that from which they had fallen: free of sin, of eternal death, and even of bodily mortality.[71]

The devil exercised power over humans by exalting his freedom from bodily death. Mortality was a manifest weakness which, Augustine explained, was more embarrassing to the proud than the iniquity from which it originated. The adherents of Satan despised the bodily suffering that was inflicted upon Christ and feared the humiliation it entailed. Christ, in contrast, proposed these injuries and embarrassments as the means of rooting out pride and overcoming the temptations of the demonic mediator. Through them, Christians were cleansed from iniquity and attained both spiritual and bodily immortality.[72]

Subjection to Satan

The devil deceived the first innocent human beings, seducing them into sin, and consequently subjecting them to bodily death.[73] He then used the fear of mortality to drag their progeny further into sin and thus into the condemnation of eternal death.[74] Adam and Eve generated their offspring not into the privileged position they had lost but into a state characterized by the consequences of their transgression: the burdens of guilt and bodily death.[75] The devil had stolen creatures that belonged to God and held Adam's posterity in service to the rebellion against God. Satan celebrated the capture and enjoyed the mastery.[76]

In this way the devil had made himself the ruler of the human world, as he was called in John 14:30. He possessed the race of Adam that he had deceived and continued to deceive; he ruled over humans by the twin powers of sin and death.[77]

Trapping and Despoiling the Deceiver

In becoming human, the Word of God took flesh that was capable of dying. As mortal, he appeared to be sinful, even though he remained free of sin and guilt. As Christ grew tired, thirsty, and hungry, as he rested, slept, ate, and drank, he deceived the devil who assumed that these signs of mortality were indicators of his sharing the common sin of humanity.[78] In his bodily life, Christ was setting a trap and baiting it with mortal flesh to capture Satan who was hungry for human death. The devil was attracted by Christ's mortality, assuming that it indicated his dominion over him, although he could find nothing of his own in him, nothing that linked him to the rebellion against God.[79] The devil then attacked that mortal flesh, enjoying the exercise of strength and domination in working the death of Christ. Thus, Augustine explained.

> The Apostle Paul says, *If they had recognized him, they would never have crucified the Lord of glory* (1 Cor. 2:8). But if he had not been killed, death would not have died, and the devil would not have been defeated by his own victory. The devil celebrated when he cast the first human

down into death. He killed the first human by trickery; by killing the ultimate human, the devil lost the first one from his snare.[80]

In taking the bait and killing Christ, in exercising power and claiming victory, the devil was defeated and his reign over humans undone.

The devil's work against Christ was done through his servants: Judas betrayed Christ; the Jewish leaders brought false charges; lying witnesses supported those charges; and evil judges condemned Christ. Christ, however, was using the iniquity of these sinners for his own good purpose. He humbled the liar who was behind the entire operation. The prince of this world found nothing on his own in Christ, no claim against him, but killed him anyway.[81]

Having killed the one whom he had no right to injure, the devil was forced to release all those whom he had seduced into his service and then held by the bonds of sin and death. Had Satan not killed that innocent one, he might have continued to hold all the guilty. Christ, however, had lived as a mortal but without sin and thus was not subject to the prince of iniquity. He accepted his death not as a punishment for sin but in obedience to the divine plan through which others would be set free. Actually, however, Christ recovered the humans whom the devil had originally stolen from him; he retrieved the goods that were rightfully his own.[82]

Killing Death and Destroying Sin

When Christ bound the devil by tempting him to attack the one human over whom he had no claim, he liberated his own disciples from the iniquity of their souls, where Satan had been ruling, rather than from some bodily captivity. By the humility of his death, Christ freed mortal human beings from their complicity with the proud mediator; he brought them to confess their sin. His justice then cleansed them from their own unrighteousness.[83] Having broken all the bonds of sin by his death, Christ killed death itself and brought his disciples to share his own immortality.[84] He turned the death that had been imposed as a penalty for sin into a means through which his disciples attained virtue, died for truth rather than sin, and thus participated in his own victory over the false mediator.[85]

Sin and Death

The connection between sin and death, highlighted for Augustine by Romans 5:12, "through one man sin entered the world, and death came through sin," and by Romans 8:3, "God sent his son in the likeness of sinful flesh," was essential to the logic of this explanation of the redemption. The theory was built upon the consent to Satan's proposal (rather than the rejection of God's command) that bound the sinners to the service of the demons.[86] This bond (*chirographum*) or pledge (*cautio*) gave the devil the power of life and death over the sinners.[87] That dominion was enforced and maintained by further sinning under the threat and the reality of death. Christ induced Satan into a violation of the freedom of an innocent human and a trespass of the limits of a master's authority over his own servants. The Savior thereby attacked and destroyed the devil's authority or power to hold sinners in servitude and subjection to bodily death. Following the logic of the "purchase" image that Augustine used so regularly, the sinner was then bound to Christ rather than to Satan. Christ could have demanded the service that the devil had exacted from the sinners; instead, he released them to reject the rebellion and to serve good freely. Even once set free, it might be noted, a Roman slave was still bound to his or her liberator and patron by duties of fidelity and service.[88]

Satan did not acquire Christ in exchange for the enslaved sinners; the devil lost both those he was holding as sinners and the innocent one he attempted to add to them. Christ both acquired those whom Satan had held and recovered the goods—his human flesh and blood—that he had expended as the cost of the transaction. In the eucharist, he lavished his life's blood on the freed captives.[89]

Summary

The interplay of justice and power that Augustine explored in the explanation of this theory of binding the strong man in his *On the Trinity* played no significant role in his sermons.[90] Instead, Augustine used the human innocence of Christ, even in mortal flesh, and the outrage done to him by the violation of his right to human life as the justification for a transformation of the sinners' servile obligation to a created, demonic master into a free service of the Lord who was both human and divine. In this explanation, the savior made no payment, either to Satan or to God; instead, he suffered a loss of human life that was soon restored, and he achieved a great dominion over the whole of humanity that he had liberated from servitude.

Few of this theory's implications were elaborated in Augustine's sermons. Instead, he preferred the violent images of Christ hanging from the cross like a bag of blood that the death-loving demon ripped open and spilled out on the ground.[91] As it poured out, however, that blood obliterated the handwriting on the pledge by which the devil had been holding human sinners.[92] The document was ruined, and its binding power destroyed. The captives were released, the slaves set free with a new and indestructible document—the gospel of Christ—that recorded his victory and their liberation. The presentation of this theory in the sermons did not elaborate the connection between the violation of Christ's right to life and the devil's loss of dominion over sinners. Nor did Augustine clearly articulate the power to free sinners from the bindings of guilt that Christ attained through his human victory over Satan. Instead, as is seen elsewhere in this volume, he linked the power to forgive sins to the gift of the Holy Spirit.[93]

On occasion, Augustine focused on the paradox of Christ's victory through the suffering of defeat.[94] He compared Christ's dealing with the Jews of his own day to the struggle between the angel and Jacob at Peniel (Gen. 32:24–32). The angel, though of superior power, allowed himself to be overcome by Jacob. Yet at the end, the winner asked a blessing from the loser and received the gift of seeing God. By submitting to their destructive power, Christ had blessed at least those Jews who were brought to faith through the preaching of the apostles.[95]

Augustine further remarked on the humility and self-abasement to which Christ had subjected himself in overcoming the demonic pride and warned his congregation against the danger of losing the benefit Christ had conferred upon them.[96]

The theory of salvation by the binding and despoiling of the slave-holding devil was closely connected to the less developed theory of purchase of slaves and redemption of captives that Augustine used most regularly. The third theory, Christ's destruction of sin in his own flesh, was compatible with these two. Augustine found it more difficult to develop.

Condemning Sin in the Flesh

The first phrase of the text of Romans 8:3 described Christ as being "in the likeness of sinful flesh." As has been seen just above, this idea was integral to Augustine's explanation of the salvific work as an overcoming of the devil by appearing as a sinner without actually owing any debt for transgression. This theory of a violated right to life through which actual debtors were set free also served as the foundation for Augustine's use of 1 Corinthians 6:19–20 that described the spilling of Jesus's blood as part of a purchase. Augustine suggested a different but complementary understanding of the saving work of Christ by considering the second phrase in this sentence of Romans 8:3–4, "so that from sin he might condemn sin in the flesh, so that the justice of the law might be fulfilled in us." To these two texts, he added 2 Corinthians 5:21, "Him [Christ] who knew no sin, for our sake, he [God] made to be sin, so that in him we might become the righteousness of God."[97] Linking these texts from Romans 8 and 2 Corinthians 5, Augustine then explained how Christ had become identified with sin, then had condemned sin, on the basis of a sin, and thereby justified Christians. To build this interpretation, Augustine identified and related the references to sin: Christ was in the likeness of sinful flesh; God made the sinless Christ "become sin"; Christ condemned sin in the flesh; and from or through sin, he condemned in the flesh the sin he had become.

The Likeness of Sin

In his initial set of sermons on the Gospel of John, preached in 406–7, Augustine had offered an interpretation of the bronze serpent that Moses raised on a pole to save the Israelites from death by the bites of snakes. The bronze serpent symbolized the death that led to sin and would be destroyed by the life-giving death of Christ. Looking at that dead snake gave bodily life to the Israelites; looking on the dead Christ provided eternal life to Christians.[98] Six years later, in June 413, Augustine used Romans 8:3 to offer a slightly different interpretation of the bronze serpent raised up in the desert as a foreshadowing of the death of Jesus and its salvific effect. The actual sin affecting humanity was represented by the serpents whose bites were killing the Israelites. The image of the serpent raised up on the pole represented the flesh of Christ that was in the likeness of that sin. As the likeness of the serpent raised up on the pole had overcome the death caused by the actual serpents, so the likeness of sin in the flesh of Christ hanging on the cross destroyed the sin and eternal death in humans. The represented or symbolized evil—in the bronze serpent and in the mortal flesh of Christ—condemned and cured the real evil in humans.[99]

God Made Christ to Be Sin

In two sermons that can be dated to 414 or 415, Augustine took up the death of Christ in the course of commenting upon the Psalms and the Gospel of John.

In his interpretation of Psalm 34, Augustine attempted to interpret the first phrase of 2 Corinthians 5:21, "He [God] made him [Christ] who knew no sin, to be sin," through the resemblance of his mortal flesh to sin. No sin could be found in the soul, the mind, or even the body of Christ. Romans 8:3, however, identified Christ as being in the likeness of sinful flesh, which Augustine understood, as has been seen, as based upon his mortality. To explain Christ's "being sin," then, he first suggested that the mortal flesh the Word assumed could be called "sin" because the subjection of flesh to death had been caused by sin. A spoken language could be called a "tongue" by reference to the bodily organ that formed its sounds, or a style of writing could be called a "hand" after the bodily member that shaped its letters. In the same way, death or mortality could be called "sin" by reference to the deviation or failure from which it had originated. Through the sin of the first parents, the whole human mass had become mortal. So when Christ took flesh from that lump through his mortal mother, he "sinned," in the sense that he clothed himself in a body that could be called "sin" because it was shaped and formed by a sinful act.[100]

In the treatment of John 8:34–35, on the liberation of the children of Abraham from slavery to sin, Augustine introduced a different understanding of Christ being sin. He explained the role of Christ as the one free of all sin who offered himself as the sacrifice to remove the sin that stood between the Jews and God. Because he was in the likeness of sinful flesh but not himself sinful, he could be the true sacrifice for sin. Augustine explained that in the Mosaic legislation (Lev. 4:3–4, in his Latin translation) that had prefigured the true sacrifice for Christ, the animal that was to be offered as a sacrifice for sin was itself called "the sin." The priests put their hands on the head of the animal, and it became the sin that was to be removed from the people. Christ was the perfect sacrificial victim because he was not only just but completely innocent, with no obligation to die. His relationship to human sin was purely representational or symbolic. As the priest offering himself, Christ effectively replaced the impeding sin and became the mediator joining the people with God.[101] In a Christmas Day sermon, preached sometime between 412 and 416, Augustine observed that unless Christ had taken the likeness of sinful flesh, humans could not have been saved.[102]

From Sin He Condemned Sin

Between 417 and 419, Augustine undertook a series of sermons on Romans 7 and 8, in one of which he returned to the questions raised by Romans 8:3: Christ being in the likeness of sinful flesh and the distinction between the sin that God condemned and the sin used to condemn it.[103] In considering these questions, he appealed again to 2 Corinthians 5:21, in which God is said to have made Christ sin, though he was without sin. He identified the sin that was condemned in the flesh (Rom. 8:3) as the sins of all humans, according to John the Baptist's identification of Christ as the Lamb of God who took away the sin of the world (John 1:29).[104]

Augustine then attempted to identify the sin by which or from which Christ had condemned the sins of all humanity. He considered that it might be the same sin that Christ had sinned according to 2 Corinthians 5:21. He then rejected the meaning of the term "sin" that he had suggested a few years earlier in his commentary on Psalm 34: that Christ had "sinned" by taking mortal flesh. Instead, he asserted that Christ had never sinned, not in his conception, not in his birth, not by his own decision (1 Pet. 2:22). The "prince of this world" found nothing to claim in him (John 14:30). Nor was his death suffered as punishment for his having or being sin; it was voluntarily endured in carrying out the divine plan.[105] Because the sin that Christ "became" was not a sinful act, he concluded, it could not be the "sin" from which he condemned sin.

Some interpreters, whom he did not name, had proposed a solution that Augustine acknowledged as possible but not right. The sin from which Christ condemned sin would be the act of another person, not something associated with Christ himself. The sin from or by which Christ condemned sin, then, might be identified as that of Judas betraying him or the sin of the Jewish leaders condemning him. These sins actually led to his death at their hands, and by dying he condemned sin. Such an explanation could not be rejected as false, Augustine admitted.[106] Indeed, he had used this very solution to explain that the devil sinned by causing the death of Christ through human agents and that thereby all of humanity had been liberated from his control.

Augustine did not accept this solution to the identity of the sin Christ used to condemn the sin he had come to be. He could not bring that proposal into conformity with his understanding of 2 Corinthians 5:21: Christ was made to be sin. The sin in that text could not be understood as referring to the sin of some other person. Nor could it be interpreted by referring to some "sin" by which Christ could be called a sinner, someone who performed a sinful action. That Pauline text, he observed, did not use a verb to say that God caused Christ "to sin" but a noun to say that God made him "to be sin."[107] In his attempt to reconcile Romans 8:3 and 2 Corinthians 5:21, Augustine found himself forced to develop an interpretation of the saving death of Christ that was different from the victory achieved by having the devil kill an innocent person who appeared to be a sinner because of his mortality.

Finally, then, Augustine returned to the interpretation he had introduced in his commentary on the Gospel of John: in the ritual of offering, a victim carried the sins of the people (Lev. 4:3–4).[108]

> In the law, sacrifices that are offered for sins are also called sins. It reads: "when the victim for a sin is brought forward," the law says, "the priests shall lay their hands on the sin," that is, on the victim for the sin. And what else is Christ if not a sacrifice for sin? "Just as Christ," he says, "loved us and delivered himself for us as an offering and a sacrificial victim to God in an odor of sweetness (Eph. 5:2)." This, then, is the sin by which he condemned sin: by the sacrifice that was made for sins, he condemned sin.[109]

By killing this "sin," a victim on which were symbolically loaded the sins of the whole people, the sins themselves were destroyed. God had made Christ to be the sin of the whole world. In his own freely accepted death as an offering, Christ had then condemned and vanquished the sins that he had become through that offering. Augustine repeated this sacrificial explanation in another sermon in the series on these central chapters of Romans.[110]

Finally, in a sermon that seems to have been preached in 420, Augustine also named the kinds of sacrificial animals that were used—a ram or a goat—but made the same point: that Christ was made to be a sacrificial offering through which sins were removed.[111] The death of Christ fulfilled the ritual of sacrifice for sin that had been given to Israel. His mortal body could symbolize sin because it did not realize sin: it was in all ways innocent and free of sin. This ritual destruction of the mortal flesh symbolizing the sin effected the destruction of the real sin and removed it as an obstacle to union with God. As priest, Christ took this sin upon himself; he not only destroyed the sin as an impediment separating humans from God; as a mediating priest who inseparably joined humanity to God, he occupied the place vacated by that sin.

Augustine did not exclude an alternative identification of the sin by which God condemned sin, as the sinful act of Satan or the enemies of Christ. Indeed, he had used just such an identification in the elaboration of the conflict between Christ and Satan. Once he had incorporated 2 Corinthians 5:21 into the analysis, however, he searched for the way to identify Christ as that sin-destroying "sin." Leviticus 4:3–4 provided that means: Christ became the sin of the whole of humanity, the sin symbolized in the mortality of his innocent flesh. In his freely accepted death, he destroyed that sin. The (earlier) theory of a Satanic attack allowed Christ to function as an innocent victim who would be vindicated by God's justice and power. It did not allow him to function as a priest whose voluntary identification with the death-dealing sin not only destroyed and removed that obstacle but made him the priest who stood between God and humans in perpetual self-offering.

CHRIST'S IDENTIFICATION WITH CHRISTIANS

The explanation of the death of Christ as the actual destruction of his mortal flesh and thus of the sin of humanity that it symbolized did not fully treat the final phrase of 2 Corinthians 5:21, "so that in him we might become the righteousness of God." That objective was accomplished through Augustine's identification of Christians as the members of Christ's body. The flesh whose mortality symbolized human sinfulness also represented the ecclesial body of Christ. In the death and resurrection of his flesh, sin was condemned in Christians and the justice of God was fulfilled in them.

Augustine asserted that in his death Christ himself was speaking and acting in union with the faithful Christians who formed his ecclesial body. His interpretation of Christ's expression of sorrow and fear on the evening when he was arrested and of his praying Psalm 22 on the cross was based on the identity between head and members that characterized his reading of the Psalms. In this instance, however, Augustine had to distinguish the speaker's confession of sinfulness from expressions of weakness and suffering of body or soul that were not sinful. In the development of these interpretations, Augustine came to a fuller understanding of Christ's identification as head with the members of his body.

The cry of dereliction that begins Psalm 22 and the confession of sinfulness that followed immediately—in his Latin version, "the tale of my sins leaves me far from salvation"—presented a dilemma for Augustine.[112] Sin could not be attributed to Christ, as divine or as an individual human and head of the church.[113] But the Gospels of Mark and Matthew attributed the entire psalm to Christ in his praying aloud of its opening and in their narrating the details of his crucifixion as the fulfillment of its prophecy (Matt. 27:46; Mark 15:34). Christians, he concluded, must interpret the whole of Psalm 22 as applying to Christ.[114] Augustine accomplished this by distinguishing the different voices in which Christ was speaking and acting as the subject of that text.

In confessing divine abandonment and the sin that provoked it, Augustine asserted, Christ was speaking not for himself as divine or even as an individual human but for the members of his body, the Christians who were joined into him.[115] Augustine invited his congregation to hear their own voices in that of Christ, as he prayed for them in the voice he shared with them.[116] All should recognize and confess sinfulness, not only as descendants of Adam and heirs of his sin, but in the failures that they had individually added to that common one. No member of Christ could claim to be free of sin.[117] Instead, they should accept Christ's words as their own, trusting that God would not reject them, just as God had not abandoned Christ who was carrying Adam's flesh that he shared with them.[118] Thereby, he explained, they would come to share the justice of Christ, who had in these words made their sins his own.[119]

Appealing to Romans 6:6, "our old self was crucified with him," Augustine assigned the words of Psalm 22 to Christ, since he represented in his mortal flesh the "oldness" of humanity that was being destroyed.[120] Christ was carrying their mortality, the punishment for the first sin, in that flesh which he had received from Adam through his mother. Thus, he spoke not only for his members but for himself, in what Augustine called "the person of his body," which was beset with human weakness.[121] Christ, he concluded, had identified not only with the Christians for whom he spoke, but with the whole of humanity whose weakness he had taken upon himself in accepting the flesh they shared. Echoes of the understanding of Christ as priest offering himself as the sacrifice that extinguished the sins symbolized in his mortal flesh could be heard in this interpretation of Romans 6:6.

On occasion, Augustine found the sadness and fear that the Synoptic Gospels present Christ experiencing on the Mount of Olives (Matt. 26:38–44; Mark 14:32–42; Luke 22:40–46) no less troubling and implausible than his confession of sin. He sometimes argued that Christ did not really fear death because he had the power both to lay down his life and to take it up again (John 10:17–18), because he knew that he was going to rise. More-over, he noted, Paul had faced death with equanimity, actually preferring to suffer it and be with Christ than to continue in earthly life (Phil. 1:23; 2 Tim. 4:6–8). The voice in which Christ spoke fearfully, Augustine sug-gested, was that of the human weakness of his members rather than his individual voice. As head, he was taking the members upon himself and speaking for them. He then exemplified for them proper conformity to the divine will when death could not be avoided.[122] In the same way, he once suggested, Paul had presented himself as a person beset by concupiscence and struggling against sin (Rom. 7:22–25).[123]

More often, however, Augustine affirmed that in voluntarily assuming mortal human flesh, Christ had also taken upon himself not only bodily mortality but the actual sadness and fear that the human soul experienced in sympathy with its body when facing danger or suffering. In comment-ing on Psalm 88:3–4, "My soul is filled with evils and my life draws near to the underworld," he explained that the body cannot suffer without the soul, although the soul can suffer without the body doing so. The gospels report that as Christ approached death, he felt sorrow and fear even be-fore he experienced any bodily pain (Matt. 26:37–38; Mark 14:34). Paul, Augustine added, had reported a similar mental sorrow and anguish as he witnessed his fellow Israelites rejecting the gospel (Rom. 9:2). These emotions were not forced upon Christ by his bodily pain; he had chosen to suffer them. He did so in order to assure his disciples, Augustine explained to his congregation, that the fear and sorrow were signs of human weak-ness, that they indicated neither personal infidelity nor divine abandon-ment.[124] Although Christ freely assumed these feelings upon himself and was not overwhelmed by them, he actually shared the emotional distress that his members experienced in similar situations. Like so many of them, he sometimes carried out the divine will in sadness rather than in joy.[125] In another instance, Augustine portrayed Christ as accepting from God the same discipline through which every father trained his heir (Heb. 12:6; Prov. 3:11–12).[126]

In his preaching, Augustine appealed to this identification of Christ with the emotions of the Christians who formed his body for two related purposes. More often, he applied it to a pedagogical goal, providing an example of conformity to the divine will in the midst of sorrow and fear.[127] Christ had endured the bodily pain and mental anguish that were punish-ments for sin; he served the divine will as they often did, in sorrow. Christ provided himself not only as an example but as a companion to his disciples.

He entered the fight and himself achieved a victory that he then invited his martyrs to share, symbolizing them in the bloody sweat that covered his body.[128] Augustine identified a second purpose of Christ's voluntary anguish by reflecting on the contrast between the appeals that Satan and Christ made to humans. When the devil approached Adam and Eve in the garden, he did not try to persuade them that the experience of the knowledge being offered by eating the fruit of the tree was more valuable than the death that had been threatened for violating its prohibition. Adam was not invited to assess and accept the risk of bodily harm in order to gain valuable knowledge. Instead, the tempter asserted that the humans would not actually suffer death for violating the prohibition. He suggested that God's command was backed by an empty threat. Christ, in contrast to the demon, spoke the truth: he freely and explicitly acknowledged and even experienced the horror that humans felt in the face of death; he asserted that the sin of disobeying God was a greater evil. Christ urged his disciples to follow him in accepting bodily death in order to avoid sin and eternal death.[129]

Augustine taught that in his passion and death no less than in his incarnation Christ had identified himself voluntarily with his members. Although he did not share their sin and guilt, he represented them as sinners not only in his mortal flesh but in his emotions and his prayer with them. Thereby, Christ exhorted and strengthened his disciples to follow the way that he had opened for them. While not in itself a full explanation of the process of salvation, this teaching elaborated and complemented the third theory, Christ's becoming and destroying sin in his mortal flesh.

Descent into the Underworld

Christ's descending to the realm of the dead seems to have been absent from the baptismal creed used in Augustine's ritual.[130] He discussed the liberation of those who had died before the coming of Christ in a letter to his friend Evodius, Bishop of Uzalis, citing the New Testament text in which it is affirmed (1 Pet. 3:19–20).[131] He seldom referred to that part of Christ's activity in his preaching.[132] On one occasion, he explained that after his death, Christ was in the grave in his body, in the underworld by his soul, but entertaining the thief with whom he had died in the paradise that he had never left in his divinity.[133]

In three sermons, however, Augustine did make the visit to the underworld a part of Christ's redemptive work. In preaching on the children who had been executed by Herod, he listed the trip to the underworld along with Christ's birth, hanging on the cross, ascending into heaven, and sitting at the right hand of the Father as efforts to seek those who had perished.[134] In his humility, he had descended not only to mortal humans but even to the dead.[135] In the underworld, he had visited those who were at rest.[136] In none of these instances, however, did Augustine explore the assertions of Christ's preaching to the dead, as he had in writing to Evodius.

RESURRECTION AND ASCENSION

In considering the saving work of Christ, Augustine treated the resurrection and ascension together as a manifestation of the efficacy of his obedient death in the heavenly exaltation of his human reality, and thereby a foundation for the hope of Christians to share his glory. The resurrection and ascension marked the true victory of Christ over the power of evil.[137] The scripture, he observed, speaks of Christ as both passive and active in the events. Augustine found in the words of Psalm 57:3, "He sent from heaven and saved me," the prayer of Christ, as a man of flesh, praising God for rescuing and raising him up. The same divine action was attested in Philippians 2:8–9. He also noted that Christ himself had claimed an active role in his resurrection when he promised to raise up the temple of his own body (John 2:19–21).[138]

To the vindication of Christ through his resurrection after an unjust killing, the ascension added the demonstration that a material body could be raised into heaven. Their belief in God's creating of the whole world from nothing and in the miracles that Christ had performed should have led Christians to affirm as well that God could transform a fleshly body into a heavenly one, that their humanity could be brought into heaven. Had Christ stripped off the humanity that he has assumed and discarded it as a temporary clothing, however, Christians might have despaired of their own bodily resurrection and glorification. This would have changed their understanding of the salvation they were promised. Augustine explained that living in a body was essential for humans, although it was an act of mercy for a divine being.[139] Moreover, he insisted, Christ had died and risen in the assumed form of a servant so that humans would not lose hope. Though they could not claim to be righteous, as he was, even as sinners they had received his promise of resurrection. As he had descended to those who had fallen, in ascending he would lift humans up with him.[140] Christ's bringing immortal flesh into heaven, then, was the appropriate completion of his saving work.[141]

Augustine realized that the resurrection and ascension of Christ was a necessary completion of his destruction of sin and vindication of his own righteousness. That, however, did not answer the question that Paul had addressed in his response to the Thessalonians: Did the resurrection of Christ imply that Christians would also be raised and glorified (1 Thess. 4:13–18)? He argued, then, that the Word of God had taken human flesh and died in that flesh not to gain a higher status for himself but as an act of mercy; he humbled himself, suffering injury and insult in the flesh. He was resurrected and he ascended in his fleshly existence in order to demonstrate to his disciples that their human reality would also be resurrected and raised into the heavens.[142]

The text of John 3:13, part of Christ's puzzling meeting with Nicodemus, provided Augustine with a focus for the question and a means of explaining the connection between the resurrection and ascension of Christ and the hope of Christians. "No one ascends to heaven except the one who descends from heaven, the Son of Man, who is in heaven" might indicate that Christ would return to heaven alone, leaving Christians behind.[143]

While acknowledging the difficulty the text presented, Augustine approached its interpretation by observing that Christ referred to himself as "Son of Man, who is in heaven." He made two points. Christ applied a title linked to his humanity to his descent from heaven. Moreover, he claimed to be still in heaven, under that same title, while speaking on earth. The Word of God, as all Christians knew, had become human in the act of descending from heaven. At the time he made the statement, he already had come from heaven but had not yet returned there in that humanity. During his earthly life, then, how could Christ speak of the "Son of Man" as having descended from heaven and as still or already being in heaven? This use of language, Augustine argued, indicated that Christ intended to call attention to the unity of his person, in both his divine and human reality. The body that he assumed from the virgin was not and did not have a personal unity distinct from that of the Word. His statement in John 3:13, then, focused on the one person who both had descended and would ascend. Even when existing in his divinity before incarnation, Augustine explained, Christ could be called Son of Man. He suggested a parallel: a person might walk down a hill clothed in one way and return dressed in an entirely different costume; still, the one who descended also ascended. Christ's intention, he inferred from this use of language, was to assert that his humanity was no obstacle to his ascent into heaven. This was precisely what had been demonstrated in the bodily ascension of Jesus, to which he referred in the same terms later in the Gospel of John (John 6:63).[144] Thus, Augustine established that the crucial text of John 3:13, when applied to Christ himself, must be interpreted through the oneness of the person descending and ascending rather than the distinction of divine and human realities.[145]

The next step in the argument for the resurrection and ascension of Christians was to extend this unity of the person of Christ, who alone descended and ascended, to the faithful who were joined into his person as members of his churchly body. To accomplish this, Augustine called attention to the unity of Christ in his humanity and the body that was composed of his faithful disciples. Two sets of scriptural texts served his purpose in this instance. In Galatians 3:16, Paul had argued that the term "seed of Abraham" was to be taken as a singular but not a collective form; it referred to Christ alone and not to the entire people that had descended through carnal generation from Abraham. Shortly thereafter, in Galatians 3:29, Paul had referred to the Christians to whom he was writing as the "seed of Abraham." Modifying his earlier rejection of a collective interpretation, Augustine observed, Paul identified both Christ and the church as Abraham's seed, in the singular.[146] Augustine made the same argument by means of Ephesians 5:29–30: Christ and the church were two in one flesh; Christians were members of the body of Christ.[147] These texts confirmed Augustine's contention that John 3:13 included Christians with Christ in his ascent into heaven to share his glory.

This interpretation of the ascension text of John 3:13 through the unity of Christ with Christians also served Augustine's insistence that belonging to the unity of the church was essential to salvation. Only those who were members of the ecclesial body of Christ could ascend in personal unity with him into heaven.[148] The resurrection and ascension had already been accomplished in the head; it would certainly follow for the members.[149]

Even prior to the glorification of Christians, moreover, Augustine asserted that their presence in heaven was established by their union with Christ. His interpretation of John 3:13 noted that Christ had claimed to be "Son of Man" in descending from heaven and to be in heaven while he was living on earth. He extended this argument to assert that as Christ did not leave heaven when he came to earth, so he did not leave the earth when he ascended, as Son of Man, to heaven. He had been persecuted by Saul on earth while he was also safe in heaven (Acts 9:4); he was served daily by his disciples as they fed and clothed the needy (Matt. 25:35). By his divinity, power, and love, Christ continued to be present on earth among Christians; by love, Christians were joined into Christ and already with him in heaven, where their names were written.[150] He was down below with them in the compassion of love; they above with him in the hope based on love.[151] Thus, Augustine explained Paul's assertions that the Christians' city was in heaven (Phil. 3:20), where they had been raised with Christ (Col. 3:1).[152]

CONCLUSION

In his preaching on the saving work of Christ, Augustine developed distinct but closely related explanations of the meaning and efficacy of his death and resurrection. Most often, he referred to Christ paying a price for the redemption or purchase of humanity that was held captive and in slavery by the devil as a consequence of both the original sin of Adam and Eve and the personal sins of their offspring. Even in this, however, he carefully qualified the transaction to prevent both the devil achieving any gain and Christ suffering any loss; the one had failed to hold what he had sought and the other regained the cost he had expended. This description served most often as the basis of moral exhortation that urged gratitude and service to Christ for the great effort he had made.

A fuller explanation of the foundations of this ransom transaction was provided in the interpretation based explicitly on the "binding and plundering of the strong man" found in the Synoptic Gospels. By taking mortal flesh, Christ had tricked the devil into assuming that he was subject to death as a punishment for sin. By causing the death of this innocent one, the devil transgressed the boundaries of his dominion over the human sinners who had voluntarily subordinated themselves to him. Christ bound the devil by that transgression and recaptured the sinners who had originally been his own property but had given themselves over to the devil. Christ emerged as the Lord of all humanity with the power and right to liberate from sin and demonic servitude.

Augustine's explanation of the death of Christ as the destruction of sin through the sacrificial killing of a surrogate to whom the guilt of humanity had been symbolically transferred combined elements of the second theory with an appropriation of the ritual practices of Israel that foreshadowed the work of Christ. Christ's innocence enabled him to symbolize human sinfulness in his own mortal flesh that was free of all sin. In the destruction of that flesh, the sin was ritually destroyed, and humanity liberated from its alienation from God. As mediator between divine and human, Christ then restored his disciples to God by uniting them into his own person. This sacramental explanation of the death of Christ was original to Augustine; it identified the human body of Christ as the symbol of the sinfulness of Adamic humanity that through his death and resurrection would be cleansed and restored to newness and justice. The reflections on Christ's confession of sin and experience of human evils in his passion and death elaborated and extended his identification with his body, the church, and with the whole of humanity.

The discussion of Christ's descent into the underworld, to greet the dead awaiting liberation and resurrection, affirmed the breadth of his victory and the universality of his dominion. Augustine's interpretation of Christ's resurrection and ascension returned to the peculiar relationship between head and members that was at the core of his sacramental understanding of the death of Christ. All humanity had been freed from the bodily mortality that was the consequence of sin; only those who were joined into the body of Christ as his members, the church with which he formed one flesh, would ascend with him into heavenly glory.

Two considerations, both derived from Pauline and Johannine teaching, filtered through Augustine's preaching about the saving work of Christ. The mortal flesh that he assumed from the heritage of Adam enabled him to identify with humans and to symbolize human sinfulness in his own person. His full innocence and freedom from sin meant that his death, by the attack of the devil and by his own self-offering as the symbolic carrier of human sinfulness, destroyed that sin and wiped out every claim over humans other than his own. He would cleanse and join the saved into himself as the new humanity; he would condemn by his own authority both the humans who refused to acknowledge him and the demons whom he had bound in their sin.

The explanation of the efficacy of Christ's death through the overcoming of the devil, the symbolic destruction of sin, and the identification with Christians can be found developed in his treatises as well as his sermons. The language of purchase or redemption from slavery or captivity, however, was peculiar to the sermons, where it was largely focused on moral exhortation to faithful service of Christ in gratitude for his generous rescue.

Augustine's use of the language of personal unity in Christ, as divine and human, was prior to and independent of the conflicts that led to the declaration of Mary as Mother of God in the Council of Ephesus the year after his death. The same language was affirmed in the agreement between the bishops of Alexandria and Antioch in the Formula of Union and was explicitly asserted twenty years later by the Council of Chalcedon. It became a standard of right and true teaching for most Christians. Augustine's use of that language for Christ himself and its extension to his unity with the faithful Christians formed into the body of Christ were based on Pauline teaching and soteriological applications that the dogmas developed in the Greek church neither suggested nor supported. Augustine's broad usage will be examined more fully below.

Chapter Nine

THE HUMAN SITUATION

F EW OF AUGUSTINE'S *Sermons to the People* in the decade following his ordination as a presbyter in 391 treat the issues that would become important to his understanding of the human condition. The central scriptural texts—1 Corinthians 15, Galatians 5, and Romans 5, 7, 8—are mentioned only in passing, if at all, in the commentaries on the psalms and other preaching; none are the subject of sustained analysis.*

Augustine did examine and discuss the fall of humanity in the first parents and the situation of their offspring in his treatises against the Manichees and the scripture commentaries that he composed in response to questions from his colleagues. The results of this work appeared later in his sermons. Hence, the review of his preaching on human sinfulness will begin with the second decade of his ministry. Because that preaching drew on the developments of the prior decade in the treatises, however, it will be prefaced with a summary of his writing on that subject during the period between his ordination to the presbyterate and his completion of the *Confessions* in 401.

THE INITIAL DECADE OF AUGUSTINE'S MINISTRY

The Original Sin and Its Consequences

In his first exposition of Genesis, directed against the Manichean dualists, Augustine explained that Satan, an already fallen angel, had exploited a

---

*For the development of the chronology of the Augustinian materials used in this chapter, please see the introduction above, pp. 5–7.

movement originating in the sense faculty of the human mind to tempt Adam and Eve to disobey the divine prohibition of eating of the Tree of Knowledge. They sinned by failing to exercise their mental power to discern and control an operation of the senses.[1] In a subsequent treatise, also against the Manichees, he offered the mental sin of cupidity or avarice as the cause of the transgression.[2]

The punishment for the first human sinning was the mortality that was imposed upon the original parents and transmitted to their offspring. The consequence of this bodily weakness was not only suffering through injury and illness, leading to death and bodily dissolution but failures in the higher human functions: an initial ignorance of moral standards and a difficulty in performing according to the moral law once it was discovered or learned.[3] Augustine insisted, however, that sinning involved personal responsibility.[4] Individuals became guilty only by failing to make the intellectual and moral progress they could or by neglecting to seek or refusing to accept the assistance that God offered them.[5] As they gained and exercised the use of their natural capacities for understanding and deliberate choice, Augustine taught, humans regularly sinned.

In the *Confessions*, he analyzed the process by which the bodily appetites that support mortal life produced illicit desires. By consenting to and acting upon these, individuals formed habits of choice and action that then chained them to patterns of evil decision and practice.[6] All humans capable of sinning soon deserved condemnation, so that salvation was not awarded on the basis of prior good merits but freely offered by Christ.[7]

Because infants were not capable of personal sin, those who died before they attained the power to act responsibly for themselves were neither granted access to the kingdom of God nor assigned any punishment. God could be trusted to make provision for those who had done neither good nor evil. Infants who were given Christian baptism and died before making any personal decisions, however, were granted access to the kingdom of God.[8]

The Condition of the Offspring of Adam and Eve

In the commentaries on the letters of Paul written during this first decade of his ministry, Augustine showed that the dependence of human life upon the satisfaction of bodily appetites, the consequent dominance of the sense faculties in guiding a child's affective development, and the delayed emergence of intellectual knowledge and responsible decisions resulted in the establishment of patterns of personal choice that opposed rather than supported the mental capacity, moral responsibility, and eternal destiny of human beings. By the time a person was capable of appreciating mental or moral goods such as justice and equity, customs of carnal desire and action had been established that militated against, and even prevented, following the standards and seeking the values of moral behavior.[9]

Commenting on Romans 7:7–13, Augustine explained that the revealed moral code—the Decalogue of the Mosaic law—displayed their moral impotence to any Christians who attempted to fulfill it. Although they retained the capacity to recognize the precepts and prohibitions of that law as right and just, their attempts to follow these norms were opposed, with regular success, by the carnal desires arising from mortality and the habitual patterns that persons had established by voluntary practice.[10] To the evil of their perverted willing, newly knowledgeable sinners added the guilt of transgressing the revealed divine law.[11] As a result, the inbred and acquired disorders in the children of Adam and Eve transformed the moral law into an agent not of improvement but of deepening failure. As Paul wrote in 1 Corinthians 15:56, death caused sin that the law then empowered.[12] Finally, even those living under the influence of the love of Christ longed for the extinguishing of those lusts in the promised resurrection of the flesh. They prayed with Paul in Romans 7:24–25 for deliverance from "the body of this death."[13] Thus, Augustine's principal use of 1 Corinthians 15:21–22 contrasted the sinning and penal death coming from Adam to the immortal and renewed bodily life promised by Christ.[14]

The Second Decade: Preaching on Human Sinfulness

Blocks of sermons preached at the same time have been identified in the second decade of Augustine's preaching ministry, extending from the completion of the *Confessions* in 401 to the beginning of the controversy with the Pelagians in 411. In these, the developments of the prior decade began to appear regularly, and with some variations on the interpretations offered earlier. The first includes a group of seven of the *Enarrationes in Psalmos* whose relation to one another has long been recognized. Parallel themes and uses of scriptural evidence have provided evidence that many sermons were preached at the same time, late 403 and early 404.[15] A second set was preached as a group a little more than two years later, December 406 through Eastertide of 407. Augustine interspersed expositions of the

Psalms of Ascent (119–33) and the first four chapters of the Gospel of John. In addition, the First Letter of John was treated during the octave of Easter in 407.[16] Scholars have assigned other sermons and psalm commentaries to this period, though that dating is less secure than that of the series on John and the Psalms.* In all of these sermons, Augustine devoted limited attention to questions of the fall of humanity in Adam and Eve and to the consequences of this failure for their offspring.

The Original Sin and its Consequences

Augustine occasionally used the narrative of the temptation and fall of Adam and Eve to illustrate a point that he was making in a sermon. Eve had been taken in by the assurance of the devil that God would not really follow through on the penalty of death for violating the prohibition of eating the fruit of the tree. Similarly, sinful Christians told themselves that, at the judgment, God would not actually condemn vast multitudes and save only the few who struggled to live well.[17] On another occasion, he offered a moral interpretation of the prohibition and its violation. A knowledge of good and evil could not have been acquired simply by eating the fruit of a tree. Instead, the reward of obedience or the punishment of disobedience would bring an experience of good or evil.[18]

The innovation of this period, however, came in Augustine's adaptation of Paul's explanation of the pattern of sinning by which humanity had fallen into idolatry. In preaching against the pagans on New Year's Day 404, he explained that although humans had been given a knowledge of God, they claimed as their own achievement both that knowledge and the other goods that had been bestowed upon them. Falling into a sin that could be understood as pride (Sir. 10:15) or avarice (1 Tim. 6:12), they refused to honor and thank God. As a punishment, they were cast down into ignorance and turned over to their sensual appetites. Thus, the first sin of pride was punished by desires and actions that were both punishments for sin and themselves sins—from which people could turn back.[19] In an exposition of Psalm 58, that may have preceded this sermon by a few days, Augustine had applied this Pauline analysis to the sin of Adam and

---

* Internal references to the development of the Donatist controversy and scriptural interpretations that parallel treatises that are securely dated to this period through the *Retractations* help to locate many, but not all, of these sermons.

Eve. The first sin was, according to Sirach 10:14–15, apostasy from God or pride. It was punished by a darkening of the mind and vices of the body that were both punishments and further sins.[20] During the same period, Augustine named pride as the root cause of the mortality, weakness, and suffering of humans.[21]

This application of the Pauline account of the origins of human ignorance and lust in a prideful refusal to acknowledge God's gracious gifts would thereafter guide Augustine's explanations of the sinning of the first parents and the punishments visited upon them. In his preaching during this period, Augustine was satisfied to note that the whole of humanity had been concentrated in this couple and had thereby suffered the threatened punishment of mortality and the affective disorders that arise from it.[22]

The Inheritance of Death and Concupiscence

As he developed an understanding of the sin of humanity in Adam and Eve, Augustine shifted the interpretations of 1 Corinthians 15:56—the sting of sin is death and the power of sin is the law—away from the earlier focus on the human resistance provoked by the prohibition of certain forms of action and on the guilt of transgression added to already customary evil desires and actions.[23] In preaching on the text, his interest was drawn to the first part of the sentence: the relation between sin and death. In addition, he began to assert that the lust driving sexual generation signaled a deeper disorder in human affections that had been imposed as a punishment for the sin, rather than developing only as a consequence of mortality.[24]

Augustine continued to name mortality that was so clearly witnessed in the Genesis account of the fall and in the Pauline letters (Rom. 5:12–21 and 1 Cor. 15:55–56) as the primary punishment for the transgression of the prohibition of eating from the Tree of Knowledge. Obedience would have brought the reward of immortality; disobedience was punished by mortality. That condition also was used to contrast Christ as the source of life and mediator of justice to Adam who brought death and Satan who mediated injustice but could not share his natural immortality.[25]

Augustine explained that bodily mortality was a chronic illness that constantly threatened a person's hold on life.* Food and drink were medi-

---

* In *Serm.* 362.11.11, Augustine compared the mortal body to an oil lamp that needed to be refilled regularly to keep burning, but whose fibrous wick eventually failed so that its light was lost.

cations required daily to replenish the mass and energy of a mortal body; they satisfied temporarily but did not extinguish that continuing need.[26] Because of its fragility, human flesh demanded constant attention and changing responses to maintain bodily life. A person could remain only so long sitting or standing, waking or sleeping; eating or drinking was followed by elimination and renewed hunger or thirst.[27] As a consequence, most human pursuits were dictated by necessity rather than inspired by love. The mind experienced its body as a prison rather than a home.[28] The fear of death, he noted, would continue to occasion sinful willing and actions until the bodily resurrection removed mortality itself.[29] Moreover, the generation necessary to keep the human race alive had to be performed in a mortal way, subject to lust.[30]

In addition to the burdens of mortality, Augustine explained, the descendants of Adam and Eve experienced a conflict in which the mortal flesh opposed the guidance provided by a mind informed by the moral law. It held the person captive to what Paul called "the law of sin" in the bodily members (Rom. 7:22–23). This law was not only a physical consequence of the original sinning but the application of a principle of justice. The right ordering of the human person required that the bodily members be subject to the mind and the mind to God. After rebelling against its lord, the mind justly experienced the revolt of its own servant. Although the bodily members continued to follow the governance of the mind in most activities, in some they failed through weakness and in others they either refused to perform or acted independently.[31] All humans, then, were born with various forms of desire that operated independently of personal governance. These accompanied their mortal condition and would be removed only in the resurrection, when the faithful were granted immortal life.[32] Although their creation in the divine image endowed them with free will and made them accountable for their choices and actions, the offspring of Adam and Eve found themselves severely restricted in the exercise of self-governance in both willing and operation.[33]

In preaching on the Christian life in the first decade of the fifth century, Augustine's interpretations of the central chapters of Romans and Galatians drew upon both mortality and concupiscence he identified as the heritage of Adam and Eve. The demands and desires of the flesh gave rise to suggestions that moved a person toward evil; acting on these, a person built up customs of sinning that exacerbated the conflict.[34] The gradual awakening of human reason allowed evil habits to become established before people learned the divinely revealed moral code and recognized their condition as sinful. That knowledge, however, did not inspire and empower humans to observe the prohibitions and fulfill the precepts of the Decalogue. Instead, it made them knowing, willing sinners; it added the guilt of transgression to the evil of their desires and actions.[35] Augustine attributed the moral impotence and unavoidable guilt arising from personal sin to mortality and lust as the roots of urgent appetites and persistent desires that wore down even a Christian's resistance and resulted in violations of the Decalogue.

At this point, Augustine did not devote significant attention to the gift of the Holy Spirit that inspired in the mind a delight in the divinely commanded good that would enable a Christian to counter the influence of the disordered desires arising from inherited mortality and lust.[36] Instead, he urged his congregation to make the determined effort necessary to refuse consent and prevent their evil desires from breaking out into action. He exhorted them to undertake the good works symbolized by the childbearing by which Eve was to attain salvation (1 Tim. 2:15).[37] They should look forward in hope to the resurrected life in which they would be liberated from the body of death that oppressed them.[38] True peace, however, would be given by the contemplation of the face of God, which would so satisfy the person that no other desire could pull the mind away.[39]

The Inheritance of Sin

In sermons that might have been preached during the winter of 403–4 or in the spring of 407, Augustine began to use language that could have been intended to indicate the transmission of sin from Adam to his descendants, so that infants would have been born not only subject to the debilitating punishments but bearing the guilt of the parental sin.

In commenting on Psalm 85, he affirmed that because all humans had been identified with Adam, they suffered what happened to him as a result of his sin. He acknowledged that once children were separated from their parents as distinct individuals, they were responsible for their own actions. They either imitated their parents and shared their fate or turned away from them and earned a different recompense for themselves.[40] He did not, however, elaborate the argument by differentiating between the progenitors of all humans and successive generators who followed them.

Using the same identification of descendants in their progenitors, in his fourth sermon on Psalm 104, Augustine affirmed that the propagation of death from the first sinners made their children subject to debt or defect as well as the punishment visited upon it. In support of the interpretation, he cited Job 14:4–5, which stated that no one, not even a one-day-old baby, was pure in God's sight. This was the heritage of death and sin from the first sin.[41]

Finally, in the sermons preached on the First Letter of John during the octave of Easter in 407, Augustine appeared to have asserted the inheritance of both the sin of Adam and its punishment. The presence of the guilt of the parental sin would seem to be indicated by its punishment, even before the child had added any personal sin. In confirmation, he cited the practice of baptizing infants, which implied the presence of sin. Finally, he contrasted birth from Adam to birth from Christ. The first brought sin and death; the second life and justice.[42]

In his sermons on the Gospel of John, preached before and after those on the letter, Augustine spoke of humans as having been born in sin. The meaning of his statements was not clearly different from the explanation offered in his earlier written commentaries and the contemporary sermons examined above: the transgression of Adam and Eve in the Paradise was punished by bodily mortality that was transmitted to their offspring, in whom it resulted in personal sinning.[43] Thus, in an exposition of John 3:36—that the wrath of God remains on those who do not believe in Christ—Augustine asserted, without fuller explanation, that humans born from Adam were subject to both mortality and the wrath of God.[44]

Thus, Augustine interpreted the moral conflict within human beings primarily as a division between mental understanding and the fleshly desires that grew stronger because of the bodily mortality that derived from the sin of Adam and Eve.[45] Despite having come to a recognition of the moral good and wanting to perform that good, mortal humans usually failed to act properly because of the contrary weight of carnal needs and desires. These sinners needed both divine forgiveness and help.[46] In Romans 7 and Galatians 5, Paul described the conflict and failure, confessing that he was or once had been such a person, oppressed by desires based on penal mortality and by the revealed moral law.[47]

In some instances, Augustine interpreted the text of Romans 7:22–25 as the prayer of a faithful Christian resisting the fleshly desires that arose from mortality.[48] Throughout their lives, Christians continued in this struggle against lusts as they worked toward salvation.[49] Augustine also interpreted that prayer for deliverance as a plea by such Christians: to be set free from the carnal desires and thereby to serve God without division or opposition.[50] He explained that this desire arose from the Christian's experience of love for God and the goods God commanded, itself a gift of God, and from a hope that God would further support and bring that love to fulfillment. He attributed the prayer to faithful Christians and even to Paul himself.[51]

That liberation, Augustine taught, would be delayed until the Christian was freed from mortality.[52] The lust that was both a sin and a punishment for the original sin had to be removed before the mortality it caused was overcome and the vision of God could be given.[53]

Christ and the Church

The Donatist controversy did not directly involve the questions of human sinfulness that Augustine had pursued in his Pauline commentaries and would take up again in the debates with the Pelagians. That conflict focused on the efficacy of the church in providing the ministry of baptism through which the saving work of Christ was applied to individuals. One further development requires attention because of its contribution to the role of the church in applying the saving power of Christ to individual Christians.

In the discussion with Nicodemus on the necessity of rebirth in the Spirit (John 3:3–15), Christ moved to the assertion that only one who first had descended from heaven could ascend there (John 3:13). Augustine applied this statement to the preceding teaching on rebirth by explaining that Christ had descended from heaven in order to join humans to himself as members of his body. They could ascend with him and so attain eternal life.[54]

Augustine then extended this explanation into the gospel's following appeal to the efficacy of the bronze serpent raised up by Moses as a foreshadowing of the liberation of humans through faith in Christ. Satan, he explained, had brought death upon Adam by deceit and that penal death had been passed down to his offspring. In them, mortality had occasioned the sins from which Christ provided liberation through his own unmerited bodily death.[55] He concluded that the death of Christ destroyed bodily death and brought eternal life to those joined into him as his members by faith and baptism.[56]

This interpretation of the necessity of the church's baptism for joining a person to Christ and thus providing access to eternal life would serve as a dogmatic foundation for Augustine's teaching on baptism. Adam brought death upon all his descendants; sin resulted from that death. Christ liberated from sin and, through baptism, joined the saved into his body and raised them to heaven.

Sin Punishing Sinning

In two contemporary sermons, Augustine elaborated the Pauline explanation of the state of Greco-Roman society and applied it to the heritage of Adam and Eve. In his exposition of Psalm 57, he undertook to explain the immediate, hidden punishment that sinners suffer—even though they seem to be spared other forms of suffering appropriate to their evil desires and deeds. For this purpose, he appealed to the statements in Romans 1:24, 28: those who had refused to acknowledge and glorify their creator were turned over to the lusts of their hearts. Appealing to Sirach 10:14–15 to interpret Romans 1:20–21, he distinguished the initial act of pride that was sin alone from the consequent lusts and evil deeds that were both sin and punishments for the prior sin. These sins would lead eventually, he added, to the suffering that was punishment alone either immediately after death or following the general resurrection.[57]

As he continued the exposition of the psalm, Augustine applied this tripartite distinction more generally to humanity. The initial sin of pride committed by the first humans was punished by the mortality and attendant delight in bodily goods with which all their offspring were born. Unless these desires were restrained by early efforts, they would grow strong through practice and divide the person.[58] In his long sermon against Roman traditional religion a week or two later, on January 1, 401, Augustine applied the text and teaching again. In this instance, he explained that the intermediate actions were called sins as well as punishments because sinners refused to draw back from them. They would have no such option to avoid the final punishment.[59] Later, Augustine would use this notion of a sin that was itself a punishment for prior sin in developing his teaching on the transmission of guilt and in disputing the Pelagian theory of human voluntary autonomy.[60]

Summary

After two decades of writing and preaching, Augustine's understanding of humanity's plight was approaching a significant change. He had named mortality, the condemnation to bodily death, as the principal punishment of the sin of Adam and Eve in the Paradise. That penal mortality gave urgency to bodily appetites that protected human life and increased the pleasure of their satisfaction. These desires and satisfactions conflicted with the moral judgments made on the basis of human reason guided and enlightened by the revealed law. Transgressing the divine law moved sinners to seek assistance from Christ, expressed in Paul's plea for liberation from guilt and its deserved punishment.

A set of Pauline texts—1 Corinthians 15:21–23 and 53–56, Romans 7:1–25, and Galatians 5:16–17—were central to this development of Augustine's thinking. The central text, Romans 7:15–25, was applied in two different ways, depending on the context. The person in process of conversion attempted and failed to fulfill the demands of the moral law. Then, in fear of condemnation, the convicted sinner appealed to Christ for help. After having received the gift of the Holy Spirit and begun to follow the law in love of its justice, the Christian would also pray for fuller assistance against and deliverance from the continuing opposition of carnal desires and established evil habits.

Augustine also noticed but did not develop a third meaning in Paul's plea for liberation. The Christian who had been assisted by Christ in resisting the desires arising from mortal flesh longed to be set free from the lifelong conflict between evil desire and good intention. That full health of body and mind would be granted only in the resurrection, through both the extinguishing of mortality and the filling of the mind with the knowledge and love of God.

As he worked his way through the initial chapters of the Gospel of John, Augustine moved toward a fuller understanding of the Pauline contrast between Adam and Christ, as the sources of death and life, for both body and soul. As humans had been harmed by birth from Adam, they were healed by being joined into Christ.

In the commentary on the First Letter of John, Augustine reconsidered the status of infants, which he had set aside a decade earlier. He would find himself surprised but not unprepared for the breakout of the Pelagian controversy.

Finally, Augustine found in Romans 1:20–32 a resource for understanding the origin and transmission of human sin and punishment that would be developed in the conflict with the Pelagians. Inherited lust would be identified as a punishment for the sin of pride that was also a sin.

The Third Decade: The Pelagian Controversy

In 411, a conflict arose in Carthage over the opinions of Caelestius, a disciple of Pelagius, who had recently arrived in the city. Among these, two assertions were particularly troubling: that death was natural to humans rather than the punishment of the primordial sin; that humans were born innocent and thus those who died as infants would enjoy eternal life. Because these children had done nothing evil, they suffered no punishments in the afterlife. Caelestius admitted, however, that they could not enter the kingdom of Christ because they had not been baptized.[61] Taken together, the teachings meant that children were born in the same condition that Adam and Eve had been created.

Augustine was brought into the ensuing argument by appeals from members of the Christian community in Carthage and requests from its bishop, Aurelius, that he preach on the topics when in the city. In addition to responding to correspondents in the city, he preached a series of sermons in the summer of 413 in Carthage and wrote a total of four treatises.[62] The scope of the conflict expanded to involve the original condition of humanity, the penal and sinful heritage of Adam and Eve, and the forms of divine assistance through which Christians were redeemed, sanctified, and brought to peace in immortal life.

The following two sections of this chapter will follow the controversy during the years 411–18, beginning with the trial of Caelestius in Carthage, continuing through the arrival in Africa in spring 416 of the reports about the trials and acquittals of Pelagius in Palestine, and ending in the condemnations of Pelagius in Carthage and Rome in May 418. During the first part of this period, Augustine carefully avoided attacking Pelagius by name. He considered the ascetic teacher wrong but well intentioned; he had hoped to convince him and his followers to abandon their erroneous ideas and accept the doctrine of the church.[63]

In June and December 415, synods were held in Jerusalem and Diospolis in Palestine to deal with charges against the teaching of Pelagius. He evaded condemnation and even prepared his own account of the trials and his defense, which he distributed in Africa and, apparently, in Rome. The Latin Christians who had brought the charges appealed to the bishop of Rome for review of the exonerations.

Reports of the events in Palestine and Pelagius's account of his defense reached Carthage the following spring during an annual provincial synod and were delivered in Hippo a little later. The bishops responded by condemning Pelagius and enlisting the bishop of Rome to join them.[64] Pope Innocent responded with appreciation and (general) agreement to the African correspondence in late 416 and early 417.[65]

Beginning with a sermon in Hippo in the spring 416, Augustine attributed the offensive doctrine to Pelagius, although he seldom mentioned him by name.[66] A small number of sermons in this period give sustained analysis and refutation of the Pelagian teaching. In other sermons, particularly a series on Romans 7–8 that were preached in Carthage in 417 or 419,[67] he elaborated a fuller understanding of the situation of humanity, and of Christians in particular, in whom the Adamic heritage of sin and death was opposed by the sanctifying gifts and operations through which the indwelling Holy Spirit moved Christians to love God and neighbor. Although Augustine included some considerations of the original condition and the consequences of the failure of the first humans, his preaching and writing in the period 416–420 devoted more attention to the situation of adult Christians than to that of infants.

After the condemnation of Pelagius in Africa and Rome, his teaching was defended by Julian, bishop of Eclanum, the leader of a group of Italian bishops who refused to accept the Roman bishop's condemnation of Pelagius. Although Julian and Augustine dueled in treatises against each other for a dozen years, their controversy does not appear in Augustine's surviving sermons.[68]

This analysis of the human situation in preaching against the teaching of Caelestius and Pelagius will be divided into two parts. The first section will deal with the transmission of both the guilt and punishment of the sin of Adam and Eve to infants generated in their line. The following part will examine the situation of adult Christians, the conflicts to which they were subject, and the resolution of those struggles in the resurrection of the body and perfection of the soul. Augustine's developing analyses of the creation and sin of Adam and Eve are considered in both parts.

Original Sin and Inherited Guilt

Augustine returned to the contrast of Adam as the originator of death and Christ as the restorer of life for humans that he had introduced nearly a decade earlier in his first sixteen commentaries on the Gospel of John, using 1 Corinthians 15:21–22.[69] In opposition to Caelestius, however, he spoke of both the punishment and the guilt coming from Adam; Christ had accepted the punishment of mortality without the sin and used his death to free humans from both. In contemporary sermons, he added the contrast of Adam and Christ in Romans 5:19 in order to stress the link between death and sin as well as the universal influence of the first sinner and the sole redeemer. Adam was the source from whom all humans were drawn, even Eve, his partner in generating. All deriving from that source through sexual propagation were born to sin and death. Through regeneration in baptism, Christ alone restored life and established justice in all who placed their trust in him.[70] Augustine would develop this contrast between the two "heads" of humanity to serve as a dogmatic foundation for the doctrine of original sin and inherited guilt that affected all humans. To this consideration, he added an appeal to the name specified for Jesus because he would save the people from their sins (Matt. 1:21).[71]

Interpretations of the narrative of the temptation and sin of Adam and Eve appeared in few of Augustine's sermons during the conflict with Caelestius; only his commentary on Psalm 71 gave it extended attention. Central to his concern in that exposition was human subordination to God, which obedience to the prohibition of the Tree of Knowledge would have performed and preserved. He judged that God could have issued a different type of command, such as the offering of sacrifice. Forbidding their eating the fruit of a particular tree in a garden filled with available and permitted fruit indicated that God's objective was that humans accept divine authority and their own dependent status. The fruit of this tree would not itself have conferred any valuable knowledge; instead, humans would have learned the difference between good and evil by experiencing the consequences of their observance or violation of the divine precept. Augustine explained that Adam and Eve had been created in the image of God. They abandoned that goodness in pursuit of an illusory likeness to the properly divine attributes of autonomy and independence. Thus, the evil—the absence of a necessary good—that resulted from their disobedience consisted in the loss of their privileged relationship to God that they abandoned and replaced with a trust of their own, necessarily lesser, power. By rebelling against divine guidance and governance, they fell away from the goodness proper to a creature.[72]

Preaching on the anniversary of a martyr's death, Augustine distinguished the saint's contempt for death from the pride and curiosity through which Adam had abandoned God and incurred guilt and mortality. Adam and Eve did not risk and suffer death in a heroic quest for valuable, necessary, and even beatifying knowledge. Instead, they rashly believed the tempter's promise that the divine threat was empty, that they would not die by tasting the forbidden fruit.[73]

These interpretations of the original sin as a failure to maintain the blessed condition in which humans had been created were illustrated by analysis of the Greek (and derived Latin) translation of Job 7:1–2. Humans were like servants who ran away from their master and then experienced a shadow of their prior life. Adam hid from God, clothing himself in the leaves that blocked out light.[74]

In his sermons as well as his extended commentary on the creation and fall narrative in Genesis, Augustine was moving toward an interpretation of the sin of both angels and humans as a failure to preserve the blessed condition in which they had been created. The mortality and internal division that were experienced by humans descended from Adam and Eve were both consequences and punishments for that sin. These conditions were also indicators that the sin itself had been transmitted from the first parents to all their offspring.

PREACHING IN CARTHAGE ON INHERITED GUILT

June 24, 413

In a sermon presented for the commemoration of the birth of John the Baptist in Carthage on June 24, 413, Augustine moved into an exposition and defense of the doctrine of inherited guilt. He compared John as heir to the sin of Adam to Christ who was not. To establish his point about John, Augustine appealed to Romans 5:12 and to 1 Corinthians 15:21–22 in contrasting Adam and Christ: one had inflicted sin and death on all humans; the other brought resurrection of the dead and the renewal of life to all. "All," he acknowledged, should be interpreted by focusing on the two "exclusive" agents rather than the many recipients: Adam was the only source of the death suffered by all humans; Christ the only source of their restoration to life.[75]

To establish that all required Christ for their salvation, Augustine appealed to the practice of baptizing dying infants. The parents who came running to the church with their children, the wailing infants themselves, and the clergy who accepted and baptized them all testified that Christ was their only hope for salvation. Would any Christian refuse to help these children?[76]

Augustine developed the argument by appealing to the angelic instruction given to Joseph on the naming of Mary's son. It specified that he was to be called Jesus because he would save his people from their sins (Matt. 1:21). God had sent Israel many saviors to deliver and protect the people from enemies, from Moses and Joshua through the judges and the kings. Only Jesus, Augustine observed, was given as savior from sin. Should the church, then, turn the infants away? Should the clergy explain that Jesus was a physician sent only for the sick (Matt. 9:12) and that infants were not "sick" because they were not yet capable of deliberate sinning? Would not the parents rushing to save their infants respond with their own scriptural text, from Job 14:4—in the Septuagint and Old Latin versions—that a day-old child was not clean in God's eyes? The child, Augustine pointed out, was in danger of death; action for its salvation was urgently needed, not a long argument. Returning to his foundational contrast, he insisted that the child entered life in the present age only through Adam; it would escape death in the age to come only through Christ.[77]

Augustine concluded the sermon by returning to his two texts and asserting that John the Baptist could have been exempted from the sin that all humans committed in Adam only by being conceived and born—as Christ had chosen to be—outside the line of sexual generation deriving from Adam and Eve.[78]

Augustine earlier had used 1 Corinthians 15:22—as in Adam all die, in Christ all shall be made alive—to contrast Adam to Christ.[79] In a sermon that might have been preached in Carthage a couple of years earlier, for example, he had applied the text to both bodily death and sin as deriving from Adam.[80] In the sermon on John the Baptist, however, he cited the Romans 5:12 text primarily to justify the application of the Corinthians text to the inheritance of sin from Adam.[81] The argument proceeded from the scripturally-based affirmation of the necessity of the life-giving and from-sin-saving work of Jesus toward the role of Adam in originating and transmitting both the death and the sin that affected humanity. Throughout the controversy on original sin and inherited guilt, Augustine consistently argued from Christ's saving role toward Adam's condemning one.[82] The exclusive positive role of Christ was the dogmatic foundation of the universal negative effect he assigned to Adam.[83]

The dramatic appeal at the end of the sermon to the plight of sick infants might have been rhetorically effective but Augustine should—and may—have realized that it did not count against the teaching of Caelestius, which privileged baptized infants by granting them access to heavenly glory while allowing that unbaptized ones evaded punishment and received a lesser form of eternal life.[84] A discerning listener could have noted that parents would have sought baptism to provide their dying infants with access to Christ's kingdom and knowledge of his Father, rather than from a fear of eternal punishment for the infant who died before the ritual was performed. Augustine would soon remove that option.

The contrast of John the Baptist to Christ at the end of this sermon on John's feast day seems to have failed to convince many of Augustine's hearers that infants, including John, were born guilty of a sin committed by Adam and Eve. His friend and host in Carthage, Bishop Aurelius, required him to return to the topic in a sermon delivered three days later.[85] The preacher arrived well prepared for the task.

June 27, 413

That next sermon began with a review of the teaching of Caelestius, who presumed that all humans were born innocent. Augustine then attempted to exclude the proposed destiny of eternal life appropriate for persons who died without either qualifying for admission to the kingdom of God by having been baptized as Christians or deserving eternal punishment for the guilt of some grave and unrepented sin. To this purpose, he made three arguments. First, he cited Christ's description of the judgment of the nations that offered only two possibilities: the kingdom prepared from the beginning of the world and the fire for the fallen angels (Matt. 25:31–46). Caelestius's proposed eternal life outside the kingdom was not being offered by Christ. Second, Augustine added Paul's warning to sinners in 1 Corinthians 6:9–11 in which he identified their threatened and anticipated condemnation as failure to attain the kingdom. Again, the proposed (happy) eternal life outside the kingdom was shown to be unavailable.[86] Third, Augustine observed that Caelestius's plan still would deprive children innocent of personal sin of the great benefit of sharing in the kingdom of God and send them into eternal exile from the angels and saints. The proposal, he concluded, failed to resolve the human objection to apparent divine injustice that had inspired it.[87] Finally, although for neither the first nor the last time, Augustine appealed to Paul's exclamation in Romans 11:33–36 on the inscrutability of divine justice.[88]

The more important issue for Augustine and his audience was the exclusion of the unbaptized from the kingdom of God that was so clearly articulated in John 3:5. He cited the text of John 3:13 in which Christ explained that only the one who first had descended from heaven could ascend there. Using Paul's teaching that the baptized were joined into Christ's body and became his members (1 Cor. 12:12), he argued that they alone could be lifted up with him into the kingdom.[89] This explanation of the necessity and efficacy of baptism for salvation, it will be recalled, had been developed in Augustine's earlier commentary on the Gospel of John.[90] In that earlier discussion, however, he had not applied it to the question of the condemnation—and therefore sinfulness—of infants who were not joined into Christ by baptism.[91]

Continuing his analysis of Jesus's discussion with Nicodemus in John 3 (whose reading for that day's liturgy he may have arranged), Augustine moved to the saving of the Israelites from death by snakebite through the ritual of looking upon the bronze serpent that Moses was instructed to set up on a staff. The Gospel of John appealed to this foreshadowing event in explaining the Christian's deliverance from sin by faith in Christ raised up on the cross. Augustine elaborated the typology linking the bronze serpent to Christ by citing Romans 8:3.

> "God sent his son," not in the flesh of sin but, as the scripture continues, "in the likeness of sinful flesh," because it came not from the marital embrace but from a virginal womb. "He sent [his Son] in the likeness of sinful flesh." To what end? "So that from a sin he might condemn the sin in the flesh" (Rom. 8:3); from a sin, the sin; from a serpent, the serpent. Who could doubt that the sin is indicated by the name of the serpent? Therefore, the sin is destroyed by a sin as the serpent was by a serpent. But this was accomplished by a likeness because in Christ was found no sin but only the likeness of sinful flesh.[92]

Christ, as virginally conceived, had taken human flesh but not its hereditary wound; during his life, he maintained his freedom from personal sin. His flesh, then, was not actually sinful; instead, it bore the likeness of sinful flesh because he accepted the mortality that punished the sin in Adam and his progeny. Adam had been bitten by the demonic serpent, whose venom made him mortal and poisoned the flesh that he passed to his offspring. As Moses's bronze serpent symbolized but did not realize the death-dealing serpents, so the mortal flesh of Christ symbolized but did not realize the death-dealing sin of Adam and his progeny. Taking and suffering the penalty of death actually, but bearing and sharing the human sin only symbolically, Christ destroyed that sin and extinguished its guilt by the sacrifice of his mortal flesh. He thereby brought salvation to those who shared the sin of Adam. They had only to look in faith upon Christ raised on the cross, as the Israelites had looked at the serpent lifted up on the pole.[93]

Infants, Augustine acknowledged, could not themselves believe in and adhere to Christ, just as they could not sin for themselves. Because they had been harmed by another person's sin, he claimed, they could be helped by another person's faith.[94] Thus, parents could present their infants for baptism and profess faith in Christ for them. The love by which the parents thereby generated them to immortal life in the future age was as strong as the sickness in their own sinful flesh by which they had generated them to mortal life in the present age.[95] Augustine reminded his hearers that the church had always recognized infants so baptized as believers and among the faithful who were not condemned. In contrast, he asserted, the unbaptized had not believed in Christ; the wrath of God remained upon them; they were judged and condemned (John 3:18, 36; 5:29).[96]

By linking Christ exalted on the cross as the source of salvation to the bronze serpent in the desert, and thence to the serpent in the paradise whose sinful power was destroyed by the death of Christ on the cross, Augustine attempted to indicate a sin and punishment that, like venom, was transmitted from Adam to all his offspring through carnal generation. In addition, he established the role of mortality in Christ's flesh as a symbol of the sin that was present in all offspring of Adam. Through the destruction of the sinless flesh in which the sin was symbolically present, that sin could be extinguished in all other mortal flesh.[97]

Augustine then considered and refuted a proposal that in Romans 5:12, Paul had linked the sinfulness of his offspring to that of Adam through imitation rather than generation. He began by observing that, as a method of transmission, imitation would have contrasted Adam, or even Satan (John 8:44; Wis. 2:24–25), as the first sinner, to Abel who was identified as the first just human. Moreover, although Adam had imitated Satan in sinning, he was not described as having sinned in him, as his source and parent. The text's contrast of Adam and Christ showed that Paul intended transmission through generation and regeneration, rather than imitation. His offspring sinned in Adam because they were present in him genetically. They were poisoned in the root of that tree; they did not follow his example, so many years later.[98]

Continuing this line of argument, Augustine contrasted the generation that was performed through the sinful flesh derived from Adam to the regeneration accomplished through spiritual union in Christ. Regeneration in Christ justified the faithful in their spirits but not in their flesh. Baptized Christians generated children by their decayed flesh that—unlike their spirits—had not yet been regenerated and purified. Acting by their sexual union in their sinful flesh, these Christians conceived and brought forth sinners. Then, acting by spiritual union in their justified spirits, they regenerated these same children as faithful Christians in baptism.[99]

June 29, 413

Two days later, June 29, Augustine preached at the celebration of the martyrdoms of Peter and Paul. He promised to focus on the apostles, as was expected of him, but he did find his way back to the sin and death inherited from Adam and Eve.[100] After briefly praising the two saints and remarking on their universal renown, he began to contrast their individual stances toward death. Paul was ready and willing to go to his promised reward (2 Tim. 4:6–8); Peter was reluctant and, as predicted by Christ, would be bound and led to execution (John 21:18–19). Christ himself, however, had recognized and accepted a human reluctance to die in his own prayer to be spared (Matt. 26:39). Death was not to be loved, Augustine concluded, but only tolerated. This horror of dying, indeed, gave value to the apostles' martyrdom.[101]

Working from this divinely approved reluctance to die, Augustine then attacked Caelestius's teachings that human mortality and death were natural rather than the punishment imposed for some original and transmitted sin.[102] Citing the texts of Romans 5:12 and Sirach 25:24 (sin began with a woman; through her we all die, Vulg. 25:33), he argued that God had not created human nature subject to death. Instead, the first parents had attached sin and the death that punished it to the nature they transmitted. Only in Christ was the punishment present without the fault. Its reluctant acceptance by both Christ and Peter indicated that death was derived from sin. Eager though he was to go to Christ, moreover, Paul had preferred that his corruptible body not be stripped away by death. He wanted its mortality to be absorbed and removed by an overlay of life (2 Cor. 5:4), so that he might avoid death and be clothed in immortality (1 Cor. 15:53–56).[103] The abhorrence of death expressed by Christ, Peter, and Paul showed that death was not natural, that it was penal.

Finally, Augustine's interpretation of *the sting of death is sin* (1 Cor. 15:56), marked a change in his thinking about the relation of death to sin. In earlier sermons, he had focused the text on the role of death in inciting to sin—that bodily mortality occasioned or caused sin by sharpening the appetites that sustained bodily life.[104] Beginning in this sermon, he argued that the text identified sin as the cause of death. The "sting of death" brought on death, like a poisoned "cup of death," killed its drinker.[105] In subsequent sermons, he repeated this interpretation of the text and its implications for the derivation of death from a prior sin.[106] The presence of death, then, became an indicator of the presence of sin. In infants, it was a clear sign of the inheritance of both.

July 15, 413

Two weeks later and still in Carthage, Augustine preached on Psalm 51. He attributed the text to David, praying in repentance for having impregnated Bathsheba and caused the death of her husband, Uriah. In confessing himself as conceived in iniquity and nourished in sins, Augustine explained, the psalmist was speaking for the whole human race and referring to the punishment of death and the iniquity that deserved such punishment, both passed down from Adam by generation. Christ alone, he explained, was free of this bondage because he alone was born without sexual intercourse.[107]

Sexual intercourse itself, Augustine hastened to add, was not the cause of sin in infants. Citing Romans 8:10, he reminded his hearers that Christian parents were alive in the spirit but dead in the flesh because of the inherited sin. Their commitment in baptism and in marriage liberated them from guilt but from neither mortality nor the Adamic sin that caused it. Christ alone was mortal without being sinful. The sexual desire operative in intercourse, then, was identified as the culprit in the transmission of morality and sin from parents to child. Once again, Augustine suggested that parents recognized this connection when they rushed their mortal— and especially dying—children to baptism.[108] In this fourth sermon on inherited guilt, Augustine was drawing a set of tight links between the sin of Adam, the mortality that punished it, and the carnal lust that transmitted it through sexual generation.

Subsequent Teaching on the Status on Infants

The consequences of the sin of Adam and Eve were discussed briefly in Augustine's initial preaching against Pelagius, beginning in spring 416. As he had in the sermons delivered during the summer of 413, Augustine identified death as the punishment for the sin of Adam and Eve. Bodily mortality was regarded as the cause of the opposition of the flesh to the mind.[109] As he had earlier, Augustine supported the role of carnal desires in transmitting sin by appeal to Christ's singular freedom from the sin and guilt of Adam. Because his conception was unaffected by lust, the penal mortality to which his mother was subject as a punishment for sin was not passed to her son.[110] Christ's own virginal conception served as a guarantee of his sinlessness, itself a necessary qualification for his work as savior.[111]

Pelagius on the Original Situation of Humanity

According to Augustine's report in his first sermon naming his opponent in the spring of 416, a principle of divine justice and graciousness was foundational to Pelagius's understanding of Christian life.[112] God bestowed the goods of the earthly realm—sunshine and rain—on good and bad alike (Matt. 5:45). In the same way, Pelagius insisted, God created all humans with the free will and power to fulfill the requirements of the moral law and thus to make themselves just. This great gift of self-determination was a basis for Christian gratitude to the creator.[113] A corollary of this principle was the belief that the power to attain moral justice was inalienable: through sinning humans would not and could not deprive themselves of the power to reverse their bad decisions and return to just willing and action.[114]

Augustine's rejection of this principle of autonomous initiative and recovery in good willing and action took different forms, but he consistently upheld the opposite principle: that human good willing and acting never became independent of divine initiative and assistance. God created voluntary beings in a condition of actually loving God and willing justly rather than at rest and responsible for initiating such good loving and choosing. Augustine did recognize that—at least in their original condition—humans were capable of cooperating with the divine gift by sustaining those good operations begun in them by God and by directing their knowledge and love to particular good works. If abandoned (or allowed to lapse), however, human loving of God as the highest and governing good—along with the just willing and action that flowed from that love and to its defining divine goodness—could be neither restored by human action nor reclaimed from God by any human meritorious willing or acting. The good human operations of just willing and action could be restarted only as they had been originally begun, by divine initiative.[115]

Augustine's discovery of this foundational principle may have been among the gifts he received through the presbyter Simplician in Milan, who introduced him to Neoplatonic philosophy.[116] Instead of appealing to a philosophical school, however, Augustine articulated this judgment in religious terms: no creature could make itself better than God made it. To be a just and righteous human, he asserted, was to be better than being human without also possessing and practicing the virtues associated with justice. Against the Pelagians, he concluded that humans were just or righteous only when God initiated and continued to support their just willing and operating by loving and serving God, self, and neighbor in proper order.[117] He identified this divine operation in faithful Christians with the indwelling of the Holy Spirit. Augustine explained that the good willing and action of a creature—like its nature and existence—truly belonged to that creature, although both the power and its operation were also dependent upon a divine causality in the person. As was so evident in the life of Paul, this divine action expanded and did not detract from the willingness and efficacy of the human activity.[118]

When humans failed to maintain the just willing inspired in them by God, they fell from that practice of good willing and action into defective and disordered desires, choices, and activities.[119] Turning from God was like moving away from heat and light: the sinner became cold, dark, and ineffective.[120] In this way, Augustine applied his understanding of evil as a failure in good being and just operation that resulted in further disorder in personal willing and action.[121]

Although Augustine's initial preaching in Carthage against Pelagian ideas was focused on the question of inherited guilt and infant baptism, he soon began to argue that the sin of the first parents and its punishments affected the efforts of adults to fulfill the moral law and of baptized Christians to attain salvation. He had, of course, dealt with these questions extensively in his early scriptural commentaries, particularly on 1 Corinthians, Galatians, and especially Romans. In those and even later writings, however, he had judged that all guilt arose from personal decisions or failures. In commenting on Romans 1:24–25, however, he had identified forms of punishment for sin that led to further sin. The phrase, "sin that is itself the punishment for sin," had been used occasionally.[122] In none of these earlier writings and sermons, however, did he argue that adult humans were subject to forms of involuntary sinning that were not derivative from their own personal decisions. Only after asserting the doctrine of inherited guilt in infants did he open the possibility that adults might be guilty of sinning not only independently of but even contrary to their own, active willing.

Conflict between Spirit and Flesh

During the time between the judgment passed on Caelestius in Carthage in 411 and the arrival of the news of Pelagius's exoneration in Palestine in spring 416, Augustine also had been addressing the situation of adult Christians. In addition to the opinions of Caelestius, he received a letter from Syracuse reporting on similar teaching being offered there and, eventually, a treatise attributed to Pelagius himself, *On Nature*.[123] All of these asserted that humans had the power to fulfill the moral law that God had revealed in the Decalogue and to recover from any violations of it that they committed. Augustine had long disagreed with such teaching, primarily on the basis of the Pauline description of the conflict between spirit and flesh within the human person.[124]

The conflict between what Augustine called the desires of the flesh and those of the spirit was not original to humans; it began only after the transgression in which humans refused to serve God and were handed over to themselves—not to enjoy the autonomy they had sought—but as captives of the devil who had deceived them.[125] He associated the rebellion of the body against the governance of the mind with bodily mortality, itself the punishment for the prior sin of Adam.[126] Its resistance would be removed only when the flesh was put off in death and recovered by the saints, freed of its lusts, in the resurrection of the body in an immortal state.[127] For Christians, baptism removed the iniquity and guilt that was inherited from Adam but not the weakness signaled by the conflict within the person.[128]

In responding to the claims of Caelestius, Pelagius, and their associates, Augustine distinguished a range of states or forms of the conflict between spirit and flesh. Humans given over to the lust resulting from mortality experienced no conflict; they followed fleshly impulses and attractions without knowing or caring about the sinfulness of their desires and actions.[129] In some, however, a mental or spiritual resistance to carnal desire was provoked by the revelation of the moral law and the threat of divine punishment for its violation. That fear of punishment, however, could restrain a person from acting in forbidden ways but did not improve the person's intentions and affections; the person would have preferred to continue performing actions now known to be evil and to escape punishment for doing so.[130] In Augustine's judgment, the restraint of practice guided by such fear remained a form of servitude to sin, although he admitted that it could assist in a transition toward love of justice.[131] A Christian successfully responded to the moral law, however, only when a delight in the justice mandated by the law of God began to oppose the lusts of the flesh.[132] Such a transformation of human desire, however, could be neither initiated nor completed by the human sinner; it was the work of God dwelling within and moving the Christian to love God and desire the good God commanded (Rom. 5:5; 13:10).[133] He considered the divine role in such a transformation so significant that Augustine even described such human delight in goodness as God loving God from within the Christian.[134] Only once a person had begun to love self not as the highest good but in proper subordination to God, he explained, could the human mind and will exercise proper governance over the fleshly powers.[135] Under the influence of the divine Spirit, then, the human person began to offer resistance to the lusts of the flesh that was both effective and morally good. In summary, Augustine compared the human person to a vessel that had been shattered; each person had become an enemy to self and unable to exercise the self-governance proper to created spirits. Sinners, he concluded, were restored to good willing and acting not by their own initiative or the exercise of inalienable natural powers but by the operation of God within them.[136]

Thus, Augustine taught that the impetus of the Holy Spirit received through baptism or restored through repentance moved Christians to loving God and thereby empowered them to oppose and restrain the desires of their mortal flesh (Gal. 5:17; Rom. 6:12–13). God, however, allowed the carnal lusts to remain and to resist the desires of a human spirit operating under the influence of the indwelling divine Spirit. Thus, in addressing baptized Christians in Galatia, Paul had not forbidden them to experience the lusts of the flesh. Instead, he exhorted them to take up the battle against those desires. Though they experienced lust, they must not fulfill and complete it (Gal. 5:16); they must restrain those desires and prevent them from breaking out into action and turning the bodily members into weapons of iniquity (Rom. 6:12–13).[137]

Indeed, the battle for self-control should be pursued into the inner person, where the evil desires could be recognized and rejected as they emerged into consciousness. To illustrate the necessary vigilance, Augustine described the ease and speed with which thought moved first to speech and then into forms of bodily actions.[138] By restraining and frustrating the evil desires, he taught, a Christian could weaken them gradually. When people failed to enter and sustain this struggle, however, the unopposed desires grew strong in the flesh and the love of God was weakened in the mind.[139]

Augustine argued that the faithful Christian was required to live in this state of active conflict between the divinely inspired holy desires in the spirit and the evil lusts derived from the Adamic heritage that were anchored in the mortality of the flesh. Commenting on Romans 7:15–20 and Galatians 5:16–17, he observed that the same person served both the law of sin with the flesh and the law of God with the spirit. Using Paul's texts, he distinguished between the lusts that arose in the person and the decision to act on them. Paul did not forbid the Christians to lust: that was impossible for them: the evil desires arose spontaneously within and belonged to the person. Instead, Paul forbade his readers to satisfy the lusts, to act on them. The desires that spontaneously welled up in consciousness must be allowed to burn out without accomplishing anything in action. By thus refusing to approve them by consent and to satisfy them in action, Christians would dissociate themselves from their own unwanted desires.[140]

In this situation of division between good and evil affections, however, the Christian never fulfilled the justice of the divine law, was never without sin.[141] The perfection of goodness, Augustine explained, required the elimination of evil. To fulfill the Mosaic law was not to lust at all (Exod. 20:17). According to Paul's own testimony in Romans 7:14-19, however, complete goodness was not possible. At most, Christians must oppose and refuse to follow their lusts (Sir. 18:30) and live under the forgiveness of God for their failures.[142]

The continuing presence of evil desires and the fragility of mortal life, Augustine insisted, required that Christians continue to practice repentance for daily sinning, even if they managed to avoid the major failures of consent and action that would separate them from the altar.[143] Christ's parable had criticized the Pharisee (Luke 18:9-14) not because he failed to thank God and claimed his virtue as his own but because in comparing himself to the sinning tax collector, he failed to notice the limits of his goodness. He neglected to beg God for the forgiveness of his sins and an increase in his justice.[144] Augustine found a parallel in Jesus's response to the Pharisee who objected to his allowing the repentant woman to touch him during a dinner party. Christians, he observed, should thank God for the sins that they avoided when God prevented a temptation or intervened in some way to disrupt situations in which they were likely to be led into sin. Divine grace worked in both their hearts and their environment.[145]

This analysis of the human condition, even that of faithful Christians, was clearly set forth in Augustine's initial preaching in response to Pelagian teaching. As the dispute developed, however, Augustine elaborated particular points and carried the argument well beyond the teaching of his earlier commentaries on the Pauline letters. He elaborated the import of the Mosaic law's prohibition of lusting; he distinguished between human and divine justice. Throughout the debate, his interpretation of Romans 7 and Galatians 5, along with parallel texts in 1 Corinthians and Ephesians 3, became increasingly precise.

Lust and the Law

In addition to the natural power of free choice, the Pelagians recognized the moral law as a or even the divine gift facilitating good willing and acting in human beings.[146] In response, Augustine repeated the teaching of his earlier commentaries on Romans and Galatians that the actual role of the revealed moral code was to demonstrate to the descendants of Adam and Eve that they were incapable of fulfilling its precepts and following its prohibitions; the law might thereby lead or drive humans to seek and accept divine forgiveness and assistance. He regularly turned to the anguished cry for liberation from the inability to fulfill the requirements of the law in Romans 7:22–25. He applied the text both to persons who had presumed upon their own powers to fulfill the law and escape the punishments it threatened,[147] and to Christians operating under the influence of the love of God but meeting the resistance of internal desires and external, social pressures.[148] In later sermons dedicated to Romans 7 and Galatians 5, he made similar points about the divine intention in revealing the Mosaic law.[149]

Augustine focused attention on lust by using "you shall not lust," as a summary for the full Decalogue. Although the term appeared in only two of the commandments, he used lust to name and indicate the general category of carnal forces that opposed the Spirit-inspired good intentions of Christians.[150] He referred to and analyzed specific types of evil activity— fornication, drunkenness, avarice—only as illustrations.[151] Even in its defective state, he claimed, the human mind was capable of recognizing that the moral law was good: that it forbade what ought to be forbidden; that it threatened punishment of behavior that ought to be punished. A person born into mortal life might presume that bodily desires were natural and their satisfaction both necessary and good; the moral law provided an important service in correcting that error.[152]

To the sinner, however, the moral law offered neither forgiveness for the guilt of past failures nor future assistance for accomplishing the righteous desiring and acting it defined. The sinner living under the law but without the assistance of the Holy Spirit received no power to withstand the desires arising from bodily mortality and the evil habits already established by repeated sinning. Augustine offered the struggles and failures of a drunkard striving to attain and maintain sobriety as an illustration of the futility of trying to follow and fulfill the law by one's own power.[153] In the absence of a divinely inspired love of the good, moreover, inbred lusts turned the moral law into a powerful weapon that sin directed against the offspring of Adam and Eve.

Augustine remarked that the prohibitions of the moral law provoked the desires of the flesh to greater urgency that subjugated a person.[154] In one who failed to recognize its evil and followed its promptings, lust flowed easily and quietly from desire into action. Once warned of the forbidden evil and threatened by the sanctions of the moral law, however, the sinner might attempt to block that smooth operation. Lust then built up like water behind a dam; its power grew and it became harder to restrain; at last, it broke down the person's resistance; it rushed down with great force, carrying all before it.[155] Awareness of the moral law, moreover, turned the new sin into transgression—violation of a prohibition—that increased its guilt and deprived the now knowing sinner of any claim on divine assistance.[156] In these descriptions of the plight of the sinner oppressed by the law, Augustine explained that Paul may have been looking back on his earlier experience, before accepting the justice offered by Christ.[157] In the absence of the divine gift of delight in the good, then, the law served sin by increasing its force, as Paul concluded in 1 Corinthians 15:56.[158]

Finally, Augustine argued that in asserting the adequacy and effectiveness of natural freedom of will and the guidance of the moral law for attaining justice, the Pelagians were opening a way for pride and self-satisfaction. This had happened with the Jews and the Greeks, both Stoics and Epicureans. To rely on human power, he insisted, was always to fall short of true goodness and to cultivate a false righteousness.[159]

True and False Justice

To build his case against the Pelagian teaching—that true justice must be inspired by a love of God and of the justice embodied in the moral law—Augustine demonstrated the inadequacies of both natural human freedom and the guidance of the Decalogue. He also contrasted the false justice that Paul had achieved and abandoned to that true justice that he later confessed himself unable to fulfill even after decades of striving.

A sermon preached in Carthage after 416, when Augustine began to name Pelagius as misguided, focused on Paul's recounting of his credentials as a Pharisee, justified according to the Mosaic law (Phil. 3:3–9).[160] In preaching on Paul's claims about his earlier achievement, Augustine admitted that a dedicated person might be able to hold evil desires in check so that they did not manifest themselves in observable activity. This form of justice could meet the standards of human judgment that attended only to behavior—since only the divine judge could accurately discern motive and identify interior consent. Even human laws, whose enforcement might be escaped and whose punishments might be evaded, he admitted, could suppress evil performance with some regularity. He illustrated this "just" performance by comparing it to the behavior of a predatory animal or a human criminal that was scared off by guards but soon returned to make further attempts. Since people generally recognized that God's knowledge and power were comprehensive, a threat of divine punishment might be even more effective than that of human enforcers in preventing forbidden actions. So, Augustine admitted that Paul and others might have attained consistent observance of the precepts and prohibitions of the moral law. He argued, however, that such performance did not fulfill the justice specified in the Mosaic law, which forbade evil desires—"you shall not lust"—as well as the actions satisfying them. Performance of the moral law, moreover, could establish an appearance of justice that did not include a true submission to God (Rom. 10:3).[161] Paul had abandoned his righteousness under the law, Augustine claimed, because he realized that it was empty.[162]

In this and contemporary sermons, Augustine made similar criticisms of legal performance that was not inspired by a love of justice and goodness. He argued that using such performance to establish one's standing before God replaced an appreciation of justice with a love of self; it led to pride and to comparing one's own level of observance to that of others.[163]

To the self-justification inspired by either fear of punishment or proud self-aggrandizement, Augustine contrasted the fulfillment of the moral law inspired by a love of divine justice.[164] Paul had accepted this righteousness based on faith in Christ that works through love, when it was offered to him (Rom. 9:30–32).[165] To illustrate the superior power of love—in contrast to fear or pride—in inspiring human behavior, Augustine offered two examples. He contrasted the attitudes of a faithful and an adulterous wife during the absence of their husbands: the one feared that he might not return safely; the other that he might arrive at an inopportune moment.[166] He also pointed to the loyalty that even a criminal might demonstrate toward associates, refusing to implicate them in crimes, even under torture. Christians who shared in the sufferings of Christ showed the power of a different form of love—charity.[167]

The power of lust in the flesh, Augustine argued, had to be countered not by fear of punishment or the desire for a good reputation but by the delight that brought a Christian into agreement with the law of God and found joy in good works.[168] This love of the good commanded by the moral law, he asserted, was inspired in the Christian by the operation of the Holy Spirit (Rom. 5:5).[169] Unlike fear of punishment or even loyalty to companions in evil, such love of God initiated and increased a person's attraction to justice and pleasure in the service of God and neighbor. Such love would move a person to observe the divine law even if God were to promise never to punish a transgressor.[170] Augustine contrasted this indwelling of the Spirit to the visit of rich and overbearing houseguests, people whose requirements and desires gradually took over the house and pushed the host family into the servant quarters. God's operation did not displace the human agent; it expanded the power and range of human good willing and working.[171]

Paul had hastened to add, Augustine noted, that the fullness of such love of God had not yet been conferred upon him (Phil. 3:11–13). The apostle had attained the perfection of a traveler moving toward a promised reward. He lived in hope of gaining possession, secure in the faith that he was on the right road, however slow and difficult his progress.[172] The love of God, rather than the promise or threat of any created reality, then, would sustain the faithful in opposing the lustful desires that remained even after the guilt of the Adamic heritage had been forgiven in baptism. These Christians fought against their lusts not as captives bound in guilt but as free and willing followers of Christ.[173] He urged his listeners to look within themselves and discern the hope and love in which they served God.[174]

The Continuing Struggle of Christian Life

In commentaries on Romans 7:14–25 and Galatians 5:16–18, Augustine explored the situation of Christians who had been freed from inherited guilt in baptism and endowed with charity, though they continued to be burdened by the mortality and lust that had punished the sin of Adam and Eve. The lives of these saints were defined by a conflict between what he described as the natural but opposing components of the human beings—mind and flesh—or as forms of intentional orientation and operation—charity and lust. The first sin had disrupted the hierarchal harmony between the mind and bodily members. Evil desires rooted in the mortality of the flesh continued to function throughout earthly life. The love of God planted in the mind by the gift of the Holy Spirit opposed these lusts, so that Christians could restrain them from moving into action, could refuse to entertain or consent to them when they emerged unbidden in consciousness. The faithful could not, however, prevent them continuing to function in the person and rising into consciousness as prompts toward action.

The texts Romans 7:15 and 7:19, with the parallel in Galatians 5:17, became increasingly prominent in Augustine's preaching against the Pelagian understanding of human autonomy. The statements of inability to accomplish what one willed provided, in his judgment, the direct contradiction necessary to his argument: "I do not do what I will; instead, I do what I hate"; "I do not the good that I will but the evil that I reject"; "you do not do whatever you will."

Augustine seems to have understood lusting—not unlike the love of God and self—as a continuous operation within the person, though often or even usually without gaining direct attention.[175] As he continued to work on these texts, he moved from the description of the conflict within the person to an analysis of Romans 7:14–25 that identified the good that the speaker intended—but was prevented from accomplishing—as the elimination of all lustful activity, including habitual desiring and intermittent prompts for action and bodily performance. In a commentary on Psalm 144 during the early years of the fifth century, Augustine had noted already that a person bothered by the continuing presence of evil desires really wished to be completely free of them. That freedom from all conflict and achievement of peace, he explained, would be attained only with the gift of immortality in the resurrection of the flesh.[176]

As the conflict with Pelagius became intense, Augustine's discussion of the heritage of death and sin provided a different context for the interpretation of Romans 7:22–25—that is, as a desire for the elimination of all lusting. He began that analysis when resuming his exposition of the Gospel of John in 414.[177] A few years later, he remarked that the extinguishing of evil lusts and illicit delights was desired by all the saints.[178] This interpretation seems to have emerged from his emphasis on the active opposition to the operation of evil desiring within the Christians who acted under the inspiration of the Holy Spirit. Anyone truly engaged in that conflict would acknowledge that its objective was peace, a triumph over the enemy rather than a series of successful battles in an unending war.[179] Augustine offered a second argument for his interpretation, based on the analysis of Romans 7:18 and Galatians 5:16 that contrasted willing the good and bringing it to completion. To bring goodness to fullness would mean the elimination of evil, which was the objective of the prohibition of lusting in the Decalogue. This extinction of evil desire was the good condition intended by the writer in the Pauline texts and the speaker they described.[180] The analysis proceeded in stages through which Augustine approached and reached the identification of Paul as describing his own divided condition in the maturity of his life as a Christian and an apostle, in Romans 7:14–25.

When Augustine preached on inherited guilt in infants in 413, he may have already been offering an interpretation of Romans 7 that applied the text to Christians assisted by the gift of charity rather than persons struggling to fulfill the moral law by their natural powers alone. In his sermons, he appealed to his congregation in Hippo to look within themselves and to identify in their own experience the truth of Paul's description. He spoke to them as Christians engaged in the fight who would recognize not only the conflict Paul described but the desire to be set free from the lusts that opposed them.[181] When he mounted his response to the Pelagian pamphlet distributed in Hippo in spring 416, he showed that Paul had provided a description of the difficulty of the Christian's attempt to live justly and well: the grace of God was opposed by the flesh and a person's own evil habits.[182] In attacking the Pelagians by name in a sermon in Carthage in the autumn of that year, Augustine offered himself as a Christian witness to the struggle, as one who prayed for liberation in the words of Romans 7:14–25. Citing the testimony of his own conscience, he admitted that he continued to lust and claimed that he did so in opposition to his deliberate willing and intention. The Pelagians were just wrong, he insisted, in asserting that people accomplished what they really wanted to do. How could they know what went on in another person's consciousness, he asked, citing 1 Corinthians 2:11? Again, he invited his hearers to look within themselves and confirm—as he had—the truth of Paul's description of the Christian's frustrated desire to be free of all lust. He suggested that persons who claimed to experience no involuntary interior conflict either felt no lust or had completely surrendered to its evil desires.[183]

Throughout the controversy over Pelagian teaching on the power of human willing, Augustine continued to assert that his hearers who were engaged in the struggle could verify his interpretation of Paul's description of Christian weakness and inability to accomplish the good they so desired: the elimination of lust. Their groans of recognition when he recalled the power of lust over a sleeping person proved, he said, that they had understood that Paul spoke the truth.[184] Christians might be ashamed of their weakness but not of asking for God's help. This breakthrough raised the further question: Might Paul be speaking not only about other faithful Christians—as he clearly was in Galatians 5:16–17—but about himself as well?

Paul Described Himself

In gradually approaching the judgment that Paul was confessing that he continued to sin even at the zenith of his career as an apostle, Augustine was careful to specify what sort of fault Paul or the person in whose name he was speaking was committing by continuing to lust. He insisted that the speaker was not accusing himself of sinful actions, such as adultery and greed, that he was powerless to restrain. Nor was he consenting to or voluntarily entertaining the evil desires that arose in his mind. These interpretations might be possible if Paul was not applying the statements to himself.[185] Instead, Augustine explained, the person Paul presented in Romans 7:14–25 was subject to a constant attraction or tendency toward forbidden carnal satisfactions that regularly or occasionally gave rise to affective movements in his consciousness.[186] Could Paul have been describing himself?

In a set of sermons on Romans 7 and 8 preached in Carthage between 417 and 419, Augustine began to attribute the sentiments expressed in Romans 7:14–25 to Paul. This great athlete of God, the Christian champion in the battle against the forces of evil, wrote this self-description as a mirror in which all faithful Christians could recognize themselves and take heart to persevere in the fight.[187] The problem that Augustine faced was determining what kind of sin and weakness Paul might be confessing.[188]

As he testified of himself elsewhere, Augustine showed, Paul had not yet attained full perfection in justice. In Philippians 3:12–13, Paul admitted that he did not enjoy the secure perfection of the angels; that, however, might have been the consequence of not yet having received bodily immortality. In 2 Corinthians 4:7, he recognized bodily weakness, describing himself and his addressees as carrying a treasure in fragile vessels. Then in 2 Corinthians 12:7, he admitted that God had to save him from pride through a bodily illness. That was a signal that he did not share angelic justice. He might have properly called himself carnal in Romans 7:14.[189] In Galatians 6:1, Paul warned that even spiritual leaders in the church could be tempted, clearly distinguishing their perfection from that of the holy angels.[190] Paul, then, could have been spiritual in mind but still carnal in his flesh. He could have experienced the temptation arising from lust that he restrained and did not satisfy (Sir. 18:30). He might have longed for the perfect justice of being free of all lusting. That same Paul, then, might well have spoken for himself as well as for other faithful Christians in acknowledging that he was still both captive and free, praying for and looking forward in hope to the liberation worked by the grace of God through Jesus Christ.[191] Still, Augustine was willing to assign the lust to Paul only if it involved weakness and "captivity" in his flesh that his mind, delighting in the law of God, opposed and even ruled.[192]

Augustine concluded that Romans 7:14–25 could be Paul's description of his actual condition. The apostle agreed with the moral law that lust was sinful; he willed not to lust; yet he continued to lust; though he rejected and refrained from satisfying that lust. Lusting was an activity, but it was not the same as consenting to that illicit desire.[193] Yet Augustine judged that these lustful movements that Paul acknowledged were both evil and sinful.

The biblical term that Augustine used to describe this evil was "the law of sin and death." He identified its rebellion as a direct consequence of the mind or spirit's disobedience to God. Paul called it a "law" in the members because it embodied a principle of justice: that a mind refusing obedience to its Lord should lose control over its own bodily servant. By this "law" the mortal body attempted to subjugate the human mind and spirit to the service of the desires arising in its members.[194] This connection between the transgression of the prohibition of the tree of knowledge and the rebellion of the members against the mind that was its just consequence and punishment also meant that Paul had inherited the sinful activity, that he had not cultivated it by prior voluntary decisions.[195] On this basis, Augustine could and did recognize Paul as confessing his sinfulness without lessening his status as a model for Christian living.[196]

Lust and the Faithful Christian

This new interpretation of Romans 7 explained that the evil lusting for whose elimination Paul prayed truly should be attributed to the apostle and to the Christians he addressed in Rome and Galatia. Augustine argued that these affective motions did not derive from or reveal the operation of some alien nature, as the Manichees claimed.[197] Paul clearly acknowledged that both the good and the evil desires operating within him were his own: "I will"; "I reject"; "I hate"; "I do" (Rom. 7:15, 19). In concluding the statement, Paul emphasized his agency: "Therefore, I myself serve the law of God with the mind but the law of sin with the flesh" (Rom. 7:25).[198]

Paul gave clear witness, moreover, that he desired not to escape from his body but to attain the fullness or perfection of life through the healing of his fleshly mortality and corruptibility.[199] In an earlier sermon on the martyrdoms of Peter and Paul, Augustine argued for this interpretation by citing Paul's desire in 2 Corinthians 5:1-4: he would have preferred not to be stripped of his mortal flesh but to put on immortality over it, so that the weakness of his mortality might be absorbed and overcome.[200]

A problem with this interpretation of Romans 7:14-25 might have been that Paul described the evil desires as beyond personal, voluntary control. Initially, Augustine had attributed the power of these desires to the prior willing and behavior of the individual—they were bad habits built by repeated personal choices.[201] Thereafter, Augustine regularly assigned the power of carnal desires to the mortality of the flesh that had been inherited from Adam and Eve.[202] Subsequently, however, he introduced a new interpretation of 1 Corinthians 15:56: sin was the sting that caused death. Although mortality could occasion sinning, sin had first caused mortality.[203] Finally, he began to treat the bodily rebellion against the mind as a punishment imposed directly on Adam and Eve, immediately after and because of their disobedience to God. Their arousal was like the sudden opening of one's eyes rather than the gradual development of bad habits in response to mortality.[204] The descendants of Adam and Eve, therefore, had inherited the illicit desires before they could have done anything voluntarily to bring lusting upon themselves.[205]

Augustine asserted as well that the inability to eliminate the operation of carnal lusting did not excuse a person from responsibility for its evil. The activity itself had been forbidden in the Decalogue.[206] Paul could distance himself from the evil desires within him by intentionally identifying with his mind and cooperating with the gift of God working in him in opposition to the "sin" dwelling in his own flesh (Rom. 7:17).[207] Still, he recognized that he did the lusting that he hated and longed to extinguish. That lust could be redirected into other forms of human sinning—pride and self-aggrandizement—but effectively restrained only through the gift of the Holy Spirit working within the Christian.[208]

Following Paul's self-description in Romans 7:14-25, therefore, Augustine defined the life of the faithful Christian, during the earthly journey from baptismal initiation into Christ to bodily death in Christ, as an ongoing conflict between lust and charity. Neither of these affective orientations and the particular desires to which each gave rise had been initiated by the Christian: the one was transmitted from Adam and Eve by sexual generation; the other was received as a free gift from God through baptism into Christ. The one could be restrained but not extinguished by personal decisions; the other was preserved by its voluntary exercise and by adherence to the unity of Christ's ecclesial body.

The greatest danger for Christians was that either the lusts of the flesh or the pride of the mind would extinguish the light and warmth of the love of God in their spirits.[209] Actually, Augustine noted, mortality and the lust in the flesh had been visited upon Adam and Eve as both a punishment and a remedy for their initial sin of pride. The forbidden lusting continued in the flesh of the faithful in order to protect them from that sin of pride. God willingly forgave the lesser sin because its regular acknowledgement, as illustrated in Romans 7:14–25, prevented the greater one.[210] Repentance and the penitential works of almsgiving, prayer, and fasting were always necessary and appropriate for Christians.[211]

Liberation and Fulfillment

Even after recognizing lust as a distinct and direct punishment for the original human failure, Augustine continued to link it closely to mortality. He stressed the role of the resurrection of the flesh in the liberation of Christians from the conflict between charity and lust. The spirit's victory was achieved by a removal of the aggressive force of death.[212] The overcoming of mortality in the bodily resurrection of the dead was also proof that human flesh was not an alien reality to be escaped but an integral contributor to human perfection that was to be healed and perfected for heavenly life.[213] When the illness of the body was finally cured, the appetites caused by that sickness would pass away and be replaced with those natural to immortal flesh (1 Cor. 15:54–55).[214] Yet the processes of bodily death and resurrection did not secure human perfection. All would indeed be raised (John 5:28–29), but those who had not been set free by the grace of Christ would be returned to a lustful body for the everlasting death of punishment.[215]

Liberation from lust was also explained as the effect of the fullness of the love of God, which had initiated the opposition to lust when the sinner was joined to Christ in baptism. The vision of God, Augustine asserted, would satisfy all human desires; God was so wonderful that, in the divine presence, nothing else could distract a person.[216] Once love of God reached its perfection, it would never grow old or wear out.[217]

In his explanations of inherited sin, Augustine regularly reminded the congregations to which he preached that this Christian understanding of conflict between mind or spirit and the bodily members was not to be confused with the Manichean doctrine that the two natures were alien and naturally opposed to one another.[218] It was the consequence of a weakness or defect introduced into a nature created stronger by God that subsequently was being cured and perfected through Christ. In the resurrection, the flesh would be cured of the mortality and lust that resulted from and punished voluntary failure and revolt. The healed flesh would be joined forever to the soul rather than being replaced by a different kind of body.[219] In Romans 8:6–7, he pointed out, Paul had said not that the nature of the body but that the prudence of the flesh could not be subjected to God.[220]

The Sinning of Adam and Eve

In the sermons directed at Pelagian teaching, Augustine made some adjustments to his explanation of the sinning of Adam and Eve, as well as its consequences and punishments. His increased attention to the role of the Mosaic law may have suggested a new interpretation of the prohibition of the fruit of the tree of knowledge. In Romans 7:11—"sin deceived and killed me through the law"—he found Paul explaining that the moral law had prompted humans to rely on their own judgment and strength to fulfill that law.[221] In applying this text to Adam and Eve, he did not suggest a prior sin that the law exposed but—against the Pelagians—a misuse of the law by relying on one's own strength to fulfill it. The serpent used the command itself to kill Eve by offering an evil interpretation of God's motive in imposing it. Instead of trusting God's guidance, she passed judgment on God and sinned.[222] Adam fell in a similar way, judging that the threat of death was a bluff that God would not enforce. He died not on an audacious quest for life-giving knowledge but by a proud trust in his own good judgment.[223]

Against the Pelagian assertion that death was natural to humans rather than the consequence of sin, Augustine continued to assert that the mortality humans experienced was the consequence of the sin of Adam and Eve.[224] He regularly continued to connect the opposition of the flesh to the mind to that inherited penal mortality.[225] In some instances, however, he attributed the division within the person directly to the original transgression of the divine command. Thus, he explained Paul's term "law of sin" or "the law in the members:" the mind that rebelled against its Lord suffered the rebellion of its bodily servant.[226] The shameful stirring of the genitals that prompted Adam and Eve to cover themselves followed immediately on the sin as its just consequence and punishment.[227] That movement also indicated that the sin would be transmitted to their offspring through sexual intercourse whose performance depended upon the lustful desires in the body rather than being under the direct control of the mind.[228] Through sin both death and lust entered into the human race; it did not remain in the source but passed down with human nature through sexual generation (Rom. 5:12). Each infant was infected by the sin and guilt of Adam and Eve before becoming capable of any personal decisions.[229]

In his commentaries on Romans 7 and Galatians 5, in the autumn of 417 or 419, Augustine piled up arguments to show that inherited lust was not only a disability or defective condition limiting the power of fallen humanity. Evil desiring was an activity, a constant affective operation within each human person who was descended from Adam and Eve. As preceding and independent of a person's voluntary direction, such desires reversed the proper order and hierarchy of being and goodness.[230] This autonomy of carnal desire was sometimes displayed, Augustine asserted and his congregation recognized, in taking over control of bodily action when a person was asleep. As such it should be recognized as sinful.[231] The lust could also be called sin because it arose from sin and punished sin.[232] He identified it as both evil and sinful by its prohibition in the moral law: "you shall not lust."[233] Its division of human affection prevented the fulfillment of the great commandment of full love of God.[234] However, Augustine also understood this inherited lust as a means of humbling the saints and thus a corrective to prevent the more dangerous sin of pride.[235] This too was a legacy of Paul's explanation of the origin of sinning and the divine response in Romans 1:24–28.

In this carnal lust, Augustine seems to have identified a human activity corresponding to the inherited sin, the carrier of guilt, that was transmitted by carnal generation from Adam and Eve to all their descendants. As its only exception, the virginally conceived Christ proved the general rule.[236] Perhaps without ever intending to do so, Augustine seems to have found in the lust operative and replicating itself in sexual generation an explanation of the transmission of the Adamic heritage of sin and death.

Conclusion

Unlike most of the essays in this volume, this study of the human condition in Augustine's preaching has revealed significant changes over time in his teaching. A brief summary of these transitions and their implications for the Christian life will be useful.

The Original Sinning

Augustine was always careful to locate the origin of the first sin of humanity in the mind rather than the body and its fleshly appetites. In his first attempt to describe the sin of the first humans, he focused on a mental failure to control an operation of the sensual faculties. In the second decade of his ministry, he identified the mental vice of cupidity or avarice as the source of the disobedience in bodily action. In that period, he also began to interpret the Genesis text through Paul's analysis in Romans 1:18–32 that focused on a sin of pride in which the creatures claimed divine gifts as their own achievement. In his treatises, Augustine continued to develop this understanding of the original sin as an act of pride that preceded the transgression of the divine prohibition and was revealed by its violation. As Paul taught in Romans 7, God imposed moral laws in order to provoke and reveal a hidden sinfulness, so that sinners might repent and seek divine assistance for obedient practice.

In the third decade of his ministry, in preaching against the Pelagians, Augustine again affirmed this connection between the interpretations of the paradisal prohibition and the Mosaic Law. The Decalogue's condemnation of the lust transmitted as the punishment for the original sin forced even the most advanced among the Christian faithful to recognize their sinfulness and place their trust in the divine mercy that would deliver them from the Adamic "body of this death" (Rom. 7:24–25).

The Consequences of the Original Sinning

Like his teaching on the sin of the first humans, Augustine's understanding of its punishment and consequences for their offspring evolved during his preaching ministry. In his early treatises and commentaries on the Pauline letters, he identified bodily mortality as the threatened and imposed punishment for the sin that affected all of humanity. Thereafter, he regularly associated the consequent bodily weakness and the fear of death as the root of humanity's moral disability. Infants born mortal advanced slowly in both understanding and willing; before they became personally responsible, they established patterns of behavior that satisfied the urgent bodily appetites that sustained their fragile lives. Even after they were capable of reflecting on and judging their decisions and actions, they established habits that would later result in their regular moral failures. Augustine was unwilling to affirm the condemnation of infants who died unbaptized. He had no such hesitations in recognizing the universality of human moral failure among adolescents and adults. Sinfulness and guilt became universal in the line of Adam and Eve.

When he began to preach about original sin, in the second decade of his ministry, Augustine continued his focus on mortality as the root of human moral disability. Three important advances in his explanation were introduced during this first decade of the fifth century. First, Augustine began to identify a "law of sin," distinct from the customs developed from penal mortality. This rebellion of the sensual powers and the bodily members against the governance of the mind was a just punishment imposed on the human mind in response to its own rebellion against the divine master. The disorder was most evident in the movement of the genital organs independently of direct personal control that followed immediately upon the transgression. Second, Augustine argued that the whole of humanity was concentrated in the first generating couple; all their offspring were implicated in their sin and justly suffered its punishments and consequences. Third, he occasionally suggested that these disordered desires and operations were both punishments for sin and sinful. Their guilt was transmitted from Adam and Eve to their offspring.

In his encounter with Pelagius and Caelestius in the third decade of his ministry, Augustine quickly expanded his explanations of the consequences of the first sin. First, he changed his interpretation of 1 Corinthians 15:56—"the sting of death is sin"—that had traced universal human sinning to penal mortality. Sin caused death rather than only following from it. Death thereby became an indicator of the presence of a sin and guilt that deserved condemnation, in both infants and adults. In preaching on Romans 7–8, he asserted that the sinful lust operative in sexual generation served as the mechanism for the transmission of sin and guilt to the descendants of Adam and Eve. The virginal conception of the Savior became the exception that proved the rule: Christ voluntarily inherited his mother's mortality but not the lust and sin that caused it in those he came to save.

Living in the Shadow of Original Sin

Augustine's teaching on the condition of Christians—burdened by the punishments of the sin common to all the descendants of Adam and Eve and supported by the redemptive work of Christ and the gift of the Holy Spirit—brought him to an understanding of the Christian life that departed radically from the consensus on human autonomy and divine assistance that he had originally shared with most other Christian teachers of that time. That change was accepted among his episcopal colleagues in Africa and gradually became the standard, albeit uneasy, position of Western Christianity.

By a careful reading of the Pauline letters, Augustine challenged the consensus on the role of the moral law. The first function of the revealed moral law was not to guide human freedom but to unmask human sinfulness—both inherited and personally committed. Through the law, God moved a self-reliant and self-satisfied sinner toward repentance, reliance on divine forgiveness and assistance for improved moral performance.

The revealed moral law branded the independent sensual desires that arose and persisted in a Christian as sinful, even though they were involuntary and could not be expunged. Baptism removed—or more accurately suspended—that guilt as long as the Christian resisted, withheld approval, and prevented the desires from breaking out into action. By persistent and vigilant effort, Christians could mitigate and weaken their inbred cupidity, but they could not eradicate it, as the Decalogue required. Full liberation from this sin would be achieved only in the purification of their bodies through death and resurrection. In this period, Augustine attributed Romans 7:14–25 to Paul describing the anguished conflict he and others experienced as new Christians.

In responding to the Pelagian understanding of the inalienable endowments of human nature, Augustine articulated a foundational principle: that a creature's moral willing and action depended on a continual divine operation within the person that initiated a loving of God as the highest good, which, in turn, inspired and guided an individual's good choices and actions. In the absence of this type of love of God, he explained, a person loved self as the primary good and loved all other goods (including God and neighbor) for the sake of self. Such a person might avoid performing forbidden actions because of a fear of threatened divine punishment but would actually prefer to sin and escape punishment. Such a desire was itself unjust, Augustine observed.

The first humans were created loving God for God's sake but failed to maintain that love and proved susceptible to the demonic suggestion that God was deceiving them and preventing them from sharing divine wisdom. Christ, in contrast, practiced that full love of God (humanly), broke the power of sin, and restored it to Christians by the gift of the Holy Spirit. The loving of God that the Spirit's indwelling inspired and sustained in Christians extended to a delight in the good works God commanded. By this love, Christians both resisted the attraction of inherited or personally developed evil desires and pursued the good works God commanded. A Christian could still fail to cooperate with the Spirit's operation, but engagement in the daily struggle against lust that was recognized by Paul as a mature Christian speaking in Romans 7:14–25 protected the person from the deadly sin of self-righteous pride. Only in heaven, when the immortal body was purified of lusts and the person filled with the knowledge and love of God, "face-to-face," was the Christian secure from failure.

In his preaching, Augustine helped his hearers to identify this conflict between delight in good and inherited evil desires in their own hearts and minds, along with their longing to be freed from the latter and attain the fullness of the former. The range of human autonomy, he taught, was narrowed by the persistent evil desires inherited from Adam on one side and the divine gift of love of God bestowed by Christ on the other side. Both were voluntary, Augustine insisted, but neither was initiated by a Christian's free choice.

Chapter Ten

CHRIST AND THE CHURCH

T HE DEVELOPMENT OF AUGUSTINE'S UNDERSTANDING of the Savior, as a divine and human individual and as head and body in the Whole Christ, was based on an already traditional interpretation of scripture that focused on the person to whom a passage referred, as subject or object of predication. As has been seen in the initial chapter of this study, Christians found the Old Testament texts, especially in the Psalms, referring to Christ in various roles and situations. This technique led toward a doctrine of the Savior as one person living, speaking, and acting simultaneously in both divine and human ways.

As has been seen in the subsequent chapters, Augustine applied this technique to a third form of activity, in which the Savior acted in and through the church and individual Christians. In this way, he identified not one but two closely related "persons." First, the Savior was at once Son of God and Son of Man. The second person or subject, whom Augustine called "the Whole Christ," joined the Savior to the Christian community as its head to a (social) body. In careful, even grammatical analysis, Augustine found that the "rules" of scriptural usage were somewhat different for the Savior as an individual than for the Whole Christ. Both human and divine attributes and operations could be assigned to the Savior. The Savior could speak and act in personal unity with the church and even individual Christians, as he did most dramatically in praying in the garden and on the cross. He was more circumspect in attributing to the Savior statements or actions of either the church as a whole and of individual Christians, particularly in the binding and loosening of sins. Still, in Augustine's teaching, Christ and the church were personally and inseparably united.

To distinguish these two persons in the current chapter, the name "Savior" will be used for the single individual who was Son of God and Son of

Man. The term "Whole Christ," or occasionally "Christ," will be used to designate the reality that included both that human-divine individual and the Christians who were personally united to form the body of the church that the Savior served as head.

In its five sections, this chapter will detail Augustine's arguments for the existence of each of these two personal unions, the ways in which each of these two persons operated in the process of salvation, and, finally, the relation between the Word and the Holy Spirit in the constitution and operation of these two, overlapping persons—the Savior and the Whole Christ. This presentation will serve as a unifying summary of this study of the theological doctrines that Augustine developed in his preaching.

The Union of Divine and Human in the Savior

Augustine's affirmation of the union of divine and human in the Savior was in accord with the standards that the Council of Chalcedon adopted twenty-one years after his death—a union of one person in two natures without the mixing or separation of divine and human.[1] In the absence of the more technical terminology that would be developed in the debates before and after that council, Augustine found ways to describe the unity of person and duality of nature. He affirmed that the Son of God had taken the initiative in joining a full human being to himself.[2] The union, moreover, was accomplished in the first moment of the human's existence, prior to every human personal willing and action that might have earned that privileged relationship.[3] Augustine described the Savior as "the Son of God having a man"—a man who never existed separately—and, thereby, was possessed of both a human soul and body, in addition to the divinity shared with the Father and the Holy Spirit.[4] Thus, the Savior was the joining of the Word of God to a united human soul and body; other humans were the unity of a soul and a body.[5] In such personal unions, he explained, the properties and actions of each component were assigned to one and the same person. In the Savior's case that person could be titled as either Son of God or Son of Man.[6] In particular, Augustine regularly applied divine titles and attributed divine activities to the Savior, as one and the same subject: the Savior, even before his birth from Mary, had spoken of himself in the Old Testament prophets.[7] This practice of assigning both divine and human properties and operations to a single subject, named as either Word or Savior, anticipated the distinctive practice of shared attributes worked out more fully in the debates following the Council of Chalcedon in 451 CE.

Augustine explored the relationship between the two—divine and human—roles of the Savior in his exposition of scriptural texts. Perhaps the most important of these analyses exploited a theme of time and place repeated in the Gospel of John. In his puzzling exchange with Nicodemus, Jesus said, "No one ascends into heaven except the one who descends from heaven, the Son of Man who is in heaven"[8] (John 3:13). Augustine assumed that the title "Son of Man" belonged to the Word because of birth from Mary in flesh she had derived from Adam.[9] Thus, the Savior could identify himself to Nicodemus as the Word of God who had descended from heaven to become human but who had not yet ascended into heaven in that human reality. Further, in saying—while living on earth—that the Son of Man was simultaneously in heaven, the Savior was claiming for himself a kind of multiple or even universal presence that was not within his competence solely as human.[10] In other sermons, Augustine made this point clearer: the Savior's existence as Son of Man began on earth; the personal unity justified the Savior's claim to share the Word's prior descent to earth and uninterrupted heavenly residence.[11] In these same expositions, moreover, Augustine explained that the Son of Man ascended as human, and thereby was joined in that ascent by the Christians who were united to him as members of his churchly body.[12]

In two later expositions of John's Gospel, Augustine repeated these interpretations. In John 6:63, Christ addressed the disciples who were puzzled by the command to eat of his life-giving flesh. Once they had seen "the Son of Man ascend where he was before," he told them, they would grasp that he was not to be butchered and consumed.[13] A little later in this sermon series, Augustine made similar observations about John 7:33–34, where Jesus asserted that he would return soon to "him who sent me" and that the disciples would be unable to find him because, "where I am you cannot come." Again, Augustine observed that in saying, "where I am," rather than, "where I will be then," the Savior was speaking on earth and claiming to be simultaneously in heaven—not only that he would be there later, after the ascension.[14] Thus, he concluded that when speaking in a human way, when referring to himself by a title derived from his assumed humanity—and thus one that originated in time—the Savior claimed for himself a divine independence of temporal and spatial limitations. The Savior said that he was in heaven both before and while he was on earth. Augustine's careful analysis of the Latin gospel text's use of the present tense of the verbs showed that the Savior was a single person who was simultaneously divine and human—one who could make human claims to the "past, present, and future" existence belonging to him in his divine reality.

Finally, Augustine used the descriptive phrase "two in one flesh" (Gen. 2:24; Eph. 5:31–32; Matt. 19:6) to characterize the union of the Word of God to the human conceived by Mary.[15] Usually, as shall be seen next, he applied this phrase to the union of the Savior and the church, as head and body.[16] Sometimes he added Isaiah 61:10, which used the titles bride and groom for the same person.[17] Though they seemed to be two, he explained, spouses were really one, and thereby represented the relation between the Savior and his churchly body (1 Cor. 12:27).[18]

Although this scriptural usage allowed the identification of two realities as a single "person," speaker, or actor, it was clearly different from the substantial or "hypostatic" understanding of the union that adopted and adapted philosophically explanatory concepts and would emerge in the debates and decisions that followed the decree of the Council of Chalcedon.[19] In the case of the Savior himself, Augustine had worked around this difficulty by insisting that the Son of Man had been joined to the Word from the first moment of his existence.* This usage eliminated not only a separate existence but all human willing or acting of the Savior that could be construed as independent of, and thereby unattributable to, the person identified as the divine Word.[20]

The Union between Christ and the Church

Augustine extended the union between divine and human in the Savior to a personal union between the Savior and the church, composed of the faithful Christians who were formed into the body which the Savior served as head. In this, he differed significantly from the theologians involved in the subsequent debates.

---

*The possibility of a prior, natural existence of the soul of Jesus never became part of Augustine's attempt to account for the sinful and penal condition with which humans entered earthly life. For Robert J. O'Connell's investigations of that doctrine, see St. Augustine's Early Theory of Man, A.D. 386–391 (Cambridge: Harvard University Press, 1968) and The Origin of the Soul in St. Augustine's Later Works (New York: Fordham University Press, 1987).

As in his consideration of the joining of divine and human in the Savior, Augustine established the existence of this personal union between the Savior and Christians through the interpretation of the scriptures. He provided a succinct summary of his practice in the opening of his exposition of Psalm 63.[21] The psalms were spoken in the one voice of the Whole Christ, by the divine and human head and by the human members of his churchly body. The divine Word was head of the church through a personal union to the human Son of Man. That human reality assumed by the Word of God was the firstfruits or foundation of the churchly body, into which Christians were joined. Had the Savior taken only a human soul and not a human body, Augustine contended, Christians would not be united to him as his members in a social body that shared his identity.[22] That churchly body was the communion of faithful Christians in the universal church. However, the social body was also unlimited in both geography and time. The body of Christ extended beyond Africa—contrary to Donatist claims*—and to all the faithful among humans from the first created to the last born (and baptized) before the return of Jesus in glory.[23]

In his expositions of the Psalms, then, Augustine used the term "Christ" for both the one person of the Son of God/Son of Man (the Savior) and for the personal union of the Savior, as head, with the saints who were gathered in the church as his "bodily" members. He distinguished these two when necessary for clarity, by adding a qualifier to identify the divine-human-churchly reality as the Whole Christ.[24]

This second personal union (the Whole Christ) differed in many ways from the personal union that constituted the Savior. Augustine recognized that, unlike the human reality in the Savior, the bodily members existed as many individuals, indeed as alienated sinners before being joined to Christ in the church by conversion and baptism. Thereafter, they continued as repentant and repenting sinners throughout their earthly lives. Their guilt and imperfections were not shared with the Savior, though he bore their penal sufferings and death.[25] The attributes and operations belonging to the Word of God, even those shared with the Savior, were neither assigned nor denied systematically to the church or to individual Christians as its members. Instead, Augustine applied these properties and actions in a

* This breakaway Christian group in Africa claimed that during and after the Diocletian persecution, all other Christians had become unfaithful to Christ by either denying Christ or tolerating Christians who did in their eucharistic communion.

variety of ways, using particular scriptural passages. The sinless head, for example, voluntarily shared the mortality and suffering of his members, but the members did not share all the perfections of their divine head: he was creator and mediator; they were not.[26] As shall be seen below, however, Augustine argued that in the Whole Christ, the body and its members—sometimes as a whole, sometimes as individuals—participated in the head's divine and human powers and operations in his redemptive and sanctifying mission, especially in forgiving sins, giving the Holy Spirit, offering sacrifice, and, occasionally, working miracles.[27]

As he had in discussing the personal unity of divine and human in the Savior, Augustine clarified the union of the Savior and the saved in the Whole Christ in the process of interpreting a series of scriptural passages. In 1 Corinthians 12:12, Paul compared the unity of diverse members in the human body to the Whole Christ: "Just as the body is one and has many members, and all the members of the body, though many, are one body, so it is with Christ." Paul did not say, Augustine observed, "so it is with Christ and the church," which would have restricted the proper name of Christ to the head—the Savior—rather than extending it to the whole, the unity of head and members. Christ, then, was to be understood as one body in all the members, including the head. To confirm this interpretation, Augustine appealed to Acts 9:4, in which the risen Savior, already safely in heaven, protested that he was being persecuted by Paul. Within the Whole Christ, he explained, the head continued to suffer the attacks directed at other members who were still on earth.[28] Speaking from the perspective of a Christian member of the body, Paul later asserted that the sufferings in his own flesh continued to fill up those of Christ (Col. 1:24). These two scriptural statements could be true only if the flesh of individual Christians was joined into the body that was the Whole Christ, whose head and members shared the same sufferings.[29]

Similarly, Augustine noted Paul's assertion that the individual members had suffered and been glorified in their head in Colossians 2:20, "you died with Christ," and Romans 6:6, "our old self was crucified with him so that the body of sin might be destroyed." He then added that Christians had not only died on the cross and risen with Christ (Col. 3:1), but that Christ continued to die and rise in them. The bodily members participated in the sufferings of the head, and the head suffered in the bodily members; head and members shared the same trials and triumphs.[30] In these interpretations, Augustine followed Paul in crossing temporal boundaries and reversing historical sequence just as he had in interpreting the Gospel of

John (3:13; 6:63; 7:33–34).[31] Christians participated in the events of Christ's death and resurrection even before their individual births, baptisms, and deaths. As the Son of Man was in heaven before and during his earthly life, so the ascended Savior continued to suffer and triumph on earth in his church.

In other scriptural texts, Augustine found attributes and operations of the Savior that were shared with Christians as a body rather than as individuals. In writing to the Galatians, Paul read the collective noun "seed" that God had used in promises to Abraham (Gen. 12:7) as a personal singular and identified the Savior as that seed (Gal. 3:16). Paul then proceeded to argue that, in baptism, Christians were joined into that identity of the Savior: they were no longer categorized by ethnic, gender, or social class identifiers derived from natural birth and family relations. The Whole Christ was thereby Abraham's seed; the members shared in the earlier promise and, like their head, were not bound by the later Mosaic law (Gal. 3:26–29).[32] In commenting on Psalm 89:4–5, Augustine made a similar claim that Christians participated in the Davidic promise of an everlasting reign; it was fulfilled not only through the Savior—who was heir to David by birth— but in the faithful Christians who were his members.[33]

In his practice of interpreting the Psalms by applying them to Christ, Augustine used all elements of the union: the divine Word of God, the human son of Mary, and the faithful Christians both as individuals and as a collective body. Particularly in handling the relation between head and members, he recognized ambiguity. Although he insisted that the Savior and the church were in one flesh and one voice, Augustine regularly described the source or basis for a particular statement by or about that unity by distinguishing the head from other members of the body. For example, any scriptural statement in which the speaker confessed sin must be assigned primarily to the Christians as members; the sinless head—the Savior—shared it only through his love for and identification with those members. In this way, as 2 Corinthians 5:21 read, "He [God] made him [Christ] who knew no sin to be sin for our sake."[34] This type of distinction within the Whole Christ paralleled the common practice of recognizing that the Savior suffered and died in his humanity rather than his divinity, even while insisting that the only begotten Son of God died for the salvation of humans.[35]

Still, Augustine looked for opportunities to apply scriptural texts to the Whole Christ, as both head and members. Thus, "My soul thirsts for you, God," could describe the longing of both the Savior and the Christians.[36]

"My soul is glued to you; your right hand lifted me up," could be read as the words of the Savior spoken either for himself or in his members and also of his bodily members speaking to God for themselves or in their head, because he and they each suffered persecution from the agents of Satan.[37] As has been seen above, Augustine occasionally applied the bridal imagery to the union of the Word and the human as one Christ or Savior.[38] More regularly, he used it for the identity of head and members in the Whole Christ.[39] Though they seemed to be distinct, in Genesis 2:24 and Ephesians 5:22–32, Christ and Christians were proclaimed to be one flesh.[40]

Augustine was conscious of significant differences between the union of divine and human in the Savior and the union of head and members in the Whole Christ. In comparing the various types of unity, Augustine identified Father and Son as one in substance, and then the Son—in the form of a servant—as one in nature with humans. Christ and Christians were together the seed of Abraham.[41] The Savior who was head of the church could be referred to in the terms of John 1:1–3—in the beginning God with God, through whom all things were made—because the Son of Man was personally united to the Word of God. Those same terms could not, however, be extended to Christians—individually or corporately— who were joined into the Savior as his members. None of them ever said, "I and the Father are one," as the Savior did (John 10:30).[42] As has been seen above, Augustine affirmed—with John 3:13 and 6:63—that the Son of Man was in heaven because of the personal union with the Word of God, even before his ascension. In contrast, he was more cautious in interpreting the statements of Colossians 3:1 that Christians had died and risen with Christ, who was already seated in heaven, where their life was hidden and would appear with him.[43] He regularly qualified that presence: Christians were in heaven in faith, hope, and love (but not yet in resurrected bodies).[44]

Augustine also was freer in speaking of the union of the head to the body of the Whole Christ than to its individual members. When he focused on the church as a united whole, he was particularly attentive to the divine operations that were also attributed to the Holy Spirit. Thus, he compared the Holy Spirit's role as the bond of unity within the Trinity to the Spirit's mission as the gift of life and love by which the Christians were joined together to become the body of Christ.[45] As the soul of a living human coordinated the activities of its diverse organs and faculties, so the Holy Spirit, through the gift of charity, inspired and formed individual Christians into the church, the body of Christ.[46] That love made many souls to be one soul, many individuals to become one heart and one mind—a single dwelling place for God.[47] Thus, the body of Christ lived by the Spirit of Christ.[48] Augustine did not, however, attribute to the church the heavenly existence proper to the Word and the Spirit. The church did not remain in and descend from heaven, as the Son of Man did according to John 3:13 and 6:63.[49] The human body and soul of the Savior, and those of his members were rooted in earthly life and, as such, were essential to the constitution of the church and thus of the Whole Christ.[50]

In order to specify further Augustine's understanding of these two forms of personal union—Word/man and Savior/church—a survey of the way he applied and used them to explain the divine and human operations that established the process of salvation will be necessary. The next two sections, then, will summarize much of what has been developed in the preceding chapters on the Savior and his relationship to the saved. Only then can the two personal unions be compared and, perhaps, understood in greater detail.

THE OPERATION OF DIVINE AND HUMAN IN THE SAVIOR'S WORK

The understanding of a personal union between divine and human in Christ enabled ancient Christian teachers to interpret otherwise puzzling scriptural statements as referring to the Savior. An earlier example would be the presence of the Son of Man in heaven prior to his conception by Mary and simultaneous with his subsequent earthly life and work.[51] All the statements in the hymn in Philippians 2:6–11 also could be attributed to the same individual existing in a heavenly condition, then in the form of a slave, then humbled unto death as human, and then exalted above all creation as Lord. No less importantly, as seen already, this understanding of the person of the Savior explained how Christians were raised to heavenly life by ascending in union with the one who had descended.[52]

This section will undertake a review of Augustine's understanding of the personal union of divine and human in the Savior in his explanation of the economy of salvation.

Christ as Mediator

Augustine described a mediator as an agent functioning between two distinct and different parties, acting either to unite or to separate them. His interest focused on God and humanity. Existing between them, the Savior was a mediator of reconciliation and union; Satan, an agent of division and separation. As the uniting mediator, the Savior was identified with both God and humans. He was, at once, fully divine and fully human.[53] As human alone or divine alone, he could not have served as a mediator of union.[54]

Augustine noted that the key biblical text, "There is one God; there is also one mediator between God and humans, Christ Jesus, himself human" (1 Tim. 2:5), affirmed the unity of God and the humanity of the mediator. His role as mediator, Augustine explained, required that he be and remain divine in the full sense of that term rather than a secondary, semidivine being.[55] By lacking or abandoning a divine status in order to "become flesh," the Word would have been disqualified as a mediator.[56]

No less important to Augustine was the full humanity of the mediator, so clearly affirmed in 1 Timothy 2:5, as "Christ Jesus, himself human."[57] In order to function as mediator, the Word of God had to take on the human reality that was not natural to one equal to the Father.[58] By receiving a human body and soul from the Virgin and becoming her son, the Son of God assumed the mediator's middle position; the Savior made the higher accessible to the lower; in his own person, he bestowed divine qualities and powers upon humanity.[59] Augustine considered the mediator's dual role in establishing both a bridge between diverse natures and an intentional union among persons.

Since humans could not rise up to God by their own power, God had descended to them by becoming human. The Savior came to humans without leaving the Father and returned to the Father without leaving humans.[60] He also overcame the moral divide that blocked humanity's access to God. To remove that obstacle of sin and guilt, the Word retained divine justice and sanctified his humanity so that he was, even as human, free of all sin.[61]

The Savior's work as mediator was also distinguished by the ontological and the moral effects he achieved. As was his practice, Augustine communicated philosophical ideas and judgments through scriptural narratives and images. He regularly cited John 3:13, "no one ascends to heaven except the one who descends from heaven," as the basis of the belief that the Savior could introduce humans into the divine realm by joining them into himself, as members of his social or ecclesial body. In his commentary on the Gospel of John, Augustine identified an essential function of baptism as the incorporation of Christians into that churchly extension of the Savior's human body, so that they would ascend not only with but also as him.[62]

In other sermons, Augustine added that Christians could understand and follow the Savior to God. He made himself the door that opened into the sheepfold and not, as other pastors, only the one who then led the flock through it.[63]

As moral mediator, the Savior removed the obstacle of sin that separated humans from God. He maintained himself free of all traces of sin and guilt that would have separated him from God and disabled him as a mediator.[64] By his sacrifice, as has been seen above, he removed the guilt that blocked others' access to God; the shedding of his blood erased the judgment passed on sinners and reconciled them to God.[65] Augustine explained that mortality was a punishment for sin but not itself sinful. Because the Savior accepted human mortality without sin, because he died voluntarily and not under condemnation, he destroyed death rather than being overcome by it. Because he shared human flesh—unlike the demons—he could mediate to other humans the bodily immortality that, as a sinless creature, was rightfully his own.[66] The Savior created humanity as God and re-created it as human.[67] He lifted the prostrate who were unable to help themselves; he illumined believers so that they might understand; he corrected, purified, and inspired human willing.[68]

The Savior was mediator not only in his being and his perfect justice but as intercessor and priest. In a long New Year's Day sermon Augustine attacked both the Roman traditional religion and the ritualized forms of intellectual ascent to the divine. He assigned both systems to the deceits of the devil, who functioned as a false mediator and attempted to block humans' access to God. Augustine then turned his attention to the claim that bishops served as mediators between God and their people.[69] In this and other sermons, Augustine explained that the Savior, in a role proper to his humanity, had prayed for his disciples on earth and continued to do so in heaven.[70] In the figure of the Savior praying on the mountain while his disciples were making a stormy, night crossing of the Sea of Galilee, Augustine identified a foreshadowing of his continuing intercession for the church, at the right hand of God.[71] He appealed also to the text of 1 John 2:1–2 that names Jesus Christ as the advocate for sinners, noting that the apostolic writer had not claimed such a role for himself.[72]

Continuing this line of interpretation, Augustine then turned to the priestly role peculiar to the Savior, which had been foreshadowed by the Israelite priesthood in two specific provisions. The freedom from bodily blemish required of the ancient priests was an indicator of the perfect sinlessness of the Savior as sole mediator.[73] Similarly, the Israelite high priest's role (as the intercessor for whom no other person interceded) had foreshadowed the mediator's office that belonged to the Savior alone, who exercised it continuously in heaven.[74] As head, Christ shared that intercessory role with his body, the church, whose members prayed for one another under his headship.[75] The priestly status of the clergy, he argued, derived from that of Christ not through an episcopal succession (as Cyprian had claimed) but through the faithful who formed the body of the Whole Christ, the church that elected the clergy to serve it as overseers and governors.[76]

The Word Exercised Divine Power Humanly as the Savior

In his early commentaries on the Gospel of John (406–7), Augustine argued that the Savior retained to himself the power to baptize with the Holy Spirit and did not transfer it to his disciples. In baptisms performed by the apostles acting as his agents, the Savior's own power and holiness guaranteed the efficacy of the ritual they performed in conferring the sacrament. Thus, he concluded, converts need not fear that the sinfulness of the bishop who received them into the church might jeopardize their salvation.[77] The Savior himself was operating with power that could not fail when a human minister acted as his agent to perform the sacramental ritual of baptism. As shall be seen shortly, Augustine qualified this explanation of the role of faithful Christians in the sanctifying operation of the ritual.

Returning to his commentary on the Gospel of John about 414, Augustine distinguished the divine powers that the Savior mediated to humans from those he exercised as human operations. In commenting on John 5:25–28, on the roles of the Father and Son in giving life to the dead, he explained the resurrection of the mind differently than that of the body. He assigned the property of "having life in oneself" to the divine nature that the Son shared with the Father. Giving life to the souls of humans depended on this power. It was exercised by the Savior, as Son of God, even during his earthly ministry, only for those who had responded positively to him.[78] In contrast, the resurrection of the body and the judgment of all humans were assigned by the Father to the Savior as Son of Man.[79] These operations required that the Savior act in a human way so that he could be perceived by both the just and the unjust. This was the reason, Augustine explained, that the Father "judged no one but gave all judgment to the Son" (John 5:22), "because he is the Son of Man" (5:27).[80] He explained that these events belonged to the Savior, using both his divine and human powers.[81] As shall be seen below, Augustine also argued that these powers were conferred upon the Whole Christ and shared by members of the Savior's ecclesial body.[82]

In a sermon preached perhaps three years later but not in the series on the Gospel of John, Augustine seems to have modified and developed his approach to the Savior's exercise and sharing of divine power.[83] During his earthly ministry, the Savior possessed, exercised, and transferred to his disciples the power to cast out demons. In Matthew 12:22–29 and Luke 11:14–22, opponents accused him of being an agent of Satan in these exorcisms. The Savior defended himself against this charge by comparing his own exorcisms to those being performed by others whom the texts name as "your sons."[84] Augustine identified these exorcists as the Savior's current disciples and the other Jews who would become faithful disciples in the future. By his own righteousness, the Savior had bound Satan and was able to liberate the children of Adam whom he had taken captive. He empowered his disciples to do the same for others through their own faith in him.[85] Later in the sermon, Augustine argued that the Savior exercised the same power, attributed to the Holy Spirit, to forgive sins. After his resurrection, the Savior had conferred that same Holy Spirit and this power of forgiving sins upon his disciples (John 20:22–23).[86]

Addressing the principal issue to which the sermon was directed, Augustine then explained why the sin of blasphemy against the Holy Spirit could not be forgiven (Mark 3:29; Luke 12:10). He argued that sins were forgiven through the Holy Spirit's indwelling and causing charity—love of God and neighbor—to operate in the Christian. To sin directly against the Spirit, then, was to reject this charity and thus lose access to forgiveness of this blasphemy, as well as all other sins.[87] In developing this point, he argued that forgiving sins was the work not only of the Holy Spirit but of the Father (Matt. 6:9, 12, 14) and of the incarnate Son (Matt. 9:6; Mark 2:10; Luke 5:24).[88]

The operation was shared by the three divine persons and involved the human activity of the Savior. Augustine turned to an analysis of the Savior's walking across the sea to illustrate the distinct divine and human causal roles in the process of forgiveness. The Father, Son, and Spirit were equally involved in performing the miracle of keeping the Savior's body above the water; the incarnate Son, who alone took flesh and had feet with which to touch the waves, did the walking.[89] Thus, he explained forgiving sins and the expulsion of demons as at once divinely supported human operations and humanly mediated divine operations. The human activity of Christ liberating and extending pardon to particular sinners was integral to the efficacy of the divine operation. In the same way, the Spirit spoke in a martyr by moving the Christian to witness to Christ (Matt. 10:20). Similarly, the Spirit cried out, "Abba, Father," in the hearts of Christians by empowering them to cry out (Gal. 4:6). These were works of the Spirit by whose indwelling charity was poured into the hearts of the faithful (Rom. 5:5).[90] Through the indwelling of the Spirit in the social body of the Savior, Augustine went on to argue, the church shared in the Savior's human activity of forgiving sins.[91]

The Savior's Human Participation in Divine Operations

These analyses of the Savior's human exercise of the divine power to baptize, to expel demons, to forgive sins, to give life to the human spirit, and to resurrect and judge both the just and the evil clearly illustrate Augustine's varied understanding of the personal unity and the operations of the Savior that required both divine and human power.

The application of this theory of divine power exercised humanly by the Savior varied with the operation under consideration. The Savior alone guaranteed the efficacy of the baptismal ritual, independently of any contribution on the part of the minister to the consecration and incorporation of the baptized into the Whole Christ. In liberating from Satan by forgiving sins and expelling demons, however, Augustine focused on scriptural passages that stressed the human participation of the Savior—the divine Son operating in a human way on earth—in that exercise of power. He also assigned to the divine power exercised by the Savior the raising and judging of the just and sinners, which the Gospel of John attributed to Christ precisely as Son of Man, as has been seen above.[92] Without contradicting his earlier teaching on baptism, Augustine seems to have opened the way, through the humanity of the Savior, for Christians to participate in the divine operations of forgiving and sanctification.

THE COLLABORATION OF THE SAVIOR AND THE CHURCH

Augustine usually and regularly employed the personal union between the Savior and the church for the interpretation of scriptural passages that would have attributed to the Savior statements and operations incompatible with his human holiness. The Savior would have spoken or performed these only because of that personal identification with Christians to whom they properly applied. No less important for Augustine's addressing the divisions between Donatist and Catholic Christian communities in Roman Africa was a proper understanding of the church's participation in the holiness and sanctifying power proper to the Savior. The personal union that joined the Christians to the Savior and established the Whole Christ enabled the Savior to mediate between the Trinity and fallen humanity. It also enabled the church as a body and even the individual Christians within it to sanctify and be sanctified by one another within the unity of the Whole Christ.

Augustine's use of the term *church*, as has become evident in this series of essays, was ambiguous. In one sense, he insisted that all those baptized into Christ, including the Donatist schismatics as well as all members of his own Catholic communion, were Christians.[93] They claimed, at least for themselves, what could be called membership in the body of Christ. Augustine also used those terms in at least two more narrowly defined senses. He acknowledged that many of the baptized, both inside and outside the unity of his communion, were not faithful to their baptismal commitment; that they failed to practice the "faith that works through love" (Gal. 5:6); that many of them might finish their earthly lives without having repented those failures. Such persons were not living in the body of Christ. Finally, when he described what he called the "dove" or "society of saints" that shared and exercised the divine operations of the Savior, he sometimes specified that he intended only those who were living in charity and would continue to do so throughout their earthly lives. These were the predestined whom God foreknew would persevere and be welcomed into eternal life (Rom. 8:28–30). This was the church or body of Christ that Augustine believed was joined in personal union to the Savior. He compared it to the firmament of the heavens and the stars set in it, to the house or temple of God, to the wool that would be spun, woven, and sewn to make the churchly robe that clothed the ascending Christ.[94] Since this group was known only to God, he addressed the entire congregation as, at least potentially, active members of that elect body and urged them to manifest the behaviors that characterized it.

Baptism as Incorporation into Christ

In early sermons of his *Tractates on the Gospel of John* preached in 406–7, Augustine argued that the power to baptize belonged to the Savior alone and not to other human ministers of the ritual. In this way, he was able to claim that baptism joined a person into Christ, that it was both effective and the same whether it was received from a holy or evil minister, inside or outside the unity of the church. To repeat the ritual would have been to distrust the power of the Savior.[95] This argument paralleled his explanation of the truth of the gospel and the divine law that was communicated through an ignorant or deceitful preacher.[96]

Next, in subsequent sermons in the series, he warned that baptism alone, though necessary and irreversible, would not guarantee the salvation of its recipient. In declaring that Christ was the one who baptized not with water alone but with the Holy Spirit, he explained, John the Baptist had meant that the ritual was salvific only through the Spirit's gift of charity—love of God and neighbor. Unlike the baptismal consecration that would be received even by the unrepentant inside or outside the unity of the church through the divine power of the Savior, the gift of the Spirit could be received, retained, and exercised only within the unity of the saints in the body of the Whole Christ.[97] These points also were made and elaborated in contemporary sermons apart from the series on the Gospel of John.[98]

Then, in preaching on infant baptism a few years later, Augustine revisited and extended the argument based on John 3:13 that a person could enter heaven only by being joined into the ecclesial body of Christ and then being lifted up with him. In preaching on inherited guilt, he made explicit the role of baptism in that incorporation.[99] For dying infants, in particular, the sacrament provided the only means of liberation from the sinful heritage of Adam. They gained access to the kingdom of God by being regenerated into Christ and through the faith expressed and charity exercised by their parents or sponsors.[100] Later, in the exploration of the meaning of unforgivable blasphemy against the Holy Spirit discussed just above, Augustine argued again that forgiveness for sins could be received and preserved only by participating in the unity of the church gathered by the Holy Spirit.[101]

Over the decade spanned by these three considerations of the efficacy of baptism, Augustine distinguished two effects of the ritual of baptism and different roles of the church in conferring the sacrament. By the Savior's exercise of divine power, baptism always consecrated or marked a person as belonging to Christ and eligible for forgiveness and salvation. For this effect, the ritual could be performed by an unworthy minister, for an unconverted recipient, even in opposition to the unity of the church.

For recipients who were both repentant and adhering to the unity of the church, the gift of the Holy Spirit, which conferred the forgiveness of sins and the sanctifying love of God and neighbor, was mediated through the communion of the faithful within that church. The most striking example of this mediation was that of the parents or sponsors who not only presented infants for baptism but professed faith for them and communicated charity to them.[102] Thus, Augustine went on to argue and explain, the members of Christ's body participated in the transmission of the gift of the Spirit, the forgiveness of sins, and the salvation of the baptized.*

Forgiving Post-Baptismal Sin through the Gift of the Holy Spirit

Augustine's understanding of the role of the church in the forgiveness of sins was developed in sharp contrast to that of Cyprian, who assigned the power to the college of bishops as the united successor of the Twelve upon whom Christ had conferred it originally.[103] As has been seen above in the chapters on forgiveness of sins and on the clergy, Augustine interpreted the giving of the power to forgive sins in the texts of Matthew 16:19 and John 20:22–23 in the light of Matthew 18:18—which Cyprian ignored—where each and every Christian was charged with exercising it.[104] Citing the parable of the unforgiving servant (Matt. 18:23–35)[105] and the commitment to forgive others in the Lord's Prayer (Matt. 6:12, 14–15),[106] he warned his people of the consequences of failing to extend to others the pardon that had been conferred upon them. He urged them to follow the example of the Savior and of Stephen in praying for the forgiveness of their persecutors, citing the efficacy of such prayer in the subsequent gifts of conversion and repentance that God bestowed first upon Stephen and, through him, upon Paul.[107] In building his case for this interpretation, Augustine recalled the Savior's defense of his own power to liberate sinners from the dominion of Satan by citing the successful use of this same power in the exorcisms performed by his disciples (Matt. 12:27).[108]

Nor did Augustine follow Cyprian's interpretation of Matthew 16:19, in which the power of binding and loosening was given to Peter as representative of the Twelve and its successor, the college of bishops. In con-

---

* Thus, in Augustine's understanding, the *ex opere operato* explanation of sacramental efficacy applied only to the never-to-be-repeated baptismal consecration, not to the sanctification of the baptized. Sanctification involved the mediation that the church shared with the Savior.

fessing the Savior and in receiving the power to bind and loosen given in response, he argued, Peter spoke for and represented the whole body of believers, to whom the question had been posed and who shared the faith he had confessed.[109]

To explain the presence and exercise of this divine gift of forgiving among Christians, Augustine appealed to the unity and mutual love that formed the ecclesial body of Christ. These were caused by the whole Trinity but assigned to the indwelling of the Holy Spirit in the faithful. Within the Trinity, the Spirit was the bond of love uniting the Father and Son.[110] The Spirit performed a similar role within the church through the gift of charity—the loving of God above all and of all else in relation to God—that reconciled and united Christians to one another. This love purified—by covering sins, according to 1 Peter 4:8—and joined Christians into one heart and mind.[111] Dissent from this love, either in open adherence to a schismatic communion or within the visible unity of the church, separated a baptized person from the Whole Christ. When such sinners repented and adhered to the intentional unity of the church, the same gift of charity was communicated to them by God through the body of the faithful and it caused the forgiveness of their sins.[112]

Thus, Augustine assigned the power to forgive sins to the Spirit-inspired union of the faithful within the church. In preaching, he referred to these Christians as the society of the saints,[113] which was being established in unity and charity.[114] Alienating oneself from this union bound a person in sin; being joined into it liberated from sin.[115] In this sense, the bonds of love between the members of Christ released the chains of sin; breaking those bonds bound a person in sin.

Augustine's understanding of the church's forgiving of sins did not violate the concerns that he raised in asserting that Christ had not transferred the power to baptize to the ministers of the sacrament. Although he seems not to have addressed the question explicitly in preaching, the necessary distinctions are evident in his surviving sermons. The church's power to forgive sins was not based upon an authorized agency conferred on the clergy or a mediatory influence merited by the fidelity of individual Christians. Instead, the church community's acts of forgiveness toward those who harmed them and prayer that God would convert and forgive these sinners were inspired and empowered by the gift of the Holy Spirit working within the Whole Christ.[116]

In pardoning sinners, then, Christians were not limited to acting as agents or ministers of the Trinity—as the ministers acted for Christ in the baptismal consecration.[117] As has been seen in the chapter on sin and for-giveness, Augustine regularly invited, exhorted, and even required Christians to participate in forgiving and thereby both sanctifying others and being sanctified themselves. This activity was illustrated in Augustine's analysis of the divine and human causality by which the Savior walked on the sea. Under the influence of the Trinitarian operation of love, attributed to the Holy Spirit, Christians performed the human act of loving and forgiving one another. In that human act of pardoning, God forgave the sins of the offender and the pardoner as well. As has been noted earlier, a victim's refusal to cooperate with the divine graciousness harmed not a penitent offender but the vengeful Christian who dared to refuse the requested pardon of a wrong suffered.[118]

In Augustine's use of Matthew 18:15–20 to interpret the texts of Matthew 16:18–20 and John 20:22–23, the divine operation assumed a human face and acted through human generosity, patience, and love to forgive sins when accepted and to bind them when rejected. In explaining the forgiving of sins, then, Augustine extended the personal union of divine and human in the Savior to the body of the faithful and even the individual members of that body. As faithful members of the Whole Christ, they cooperated in the divine operation of forgiving sins.

The Eucharistic Body of Christ

Augustine's teaching on the eucharist is to be found primarily in special sermons preached on Easter Sunday to the newly baptized,[119] and in his commentary on the Bread of Life discourse in the Gospel of John. In these presentations, he insisted that the Whole Christ—head and members—was offered and shared in the consecrated bread and wine. He also asserted that the flesh and blood that the Savior had offered on the cross was received by the faithful, though he did not appeal to its sharing in explaining the efficacy of the ritual.[120]

Through the long initiation process of the catechumenate and the ritual of baptism that they had just completed, Augustine told the new Christians, they had been incorporated into the churchly body of Christ. In receiving the eucharist, they then shared the reality they had just become.[121] The "amen" with which Christians accepted the bread and cup affirmed their adherence to the Whole Christ and pledged them to live in a manner that would preserve their participation in that body. Those who failed to honor that commitment would receive not Christ but only the sacramental signs of bread and wine, and that to their detriment.[122] Thus, Augustine explained the eucharistic ritual as a means not of being joined into the body of Christ but of celebrating and maintaining that union.

The Pauline teaching of 1 Corinthians 12:27 that Christians "are the body of Christ and his members" determined Augustine's interpretation of the eucharist as the sacrament of the Whole Christ. The many Christians joined to Christ in one body made the many loaves placed on the altar in the church and on similar altars spread across the world to be one bread. Augustine redirected in the same way the meaning of the text of 1 Corinthians 10:17: "one bread, we many are one body." The body of the Savior made the many Christians to be one in him and bestowed their unity on the shared bread.[123] Again, he reversed the meaning of John 6:56: "Those who eat my flesh and drink my blood remain in me and I in them." Being united to Christ in his church was the meaning, he explained, not the effect, of ritually eating his flesh and drinking his blood. Receiving baptism joined a person into Christ; participating in the eucharistic ritual affirmed, maintained, and celebrated the Christian's commitment to life in the unity of Christ's ecclesial body.[124]

Augustine's understanding of the life-giving power attributed to eucharistic participation focused, then, not on the bodily immortality to follow the resurrection but on the eternal life already possessed by the faithful saints whom it formed into the ecclesial body of Christ.[125] As John 6:63 said, "the spirit is what gives life; the flesh can accomplish nothing;" the life that the Savior offered in the eucharist was the fellowship of the saints in himself.[126]

Augustine could and did affirm that the saints received the body, blood, and soul of the Savior. By taking these, the Word of God had become the head of the larger, churchly body, into which the saints were joined.[127] He found that saving body better illustrated by the Jerusalem community in which the many Christians were one soul and one heart in God (Acts 4:32).[128] The Whole Christ was realized in each Christian community that gathered in faith to share and exercise that love, manifesting in reality what they received and shared sacramentally.

Priesthood and the Body of Christ

As has been seen in the chapter on clerical orders, Augustine argued that the Israelite priesthood foreshadowed the role of Christ as the pure and holy intercessor who prayed for the people but for whom no one else interceded.[129] In particular, he observed that the presider at Christian eucharistic worship stood with the standing people gathered in the church rather than being hidden behind a veil in a sanctuary, as the Israelite high priest had been.[130] The entire Christian people affirmed with their "amen" the prayer spoken by its leader.[131] The Savior, and not the Christian bishop or presbyter presiding at the eucharist, he insisted, was the only priest and intercessor foreshadowed by the Israelite priesthood.

Augustine argued that the whole church, as the body of Christ, participated in the anointed offices of Israel that belonged to the Savior by both birth and divine mission: the Levitical priesthood and the Davidic kingship. All faithful Christians shared them through the one—and only—anointing that was usually conferred immediately after baptism. The priestly title was used for the bishop—the only cleric to whom it was applied in Augustine's day—because he was the leader of a priestly people (1 Pet. 2:9).[132] In the resurrection, all the saints would be joined with Christ in the heavenly sanctuary for the unending offering of the one perfect sacrifice.[133] The priestly office of the Savior, therefore, was shared with and exercised by his body— but as a whole and not as individual members.

Thus, Augustine treated the bishop's priestly office in leading the community in the eucharistic ritual very differently than he had the role of administering baptism—and more like the ministry of reconciling formal penitents. The prayers of offering and intercession were made by the whole community; the bishop had no mediating role as the Savior's agent.[134] Unlike the baptismal ritual that must not be repeated, the eucharist was celebrated more often, even daily. Rather than initiating the participants' incorporation into the Whole Christ, the efficacy of the eucharist was derived from the baptismal consecration and sanctification.

Because of his role as teacher and overseer, the bishop might have claimed and been accepted, in practice, as exercising a governing authority derived from Christ. Yet, Augustine treated the offices of priest and king in parallel, as belonging to the Whole Christ. Moreover, as has been seen above in his discussion of Jesus's own warning about the teaching of the Jewish leaders in Matthew 23:2, he recognized and urged the responsibility of the laity to question and even to refrain from following the teaching, as well as the example, of misguided or malicious clergy.[135]

The Body of Christ in the Redemption

The passion narrative in each of the gospels begins with the Savior's struggle to accept the rejection and death facing him (Mark 14:36–42; Matt. 26:36–46;

Luke 22:42–44; John 12:23–29). In his commentaries on these passages and on Psalm 42:5, which Jesus quoted (Matt. 26:38; John 12:27), Augustine appealed to the head's personal unity with his members to interpret the Savior's fear and his obedient submission to the Father's will. Although he insisted that the Savior was free of all disordered desires and emotions, Augustine affirmed that he truly felt the fear of execution that arose from his freely accepted mortality. He insisted that the Savior, in his individual body and soul, had experienced that terror—just as he had the fatigue, hunger, and thirst recounted in the gospels.[136] In doing so, his human willing never deviated from the divine willing (that he shared with the Father and Spirit). Even though he had the power to take it up again, the Savior was sorrowful in laying down his life, as he knew many of his disciples would be in accepting the divine will that they do the same.[137] As head, then, the Savior freely identified with the fear of his churchly body, so that his members might identify with him in trusting that God had not abandoned them but was leading them through death toward glorious life.[138] Augustine offered a similar interpretation of John 11:33 in which Jesus was deeply moved at the death of Lazarus and the grief of his sisters. He had freely entered the sadness that affected his members as they faced death.[139]

Similarly, Psalm 22, which the Gospels of Mark and Matthew placed on the lips of Christ crucified (Mark 15:34; Matt. 27:46), was interpreted by Augustine from the perspective of the Christian faithful. He invited his hearers to identify themselves in the psalm's prayer of repentance and plea for deliverance that their head had offered, not for his own failures and abandonment, but in solidarity with them.[140] Using Romans 8:3, that God sent his Son in "the likeness of sinful flesh," Augustine interpreted Christ's mortality as the symbol of the Adamic and personal sins it punished. In the destruction of his sin-symbolizing flesh on the cross, Christ had extinguished the sins and liberated Christians from the resulting guilt and punishment. Augustine appealed to Romans 6:6 and Colossians 2:20 to exhort the members of Christ's body to find themselves dying and being liberated from sin in the mortal flesh of their head, so that they might both die and rise with him.[141] Christ was inviting all to join him in praying Psalm 22 and to offer themselves with him in the mortal flesh that was being purified from sin by his death. In this instance, the head was taking upon himself the experience of weakness of his members and transforming them in himself.

In each of these identifications of the suffering and dying Christ with his faithful followers, Augustine applied the personal union by which the head could speak and act for his members and the members pray and offer themselves in and through their head. Not only did this unity of the Whole Christ explain the words and actions of the Savior but revealed their significance for his members in the church. The mystery of their lives and deaths were being enacted, displayed, and revealed in his. They were being called to recognize themselves in him: to feel the same fear and pain, to exercise the same trust in the Father. By willingly participating in his death, they were being lifted into his glorious life (Rom. 6:5–11).[142]

Christians Share in Judging at the End of Time

As was seen in a prior section, Augustine recognized that the text of John 5:25–28 assigned the role of judgment at the end of time to the Savior precisely as Son of Man—so that he could be perceived by the condemned.[143] In Matthew 19:25–29, just such a role was promised to the disciples of Jesus who had left all to follow him: they would sit on twelve seats, judging the twelve tribes of Israel.[144]

Augustine then expanded the available judicial positions to fit the members of Christ. Since the apostle Paul, who had worked harder than all the rest, could not be excluded, the number of seats would not limit the number of judges. He suggested that the number twelve indicated the universality of Israel and thereby symbolized the universality of humanity to be judged (the four quarters of the earth multiplied by the three persons of the Trinity).[145]

More regularly, Augustine recognized that having abandoned one's property to follow Christ was a judicial qualification (Matt. 19:29)—though it did not imply the condemnation of the faithful who had retained property.[146] He found a different judicial qualification in Psalm 94:15. Christians should acquire justice and a right heart by patiently enduring evil persons on earth; that justice would be turned into judgment at the end.[147] Similarly, Psalm 101:6 specified that all who had been faithful on earth would sit with the Savior to judge.[148] Even more regularly, Augustine appealed to 1 Corinthians 6:1–3, where Paul urged Christians not to take one another to imperial courts. Since they were to judge not only the world but even the angels, they must settle their own disputes.[149]

Augustine's efforts to extend participation in the Savior's judging of the world to his ecclesial body clearly indicated an understanding of the union between head and members within the Whole Christ. A divine power proper to the head but exercised in a human manner was shared by his body, the church.

The Bridal Union of the Church to Christ

In its relation to Christ as spouse, Augustine focused on the fidelity of the church in its exclusive and complete dedication. That commitment was lived in three different ways: as married spouses, as dedicated virgins, and as widows. Of itself, bodily integrity had no particular religious value; in dedicated virgins, however, it symbolized the integrity of the faith that was to be maintained by all Christians.[150] Thus, Augustine explained that the virgins were brides of Christ only by participating in his marriage to the whole church.[151] Similarly, the widow who vowed not to marry again symbolized the church's faith and hope as she lived in expectation of the return of her beloved husband.[152] By their mutual sexual fidelity, the married symbolized and participated in Christ's marriage to the church.[153] In presenting their children for baptism, they regenerated to eternal life those whom they had brought into mortal life.[154] To the love realized in that fidelity and mutual care, moreover, Augustine assigned the power of forgiving the sins of their sexual union when it did not include an intention to procreate.[155]

Summary

In various ways, Augustine attempted to demonstrate that the Savior, himself constituted by a personal union of divine and human, was joined in a similar personal union to the faithful who formed his body, the church. That union could be indicated in various ways: the suffering and dying body of the innocent Jesus revealed the church's sinfulness and its purification; his resurrected flesh manifested its future glory; the Jerusalem Christian community illustrated its unity of heart and mind; the eucharistic elements symbolized its universality and their sharing confirmed the adherence of its members.

More importantly for current purposes, the activities of the Christians who were joined into that ecclesial body continued and completed the work of the Savior on earth. Head and members collaborated in offering the one sacrifice on earth and in heaven, in prayer of praise and petition, in forgiving sins, in mutual love.

The Holy Spirit, to whom the Pauline letters and the Johannine Gospel assigned the unification, sanctification, and guidance of the church, played a major role in Augustine's explanations of the Whole Christ. Through the operation of love of God and neighbor in the Christians, the Spirit acted as the soul of the body of Christ, guiding and directing all its operations. In particular, the Spirit empowered the Christians to forgive sins both on earth and in heaven, before God and Christ.

Through these explanations of the differentiated union of the Savior to the church as a whole and to the individual faithful within it, Augustine consistently eliminated the privileged role of the clergy as mediators between God and the people that was at the heart of the Donatist controversy over the fidelity of the bishops. The mediating role belonged to Christ. The full body of the faithful was endowed with the powers and charged with the mission of its Savior, head, and bridegroom. The role proper to the church's officers was oversight and maintaining order.

Explaining the Union of Christ and the Church

Unlike his extended consideration of the unity and diversity in the Trinity,[156] Augustine's discussion of the two personal unions between the Word of God, the Son of Man, and the church did not produce a search for a similar model. His explanations remained close to the language and metaphors used in the scripture. His justifications for shared operations and attributes were often grammatical: by attention to the subject, object, person (I, you, they), tense (past, present, future), or number (singular, plural) of a verb.

Indeed, Augustine's preferred "model" for the union of divine and human in the Savior was that of soul and body: the three components in the Savior were joined like the two in other humans. He attempted to extend this model to the union of the Savior and the church by identifying the Holy Spirit as the soul of the church and directing attention to the life-giving and integrating functions of the human soul. Yet he recognized that the church, designated as the body in the Whole Christ, continued to involve many hearts and minds, indeed, many individual souls and persons. The dwelling of the Spirit in many Christians did not establish the same kind of individual unity as that claimed for the incarnation of the Word in the human reality of the Son of Man. Many but not all attributes and operations shared by the Son of God and Son of Man as the Savior were also extended to the church and its individual members. The most important of these were the power to sanctify Christians by removing the guilt of both inherited and personal sin and their liberation from the affective disorder of lust that they attained only in the bodily resurrection.

In an attempt to distinguish and relate the two personal unions through which the Whole Christ was constituted, an examination of Augustine's explanations and illustrations of the joining of Christ and the church will be useful.

The Savior United to the Bodies of Christians

In a sermon on 1 Corinthians 6:15, concerning the use of prostitutes by the members of Christ, Augustine addressed the connection between the ecclesial body of Christ and the individual bodies of the faithful. He explained that if Christ had taken only a human soul, then the souls of Christians but not their bodies would have become his members. By taking a body, however, he became their head, and their bodies also became his members. He buttressed the argument by noting that in the same letter, Paul had called the body of the Christian a temple of the Holy Spirit.[157]

In other sermons, Augustine implied that the flesh of Christ was a necessary component in establishing his union with the church.[158] By being joined to the flesh in the womb of the Virgin, the Word became one with that flesh, became head of the church, and made believers his members.[159] By assuming the flesh, the Savior assumed the church.[160] In this sense, Augustine called the flesh of Christ the beginning or firstfruits of the church. Thereby, the disciples eating with him in Emmaus recognized the Savior in the breaking of bread.[161]

In his explanation of the efficacy of the Savior's death, Augustine relied on bodily mortality as the symbol of the human sinfulness it punished and thereby accounted for the extinction of both in the killing of the pure and sinless body of the redeemer.[162] As was noted in the prior section, without specific reference to this explanation of the death of the Savior, Augustine asserted that the resurrection of human bodies was accomplished through the Son of Man, indicating the humanity of the Savior. He was also contrasted with the devil as a successful mediator because he could provide bodily immortality to humans through his own flesh.[163] Unlike the resurrection of the soul into holy life even before death, the resurrection of the flesh into an immortal condition on the last day was common to all humans.[164] Augustine may have intended this universal bodily resurrection as the effect of the Word's incarnation, death, and resurrection. In preaching, however, he did not attempt to establish that connection, even for Christians.

The Savior United to the Souls of Christians

In the first sermon on the text of 1 Corinthians 6:15 cited just above, Augustine seems to have assumed that by taking a human soul, the Word was making the souls of Christians his members.[165] Yet, in other sermons, he insisted that the soul of the Savior—like that of other humans—animated only his human body, and not those of Christians.[166] In his analysis of the union of Christians to form the church and the operations they shared with the Savior, Augustine regularly appealed to an operation of the Holy Spirit in the churchly body of Christ that was analogous to that of a human soul in an individual human body. Those many souls became one heart and soul, then, through the gift and operation of the Holy Spirit within them.[167] As the human soul gave life to each of the bodily organs, worked in them all, and coordinated their disparate operations, so the Holy Spirit gave life and guidance to all the members of the body of Christ. Augustine appealed to the Pauline description of the many gifts that the Spirit bestowed on the church to provide an illustration of the ways that many operations arose from the gift of charity (1 Cor. 12). In the Jerusalem community, that unity was manifest in the sharing of goods.[168]

In building this interpretation, Augustine compared the mission of the Holy Spirit in the Christian church to its role in the divine Trinity. The Father and Son were confessed individually as God but together as one God. The perfect charity, peace, and concord of the third divine person made them one God, indeed a single soul.[169] In Christians, the Spirit first cleansed the community to remove the sins that were obstacles to unity, then drew the members ever closer to God and one another in mutual love.[170] Thus, Augustine used the Jerusalem community to illustrate the unity of the Trinity and to identify an effect of that same divine love. He explained that the bond of charity was the unifying and life-giving principle of the Whole Christ, head and members.[171] That unity, however, did not suppress the multitude of individual souls and hearts.[172] As will be recalled, Augustine insisted that the divine operation elevated and expanded the corresponding human desires and actions rather than suppressing or rendering them superfluous.[173]

Thus, when Augustine identified the Holy Spirit as the soul of the body of Christ, he was using the term in a transferred or analogous sense: the Spirit was the principle of life and action that established a personal unity among Christians and with their Savior, joining the many into a complex and differentiated unity—an organized, living body.[174] He named faith and love as its foundational operations.*

This explanation of the operation of the Holy Spirit in the individual faithful Christians and in the church as a whole rested upon an extensive analysis of the creature's adherence to God in love in the early commentaries on the Pauline Letters, the works of the Pelagian controversy, and the analysis of the creation and failure of both angels and humans in later sermons and treatises. That divine operation did not, however, establish a personal union between the Holy Spirit and the church similar to that between the Word and the Son of Man in the Savior. In that sense, it manifested both Augustine's lack of interest in a systematic exposition of this personal union and the importance of the bodily union between Christ and humanity that went largely unexplored. Indeed, in his treatment of the unity celebrated in the eucharistic communion, he discounted the role of the human body of the Savior.[175]

Personal Unity in Christ and in Adam

The personal unity between the Savior and the church was developed in contrast to Augustine's explanation of the unity of all his offspring in Adam, relying primarily on the texts of 1 Corinthians 15:21–22 and Romans 5:12–21. The first contrasted these two as the portals through which death and immortal life entered and spread. The second—particularly when read as a whole rather than by isolating the initial verse—identified the two as agents whose failure and success had affected all humans who were unified in them.[176]

Particularly during the initial stage of the Pelagian controversy, when the focus was on the condition of infants who were incapable of self-determination, Augustine insisted on the personal unity of his offspring in their first parent. His disobedience and condemnation to the punishments of lust and death affected all who were genetically united in Adam.[177] He appealed to Paul's denial in Romans 9:11 that Esau and Jacob had been able to distinguish themselves by sin or merit prior to their birth to argue that they, and all others,

---

* In *Serm.* 169.12.15–13.16, he contrasted God's action to that of an unwelcome and overbearing house guest whose family and retainers displaced a family in its own dwelling and forced them into an outbuilding. In *Serm.* 71.16.26–27, he illustrated the complementarity of divine and human operation in the Savior's walking on the sea.

were all that one Adam when he sinned.[178] Augustine then explained that the affective disorder that God had visited on the initial sinners worked its own transmission—and that of the sin it punished—through sexual generation, so that it afflicted all born in Adam's line. The Savior escaped that contagion only through his noncoital conception.[179] All born of Adam but not liberated and joined into Christ would die his penal death and be resurrected into a bodily life of unending pain. Those who confirmed that Adamic identity by their sinful choices and actions would suffer all the more.[180]

Liberation from the genetically transmitted unity of person in Adam was accomplished only by voluntary incorporation into the person of Christ. This union was initiated by regeneration in the ritual of baptism and accomplished by persevering collaboration with the operations of the Holy Spirit dwelling within the church and the individual Christians. It was perfected by death in Christ, resurrection into purified and immortal flesh, and the fullness of loving God.[181]

This union of humans in Christ was primarily intentional, in contrast to the genetic Adamic unity. Even the genetically based promises made to Abraham and David were fulfilled in the Whole Christ by intentional rather than genetic solidarity.[182] The reality corresponding to the genetic solidarity in Adam would have been the resurrection of all humans into immortal and perfected bodies. That unity, however, was divided into the kingdom of heaven and the realm of the demons.

In its development by Augustine, the doctrine of the personal unity of humanity in Adam seems to have been derived from the personal unity of Christians in the Savior.

Conclusion

Augustine's understanding of the personal unity of divine and human in Christ was both based upon and limited by his method of scriptural interpretation. He noted that contrary statements were made about the person of the Savior, whom the New Testament writings presented as speaking and acting as both human and divine. The same technique allowed him, following a well-established tradition, to interpret much of the Old Testament by direct reference to the Savior. In dealing with the Savior, he did not have conciliar decrees and creeds to defend and explain, as he did with the Trinity. Thus, his Christology consisted in defending the integrity of the Lord's humanity and his personal unity as a speaker and actor. In this sense, his surviving writings do not provide a major resource for any one of the different parties involved in the Chalcedonian debates in the centuries following his own.

The doctrine of the Whole Christ was based on Augustine's careful reading of Paul and his sustained attempt to develop an understanding of the holiness of the church that would convince his Donatist counterparts to embrace the unity of the worldwide church. The doctrine of the personal unity of the Savior and his members did open the way to new interpretations of scripture, such as the meaning of the Agony of the Garden and the death of Jesus as a sacrifice that extinguished guilt and destroyed death. It provided the basis for a more comprehensive understanding of the efficacy of the rituals and the ministry of all the faithful in the economy of salvation as operations of the Savior with, in, and through his body. In itself, however, the doctrine is a series of images and analogies rather than explanations. It points to a union that is more than voluntary but not fully physical, much less "hypostatic."

NOTES

Introduction

1. *Serm. Dolb.* 23(374 augm).19.

2. For a review of the development of the chronology of some of the sets of sermons treated in this book, see J. Patout Burns, "Situating and Studying Augustine's Sermons," *Journal of Early Christian Studies* 26 (2018): 307–22.

3. Anne-Marie La Bonnardière, "Les Enarrationes in Psalmos Prêchées par Saint Augustin à Carthage en Décembre 409," *Recherches Augustiniennes* 11 (1976): 52–90; *Augustin d'Hippone, Vingt-six Sermons au Peuple d'Afrique*, ed. François Dolbeau, Collection des Études Augustiniennes, Série Antiquité 147 (Paris: Institut d'Études Augustiniennes, 2009); Pierre-Marie Hombert, *Nouvelles Recherches de Chronologie Augustinienne*, Collection des Études Augustiniennes, Série Antiquité 163 (Paris: Institut d'Études Augustiniennes, 2000), 563–88.

4. Anthony Dupont, *Gratia in Augustine's* Sermones ad Populum *during the Pelagian Controversy: Do Different Contexts Furnish Different Insights?*, Brill's Series in Church History 59 (Leiden: Brill, 2013).

5. *Eu. Io.* 25–27.

6. *Serm.* 227; 272; *Serm. Guelf.* 7(229A).

7. Augustine, *Expositions on the Psalms*, ed. John E. Rotelle, WSA III/15–20 (Hyde Park, NY: New City Press, 2000–2004).

8. Allan D. Fitzgerald, ed., *Augustine through the Ages: An Encyclopedia* (Grand Rapids: Eerdmans, 1999).

Chapter One

1. *Conf.* 12.25.34–35. See also the citations from *Doct. Chr.* in nn. 26–32 below.

2. *Doct. Chr.* 2.39.59.

3. For example, *Serm.* 169.1.1; 180.5.5; *Psal.* 44.19; 121.9; 123.8; 135.4.

4. See the analysis in the chapter on the human condition, pp. 245–46.

5. *Serm.* 293.12; 294.14.15–15.15.

6. For example, in *Conf.* 8.2.4, 5.10–12.30; 9.8.18; 6.7.11.

7. Lamenting that most people's days are bad, he compared a good day to a disinterested friend who walks right by without stopping to talk. *Serm. Cail.* 2.92(346C).2.

8. *Serm.* 263.3; *Serm. Denis* 17(301A).1.

9. *Serm.* 2.5–6; 17.1, 3. Even the literate were accustomed to having texts read aloud to them, especially in proceedings or meetings. The written text was primarily a score for performance—public or private—rather than a silent form of communication. See Konrad Vössing, "Saint Augustin et Ecole Antique: Traditions et Ruptures," in S*aint Augustin: Africanité et Universalité. Actes du Colloque International,* ed. Pierre-Yves Fux, Jean-Michel Roessli, and Otto Wermelinger (Fribourg: Éditions Universitaires, 2003), 1:153–66.

10. *Eu. Io.* 24.2; 25.2, 5; *Serm.* 98.3; *Serm. Dolb.* 21(159B).1–11.

11. *Serm. Dolb.* 22(341 augm).11, 19; *Psal.* 61.4; 64.2; 90.2.1; 118.29.9; 128.2; 142.3.

12. *Serm. Dolb.* 23(374 augm).16–20.

13. *Serm.* 2.7.

14. *Serm.* 352.1.3; *Serm. Mai* 14(350A).2; *Serm. Dolb.* 21(159B).16.

15. *Serm.* 300.5; *Psal.* 30.2.3.9.

16. *Serm. Dolb.* 26(198 augm).50–54.

17. *Serm.* 363.1–2.

18. *Serm.* 22.1–2; 51.1.2; *Psal.* 43.8.

19. *Serm.* 27.5.

20. *Psal.* 103.2.7; 113.1.4; 125.10.

21. *Serm.* 56.3.3; *Psal.* 34.1.8.

22. "The waters will overtop the mountains," referred to the flood of Noah's time. *Psal.* 103.2.7.

23. *Serm. Dolb.* 26(198 augm).52. For details see below, pp. 170–73.

24. *Doct. Chr.* 2.9.14; 3.10.14; 3.12.18; 3.15.23. See Hervé Savon, *Saint Ambroise devant l'Exégèse de Philon le Juif,* Collection des Études Augustiniennes, Série Antiquité 72–73 (Paris: Institut d'Études Augustiniennes, 1977).

25. *Serm.* 53.11.12–14.15; *Psal.* 18.2.3.

26. *Doct. Chr.* 4.7.15.

27. *Doct. Chr.* 3.27.38.

28. *Doct. Chr.* 2.9.14; 3.27.38–28.39.

29. *Doct. Chr.* 2.6.7–8; such may even have been the intention of the inspired author, 4.8.22.

30. *Doct. Chr.* 4.8.22.

31. *Doct. Chr.* 4.13.29, 26.56.

32. *Doct. Chr.* 4.25.55.

33. The literal meaning was required in *Serm.* 293.2 but was absent in the psalm text being treated in *Psal.* 103.1.18. An example of an additional, hidden meaning is to be found in *Serm. Dolb.* 22(341 augm).22.

34. *Psal.* 138.31; 140.1; 149.14.

35. *Psal.* 77.44; 94.11; *Serm. Denis* 15(313B).3.

36. *Serm.* 98.4–7; *Serm. Mai* 125(139A).2. The similar interpretation was offered in *Serm. Dom.* 1.12.35. See below, pp. 68–69.

37. *Serm.* 248.1, 3; *Psal.* 47.9. This was repeated in *Eu. Io.* 122.8, which was not preached but may have been intended as a guide for preachers. See, Marie-François Berrouard, *Introduction aux Homélies de Saint Augustin sur l'Évangile de Saint Jean*, Collection des Études Augustiniennes, Série Antiquité 170 (Paris: Institut d'Études Augustiniennes, 2004), 181–86.

38. *Serm.* 119.7; 131.6; 171.2–3; 264.5; 365.3; 366.2; *Serm. Wilm.* 2(179A).7–8; *Serm. Dolb.* 22(341 augm).10; 26(198 augm).44; *Psal.* 31.2.7; 125.15; 136.7. It occurred in *Psal.* 118.15.6, which was not preached. The interpretation was used in Irenaeus of Lyons, *Haer.* 3.17.3 in the late second century.

39. The most comprehensive study of this practice is that of Marie-Josèphe Rondeau, *Les commentaires patristiques du psautier*, Orientalia Christiana Analecta, 219–20, (Roma: Pontificale Institutum Studiorum Orientalium, 1982). For Augustine's usage, see Michael Cameron, *Christ Meets Me Everywhere: Augustine's Early Figurative Exegesis*, Oxford Studies in Historical Theology (Oxford: Oxford University Press, 2012), especially chapters 4 and 6.

40. In *Psal.* 2.6 and *Ep. Io.* 2.5, Augustine applied the text to the eternal Son.

41. Augustine used these two texts to explain the first two forms of attribution in *Serm. Dolb.* 22(341 augm).2–3, 11. Psalm 2:7 was applied to the everlasting Christ in *Psal.* 60.8 and *Serm.* 86.9.10.

42. "Totus Christus in plenitudine ecclesiae." *Serm. Dolb.* 22(341 augm).2.

43. *Serm. Dolb.* 22(341 augm).2, 19; *Serm.* 157.3.3; *Eu. Io.* 21.8; *Serm. Mai* 20(64A).3. Augustine's text of Eph. 1:22–23 read "ipsum dedit caput super omnia ecclesiae, quae est corpus eius, plentitudo eius, qui omnia in omnibus impletur." "He gave him as head over the whole of the church which is his body, his fullness, who is filled by all in all," though the passive voice of the final verb in the Latin text is hard to render. Augustine cited it only in *Ciu.* 22.18, CCSL 46:837.37–38.

44. *Serm.* 345.4.

45. *Psal.* 85.1; see also *Psal.* 140.3.

46. *Psal.* 37.6; 58.1.2.

47. *Eu. Io.* 38.8; 43.17.

48. *Psal.* 2.6; 44.4–5, 19.

49. *Psal.* 119.2; *Serm.* 141.1, 4; 142.2.

50. *Serm.* 174.2.2; *Serm. Guelf.* 11(229G).6.

51. *Serm.* 186.1, 3.

52. *Eu. Io.* 12.8.

53. *Psal.* 138.2.

54. *Eu. Io.* 37.9.

55. *Eu. Io.* 40.5. In *Psal.* 118.22.3, which was among his mature works, he considered interpreting the learning as the divine generation from the Father but rejected it as inappropriate.

56. *Psal.* 70.1.12.

57. *Psal.* 93.19.

58. *Psal.* 29.2.1.

59. *Serm. Dolb.* 26(198 augm).37–40.

60. *Psal.* 56.1; 118.16.6; 142.3.

61. *Psal.* 30.2.3.1.

62. *Psal.* 40.6; 101.1.2; 118.22.5; 140.6.

63. As sad, *Psal.* 31.2.26; 88.2.7; *Eu. Io.* 52.2; or fearful *Psal.* 21.2.4; 42.7; 63.18; *Eu. Io.* 52.3. The martyrs were symbolized by the bloody sweat of his body, *Psal.* 93.19; 140.4.

64. *Psal.* 21.2.3; 34.2.5; 58.1.2; in the name of Adam, abandoned by God, *Psal.* 37.27. Humanity's old self was crying out in him, *Psal.* 70.1.12.

65. *Serm.* 137.2.2; *Ep. Io.* 10.8.

66. *Psal.* 60.1–2; 62.5; 74.4; 101.1.18; 103.1.2; 118.32.1; 119.7; 122.2; 130.1.

67. *Serm.* 345.4; *Serm. Guelf.* 16(229N).3; 17(229O); *Psal.* 30.2.1.3; 123.1.

68. For example, *Serm.* 345.4.

69. *Psal.* 100.3.

70. Cypr. *Unit. eccl.* 4–5, contrasted the giving of sanctifying power to Peter alone (Matt. 16:19) and later to all the apostles (John 20:22). The first signified that it was a single power; the second that it was shared by all. The bishop whom Tertullian opposed held a similar interpretation of the Matthew text, *Pud.* 22.

71. On Peter's confession, see *Serm.* 232.3–4; 244.1; 254.7; 257.2–3; 270.2; 295.3.3; *Serm. Lamb.* 3(229P).1. The power of the keys: *Serm.* 149.6.7; 295.2.2; *Serm. Guelf.* 16(229N).2. Christ entrusting the sheep: *Serm.* 253; *Serm. Lamb.* 3(229P).4.

72. *Serm.* 75.1.1–2.3; Matt. 14:22–23.

73. In this, Augustine differed from Tertullian's interpretation of the powers as given only to Peter and for a specific, time-limited mission. *Pud.* 21–22. His position reflected that of Tertullian in *Paen.* 10, where the church was identified with Christ in interceding for the forgiveness of sin.

74. "Quotienscumque alter alteri uoluntate miscetur *unum* sunt, sicut Dominus dicit: Ego et pater *unum* sumus. Quotiens autem et corporaliter miscentur et in unam carnem duo solidantur *unus* sunt." Tyc. *Reg.* 1, Burkitt 7.21–23. Here, Tyconius applied John 10:30 to the man "mixed" with the Word rather than to the eternal Son of God.

75. Tyc. *Reg.* 4, Burkitt 31.6. William Babcock's translation in *Tyconius: The Book of Rules* (Atlanta: Scholars Press, 1989), 55, offers these terms as equivalents in Tyconius's scripturally derived usage.

76. Tyc. *Reg.* 4, Burkitt 37.11–39.17.

77. Thus, Augustine said that Peter or the disciples, "bore the person of the church," *personam ecclesiae gerebat. Serm.* 295.2.2; *Psal.* 108.18; *Bapt.* 3.18.23. The relationship claimed between Peter and the subsequent bishops of the city of Rome would seem to be more like that "bearing the person" than the personal unity characteristic of Christ and the church. Augustine seldom spoke of the Roman bishops in this way and never considered their personal unity as a basis for sharing gifts conferred upon Peter.

78. *Parm.* 1.1.1; 2.21.40; 3.3.17; 3.6.29; *Ep.* 93.10.44.

79. *Parm.* 2.8.15–16; *Serm. Dolb.* 26(198 augm).49–53.

80. Tyc. *Reg.* 1, Burkitt 6.19–7.23. Aug. *Serm.* 67.4.7; *Corrept.* 11.30.

81. *Serm. Dolb.* 23(374 augm).19.

82. *Psal.* 102.25.

83. *Ep.* 29.11.

84. See below, p. 200.

85. Anne-Marie La Bonnardière exploited these constellations of texts to develop a chronology of the writings and sermons of Augustine. See the concluding tables in her *Biblia Augustiniana. A. T.: Le Livre de la Sagesse*, Collection des Études Augustiniennes, Série Antiquité 42 (Paris: Institute d'Études Augustiniennes, 1970).

86. See the second paragraph of this chapter (p. 9). What was to be recognized as the common, or Vulgate, translation of the Latin church was completed during Augustine's career and adopted only gradually and sporadically. For an excellent treatment of the Bible as he had and used it, see H. A. G. Houghton, "Scripture and Latin Christian Manuscripts from North Africa," in

The Bible in Christian North Africa, Part 1: *Commencement to the Confessions of Augustine*, ed. Jonathan P. Yates and Anthony Dupont (Berlin: de Gruyter, 2020), 15–49.

87. See pp. 116–23.

88. See pp. 95, 161–63.

89. *Psal.* 96.3; 109.12; 146.11.

90. *Serm.* 52, with its explanation of Trinitarian relations, was unique but *Serm.* 126.6.8–10.13 includes an explanation of the unity of works of the Father and Son.

91. *Serm.* 131 was preached at the Mensa Cypriani in Carthage. *Serm. Dolb.* 30(348A) was preached in Hippo but on the occasion of the receipt of the news that Pelagius had been exonerated by a court in Palestine and of a pamphlet in which he defended himself. See below, p. 244.

92. See, for instance, the first expositions of Psalms 1–32 and all the thirty-three expositions of Psalm 119. The first fifty-four lectures on John were preached; the following seventy were written. See Marie-François Berrouard, *Introduction aux Homélies de Saint Augustin sur l'Évangile de Saint Jean*, 177–97.

Chapter Two

1. *Ep.* 157.4.39; *Serm.* 355.2.

2. This was one of the charges against Caelestius, in his trial at Carthage in 411. Pelagius dissociated himself from the teaching at his trial in Palestine. *Gest. Pel.* 11.24. Hilary, a layman at Syracuse in Sicily, reported this teaching to Augustine, who responded. *Ep.* 156; 157.4.23–39.

3. *Diuitiae*, PLS 1:1380–418.

4. His analysis of Matt. 19:23–24 in *Ep.* 157.4.27–29, for example, focused on the question of divine grace and free will rather than on the specifics of using rather than renouncing wealth that is central to *Diuitiae* 18.5–6. Specific parallels and contrasts to this treatise will be noted in the exposition of Augustine's teaching.

5. *Psal.* 34.1.7; 26.2.5, 73.2. The treatise *De diuitiis*, in contrast, challenged all appeals to the Old Testament to legitimate wealth, insisting that the inequities it involved were tolerated rather than approved by God. *Diuitiae* 9.

6. *Psal.* 35.7; 62.7.

7. *Psal.* 62.10; 120.8–9.

8. *Serm.* 14.2, 5; 178.3.3; *Serm. Denis* 21(15A).5; *Serm. Lamb.* 24(20A).9; *Serm. Mai* 13(113B).2, 4; *Psal.* 51.14–15; 85.3.

9. *Serm. Denis* 21(15A).6; *Psal.* 120.8.

10. *Psal.* 85.3.

11. *Psal.* 53.3. The author of *De diuitiis* argued that Christ had rejected wealth and required this of his disciples. *Diuitiae* 10.

12. *Psal.* 85.3.

13. *Psal.* 36.3.1–2.

14. *Psal.* 127.1–5, 10–16.

15. *Psal.* 26.2.5; 34.1.7; 120.9.

16. *Psal.* 90.1.11.

17. *Psal.* 51.16; 73.2–3.

18. *Psal.* 62.14.

19. *Psal.* 66.2–3. The treatise *De diuitiis* argued instead that the equal distribution of rain and sunlight was the standard that God intended for the sharing of all the earth's goods. *Diuitiae* 8.

20. *Psal.* 35.7; 53.3; 73.1; 72.9; 79.14; *Serm. Denis* 21(15A).2.

21. *Psal.* 72.6; 73.3.

22. *Psal.* 90.1.7.

23. *Psal.* 48.2.1–6; 62.6; 91.1.

24. "In nomine Christi et in timore eius exhortor uos, ut quicumque ista non habetis, non cupiatis; quicumque habetis, non in eis praesumatis. ecce dixi uobis: non dico: damnamini, quia habetis; sed: damnamini, si de talibus praesumatis, si de talibus inflemini, si propter talia magni uobis uideamini, si propter talia pauperes non agnoscatis, si generis humani conditionem communem propter excellentem uanitatem obliuiscamini. Tunc enim deus necesse est retribuat in nouissima, et in ciuitate sua imaginem talium ad nihilum redigat. qui autem diues est, hoc modo sit quo praecepit apostolus: *praecipe*, inquit, *diuitibus huius mundi non superbe sapere; neque sperare in incerto diuitiarum suarum, sed in deo uiuo, qui praestat nobis omnia abundanter ad fruendum* (1 Tim. 6:17)." *Psal.* 72:26, CCSL 39:999.17–1000.30.

25. *De diuitiis* argues that in holding wealth that they could renounce, the rich betray an avaricious love of property. *Diuitiae* 4.1–3.

26. *Serm.* 14.6; *Psal.* 34.1.6.

27. *Serm.* 345.1.

28. *Psal.* 83.3.

29. *Serm.* 32.21; 239.4.5; *Psal.* 39.28; 64.9. *De diuitiis* generalizes this view of economic injustice: wealth is acquired and maintained only by extortion, robbery, and fraud. *Diuitiae* 7.2–5; 17.1.

30. *Psal.* 43.25; 145.8.

31. *Psal.* 149.15. Peter Brown shows that the change in social status and style of life could be immediately evident although the property was only gradually

alienated, at the discretion of its owners. Peter Brown, *Through the Eye of a Needle: Wealth, the Fall of Rome, and the Making of Christianity in the West, 350–550 AD* (Princeton: Princeton University Press, 2012), 224–40, 291–307, on Paulinus, on Melania and Pinian.

32. *Ep.* 26.5; 27; 31; 42; 45; 80; 95; 149; 186.

33. *Ep.* 124–26.

34. See the chapter on marriage, pp. 149–50, for a discussion of this issue.

35. *Serm.* 351.4.8.

36. *Serm.* 142.3, 14; 345.6.

37. *Psal.* 90.1.9. Augustine claimed that this had happened in the past, during persecution, but did not name anyone in particular who had renounced property and then failed.

38. *Conf.* 6.14.24; *Serm.* 356.2.

39. The Donatists accused him of introducing this novelty into Africa. *Petil.* 3.40.48.

40. *Serm.* 355.2.

41. *Psal.* 131.5.

42. *Psal.* 132.6.

43. *Serm. Dolb.* 26(198 augm).48.

44. *Psal.* 103.3.16; *Serm. Denis* 17(301A).2; *Serm. Dolb.* 22(341 augm).3. This problem is more fully discussed in Augustine's *Op. Mon.*

45. For additional information, see p. 150.

46. *Serm.* 355, 356. Augustine seems not to have included presbyters and others serving rural parishes. The practice of these is uncertain.

47. *Serm.* 356.13.

48. *Serm.* 356.15; *Psal.* 103.3.16.

49. *Serm.* 356.3, 4.

50. *Serm. Lamb.* 5(107A).1.

51. *Serm.* 107.1.2–4.5.

52. *Psal.* 149.15.

53. *Psal.* 136.13–14.

54. *Serm.* 85.1.1.

55. *Psal.* 103.3.16.

56. *Serm. Denis* 17(301A).5.

57. *Psal.* 43.25.

58. *Serm. Dolb.* 5(114B).11; *Serm.* 85.2.2; *Psal.* 51.14–15. The treatise *De diuitiis* explains that the apostles mistakenly thought that the resources of the rich facilitated their observance of the law. Christ had opened a different way of salvation by valuing poverty. *Diuitiae* 18.

59. *Serm.* 39.2–3; 85.5.6; *Serm. Denis* 16(299D).3; *Serm. Morin* 11(53A).3.

60. *Serm.* 346.1; 36.5; *Psal.* 51.15.

61. *Serm.* 345.1; *Psal.* 48.1.10.

62. *Serm.* 36.5; 85.3.3; 177.8; *Serm. Dolb.* 5(114B).13; *Serm. Morin* 11(53A).4. For the definition, see *Beat.* 2.11; 4.25.

63. *Serm.* 39.4; 61.9.10; 177.7; *Serm. Morin* 11(53A).4; *Psal.* 136.13.

64. *Psal.* 48.1.3.

65. *Psal.* 93.7.

66. *Serm.* 14.2.

67. *Psal.* 146.16; 48.1.3; *Serm.* 36.2.

68. *Psal.* 72.26; 93.7; 131.26; 132.4.

69. *Psal.* 85.3.

70. *Serm. Dolb.* 5(114B).8–13.

71. *Serm.* 36.5; *Psal.* 72.26.

72. *Serm.* 177.7; *Serm. Dolb.* 5(114B).12; *Psal.* 72.13.

73. *Serm.* 117.5.8.

74. *Serm.* 39.2–3; 85.5.6; *Serm. Denis* 16(299D).3; *Serm. Morin* 11(53A).3.

75. *Serm.* 36.6; 177.10; *Serm. Morin* 12(25A).4.

76. *Psal.* 49.13, 15, 17.

77. *Serm.* 85.4.5.

78. "Demus inde quamdam partem. quam partem? decimam partem. decimas dabant scribae et Pharisaei. erubescamus, fratres; decimas dabant, pro quibus Christus nondum sanguinem fuderat. decimas dabant scribae et Pharisaei: ne forte aliquid magnum facere te putes, quia frangis panem pauperi; et uix est millesima ista facultatum tuarum. et tamen non reprehendo: uel hoc fac. sic sitio, sic esurio, ut et ad istas micas gaudeam. sed tamen quid dixerit uiuus, qui pro nobis mortuus est, non tacebo. Nisi abundauerit iustitia uestra, inquit, super scribarum et Pharisaeorum, non intrabitis in regnum caelorum [Matt. 5:20]. ille nos non palpat: medicus est, usque ad uiuum peruenit. nisi abundauerit iustitia uestra plus quam scribarum et Pharisaeorum, non intrabitis in regnum caelorum [Matt. 5:20]. scribae et Pharisaei decimas dabant. quid est? interrogate uos ipsos. uidete quid faciatis, de quanto faciatis; quid detis, quid uobis relinquatis; quid misericordiae impendatis, quid luxuriae reseruetis." *Serm.* 85.4.5, PL 38:522.28–46.

79. *Serm.* 61.11.12.

80. *Serm.* 177.11.

81. *Serm.* 36.6; 39.5; 61.10.11; 177.10; 346.1.

82. *Serm.* 346.1; *Serm. Morin* 11(53A).5; *Eu. Io.* 22.3.

83. *Psal.* 131.26.

84. *Psal.* 48.1.14; 131.19.

85. *Serm.* 86.4.4.

86. *Serm.* 38.7; 61.10.11; 86.4.4; 389.4; *Psal.* 48.1.9.

87. *Serm. Lamb.* 2(335C).8.

88. *Serm.* 177.10; *Psal.* 48.1.9; 132.4.

89. *Serm. Morin* 11(53A).5.

90. *Serm.* 38.7; *Psal.* 36.3.8; 48.2.1.

91. *Psal.* 146.17.

92. See pp. 148–50.

93. *Serm.* 39.3–4; *Serm. Morin* 11(53A).4; 12(25A).2.

94. *Serm.* 14.

95. *Psal.* 51.9.

96. *Psal.* 147.4.

97. *Serm.* 9.21; 25.8; 38.8; 86.3.3; 206.2; 236.3; 239.4.4–6.7; *Serm. Mai* 13(113B).4; *Serm. Lamb.* 4(359A).11; *Psal.* 36.3.6.

98. *Serm.* 103.1.2; 239.3.3–4.4; 277.1.1.

99. *Serm.* 41.6–7; 389.6.

100. *Didache* 1.6.

101. *Psal.* 102.12–13; 103.3.10; 146.17.

102. *Psal.* 102.13–14.

103. *Serm.* 41.7.

104. *Serm. Lamb.* 28(164A).1–4.

105. *Serm.* 41.7; *Serm. Lamb.* 4(359A).11.

106. *Psal.* 32.2.2.29; 46.5.

107. *Serm.* 66.5.

108. *Psal.* 95.7.

109. *Serm.* 39.6; 47.30; *Serm. Dolb.* 26(198 augm).20; *Psal.* 125.12; 49.13; 111.3; 121.11; *Serm. Lamb.* 4(359A).11; 5(107A).8.

110. *Serm. Dolb.* 26(198 augm).20; *Serm.* 39.6; 47.30; *Serm. Lamb.* 1(105A).1; 4(359A).12; 5(107A).7; *Psal.* 49.13.

111. *Serm.* 91.7.9; *Psal.* 36.2.13; 125.11–13.

112. *Psal.* 121.11; 125.12; 47.30; *Serm. Lamb.* 5(107A).8.

113. *Ep. Io.* 5.12–6.1.

114. *Serm.* 61.12.13; 206.2; *Serm. Haffner* 1(350B).1; *Serm. Etaix* 3(350C).1–2; *Psal.* 49.20.

115. *Serm.* 9.17–18, 21; 42.1; 39.6; 83.2.2.

116. *Serm.* 39.6.

117. *Serm.* 113.2.2; *Serm. Lamb.* 4(359A).13.

118. *Serm.* 178.4.4–5.5.

119. The question of alms from ill-gotten gains was treated again in *Ciu.* 21.27.

120. *Serm.* 18.4; 38.8–9; 345.4–5.

121. *Serm.* 390.2; 345; *Serm. Morin* 11(53A).6.

122. *Serm.* 38.9; 339.6; *Serm. Dolb.* 26(198 augm).4.

123. *Psal.* 38.12.

124. *Serm.* 36.9; 38.9; 60.6; 302.8; 389.3; *Serm. Morin* 11(53A).6.

125. *Serm.* 9.20; 86.11.12; see also *Psal.* 131.19.

126. *Serm.* 86.11.13–12.14; *Psal.* 48.1.14.

127. *Serm.* 86.3.3; 239.4.5; *Psal.* 36.3.6.

128. *Serm.* 38.8; 345.2–3; 389.4; *Serm. Lamb.* 2(335C).8–9.

129. *Serm.* 390.1; *Psal.* 36.3.6; 48.1.9.

130. *Serm.* 389.4.

131. *Eleem.* 15–19.

132. *Serm.* 209.3; 210.10.12; 390.1.

133. *Ciu.* 21.27.

Chapter Three

1. *Psal.* 31.2.16; 40.6; 58.1.14; 91.3; 128.9; 140.9.

2. *Psal.* 91.3; the Latin text is too brief to be clear.

3. *Psal.* 35.10; that inability to recognize one's own failure was the condition of the demons.

4. *Psal.* 35.3.

5. *Psal.* 90.1.6.

6. *Serm.* 82.8.11, 10.13.

7. *Serm.* 82.3.4–5.

8. *Psal.* 52.2; see *Psal.* 53.1.

9. *Psal.* 49.28.

10. *Serm.* 75.5.8–6.9.

11. *Psal.* 47.9; 52.4.

12. *Eu. Io.* 36.4; *Serm.* 32.12.

13. *Eu. Io.* 33.5–6.

14. *Eu. Io.* 33.8.

15. The treatise *De diuitiis* reports and rejects an attempted distinction between salvation and the kingdom of God. *Diuitiae* 18.6.

16. By Augustine's time, only servants were deprived of the privilege of imperial citizenship.

17. *Serm.* 351.4.8.

18. In *The City of God*, Augustine provided a more systematic and extensive catalog of Christian attempts to identify exemptions that would allow them to escape the demands of divine judgment. *Ciu.* 21.17–22.

19. *Psal.* 49.7; 102.17.

20. *Psal.* 134.14; 57.21.

21. *Serm.* 19.2; *Psal.* 44.18.

22. *Psal.* 91.4; 138.15.

23. *Psal.* 110.2.

24. *Serm.* 67.1.1. The conflict of the converting will against itself was, of course, most fully illustrated in Augustine's own conversion. *Conf.* 8.9.21–12.28.

25. *Serm.* 361.21.20; *Psal.* 50.11.

26. *Psal.* 44.18; 31.2.12–13.

27. *Psal.* 140.14–15.

28. *Serm.* 389.6: penitential works were always acts of mercy toward others, especially almsgiving and the self-denial that enabled it.

29. *Psal.* 44.18; 102.13.

30. *Psal.* 31.2.17; 70.1.19; 83.10; 90.2.8; 129.3; *Eu. Io.* 3.2, 11, 14, 16; 17.2; *Serm. Mai* 158(272B augm).3.

31. *Serm. Dolb.* 23(374 augm).22–23.

32. *Psal.* 50.15; 55.13.

33. *Psal.* 54.4.

34. *Psal.* 44.17; 50.15.

35. *Psal.* 91.14.

36. *Serm.* 20.3–4; 40.1–5; 82.11.14; 87.9.11; 339.7; *Serm. Denis* 25(72A).1–2; *Psal.* 144.11.

37. *Serm. Dolb.* 14(352A).7.

38. *Serm.* 361.21.20–22.21; *Serm. Dolb.* 5(114B).3.

39. *Psal.* 32.2.1.10; 51.13; 55.6.

40. *Psal.* 84.8.

41. *Serm.* 224.3; *Psal.* 110.3.

42. *Eu. Io.* 49.19; a similar point is made in *Eu. Io.* 26.5–9.

43. *Serm.* 67.1.2–3.5; 98.5–7; 352.3.8.

44. *Conf.* 10.29.40–39.64.

45. *Serm. Dolb.* 12(354A).9, 12.

46. *Serm.* 351.3.3–5.

47. *Serm.* 56.7.11–9.12; 261.10; 278.12.12–13.13; *Serm. Dolb.* 26(198 augm).52; *Eu. Io.* 12.14.

48. *Serm.* 351.3.6; 181.6.8; 278.12.12–13.13.

49. "Forgive and you will be forgiven; give and it will be given to you."

50. *Serm.* 42.1; 56.9.12–12.16; 261.10; 351.3.6; *Eu. Io.* 12.14.

51. This understanding of sinfulness as a condition was most dramatically articulated in his developing analysis of Romans 7:14–25. See, in particular, *Serm.* 154.

52. *Serm.* 211.6.

53. *Serm.* 57.8.8; 58.7.8; 59.4.7.

54. *Psal.* 102.11.

55. *Serm.* 58.7.8.

56. *Serm.* 211.6.

57. *Serm.* 82.2.3.

58. The argument focused on the parable of the wheat and weeds. The Donatists identified the field as the world rather than the church, and the Caecilianists (Catholics) insisted that it represented the church spread throughout the world rather than confined to Africa. See *Bapt.* 4.9.13; *Cresc.* 3.66.75; *Gaud.* 2.5.5–6.6; *Parm.* 1.14.21; 2.2.5; 2.22.42–23.43; 3.2.13; *Petil.* 2.78.174.

59. *Serm.* 82.3.4–5.

60. *Serm.* 4.14.

61. *Serm.* 5.8.

62. *Serm.* 73; *Serm. Cail.* 2.5(73A).1, 3.

63. *Serm.* 248.2–3; 249.2; 250.2–3; 251.1.1–2.2; 270.7.

64. *Serm.* 250.2–3; 270.7.

65. *Serm.* 214.11; 223.2; 259.2.

66. *Serm.* 15.9.

67. *Serm.* 76.3.5–6.9.

68. *Serm.* 47.5–6, 16; 73.4; *Serm. Cail.* 2.5(73A).1, 3; *Psal.* 100.12–13.

69. *Serm.* 88.20.23–22.25.

70. *Serm.* 211.1–2.

71. *Serm.* 82 provides a sustained and systematic analysis of the first passage.

72. *Serm.* 82.3.4–5.

73. *Serm.* 82.4.6.

74. *Serm.* 59.4.7; 211.5; 278.6.6, 10.10–11.11; 315.7.10; *Serm. Wilm.* 2(179A).1, 6–7; *Psal.* 54.14; 147.13.

75. *Serm.* 57.11.12; 278.6.6, 11.11–12.12.

76. *Serm.* 211.4; 386.1–2.

77. *Serm.* 82.4.7.

78. *Serm.* 82.7.10; 83.7.8.

79. *Serm.* 4.20.

80. *Serm.* 56.13.17; *Serm. Dolb.* 21(159B).4.

81. *Psal.* 50.24.

82. *Serm. Frang.* 5(162B).2–3; 9(114A).5.

83. *Serm.* 5.2; 100.8.

84. *Serm.* 5.2; 83.7.8.

85. *Serm.* 82.2.2–3.

86. *Serm. Dolb.* 12(354A).9, 12; *Serm.* 51.13.22.

87. *Psal.* 102.14; *Serm. Frang.* 5(162B).4.

88. *Serm.* 88.18.20; *Psal.* 37.22; 129.4.

89. *Serm.* 211.5; *Psal.* 54.8–11.

90. *Serm.* 211.4.

91. *Serm. Denis* 20(16A).7–8.

92. *Serm.* 167.3.4; *Psal.* 25.2.13; 32.2.1.12.

93. *Psal.* 143.8; 147.13.

94. *Serm.* 339.

95. *Eu. Io.* 27.8.

96. *Serm.* 98.5, 7.

97. Augustine explained such admonitions in *Simpl.* 1.2.12–13 and amply illustrated them in describing his own conversion (*Conf.* 8.5.10–12.30) and the conversions of others (*Conf.* 8.2.4; 8.6.15; 8.12.29–30; 9.8.18; 6.7.11).

98. *Serm.* 98.5, 7.

99. *Serm.* 98.5; 67.1.2.

100. *Serm.* 67.3.5; 98.6, 7; 352.3.8; *Eu. Io.* 49.24. This observation indicated that the penitential practices were intended to purify the sinner and assure the community of repentance rather than to make satisfaction to God or repay a debt owed in divine justice.

101. *Serm.* 224.3; 392.5.

102. *Serm.* 82.9.12.

103. *Serm.* 296.13–15. The congregants judged that the Donatist was converting only to protect his property from confiscation, presumably under an imperial law such as those of *C. Th.* 16.5.21 (392 CE) and 16.2.29 (395 CE).

104. *Serm.* 302.10–22.

105. *Serm.* 392.4.

106. African church law forbade him to expose the sinner. *Reg. Carth.* 132–33.

107. *Serm.* 82.8.11–9.12; 351.4.10.

108. *Serm.* 392.5; 132.4.

109. *Serm.* 17.6.

110. *Serm. frg. Verbr.* 7(77C); *Serm.* 137.10.12.

111. *Serm.* 82.8.11.

112. *Serm.* 14.

113. *Serm.* 224.1; 260; *Serm. Guelf.* 18(260D).2.

114. *Psal.* 90.1.4; 93.20.

115. *Psal.* 119.3–4.

116. *Psal.* 30.2.3.6; 139.6–7; 68.2.6.

117. *Serm.* 115.4; 151.5.5; 152.3; 153.11.14; 294.11.12.

118. *Serm.* 67.1.2–3.5; 98.6, 7; 295.2.2; 352.3.8; *Serm. Mai* 125(139A).2; *Psal.* 101.2.3; *Eu. Io.* 49.24. This distinction between guilt and a sinful state of mind occurs primarily in the case of sin that would separate from the communion of the church and the kingdom of God.

119. *Serm.* 351.5.12; 389.6; *Serm. Mai* 125(139A).2.

120. *Serm.* 351.5.12.

121. *Serm.* 351.4.9; 392.3–4.

122. *Serm.* 351.5.12.

123. *Serm.* 149.6.7; 232.3; 295.2.2; *Serm. Lamb.* 3(229P).1; *Serm. Guelf.* 16(229N).2; *Eu. Io.* 50.12.

124. *Serm.* 149.6.7; 351.5.12.

125. *Serm.* 232.8; 392.1; *Serm. Lamb.* 26(335H).3.

126. *Serm.* 351.5.12; *Serm. Mai* 125(139A).2.

127. *Serm. Cail.* 2.11(112A).5; *Psal.* 147.24.

128. "Sicut enim comes paenitentiae dolor est; ita lacrymae sunt testes doloris." *Serm.* 351.1.1, PL 39:1536.

129. *Serm.* 389.6.

130. *Serm.* 207.2; 210.1.1, 3.4; *Serm. Wilm.* 14(223H).

131. *Serm.* 210.10.12.

132. *Serm.* 210.2.3.

133. *Serm.* 208.2; 252.11; 264.5; 270.3.

134. *Serm.* 210.6.9.

135. *Psal.* 42.8; *Serm.* 205.2; 208.2; 390.1.

136. *Serm.* 389.5–6; 39.6; *Psal.* 44.27–28; 65.20; 121.9.

137. *Serm.* 259.4; *Serm. Etaix* 3(350C).1–2; *Serm. Haffner* 1(350B).1; *Serm. Lamb.* 4(359A).15–17.

138. *Serm.* 389.5–6; *Serm. Lamb.* 4(359A).11.

139. *Psal.* 37.24.

140. *Serm.* 149.7.8.

141. *Serm.* 14:3–5; 41:4; 367.2–3.

142. *Serm. Denis* 21(15A).5; 24(113A).6; *Serm. Lamb.* 24(20A).9; *Serm. Mai* 13(113B).3–4; *Serm. Guelf.* 30(299E).3; *Psal.* 85.3.

143. *Serm.* 42.1–2; 206.2; *Psal.* 129.3–5.

144. *Serm.* 83.2.2; 114.5; 259.4; *Serm. Wilm.* 2(179A).1.

145. *Serm. Dolb.* 7(142).2–3.

146. Augustine did not threaten such persons with punishment or painful purification in the period between death and resurrection. *Serm.* 181.5.7.

147. *Ep.* 153.3.7.

148. *Serm.* 67.1.2–3.5.

149. *Serm.* 98.5, 7.

150. *Serm.* 67.1.2–3.5; 98.5–7; 352.3.8.

151. *Serm.* 67.1.2; 295.2.2; *Serm. Mai* 125(139A).2; *Psal.* 101.2.3.

152. *Serm.* 224.3. The same point was made in *Serm.* 152.1; 153.1.1.

153. *Serm.* 316.3–4; 317.2.2–5.5; 382.2–5. He added Cyprian in *Serm. Denis* 15(313B).4.

154. *Serm.* 392.3; *Psal.* 101.2.3; *Ep. Io.* 10.10; *Eu. Io.* 49.24.

155. *Serm. Guelf.* 16(229N).2.

156. *Serm.* 99.6; 295.2.2.

157. *Serm. Guelf.* 16(229N).2.

158. *Serm. Lamb.* 3(229P).1; *Serm.* 232.3.

159. *Psal.* 108.1; *Eu. Io.* 50.12.

160. *Serm.* 232.3–4; 244.1; 254.7; 257.2–3; 270.2; *Serm. Dolb.* 4(299A augm).5; *Serm. Lamb.* 3(229P).1.

161. *Serm.* 253.2; 296.13; *Serm. Lamb.* 3(229P).4; *Serm. Guelf.* 16(229N).2.

162. *Serm.* 149.6.7.

163. *Ep. Io.* 10.10; *Serm.* 149.6.7.

164. *Serm.* 295.2.2.

165. *Serm.* 295.2.2; Cypr. *Unit. eccl.* 4–5, TR.

166. *Serm. Guelf.* 16(229N).2; *Serm.* 149.6.7.

167. For a fuller discussion of the contrast between Cyprian and Augustine's on this point, see J. Patout Burns and Robin Margaret Jensen, *Christianity in Roman Africa: The Development of Its Practices and Beliefs* (Grand Rapids: Eerdmans, 2014), 313–53.

168. Tert. *Pud.* 21. See especially *Pud.* 21.15.

169. Cypr. *Unit. eccl.* 4–5.

170. This argument was developed in *Bapt.* 3.18.23; 4.3.4–4.5; 5.16.21, 18.24, 21.29; 7.44.87, 47.93, 44.97, 51.99.

171. *Serm.* 295.2.2.

172. *Ep. Io.* 1.6; *Serm. Lamb.* 7(335E).4; the text is used against the Donatists in *Bapt.* 1.18.27; 6.24.45; *Gaud.* 1.12.13; 1.39.54; *Cresc.* 2.12.15; 4.11.13.

173. *Ep. Io.* 10.10; *Eu. Io.* 50.12; *Serm.* 82.4.7; 149.6.7; 232.3; *Serm. Lamb.* 3(229P).1. Additional uses are found in *Cons.* 2.53.108 and *Eu. Io.* 124.5, neither of which was preached.

174. *Ep. Io.* 10.10; *Eu. Io.* 50.12; *Serm.* 149.6.7. Also, in *Eu. Io.* 124.5 that was not preached.

175. *Serm.* 295.2.2; *Serm. Guelf.* 16(229N).2.

176. *Serm.* 67.3.5; 98.6; 295.3.2; 352.3.8; 392.3; *Serm. Mai* 125(139A).2; *Psal.* 101.2.3; *Eu. Io.* 22.7; 49.24.

177. *Serm.* 99.6; 295.2.2.

178. *Serm.* 295.2.2; 392.3. An additional six uses are found outside the sermon literature: *Ep.* 185.10.45; *Ep. Divj.* 1.1; *Spec.* 25; *Fid. et op.* 3.4; *Ciu.* 20.9; *Leg.* 1.36.

179. *Serm.* 82.4.7.

180. *Psal.* 131.13; 146.9; 147.20, 23, 26.

181. *Psal.* 101.2.10–11.

182. This viewpoint was reflected in his assertion that the witnesses to a sin against an individual should be involved in the accusation, apology, and forgiveness through which it was forgiven. *Serm.* 82.7.10; 83.7.8. See discussion above at note 78 in the section titled "Beyond Patience toward Forgiveness" (p. 64).

183. For a discussion of the role of the presider in the eucharist, see pp. 171–73.

Chapter Four

1. *Serm.* 106.1.1; *Serm. Mai* 94(260C).2.

2. *Eu. Io.* 6.19. See also *Psal.* 130.1; 147.4; *Serm.* 264.5; *Serm. Dolb.* 5(114B).1–2; 18(306E).3.

3. *Serm.* 264.5.

4. *Psal.* 127.15. The textual variant, perhaps deriving from the *Vetus Latina*, is found elsewhere in Augustine's writings and preaching. See *Eu. Io.* 6.19; 7.3; *Psal.* 127.13, 15; *Faust.* 12.20.

5. *Serm.* 352.1.6; 353.4.2; *Psal.* 72.5.

6. *Serm.* 4.9; 363.2; *Mai* 89(260B).1; *Psal.* 80.8; 105.10; 106.3; 113.1.3–4.

7. *Serm.* 4.9; 213.9; 352.1.6; 353.4.2; 363.2–3; *Serm. Wilm.* 5(223E).2; *Serm. Mai* 89(260B).1; *Psal.* 72.5; 80.8; 113.1.4; 135.9.

8. *Serm.* 213.9; 352.1.3; 353.4.2; *Serm. Mai* 89(260B).1; *Serm. Wilm.* 5(223E).2; *Psal.* 80.8; 105.10; 106.3.

9. *Serm.* 4.9; *Psal.* 72.5; 135.9.

10. *Serm.* 4.9; 352.1.6; *Serm. Mai* 89(260B).1; *Psal.* 72.5.

11. *Serm.* 4.9; *Serm. Mai* 89(260B).1; *Serm. Wilm.* 5(223E).2.

12. *Serm.* 4.10; 352.1.2; 363.3; *Psal.* 72.5.

13. *Serm.* 352.1.6; 363.2; *Psal.* 72.5.

14. For example, *Serm.* 316.12; *Serm. Etaix.* 2(196A).
15. For example, *Serm.* 210.2.3; 231.2; *Serm. Denis* 8(260A).4.
16. *Serm.* 293.12; 294.20.19.
17. *Serm.* 351.5.12; *Serm. Cail.* 2.11(112A).8.
18. *Serm.* 294.16.16.
19. *Serm.* 292.3.3–4.4.
20. *Serm.* 292.4.4; 293.12; *Psal.* 90.2.6; *Eu. Io.* 4.13–14; 5.3.
21. *Serm.* 292.4.5.
22. *Eu. Io.* 4.14; 5.5.
23. *Eu. Io.* 5.6–9, 11, 13.
24. *Serm.* 57.8.8; 131.6; 152.3.
25. *Serm. Lamb.* 23(335M).4; *Serm. Guelf.* 33(77A).1; *Psal.* 80.10.
26. *Serm.* 71.12.20.
27. *Serm.* 131.6.
28. *Serm.* 316.3; *Serm. Guelf.* 9(229E).2; 28(313E).4; *Psal.* 45.4.
29. *Serm.* 351.1.1–3.3; 352.1.2; *Serm. Dolb.* 14(352A).4, 9.
30. *Serm.* 56.9.13; 57.8.8; *Psal.* 142.7.
31. *Serm.* 56.7.11; 57.9.9; 152.3; 363.2.
32. *Serm.* 151.5.5; *Serm. Guelf.* 33(77A).1–2.
33. *Serm.* 151.4.4–5.5.
34. *Serm.* 151.4.4.
35. *Serm.* 56.7.11; 58.7.8; 59.4.7; 83.6.7; 351.3.3; *Serm. Lamb.* 23(335M).4; *Serm. Wilm.* 2(179A).6.
36. *Serm.* 392.2–3.
37. *Serm.* 5.2; *Psal.* 142.7.
38. *Serm. Dolb.* 14(352A).9.
39. *Psal.* 47.8; *Serm.* 71.19.32; *Serm. Denis* 8(260A).2.
40. *Psal.* 48.2.1; 77.2.
41. *Psal.* 80.20; *Serm.* 393.2–7. See above, pp. 75–76.
42. The neophytes were segregated by their location and special garments during the service for the week following their baptism. *Serm. Dolb.* 27(306C).7.
43. *Serm.* 260; 376A.4.
44. *Serm.* 392.6. Elsewhere, Augustine affirmed that a core of predestined "saints" within the church secured the church's unity and power to sanctify through their exercise of charity. See *Psal.* 47.8; 101.2.10–11; 131.13; 146.9; 147.20, 23, 26; *Eu. Io.* 26.15.
45. *Serm. Guelf.* 18(260D).3; *Serm. Lamb.* 23(335M).4–5.
46. *Psal.* 75.15.
47. *Psal.* 85.4.

48. Tert. *Bapt.* 18.4.

49. Cypr. *Ep.* 64.4.1–6.2. He did speak of them as infected by mortality.

50. Augustine acknowledged their position in *Serm.* 183.8.12.

51. *Serm.* 174.6.7; 176.2; 293.9–11; *Psal.* 50.10.

52. *Serm.* 183.8.12.

53. *Serm.* 324. On the giving of the eucharist, note that the text specifies the fulfilling of all the sacraments before his death. See also *Serm.* 174.6.7 for infants sharing the eucharist.

54. June 27, 413; see Pierre-Marie Hombert, *Nouvelles Recherches de Chronologie Augustinienne*, Collection des Études Augustiniennes, Série Antiquité 163 (Paris: Institut d'Études Augustiniennes, 2000), 385–86.

55. *Serm.* 294.1.2–2.2. The placement of the sermon in Carthage is indicated by a reference to Cyprian having been bishop of the congregation to whom Augustine was preaching. *Serm.* 294.20.19.

56. *Serm.* 294.3.3–7.7. He further argued that exile from the company of Christ, angels, and saints in the kingdom of heaven would be a punishment for all but those who—perversely—failed to desire it.

57. *Serm.* 294.7.8–8.8.

58. The final phrase, which was essential to Augustine's argument, is not present in most ancient texts of the gospel. It was in Augustine's Latin text and the Vulgate but is not included in modern editions and translations.

59. *Serm.* 294.8.9–9.9.

60. *Serm.* 294.10.10.

61. *Serm.* 294.10.11.

62. *Serm.* 294.11.12, 17.17–19.17. This interpretation is confirmed in the contemporary *Ep.* 98.2–5 that attributes the effect to the Holy Spirit operating in both the child, the sponsor, and the entire body of the Christian faithful.

63. In Cyprian's day, some 150 years earlier, they participated in the eucharistic ritual by receiving the bread and wine. *Laps.* 25.

64. *Serm.* 294.13.14. For infant participation in the eucharist see at note 53 above.

65. The audience would have recognized, though Augustine did not here mention it, that once baptized the infants shared the eucharistic body of Christ. See p. 91 and n. 53 above.

66. *Serm.* 27.6; 165.5.5.

67. See the horrified response to Augustine's mention of the death of a son in *Serm.* 86.11.12–12.14.

68. In contrast, his earlier exposition of John 3:5–15 in *Eu. Io.* 12.5–12 focused on mortality as the consequence of Adam's sin and was unconcerned with infants.

69. The terminology *sacramentum* and *res* was developed in the medieval appropriation of Augustine. *Serm. Denis* 8(260A).4. In the treatises against the Donatists, the terminology seems to have been used only in *Petil.* 2.40.96 and *Cresc.* 4.20.24.

70. Such as the grace or power of the sacrament, the unity of the congregation, charity, the gift of the Holy Spirit, the fruit of salvation. *Serm.* 71.19.32, 22.36; 90.5; 99.11; 268.2; 269.2; *Serm. Denis* 8(260A).2; *Psal.* 77.2; 103.1.9; *Eu. Io.* 5.15.

71. *Serm.* 71.12.19; 109.1.

72. Matt. 3:11; Mark 1:8; Luke 3:16; John 1:33.

73. *Serm.* 292.4.8; 293.6; *Psal.* 131.27–28.

74. Especially for 1 Cor. 1:13, which Augustine sometimes interpreted as implying that the holiness would derive from the person in whose name the baptism was performed. *Psal.* 54.24; *Ep. Io.* 2.4; *Serm.* 76.3.5; 295.5.5; 358.3, 5; 379.7; *Serm. Dolb.* 19(130A).3; 26(198 augm).15.

75. *Eu. Io.* 5.6–7. He recognized that the dispositions of individual recipients could affect the outcome of the ritual. See above, pp. 87–89.

76. *Eu. Io.* 5.18. Augustine did not deal here with the question of how the original disciples of Christ had received his baptism.

77. By reference to the baptism narrative in Matt. 3:14, Augustine was able to specify that the Holy Spirit did not descend upon Jesus until after his baptism, but that John knew who Jesus was before his baptism. Hence, Augustine had the obligation (and opportunity) to specify something else that John learned through the descent of the Spirit upon Jesus: that he was the one who baptized (with the Holy Spirit) whenever anyone conferred his baptism. *Eu. Io.* 4.15–16; 5.2–5, 8; 6.7. He first called attention to the problem in *Cons.* 2.15.32.

78. *Eu. Io.* 5.8–11, 13.

79. *Eu. Io.* 5.6–7.

80. Hombert, *Nouvelles Recherches*, 574n69, assigns the sermon to the period 402–5, contemporary with Augustine's treatise against Petilian and a few years before the initial commentaries on the Gospel of John were preached in 406–7.

81. *Serm.* 292.4.6, 4.8.

82. *Serm.* 292.4.7. This solution, which Augustine offered the Donatists, would become the basis for the Roman Catholic doctrine of *ex opere operato*: that God supplied for the minister's deficiency either directly or through the church.

83. *Psal.* 145.9. The Donatists may not have claimed to be the source of baptismal holiness, but they did require a holy mediator to deliver that holiness.

84. *Eu. Io.* 5.15.

85. *Eu. Io.* 11.9.

86. *Eu. Io.* 11.11.

87. *Serm.* 71.12.19: in that context the forgiveness of sins and the casting of demons were considered in parallel. This sermon is generally dated a decade or more after *On Baptism* where Augustine first exploited the implications of Matt. 16:19 and John 20:21–13; *Bapt.* 3.17.22–18.23; 4.1.1. For the dating of the treatise and the sermon, see Hombert, *Nouvelles Recherches*, 93–94, 370n17.

88. *Eu. Io.* 4.12.

89. *Serm. Frang.* 8(293B).3.

90. *Serm. Dolb.* 3(293A augm).11, 13–15.

91. *Serm.* 99.10; 266.3–4; 269.2.

92. *Serm.* 99.10–11; 266.3–4.

93. *Serm.* 266.2, 4; 269.2.

94. *Serm.* 99.11; 266.4–5; 269.2. Augustine's reading of the text is witnessed in *Serm.* 266.4: they descended into the water and Philip baptized him; after they had stepped out of the water, the Holy Spirit came upon the eunuch (instead of coming upon Philip). PL 38:1227.

95. *Serm.* 99.12; 266.6–7; 269.2.

96. See, for example *Eu. Io.* 6.16–26.

97. For Simon as an example of a baptized person who did not receive the Spirit, see *Eu. Io.* 6.18; *Serm. Denis* 8(260A).2; *Serm. frg. Lamb.* 4(229U).

98. *Serm.* 71.19.32.

99. *Psal.* 103.1.9.

100. *Serm.* 90.5.

101. *Psal.* 77.2.

102. Military: *Psal.* 39.1; *Eu. Io.* 6.15–16; 13.17; *Serm.* 317.4.5; 359.5; *Serm. Denis* 8(260A).2; *Serm. Dolb.* 3(293A augm).16. Animals: *Serm.* 295.5.5; *Serm. Dolb.* 4(299A augm).2. Assigning ownership: *Ep. Io.* 5.6; *Serm. Guelf.* 17(229O).3.

103. *Serm.* 317.4.5; *Psal.* 30.2.3.3.

104. *Serm.* 160.6; 302.3; 342.1; *Serm. Denis* 17(301A).8; *Psal.* 50.1; 59.9; 73.6; 85.13; 141.9; *Eu. Io.* 3.2; 11.3; 43.9; 50.13.

105. *Serm.* 359.5; *Serm. Denis* 8(260A).2.

106. *Serm.* 268.2.

107. *Serm.* 146.2; *Serm. Dolb.* 4(299A augm).2.

108. *Psal.* 54.20.

109. In his preaching, Augustine did not deal with the complex question of whether charity could not be received by the unconverted or could be received but not retained. It was discussed multiple times but left unresolved in *Bapt.* 1.12.19–13.21; 3.13.38; 4.11.17; 5.8.9; 5.21.29; 7.3.5.

110. *Serm.* 71.2.4. For dating, see Hombert, *Nouvelles Recherches*, 370n17.

111. *Serm.* 71.3.5–7.12.

112. *Serm.* 71.8.13–10.16.

113. *Serm.* 71.12.18–19. He then returned to the question of attribution of common works to one person of the Trinity in *Serm.* 71.15.25–17.28, 20.33.

114. *Serm.* 71.12.20–13.22.

115. *Serm.* 71.17.28, 19.32–21.35.

116. For a fuller discussion, see sections of the prior chapter on sin and forgiveness, the power to forgive, pp. 79–82.

117. *Serm.* 99.9, preached in the summer of 411 or 412. For dating, see Hombert, *Nouvelles Recherches*, 295n14.

118. *Serm.* 71.23.37. Here Augustine alluded to a point he elaborated more fully in controversial writings. *Bapt.* 1.11.15; 3.18.23; 5.21.29; 6.1.1, 3.5, 14.23.

119. *Serm.* 269.2.

120. *Serm. Denis* 8(260A).3–4.

121. *Serm. Guelf.* 7(229A).1; *Serm.* 228.3.

122. *Bapt.* 1.11.15; 3.18.23; 5.21.29; 6.1.1, 3.5, 14.23.

123. *Eu. Io.* 11–12; *Ep.* 98.5.

124. *Serm.* 294.13.14; *Ep.* 98.9–10. In the letter, Augustine insisted that the infant had the sacrament of faith rather than the mental operation of faith, which it was not yet capable of either accepting or rejecting.

125. *Serm.* 71.2.4, compared to the attempt in *Rom. inc.* 15–16.

Chapter Five

1. *Serm.* 77.2.4; 80.5; 87.11.14; *Serm. Casin.* 2.114(97A).2; *Serm. Denis* 15(313B).4; *Serm. Guelf.* 9(229E).2; 28(313E).4; *Serm. Mai* 26(60A).2; 86(229I).3; *Psal.* 45.4; 66.9; 93.8; 134.22; *Eu. Io.* 31.9; 38.7; 40.2; *Ep. Io.* 1.9.

2. See the following section and n. 4 below.

3. *Serm.* 227; 272; *Serm. Guelf.* 7(229A); *Serm. Denis* 3(228B) and 6(229) are similar but cannot be assigned to Augustine himself with adequate certainty. Little of substance is lost in omitting them from the analysis. See Hubertus R. Drobner, *Augustinus von Hippo: Sermones ad Populum* (New York: Lang, 2010), 41.

4. "Quid est quod occultum est, et non publicum in ecclesia? sacramentum baptismi, sacramentum eucharistiae. opera enim nostra bona uident et pagani, sacramenta uero occultantur illis; sed ab his quae non uident, surgunt illa quae uident; sicut a profundo crucis quod in terra figitur, surgit tota crux quae apparet et cernitur." *Psal.* 103.1.14; CSEL 95/1:130.18–131.23. See also *Serm. Mai*

86(229I).3; *Serm.* 234.2; 235.3. This practice was named the *disciplina arcani* in seventeenth-century debates.

5. *Serm. Guelf.* 7(229A).3.

6. *Serm.* 226; 228.3; for details, see William Harmless, *Augustine and the Catechumenate* (Collegeville, MN: Liturgical Press, 1995), 316–17.

7. *Serm.* 227; 228.3; *Serm. Guelf.* 7(229A).1.

8. *Serm.* 227; *Serm. Guelf.* 7(229A).3.

9. *Serm. Guelf.* 7(229A).2; *Serm.* 272.

10. "Panis ille quem uidetis in altari sanctificatus per uerbum dei, corpus est Christi. calix ille, immo quod habet calix, sanctificatum per uerbum dei, sanguis est Christi. per ista uoluit dominus Christus conmendare corpus et sanguinem suum quem pro nobis fudit in remissionem peccatorum. si bene accepistis, uos estis quod accepistis. apostolus enim dicit: *unus panis, unum corpus multi sumus* (1 Cor. 10:17). sic exposuit sacramentum mensae dominicae: *unus panis, unum corpus multi sumus* (1 Cor. 10:17)." *Serm.* 227, SC 116:234.10–236.18.

11. *Serm.* 227; 272; *Serm. Guelf.* 7(229A).1, 3.

12. "Quod uidetis in mensa domini, quantum pertinet ad ipsarum rerum speciem, et in uestris mensis uidere consuestis: ipse est uisus, sed non ipsa uirtus. nam et uos idem ipsi estis homines, qui eratis: neque enim ad nos nouas facies attulistis. Et tamen noui estis: ueteres corporis specie, noui gratia sanctitatis, sicut et hoc nouum est. adhuc quidem, quomodo uidetis, panis est et uinum: accedit sanctificatio, et panis ille erit corpus Christi, et uinum illud erit sanguis Christi. hoc facit nomen Christi, hoc facit gratia Christi, ut hoc ipsum uideatur quod uidebatur, et tamen non hoc ualeat quod ualebat. antea enim si manducaretur, inpleret uentrem; modo cum manducatur, aedificat mentem." *Serm. Guelf.* 7(229A).1; *MA* 1:462.9–19.

13. *Serm. Guelf.* 7(229A).1.

14. "Unus panis, dixit. quotquot ibi panes positi fuerint, unus panis: quotquot panes fuerint in altaribus Christi hodie per totum orbem terrarum, unus panis est. sed quid est, unus panis? exposuit breuissime: unum corpus multi sumus (1 Cor. 10:17). hoc panis corpus Christi, de quo dicit apostolus, alloquens ecclesiam: uos autem estis corpus Christi et membra (1 Cor. 12:27). quod accipitis, uos estis, gratia qua redempti estis; subscribitis, quando amen respondetis. hoc quod uidetis, sacramentum est unitatis." *Serm. Guelf.* 7(229A).1, *MA* 1:463.5–12.

15. As was noted in the discussion of the sacrament of baptism, Augustine clearly distinguished the sacramental ritual and signs from the effect produced

in the participants. He used the distinction between *signum* or *sacramentum* and *res* rarely. *Serm.* 227; *Eu. Io.* 26.15, 18.

16. *Serm.* 272.

17. "Ista, fratres, ideo dicuntur sacramenta, quia in eis aliud uidetur, aliud intellegitur. quod uidetur, speciem habet corporalem, quod intellegitur, fructum habet spiritualem. corpus ergo Christi si uis intellegere, apostolum audi dicentem fidelibus, uos autem estis corpus Christi, et membra (1 Cor. 12:27). si ergo uos estis corpus Christi et membra, mysterium uestrum in mensa dominica positum est: mysterium uestrum accipitis. ad id quod estis, amen respondetis, et respondendo subscribitis. audis enim, corpus Christi; et respondes, amen. esto membrum corporis Christi, ut uerum sit amen." *Serm.* 272, PL 38:1247.

18. "Quando exorcizabamini, quasi molebamini. quando baptizati estis, quasi conspersi estis. quando spiritus sancti ignem accepistis, quasi cocti estis. estote quod uidetis, et accipite quod estis." *Serm.* 272, PL 38:1247–48.

19. "Fratres, recolite unde fit uinum. grana multa pendent ad botrum, sed liquor granorum in unitate confunditur. ita et dominus Christus nos significauit. nos ad se pertinere uoluit, mysterium pacis et unitatis nostrae in sua mensa consecrauit." *Serm.* 272, PL 38:1248. Parallel descriptions of the symbolism of the bread and wine were used in *Serm.* 227 and in *Serm. Guelf.* 7(229A).2.

20. "Qui accipit mysterium unitatis, et non tenet uinculum pacis, non mysterium accipit pro se, sed testimonium contra se." *Serm.* 272, PL 38:1248.

21. *Serm.* 272.

22. "Quod uides transit, sed quod significatur inuisibile non transit, sed permanet. Ecce accipitur, comeditur, consumitur. numquid corpus Christi consumitur? numquid ecclesia Christi consumitur? numquid membra Christi consumuntur? absit. Hic mundantur, ibi coronantur. manebit ergo quod significatur." *Serm.* 227, SC 116:242.75–81.

23. David Wright's study of the manuscript tradition, "The Manuscripts of St. Augustine's *Tractatus in Euangelium Iohannis*: A Preliminary Survey and Check List," *Recherches Augustiniennes* 8 (1972): 55–143, and M.-F. Berrouard's elaboration of the evidence provided by Augustine's letter probably sent to Possidius of Calama in early December 419 (*Ep. Divj.* 23 [23A*]), *Introduction aux Homélies de Saint Augustin sur l'Évangile de Saint Jean*, Collection des Études Augustiniennes, Série Antiquité 170 (Paris: Institut d'Études Augustiniennes, 2004), 181–86, established what had long been proposed.

24. *Psal.* 103.1.14. See the text at pp. 106–7 above.

25. *Eu. Io.* 25.17; 27.12.

26. *Eu. Io.* 27.12.

27. *Eu.. Io.* 27.17.

28. For the omission of a specific detail of the eucharistic ritual, see below, p. 309 n. 35.

29. The four sermons on inherited guilt preached between June 24 and July 15, 413, in Carthage similarly work on a single theme, but not a continuous scriptural text. *Serm.* 293, 294, 299, and *Psal.* 50. See the analysis below, pp. 224–33.

30. *Eu. Io.* 11.12 (the persecution of Isaac by Ishmael); 12.11 (the brazen serpent); 17.1 (the bodily cures).

31. *Eu. Io.* 25.13. He had used *sacramentum* in *Serm.* 227 and *Serm. Guelf.* 7(229A).1. The pair *sacramentum* and *res* appears once in *Serm.* 272.

32. *Eu. Io.* 25.13.

33. *Eu. Io.* 11.5–6.

34. *Eu. Io.* 26.11.

35. *Eu. Io.* 26.11. The preparatory action was a necessary means of maintaining the unity of the body of the Whole Christ that the Christians were about to share sacramentally. Augustine did not make this point explicit. Omission of a more detailed reference might be a sign of Augustine's attention to the discipline of secrecy in regard to the ritual actions.

36. *Eu. Io.* 26.12. The importance of Paul's identification of the rock as Christ was more fully developed in *Serm.* 352.1.3. See also *Psal.* 77.2.

37. *Eu. Io.* 26.12.

38. "Hoc quando caperet caro, quod dixit panem, carnem? uocatur caro, quod non capit caro, et ideo magis non capit caro, quia uocatur caro." *Eu. Io.* 26.13, CCSL 36:266.5–8.

39. *Eu. Io.* 26.13.

40. "O sacramentum pietatis! o signum unitatis! o uinculum caritatis! qui uult uiuere, habet ubi uiuat, habet unde uiuat. accedat, credat, incorporetur, ut uiuificetur." *Eu. Io.* 26.13, CCSL 36:266.26–29. Note that the life-giving function is assigned to the ecclesial body of the Whole Christ rather than to the flesh proper to the Savior as its head.

41. *Eu. Io.* 26.13.

42. *Eu. Io.* 26.14.

43. Both verbs are in the present tense: the one who eats now has eternal life now.

44. *Eu. Io.* 26.15.

45. "In hoc uero cibo et potu, id est corpore et sanguine domini, non ita est.

nam et qui eam non sumit, non habet uitam; et qui eam sumit, habet uitam, et hanc utique aeternam." *Eu. Io.* 26.15, CCSL 36:267.24–27.

46. "Hunc itaque cibum et potum societatem uult intellegi corporis et membrorum suorum." *Eu. Io.* 26.15, CCSL 36:267.27–28.

47. "Quod est sancta ecclesia in praedestinatis et uocatis, et iustificatis, et glorificatis sanctis, et fidelibus eius. quorum primum iam factum est, id est, praedestinatio; secundum et tertium factum est, et fit, et fiet, id est, uocatio et iustificatio; quartum uero nunc in spe est, in re autem futurum est, id est, glorificatio." *Eu. Io.* 26.15, CCSL 36:267.27–33. The reference is to Rom. 8:30.

48. This explanation is an unusual affirmation of divine predestination (as distinguished from foreknowledge) in a sermon. The following sermon in the series can be dated to August 10 by reference to the feast of the Roman martyr Lawrence (*Eu. Io.* 27.10, 12). M.-F Berrouard argues that the year was 414. See *Introduction aux Homélies*, 97–99.

49. "Huius rei sacramentum, id est, unitatis corporis et sanguinis Christi alicubi quotidie, alicubi certis interuallis dierum in dominica mensa praeparatur, et de mensa dominica sumitur: quibusdam ad uitam, quibusdam ad exitium; res uero ipsa cuius sacramentum est, omni homini ad uitam, nulli ad exitium, quicumque eius particeps fuerit." *Eu. Io.* 26.15, CCSL 36:267.33–268.39.

50. *Eu. Io.* 26.15.

51. *Eu. Io.* 26.16.

52. In discussing the efficacy of baptism against the Donatists, Augustine had identified this unity as the group that held and shared sanctifying power within the visible church. *Bapt.* 3.17.22–18.23, 19.26; 5.21.29; 6.3.5–5.7.

53. *Eu. Io.* 26.17.

54. "Hoc est ergo manducare illam escam, et illum bibere potum, in Christo manere, et illum manentem in se habere. ac per hoc qui non manet in Christo, et in quo non manet Christus, procul dubio nec manducat carnem eius, nec bibit eius sanguinem, sed magis tantae rei sacramentum ad iudicium sibi manducat et bibit." *Eu. Io.* 26.18, CCSL 36:268.4–9.

55. *Eu. Io.* 26.18.

56. *Eu. Io.* 26.19–20.

57. *Eu. Io.* 27.1.

58. *Eu. Io.* 27.1–2.

59. *Eu. Io.* 27.3.

60. *Eu. Io.* 26.14.

61. *Eu. Io.* 27.5.

62. *Eu. Io.* 26.13–14. See above, pp. 118–20 at nn. 46–49. The congregation

might have been slightly different; he must have considered the argument worth repeating.

63. *Eu. Io.* 27.6.

64. "Ut autem simus membra eius, unitas nos compaginat. ut compaginet unitas, quae facit nisi caritas? et caritas dei unde? apostolum interroga. caritas, inquit, dei diffusa est in cordibus nostris per spiritum sanctum qui datus est nobis (Rm 5:5). ergo spiritus est qui uiuificat (Io 6:64); spiritus enim facit uiua membra. nec uiua membra spiritus facit, nisi quae in corpore quod uegetat ipse spiritus, inuenerit." *Eu. Io.* 27.6, CCSL 36:272.6–13.

65. *Eu. Io.* 27.6.

66. *Eu. Io.* 26.15; 27.5–6.

67. *Serm. Dolb.* 26(198 augm).57.

68. This practice had been mandated at the Council of Arles in 314. See above, the chapter on baptism, pp. 125–26.

69. See above, the chapter on baptism, p. 99 n. 102.

70. *Eu. Io.* 17.1; *Serm. Dolb.* 25(360B).2; *Bapt.* 3.10.15; 4.25.32.

71. Aug. *Serm.* 295.2.2; *Serm. Guelf.* 16(229N).2; *Eu. Io.* 26.15, 17; 121.4; *Bapt.* 1.11.15; 3.18.23; 5.21.29; 6.1.1, 3.5, 14.23. For use of the term *columba* for the church joined in love see *Serm.* 96.7.9; 183.7.11; 262.6.5; *Psal.* 127.13; 141.7; 147.10.

72. In his treatises, he considered the possibility that the performance of baptism would actually confer the sanctification of the Spirit, and that this life would be lost by rejection of the unity of the church either through schism or a failure to repent and convert. *Bapt.* 1.11.15–1.12.20; 3.13.18; 16.21–17.22.

73. See, for example, *Eu. Io.* 44.6; 45.15; 53.9; *Ep. Io.* 10.1–2; *Psal.* 31.2.3–6.

74. *Serm. Guelf.* 2(218B).2.

75. *Eu. Io.* 26.15. See above, pp. 119–21.

76. "Ergo eucharistia panis noster cotidianus est. sed si accipiamus illum non solum uentre, sed et mente. uirtus enim ipsa, quae ibi intellegitur, unitas est, ut, redacti in eius corpus, effecti membra eius, simus quod accipimus." *Serm.* 57.7.7. The Maurist edition of this sermon adds *reficiamur* after *mente* in the second sentence, thereby giving the mental reception a transformative effect. Verbraken's edition (pp. 418.108–419.111) eliminates this variant and brings the text into line with Augustine teaching elsewhere. Pierre-Patrick Verbraken, "Le Sermon 57 de Saint Augustin pour la Tradition de l'Oraison Dominicale," *Homo Spiritualis: Festgabe für Luc Verheijen su seinem 70. Geburtstag,* ed. Cornelius Petrus Mayer and Karl Heinz Chelius (Würzburg: Augustinus Verlag, 1987), 411–24.

77. *Serm. Mai* 129(132A).2.

78. *Serm.* 71.11.17, ed. Pierre-Patrick Verbraken, *RBén* 75 (1965): 80.340–81.360.

79. *Serm. Mai* 129(132A).1–2.

80. *Eu. Io.* 26.16.

81. *Serm.* 144.4.5; 161.1.1; *Serm. Mai* 98(263A).1; *Psal.* 122.1.

82. *Serm.* 154.11.16; 128.3.5; *Serm. Dolb.* 26(198 augm).33; *Psal.* 57.17–18.

83. *Eu. Io.* 27.5–6.

84. *Serm. Guelf.* 9(229E).4; *Serm.* 131.1; *Psal.* 98.9.

85. See above, p. 306 n. 1.

86. *Serm.* 17.17; see also *Psal.* 33.1.10.

87. *Serm. Mai* 129(132A).1.

88. In *Serm.* 161.1.1. The argument is based on 1 Cor. 6:15.

89. *Serm.* 220; *Serm. Guelf.* 2(218B).1; *Psal.* 21.2.1; 39.12.

90. *Serm. Guelf.* 7(229A).2; *Serm.* 272.

91. *Serm.* 227; 272; *Serm. Guelf.* 7(229A).1–2. For the texts, see pp. 307–8 nn. 12, 14, 17 above.

Chapter Six

1. Pierre-Marie Hombert dates *Serm.* 51 at the end of December 403, pp. 82–83. *Serm. Dolb.* 12 (354A) is dated 403–4, pp. 417–32; *Serm.* 8 is dated in 403, pp. 98–99. *On the Good of Marriage* is dated 403–4, pp. 105–8. The second sermon on the Decalogue (*Serm.* 9) remains undated. Pierre-Marie Hombert, *Nouvelles Recherches de Chronologie Augustinienne*, Collection des Études Augustiniennes, Série Antiquité 163 (Paris: Institut d'Études Augustiniennes, 2000).

2. *Serm.* 392.

3. *Serm.* 278.9.9–10.10.

4. *Serm.* 332.4, PL 38:1462–63.

5. *Serm.* 9.18. Excessive sexual intercourse with a spouse could be so forgiven.

6. *Serm.* 132.2; 392.2–3.

7. *Serm.* 9.4; 392.4.

8. *Serm.* 392.4.

9. *Serm.* 332.4; 392.4; *Serm. Dolb.* 12(354A).4.

10. *Serm.* 9.4; 392.5; 332.5.

11. *Serm.* 51.11.18, 13.21.

12. *Serm.* 51.20.30.

13. *Psal.* 136.17.

14. *Serm.* 9.3, 4, 11; 132.2; 332.4; 392.5.

15. *Psal.* 143.6. Augustine did not use 1 Cor. 11:3 for this purpose in his sur-viving sermons, perhaps because it was not focused on marriage.

16. *Serm.* 9.12; 132.2; 332.4.

17. *Serm.* 9.11; 392.5.

18. *Serm.* 9.11.

19. *Serm.* 392.4.

20. *Serm.* 132.2.

21. Bishops could not yet discipline them by exclusion from the eucharist, which they were not permitted to receive until after accepting baptism.

22. *Serm.* 392.2.

23. *Serm.* 349.4.

24. *Serm.* 349.3.

25. "Dicere habet nescio quis: sed meretrix non est, concubina mea est. habes uxorem, qui hoc dicis? habeo. illa ergo, uelis nolis, meretrix est. uade, et dic quia iniuriam tibi fecit episcopus, si habes uxorem, et alia tecum dormit. quaecumque illa est, meretrix est. sed seruat tibi forsitan fidem, et non nouit nisi te unum, et non disponit nosse alium. cum ergo illa sit casta, tu quare for-nicaris? si illa unum, tu quare duas? non licet, non licet, non licet. in gehennam eunt." *Serm.* 224.3, *RBén* 79 (1969): 203.53–204.59.

26. She vowed not to take another partner when she was sent away. Augus-tine soon replaced her. *Conf.* 4.2.2; 6.15.25.

27. *Serm.* 61.1.1.

28. *Serm. Denis* 17(301A).8, *MA* 1:88.30–34. Implicit in this argument may be the supposition that the women were not free to reject the work. This would be one of the unusual instances in which Augustine promoted the religious rights of slaves.

29. *Serm.* 278.7.7–8.8; 332.4.

30. *Serm.* 161.2.2.

31. *Serm.* 349.4.

32. *Serm.* 278.10.10. This was as close as Augustine came to using a notion of ritual impurity. The defiling action, it should be noted, was itself immoral. He never implied that sexual relations with a spouse had any such effect on one's standing before God.

33. *Serm.* 343.7.

34. *Serm.* 161.8.8–12.12.

35. See above, pp. 92, 128–30.

36. Augustine considered 1 Cor. 7:14 on the sanctification of a non-Chris-tian spouse by a Christian only once in his preaching and granted it salvific significance only if it led to baptism. *Serm.* 294.19.18.

37. *Serm.* 51.14.23.

38. This attitude is especially evident in his discussion of the marriage and parentage of Joseph and Mary. *Serm.* 51.14.23–15.25.

39. *Serm.* 51.13.22–15.25; *Serm. Dolb.* 12(354A).11.

40. *Serm.* 51.13.22.

41. *Serm.* 278.9.9–10.10, 14.14.

42. *Serm.* 51.13.22–14.24; 278.9.9.

43. *Serm.* 278.9.9–10.10.

44. *Serm. Dolb.* 12(354A).11.

45. *Serm.* 8.8; 9.18; 51.13.22; 351.3.5.

46. *Serm.* 51.13.22; 351.3.5.

47. *Serm. Dolb.* 12(354A).8–9.

48. *Serm.* 351.3.5.

49. *Psal.* 147.4.

50. *Serm.* 51.13.22; *Psal.* 121.10; *Serm. Dolb.* 12(354A).8–9, 12.

51. "Inuicem amate. potest uir, non potest mulier: non exigis debitum, redde. et in eo quod reddes qui non iam exigis, si non exigis, misericordiam facis. omnino audeo dicere: misericordia est. si enim non reddideris, concupiscentia uicta coniux, aut si non reddideris tu mulier, concupiscentia uictus uir adulter futurus est. nolo te sic amplius honorari ut illum uelis damnari." *Serm. Dolb.* 12(354A).13. *Augustin d'Hippone, Vingt-six Sermons au Peuple d'Afrique,* ed. François Dolbeau, Collection des Études Augustiniennes, Série Antiquité 147 (Paris: Institut d'Études Augustiniennes, 2009), 84.206–11.

52. "Quid quod si iam non exigis, sed tantum reddis: continentiae deputatur. non enim libidine exigitur, sed misericordia redditur. prorsus dic deo tuo: domine, tu in me nosti quod dedisti, sed audio etiam quod monuisti, quia et me et coniugem tu fecisti, et neminem perire uoluisti." *Serm. Dolb.* 12(354A).13, *Augustin d'Hippone, Vingt-six Sermons,* 84.211–16.

53. *Ep. Io.* 5.3. This was the only letter of John in Augustine's Bible.

54. *Serm.* 9.18; *Serm. Dolb.* 12(354A).12.

55. *Serm.* 278.10.10–11.11.

56. *Serm.* 51.13.21.

57. *Serm. Dolb.* 12(354A). See, David G. Hunter, "Augustine, Sermon 354A*: Its Place in His Thought on Marriage and Sexuality," *Augustinian Studies* 33, no. 1 (2002): 39–60. At pp. 58–59, Hunter suggests that husbands may have been seeking to leave their marriages to become monks.

58. *Serm.* 51.13.21; *Serm. Dolb.* 22(341 augm).20. See above, pp. 142–44, for the different ways Augustine interpreted 1 Thess. 4:4–5.

59. Clergy were required to practice continence within their marriages once

they had become deacons (or even subdeacons), usually after age twenty-five. See Council of Carthage, 390, c. 2; Canons in the Case of Apiarius Ap. 16, 25 and selections from *Reg. Carth.* 70, 126; CCSL 148:13, 138–39, 201, 227. The same age limit seems to have been applied to the dedication of virgins.

60. *Serm.* 51.15.26–16.26; *Serm. Dolb.* 12(354A).11.

61. *Serm. Dolb.* 12(354A).3.

62. "Non potest inde tale arbitrium habere uir, ut dicat: continere iam possum. si potes, hoc age mecum; si non potes, nullo modo me impedies: ego facio quod possum. quid ergo? uis, o uir, ut pereat latus tuum? si enim continere non potest caro infirmior, uoluntas languidior fornicabitur, fornicando damnabitur. absit ut illius poena tua sit corona! falleris: non erit, non erit sic." *Serm. Dolb.* 12(354A).5, *Augustin d'Hippone, Vingt-six*, 79.65–71.

63. "Non erit ut dicas mihi quoniam fornicando damnabitur, melius ipsa sola quam simul. si hoc dicis, falleris. non enim damnatur coniugium, non damnatur *quod deus coniunxit, tantum homo non separet* [Mt 19,6]. tu homo es; adripiendo continentiam sine consensu coniugis tuae, sicut homo, uis separare quod deus dignatus est copulare. sed deus, inquit, separat, quia propter deum facio. plane si hoc alicubi legeris deum dixisse: si commixtus fueris uxori tuae, damnabo te, fac quod uis, ne simul damneris." *Serm. Dolb.* 12(354A).5, *Vingt-six Sermons*, 79.71–80.78.

64. "Cum uero audias apostolum Christi dicentem: *uxor non habet potestatem corporis sui, sed uir. similiter et uir non habet potestatem corporis sui, sed mulier. nolite fraudare inuicem* (1 Cor. 7:4–5) <. . . >. *fraudare* [1 Cor. 7:5] dixit: negando debitum, non faciendo adulterium. de reddendis enim debitis loquebatur, et ad reddenda inuicem debita coniugia constringebat." *Serm. Dolb.* 12(354A).5–6, *Vingt-six Sermons*, 80.79–84.

65. *Serm. Dolb.* 12(354A).6–7, 12–13. *Psal.* 149.15 develops the same teaching by allegorizing a reference to iron chains.

66. *Serm. Dolb.* 12(354A).10.

67. *Serm. Dolb.* 12(354A).12–13.

68. *Serm.* 392.2.

69. See Judith Evans Grubbs, *Women and the Law in the Roman Empire: A Sourcebook on Marriage, Divorce, and Widowhood* (London: Routledge, 2002).

70. *Eu. Io.* 9.2.

71. *Serm.* 51.6.9.

72. *Serm.* 9.11; 392.5.

73. *Psal.* 149.15.

74. *Serm.* 137.8.9; *Psal.* 55.17; 72.33.

75. *Serm.* 9.20.

76. *Serm.* 9.20; 86.9.11–11.12.

77. *Psal.* 48.1.14.

78. *Serm.* 86.11.13–12.14; *Psal.* 48.1.14.

79. *Serm.* 355.4–5; 356.11.

80. *Serm.* 356.7.

81. *Serm.* 355.4.

82. See above, p. 149.

83. A connection that Augustine repeated using the text in *Serm.* 349.3.

84. See above, pp. 128–30.

85. *Psal.* 34.2.1; 37.6; 54.3; 68.2.1; 142.3; *Serm.* 129.3.4.

86. For the fuller discussion, see the chapter on scriptural interpretation, pp. 15–19.

87. "Sic autem aliquando, ut intellegas caput et corpus, exponente ipso apostolo apertissime quod dictum est de uiro et uxore in Genesi: et erunt, inquit, duo in carne una (Eph. 5:32). adtendite ipsum exponentem, ut non coniecturis nostris aliquid ausi dicere uideamur. et erunt, inquit, duo in carne una (Eph. 5:32), et addidit: sacramentum hoc magnum est (Eph. 5:32). et ne adhuc putaret quisquam in uiro esse et uxore secundum naturalem utriusque sexus copulationem corporalemque immixturam: ego autem, inquit, dico in Christo et in ecclesia (Eph. 5:32). secundum hoc ergo quod in Christo et in ecclesia (Eph. 5:32), accipitur quod dictum est: erunt duo in carne una: non iam duo, sed una caro est (Matt. 19:5–6). quomodo sponsus et sponsa, sic caput et corpus, quia caput mulieris uir (1 Cor. 11:3). Siue ergo dicam caput et corpus, siue dicam sponsus et sponsa, unum intellegite." *Serm. Dolb.* 22(341 augm).19, *Vingt-six Sermons*, 572.474–82.

88. *Serm. Dolb.* 22(341 augm).20.

89. *Psal.* 138.2. See *Serm. Mai* 20(64A).3 for a similar use of some to these texts.

90. *Psal.* 138.2, CSEL 95/4:127.8–128.32. This analysis was repeated in an abbreviated form in *Psal.* 126.7.

91. *Eu. Io.* 9.10; see the parallel in *Psal.* 44.12.

92. This point is made in *Serm. Etaix.* 1(65A), which bases the relationship of the church to Christ on doing the will of the Father.

93. *Psal.* 10.10; 30.2.1.4. One of the examples of this that Augustine enjoyed was the Old Latin text of Isaiah 61:10, in which the same person received the symbols of marriage as both masculine and feminine, *Serm.* 91.7.9; *Serm. Dolb.* 22(341 augm).19; *Psal.* 30.2.1.4; 74.4; 101.1.2; *Ep. Io.* 1.2.

94. *Serm.* 51.11.18–13.21. For the dating of these sermons, see above, p. 312 n. 1.

95. See above, pp. 135–36.

96. This connection is made explicitly in *Eu. Io.* 2.14.

97. *Serm.* 192.2; 196.2.

98. *Serm.* 188.3.4; 191.2.3. Augustine was unsure whether the term "virgin" could be used for males; perhaps their bodies did not lose their "integrity" by sexual intercourse. *Eu. Io.* 13.12.

99. *Serm.* 188.3.4; 191.2.3; 213.8; *Serm. Denis* 25(72A).8; *Psal.* 90.2.9; 147.10; *Eu. Io.* 13.12.

100. *Serm.* 191.2.3. Not all Christians, of course, had been saved from prostitution or idolatry, at least in Augustine's day, but their wholeness remained the work of Christ. *Serm.* 213.8.

101. *Serm.* 93.3.4.

102. *Serm.* 213.8.

103. *Serm.* 184.1.1; 188.3.4.

104. *Eu. Io.* 9.2.

105. *Serm.* 192.2; 195.2; *Serm. Denis* 25(72A).8.

106. *Serm. Denis* 25(72A).8.

107. *Serm.* 192.2.

108. *Serm.* 192.2.

109. *Serm.* 192.2; *Psal.* 131.23; 145.18.

110. Faithful wives were credited with preserving in their hearts the bodily integrity that they had given up in generating. *Serm.* 192.2.

111. *Serm.* 161.1.1; 349.3; *Serm. Denis* 17(301A).8.

112. See J. Patout Burns, "Marital Fidelity as a *remedium concupiscentiae*: An Augustinian Proposal," *Augustinian Studies* 44 (2013): 1–35.

113. On sexual intercourse in paradise, see *Gen. litt.* 9.3.6–4.8; 11.1.3; on the glory of the gendered and resurrected body, *Ciu.* 22.17–19.

Chapter Seven

1. *Serm.* 266.1. Pierre-Marie Hombert dates this sermon in the period 403–8, primarily on the basis of its parallels with the treatises against the Donatists Petilian, Parmenian, and Cresconius written during that period. Pierre-Marie Hombert, *Nouvelles Recherches de Chronologie Augustinienne*, Collection des Études Augustiniennes, Série Antiquité 163 (Paris: Institut d'Études Augustiniennes, 2000), 289–99.

2. *Serm.* 266.1. See also *Psal.* 140.13, 17–19. Hombert dates the Psalm commentary to 404, *Nouvelles Recherches*, 344n8.

3. The central event was the attempt of Simon Magus to acquire for himself

the power to give the Spirit, Acts 8:14–14. See *Serm.* 266.3–8; 269.2. For the dating, see Hombert, *Nouvelles Recherches*, 265–66. For a more detailed treatment of the argument, see the chapter on baptism, pp. 97–100.

4. *Serm.* 266.3–4.

5. As was noted in the chapter on baptism, Augustine's text of this passage was unusual. See above, p. 305 n. 94.

6. *Serm.* 266.4–5.

7. *Serm.* 266.6–8. For a summary of this teaching see *Serm.* 269.2; for dating, see Hombert, *Nouvelles Recherches*, 265–66.

8. The chronology of these sermons has been the subject of intensive work for nearly a century. A consensus has developed that places the first sixteen of these between December 405 and June 406, about the same time as *Serm.* 266 and 269, but well before *Serm.* 99, to be considered below. For a summary of the process, please see J. Patout Burns, "Situating and Studying Augustine's Sermons," *Journal of Early Christian Studies* 26 (2018): 307–22.

9. *Eu. Io.* 4.14–15.

10. *Eu. Io.* 5.18.

11. *Eu. Io.* 5.1–2, 7–9.

12. *Eu. Io.* 5.13.

13. *Eu. Io.* 5.11, 18.

14. *Eu. Io.* 5.15.

15. *Eu. Io.* 6.6–8. See the parallel treatment of this passage in chapter on baptism, pp. 95–96.

16. *Eu. Io.* 6.18.

17. *Psal.* 131.14, 27.

18. See above, pp. 98–99.

19. See above, pp. 79–83.

20. The efficacy of the ritual of ordination, through which clergy were linked to certain powers of Christ, was considered as an authorization of the clergy to perform the ritual of baptism, but only in Augustine's treatises. "sicut habet in baptismo quod per eos dari possit, sic in ordinatione ius dandi; utrumque quidem ad perniciem suam, quamdiu non habent unitatis." *Parm.* 2.13.28, CSEL 51:79.26–80.1. See also *Bapt.* 1.1.2. The bishops ordained in the Donatist schism were accepted into Catholic communion as bishops and allowed to practice their ministry. See *Ep.* 43.5.16 and *Reg. Carth.* 68.

21. Hombert places it in the summer, not long after the Colloquy of Carthage in 411, *Nouvelles Recherches*, 295n14.

22. *Serm.* 99.10–12; see the discussion of *Serm.* 266, pp. 97–98 above.

23. *Serm.* 99.9. For the interpretation of the third conferral of this power, on Peter as a symbol of the whole church, in Matt. 16:19, see the following section.

24. *Serm.* 99.13.

25. See above, pp. 63–67.

26. See above, pp. 99–100.

27. *Serm.* 67.1.2–2.3; 98.6; 352.3.8; *Serm. Mai* 125(139A).2; *Psal.* 101.2.3; *Eu. Io.* 22.7; 49.22, 24.

28. *Serm.* 67.2.3; 295.2.2; *Eu. Io.* 49.24.

29. *Serm.* 392.3; *Serm. Mai* 125(139A).2.

30. Cypr. *Unit. eccl.* 4–5. It should be noted that Cyprian interpreted the group in John 20 as the twelve apostles, and thus the predecessors of the bishops. Augustine followed the Johannine text's "disciples," and thus interpreted the recipients as including all faithful Christians.

31. In this, Augustine was developing the teaching of Tertullian, an earlier African lay theologian, who opposed his own bishop's identification of Peter as a symbol of bishops alone. See Tertullian's *Pud.* 21.

32. *Serm.* 295 was dated as 400–410 by Hombert, *Nouvelles Recherches*, 238n7. Thus, it was preached during the conflict with the Donatists over the church's power to forgive sins.

33. "Dominus Iesus discipulos suos ante passionem suam, sicut nostis, elegit, quos apostolos appellauit. Inter hos paene ubique solus Petrus, totius ecclesiae meruit gestare personam. propter ipsam personam, quam totius ecclesiae solus gestabat, audire meruit, tibi dabo claues regni caelorum (Matt. 16:19). has enim claues non homo unus, sed unitas accepit ecclesiae. hinc ergo Petri excellentia praedicatur, quia ipsius uniuersitatis et unitatis ecclesiae figuram gessit, quando ei dictum est, tibi trado (Matt. 16:19), quod omnibus traditum est." *Serm.* 295.2.2, PL 38:1349.

34. "Nam ut noueritis ecclesiam accepisse claues regni caelorum, audite in alio loco quid dominus dicat omnibus apostolis suis. accipite spiritum sanctum (John 20:22). et continuo: si cui dimiseritis peccata, dimittentur ei; si cuius tenueritis, tenebuntur (John 20:23)." *Serm.* 295.2.2, PL 38:1349. The parallel statements preceding and following in the same paragraph show that Augustine was not limiting "omnibus apostolis suis" (all his apostles) to the Twelve, as Cyprian had.

35. "Hoc ad claues pertinet, de quibus dictum est, quae solueritis in terra, soluta erunt et in caelo; et quae ligaueritis in terra, ligata erunt et in caelo (Mt 18:18) sed hoc Petro dixit." *Serm.* 295.2.2, PL 38:1349. The transition from the singular (Matt. 16:19) to the plural (Matt. 18:18) might be attributed to scribal error or substitution, but Augustine's following comments show that the substitution was his own and intentional.

36. "Ut scias quia Petrus uniuersae ecclesiae personam tunc gerebat, audi quid ipsi dicatur, quid omnibus fidelibus sanctis: si peccauerit in te frater tuus,

corripe illum inter te et ipsum solum. si non te audierit, adhibe tecum unum aut duos: scriptum est enim, in ore duorum aut trium testium, stabit omne uerbum. si nec ipsos audierit, refer ad ecclesiam: si nec ipsam audierit, sit tibi tanquam ethnicus et publicanus (Matt. 18:15–17). amen dico uobis, quia quae ligaueritis in terra, ligata erunt et in caelo; et quaecumque solueritis in terra, soluta erunt et in caelo (Matt. 18:18). columba ligat, columba soluit; aedificium supra petram ligat et soluit. timeant ligati, timeant soluti." *Serm.* 295.2.2, PL 38:1349.

37. See *Bapt.* 3.17.22–18.23; 4.3.4–4.5; 5.21.29.

38. *Eu. Io.* 50.12.

39. *Serm.* 149.6.7.

40. "Si uni Petro dictum est, solus hoc fecit Petrus: obiit, et abiit; quis ergo ligat, quis soluit? Audeo dicere, claues istas habemus et nos. et quid dicam? quia nos ligamus, nos soluimus? ligatis et uos, soluitis et uos. qui enim ligatur, a uestro consortio separatur: et cum a uestro consortio separatur, a uobis ligatur: et quando reconciliatur, a uobis soluitur, quia et a uobis deus pro illo rogatur." *Serm. Guelf.* 16(229N).2, MA 1:493.24–30.

41. See above, pp. 79–82 and 100–102. Neither the scriptural texts nor Augustine's analysis offers any foundation for distinguishing the "prayer" offered by the laity and from a different type of action by the clergy.

42. See above, pp. 76–77.

43. J. Patout Burns and Robin Margaret Jensen, *Christianity in Roman Africa: The Development of Its Practices and Beliefs* (Grand Rapids: Eerdmans, 2014), 339–41.

44. *Serm.* 82.8.11–9.12; 232.8.

45. See the chapter on forgiveness, pp. 79–82.

46. *Bapt.* 3.17.22–18.23; 4.3.4–4.5; 5.21.29.

47. *Psal.* 47.1, 8; 131.13; 146.9; 147.20, 23, 26.

48. *Psal.* 101.2.10–11.

49. *Eu. Io.* 17.11; 25.4–5; *Psal.* 64.6; 130.4; *Serm. Dolb.* 26(198 augm).49, 53, 54.

50. *Serm. Dolb.* 26(198 augm).49.

51. *Serm. Dolb.* 26(198 augm).54.

52. *Eu. Io.* 17.11; *Psal.* 26.2.2; 42.5; 64.6; 129.7; 130.4; *Serm. Dolb.* 26(198 augm).50, 53, 57.

53. *Psal.* 42.5; *Serm.* 351.4.7; *Serm. Dolb.* 26(198 augm).57.

54. *Serm. Dolb.* 26(198 augm).49, 54. See also the contemporary *Psal.* 36.2.20.

55. *Psal.* 64.6; 129.7.

56. Augustine regularly used the exchange that preceded the eucharistic

prayer to exhort the congregation to rise above the temporal and mundane; occasionally he referred to the glorified Christ enthroned in heaven. For the liturgical use, see *Serm.* 229.3; for the moral exhortation, *Serm.* 25.2, 7; 86.1.1; 227; 237.3; 261.1; 362.14.16; *Serm. Dolb.* 5(114B).14; 17(110A).6; 21(159B).18; *Serm. Guelf.* 7(229A).3; 20(265C).2.

57. *Serm. Dolb.* 26(198 augm).53.

58. See Burns and Jensen, *Christianity in Roman Africa*, 287–89.

59. *Psal.* 42.5; 130.4; *Eu. Io.* 17.11.

60. *Serm. Dolb.* 26(198 augm).52; See *Parm.* 2.7.14–8.16.

61. *Serm. Dolb.* 26(198 augm).53; *Psal.* 36.2.20; see also *Parm.* 2.7.14–8.16.

62. *Serm. Dolb.* 26(198 augm).54; *Eu. Io.* 25.4–7.

63. *Serm.* 351.4.7; *Psal.* 26.2.2; 64.6.

64. *Serm. Dolb.* 26(198 augm).50; *Psal.* 26.2.2.

65. *Psal.* 26.2.2.

66. *Dolb.* 26(198 augm).49, 50, 51, 53, 57. Apparently, the rituals of ordination of the clergy did not include a distinct anointing; the church's officers were distinguished from the laity by the imposition of hands.

67. "Nos autem omnes episcopi sacerdotes ideo dicimur, quia praepositi sumus. uniuersa tamen ecclesia corpus est illius sacerdotis. ad sacerdotem pertinet corpus suum. nam et apostolus Petrus ideo dicit ad ipsam ecclesiam: plebs sancta, regale sacerdotium (1 Pet. 2:9)." *Serm. Dolb.* 26(198 augm).49; *Augustin d'Hippone, Vingt-six Sermons au Peuple d'Afrique*, ed. François Dolbeau, Collection des Études Augustiniennes, Série Antiquité 147 (Paris: Institut d'Études Augustiniennes, 2009), 404.1207–405.1210.

68. *Psal.* 49.23; *Ep. Io.* 6.14; *Serm.* 46.6; 137.8.9.

69. *Serm.* 51.3.4; *Eu. Io.* 46.6.

70. *Eu. Io.* 46.6; *Serm. Guelf.* 32(340A).11; *Serm.* 137.11.13.

71. *Psal.* 100.10.

72. *Serm. Guelf.* 32(340A).9.

73. *Serm.* 46.6; *Eu. Io.* 46.6.

74. *Psal.* 115.1; *Eu. Io.* 46.5–6.

75. *Psal.* 36.3.20; 128.6.

76. *Serm.* 137.7.7; *Serm. Guelf.* 32(340A).9.

77. *Serm.* 179.10. Hombert, building on the work of LaBonnardière, placed this sermon before 411, *Nouvelles Recherches*, 378n5. Augustine made a similar observation about Peter's failure to anticipate his future failure. *Serm.* 147.3.

78. *Serm. Guelf.* 32(340A).10; *Serm.* 74.3–4; *Psal.* 51.4.

79. *Serm.* 46.22; 74.4; 137.11.13; *Serm. Guelf.* 32(340A).10; *Eu. Io.* 46.6.

80. *Serm.* 153.1.1; *Psal.* 96.3; 146.11.

81. Among the best examples was his attempt to specify the unforgivable blasphemy against the Holy Spirit. *Serm.* 71.

82. *Eu. Io.* 45.7.

83. *Psal.* 115.1; 103.2.11; 106.14.

84. *Serm.* 137.10.12.

85. *Serm.* 46.10–12.

86. *Serm.* 137.8.8–9.

87. *Serm.* 137.7.7.

88. *Serm. Guelf.* 32(340A).11; *Eu. Io.* 46.6.

89. *Psal.* 49.23; 115.1; *Serm.* 46.6; 137.5.5; *Ep. Io.* 6.14.

90. *Psal.* 61.8; 51.4.

91. *Eu. Io.* 26.7–9; *Psal.* 66.1; 134.22; *Serm. Cail.* 2.11(112A).11; *Serm.* 152.1; 153.1.1; 179.7; 224.3.

92. *Serm.* 137.7.7; *Eu. Io.* 26.7.

93. In *To Simplician*, for example, he reflected on the way that God guided the preacher, all unknowing, to present the motives and considerations that would actually move the hearts of those God had elected and was calling. See *Simpl.* 1.2.13–14. He illustrated this process on multiple occasions in the *Confessions*, in some of which the speaker was ignorant or malicious (*Conf.* 8.2.4; 8.5.10; 8.6.13–7.18; 8.11.27–12.30; 9.8.18). In the controversy with the Pelagians, he called attention to the implications of Jesus's statement in John 6:43–45 that the Father himself draws and teaches those in whom the gospel takes root. *Grat. Chr.* 10.11; 14.15.

94. *Psal.* 87.10.

95. In *Eu. Io.* 11.9 the parallel to baptismal ministry was explicit.

96. *Psal.* 51.4; 115.1; *Eu. Io.* 11.9; 46.6; *Serm.* 137.5.5, 9.10–11; 251.4.3.

97. *Serm.* 261.2; 298.5.5.

98. *Serm.* 153.1.1; *Psal.* 96.3.

99. *Psal.* 146.11.

100. *Psal.* 36.3.20.

101. *Serm.* 46.24.

102. *Eu. Io.* 47.2; *Serm.* 138.1.1, 3.3–5.5; 146.1; 253.2; 296.4.

103. *Serm.* 46.23; 137.3.3; 285.5; 295.2.2; *Serm. Lamb.* 3(229P).1.

104. *Eu. Io.* 46.5, 7; 47.1; *Serm.* 46.30; *Serm. Guelf.* 16(229N).3; *Psal.* 126.3.

105. *Serm.* 285.5; *Serm. Guelf.* 17(229O).3.

106. *Serm.* 46.26, 30.

107. *Serm.* 138.5.5; 296.13; *Eu. Io.* 46.5.

108. For the equivalence, see *Ciu.* 19.19.

109. *Serm. Dolb.* 10(162C).2; *Psal.* 106.7; 126.3.

110. *Serm.* 146.1; 339.1–2 show Augustine's fear at the responsibility placed upon bishops.

111. *Serm.* 339.8–9; *Eu. Io.* 46.8.

112. *Psal.* 126.3.

113. *Serm. Dolb.* 10(162C).2; *Serm.* 146.1.

114. *Serm. Dolb.* 10(162C).2.

115. *Serm.* 102.1.1.

116. *Serm. Denis* 17(301A).2; *Psal.* 126.3.

117. Cypr. *Ep.* 66.1.1–3.3.

118. *Parm.* 1.2.2–4.6; 2.8.15–16.

119. Cypr. *Unit. eccl.* 4–5; Aug. *Serm.* 295.4.4. In this passage, Peter was named as representative, as he had been in Matt. 16:19.

120. "Patres missi sunt apostoli, pro apostolis filii nati sunt tibi, constituti sunt episcopi. Hodie enim episcopi, qui sunt per totum mundum, unde nati sunt? ipsa ecclesia patres illos appellat, ipsa illos genuit, et ipsa illos constituit in sedibus patrum." *Psal.* 44.32, CCSL 38:516.15–19. This was preached on September 2, 403. Hombert, *Nouvelles Recherches*, 28.

121. "Omnes simul unam domum dei faciunt, et unam ciuitatem. ipsa est Ierusalem. habet custodes; quomodo habet aedificantes, laborantes ut aedificetur, sic habet et custodientes. nam ad custodiam pertinet quod dicit apostolus: *timeo ne sicut serpens Euam seduxit adstutia sua, sic et uestrae mentes corrumpantur a castitate quae est in Christo* (2 Cor. 11:3). custodiebat, custos erat, uigilabat, quantum poterat, super eos quibus praeerat. et episcopi hoc faciunt." *Psal.* 126.3, CSEL 95/3:189.13–20.

122. Although this proposal was made and accepted in a live exchange, it was recorded as a written document and preserved as *Ep.* 213.

123. The argument for ordination is not found in the surviving sermons. See Burns and Jensen, *Christianity in Roman Africa*, 411–15, 424–30.

Chapter Eight

1. A summary of the transaction and comparison to other ones was offered in *Serm.* 117.1.1. In his preaching, Augustine preferred the term *diabolus* to *satanas*; he used the latter sparingly in comparison (612 and 95 passages) and usually when *satanas* appeared in the scripture passage upon which he was commenting, such as Matt. 4:10; 16:23; Luke 22:31; John 13:26; 1 Cor. 7:5; or 2 Cor. 12:7.

2. *Serm.* 82.10.13; 121.5; 278.7.7.

3. *Psal.* 21.2.29; 36.2.15; 37.5; 122.5; 147.6; *Serm.* 5.2; 71.2.4; 86.7.7; 107.3.4; 110.3;

163.3.3; 259.1; 265.1.2; 349.3; *Serm. Denis* 5(375B).4; 12(147A).2; *Serm. Dolb.* 4(299A augm).2; 21(159B).17; 23(374 augm).20; 26(198 augm).3.

4. *Serm.* 296.4.

5. *Falsum, Serm.* 92.3.

6. *Serm.* 21.7.

7. For the redeemed, *Psal.* 63.18; 144.5; *Serm. Guelf.* 18(260D).2; *Serm. Lamb.* 27(335I).1. From the enemy, *Psal.* 129.3; from the devil, *Psal.* 105.10.

8. For Christians, *Psal.* 25.1.1; the whole world, *Psal.* 95.5; *Serm. Mai* 94(260C).8.

9. *Serm.* 162.1.

10. *Psal.* 102.6.

11. *Serm.* 22.9; 278.7.7.

12. *Psal.* 32.2.2.14; *Serm.* 36.8.

13. *Serm.* 328; 329.1; *Eu. Io.* 47.2; *Psal.* 115.5–6; *Serm. Lamb.* 7(335E).2; 27(335I).1.

14. *Serm.* 130.2; 131.1; *Serm. Denis* 3(228B).3.

15. *Psal.* 31.2.17; 95.5; 125.2; 129.12; *Serm.* 21.6; 30.2; 171.5; 220; 363.2.

16. *Serm.* 30.2.

17. *Psal.* 95.5; 125.2; 129.12.

18. *Psal.* 129.12.

19. *Psal.* 95.5.

20. *Serm.* 21.6; 363.2; 171.5; 220.

21. *Serm* 4.34; 137.10.12; *Serm. Denis* 12(147A).2.

22. *Psal.* 68.1.9; 95.5; *Serm.* 130.2; 363.2. In Roman practice, the slave or free status of a child was determined by that of its mother.

23. *Eu. Io.* 47.2; *Psal.* 46.5; *Serm.* 94; 129.3.3; 213.4–5; 263.1; *Serm. Dolb.* 21(159B).18; *Serm. Guelf.* 23(229B).2.

24. *Eu. Io.* 7.7.

25. *Eu. Io.* 47.2; *Psal.* 46.5; *Serm.* 94; 129.3.3; 213.4–5; *Serm. Dolb.* 21(159B).18; *Serm. Guelf.* 23(229B).2.

26. 2 Cor. 15:21; *Psal.* 55.17; *Serm. Dolb.* 26(198 augm).5.

27. *Eu. Io.* 7.6.

28. *Serm.* 130.2; 254.6; *Serm. Lamb.* 27(335I).5; 21(335K).7; *Psal.* 139.11. See also p. 187 above.

29. *Serm.* 130.2; 254.6; *Serm. Lamb.* 27(335I).5.

30. *Psal.* 34.1.15; *Serm.* 171.5; 254.6; 317.2.3; *Serm. Lamb.* 27(335I).5.

31. *Serm.* 21.7; 27.2; 86.7.7; 196.4.

32. *Serm.* 162.1; 278.7.7; 349.3.

33. *Serm.* 9.4; 62.8.9; *Ep. Io.* 5.12.

34. *Serm.* 296.4; *Serm. Guelf.* 23(299B).2.

35. The text read this way in Augustine's Latin version. *Psal.* 115.6; *Serm.* 329.1; *Serm. Lamb.* 27(335I).1.

36. *Serm.* 274.

37. *Serm. Denis* 13(305A).2.

38. *Serm. Dolb.* 4(229A augm).2.

39. *Psal.* 147.16.

40. *Psal.* 21.2.30–31; 46.4; 62.20; 97.3.

41. *Eu. Io.* 13.13; *Serm. Dolb.* 21(159B).17.

42. *Eu. Io.* 6.10; *Serm.* 265.5.6.

43. *Psal.* 95.15.

44. *Psal.* 21.2.29.

45. *Eu. Io.* 13.14; *Serm. Guelf.* 32(340A).11.

46. *Ep. Io.* 1.8; *Psal.* 120.12; 147.18.

47. *Serm.* 71.2.4.

48. *Psal.* 95.5.

49. *Serm.* 4.34; *Serm. Denis* 12(147A).2.

50. See above, pp. 187–88 at nn. 16, 22.

51. *Serm.* 336.4.

52. *Serm.* 336.4; *Eu. Io.* 7.7; *Psal.* 68.2.11.

53. *Psal.* 138.2.

54. *Serm.* 130.2; 336.4.

55. *Psal.* 130.7; 138.2; *Serm.* 130.2; *Serm. Mai* 26(60A).2.

56. *Serm.* 130.2; *Serm. Dolb.* 4(229A augm).2.

57. *Psal.* 138.2; 88.1.11; *Serm.* 130.2; *Serm. Guelf.* 6(223C); 9(229E).2.

58. *Serm. Dolb.* 23(374 augm).20.

59. *Serm.* 163.3.3.

60. *Psal.* 130.7.

61. *Serm.* 130.2.

62. *Serm.* 359.2.

63. *Lib.* 3.10.31; *Trin.* 4.12.15–13.18; 13.10.13–18.23.

64. Matt. 12:24 names them Pharisees; Mark 3:22, scribes; Luke 11:14–15, part of the onlooking crowd.

65. Matt. 12:29; Mark 3:27; Luke 11:22–23.

66. Beginning with Irenaeus, *Haer.* 5.21.1–3.

67. See above, n. 63.

68. On this topic, see J. Patout Burns, "How Christ Saves: Augustine's Multiple Explanations," in *Tradition and the Rule of Faith in the Early Church,*

ed. Ronnie J. Rombs and Alexander Y. Hwang (Washington, DC: Catholic University of America Press, 2010), 193–210.

69. *Serm.* 134; 263; *Serm. Morin* 17(265D); *Serm Guelf.* 9(229E); *Psal.* 67; 71.

70. *Serm. Dolb.* 26(198 augm), *Augustin d'Hippone, Vingt-six Sermons au Peuple d'Afrique*, ed. François Dolbeau, Collection des Études Augustiniennes, Série Antiquité 147 (Paris: Institut d'Études Augustiniennes, 2009), 366–417.

71. *Serm. Dolb.* 26(198 augm).40–41.

72. *Serm. Dolb.* 26(198 augm).41; see also *Psal.* 58.2.5; 87.7, in which Augustine referred to Gal 3:13 and the apparent cursing of Christ because of his crucifixion and *Serm. Guelf.* 31(335B).2 where he explained that Satan encouraged his adherents to disbelieve that they would actually die.

73. *Serm.* 134.3.4, 5.6; 263.1.

74. *Psal.* 71.7.

75. *Serm. Guelf.* 9(229E).2; 31(335B).1.

76. *Psal.* 68.1.9; *Serm.* 263.2.

77. *Serm. Morin* 17(265D).4.

78. *Serm.* 134.3.4; 152.8.

79. John 14:30. *Serm. Morin* 17(265D).4–5; *Serm.* 134.3.4, 5.6.

80. "Quando quidem dicit apostolus Paulus: *Si enim cognovissent, numquam Dominum gloriae crucifixissent* (1 Cor. 2:8). Sed si ille non occideretur, mors non moreretur: trophaeo suo diabolus victus est. Exsultavit enim diabolus, quando hominem primum seducendo deiecit in mortem. Primum hominem seducendo occidit: occidendo novissimum, de laqueis primum perdidit." *Serm* 263 (*Guelf.* 21).1, *MA* 1:508.5–10.

81. *Psal.* 67.16; 71.7; *Serm. Wilm.* 15(223I).

82. *Psal.* 58.1.6; 68.1.9; *Serm. Guelf.* 31(335B).1–2; *Serm. Morin* 17(265D).4–5.

83. *Psal.* 67.16; *Serm.* 134.5.6; *Serm. Dolb.* 26(198 augm).41.

84. *Serm. Morin* 17(265D).5. In *Serm. Casin.* 2.76(265B).4, Augustine interpreted the killing of death by life as a consequence of its unjust attack on one who was innocent of sin. *Serm. Dolb.* 26(198 augm).40.

85. *Serm. Guelf.* 31(335B).2.

86. The original sinning is treated above on pp. 214–17, 225–27, 249.

87. *Serm.* 134.4.5; *Serm. Morin* 17(265D).4; *Serm. Guelf.* 6(223C); 9(229E).2; *Serm. Dolb.* 23(374 augm).20; *Psal.* 61.22; 138.2.

88. For a study of the relations of masters to their freed slaves, see Pedro López Barja de Quiroga, "Patronage and Slavery in the Roman World: The Circle of Power," in *The Oxford Handbook of Greek and Roman Slaveries*, ed. Stephen Hodkinson, Marc Kleijweft, and Kostas Vlassopoulos (New York: Oxford University Press, 2020). See especially the section, "From *Imperium* to *Beneficium*," https://doi.org/10.1093/oxfordhb/9780199575251.013.31.

89. *Serm.* 130.2; 131.1.

90. *Trin.* 13.13.17–16.21.

91. *Psal.* 21.2.28; 146.4; *Serm.* 336.4–5; 329.1; *Serm. Dolb.* 26(198 augm).5; *Serm. Lamb.* 16(265E).2; 27(335I).5; *Eu. Io.* 28.2.

92. *Psal.* 61.22; 88.1.11; 129.3; 138.2; *Serm.* 134.4.5; 152.10; *Serm. Dolb.* 23(374 augm).20; *Serm. Morin* 17(265D).4.

93. See above, pp. 79–82, 100–102, 164.

94. *Psal.* 149.6.

95. *Serm. Guelf.* 10(229F).2.

96. *Serm. Dolb.* 26(198 augm).40–41; *Psal.* 58.2.5; 61.22; 71.7.

97. See, for example, *Serm.* 134.3.4–4.5; 152.10. The wording of the texts is stable across Augustine's works.

98. *Eu. Io.* 12.11.

99. *Serm.* 294.10.11–12.13. The sermon was preached on June 27, 413, according to Pierre-Marie Hombert, *Nouvelles Recherches de Chronologie Augustinienne*, Collection des Études Augustiniennes, Série Antiquité 163 (Paris: Institut d'Études Augustiniennes, 2000), 385–86.

100. "Sic ergo peccatum domini, quod factum est de peccato, quia inde carnem assumsit, de massa ipsa quae mortem meruerat ex peccato." *Psal.* 34.2.3, CCSL 38:314.52–54. The interpretation depends upon the use of the possessive genitive form of *domini*: This was the sin of the Lord, that he was made from sin, because he assumed flesh from sin, from the mass that merited death from sin. Augustine would examine this interpretation again in *Serm.* 152.9 for the purpose of challenging it.

101. *Eu. Io.* 41.5–7; *Serm* 155.7.7–8.8.

102. *Serm.* 185.1. This sermon is assigned to the period 412–16; Hombert, *Nouvelles Recherches*, 218n20.

103. *Serm.* 152.8–11.

104. *Serm.* 152.8–9.

105. *Serm.* 152.9.

106. *Serm.* 152.10.

107. "Deus, cui uos obsecramus reconciliari, *eum qui non nouerat peccatum*—id est Christum Deum, eum Christum qui non nouerat peccatum—*peccatum pro nobis fecit, ut nos simus iustitia dei in ipso* (2 Cor. 5:21). Numquid hic potest intellegi peccatum Iudae, peccatum Iudaeorum, peccatum cuiusque alterius hominis, cum audias: *Eum qui non nouerat peccatum, peccatum pro nobis fecit*? Quis? Quem? Deus. Christum. Deus Christum fecit pro nobis peccatum. Non dixit, 'fecit pro nobis peccantem', sed: 'fecit eum peccatum.'" *Serm.* 152.10, CCSL 41Ba:44.230–45.238.

108. *Eu. Io.* 41.5–7.

109. "In lege peccata uocabantur etiam sacrificia, quae pro peccatis offere-bantur. Habes: *cum uictima pro peccato adduceretur,* dicit lex, *ponant manus suas sacerdotes super peccatum* (Lev. 4:29)—id est: super uictimam pro peccato. Et quod est aliud quam Christus sacrificium pro peccato? *Sicut et Christus,* inquit, *dilexit uos, et tradidit semetipsum pro uobis oblationem et hostiam deo in odorem suauitatis* (Eph. 5:2). Ecce de quo peccato damnauit peccatum: de sacrificio quod factus est pro peccatis, inde damnauit peccatum." *Serm.* 152.11, CCSL 41Ba:45.249–46.257.

110. *Serm.* 155.8.8.

111. *Serm.* 134.4.5. The date of 413 proposed by Othmar Perler and Jean Louis Maier would place it before the two sermons just considered, which belong to the period 417–19, according to their editors. See *Les Voyages de Saint Augustin,* Collection des Études Augustiniennes, Série Antiquité 36 (Paris: Institut d'Études Augustiniennes, 1969), 320. Moreover, other citations of this section of the verse are grouped in the period between 417–20. Augustine's *Hept.* 4.12 (419–20) offers a similar explanation for the text of Numbers 6:14. Anne-Marie La Bonnardière assigned this *Serm.* 134 to 420, which seems more likely.

112. Following Maria Boulding's translation, WSA 3/15:228.

113. *Psal.* 21.2.3; 37.27; 43.2; 140.6.

114. *Psal.* 21.1.2; 30.2.1.11; 37.6; 90.2.1; 140.6.

115. *Psal.* 21.2.3; 30.2.1.11; 34.2.5; 37.6; 40.6; 41.17; 43.2; 53.5; 90.2.1.

116. *Psal.* 70.1.12; 140.5.

117. *Psal.* 68.2.11; 140.6.

118. *Psal.* 37.27.

119. *Psal.* 21.2.3.

120. *Psal.* 140.5.

121. *Psal.* 21.1.1; 37.27; 58.1.2; 68.2.11; 70.1.12.

122. *Psal.* 40.6; 100.6; 103.3.11; 142.9.

123. *Psal.* 42.7. Later, Augustine insisted that Paul was speaking in his own person, as a mature Christian and an apostle. See *Serm.* 154.7.9–10.14.

124. *Psal.* 87.3.

125. *Serm.* 31.3; see also *Serm. Guelf.* 9(229E).1.

126. *Psal.* 31.2.26.

127. *Psal.* 32.2.1.2; 63.18; *Eu. Io.* 52.3; *Serm. Denis* 5(375B).3.

128. *Psal.* 40.1; 68.1.9; 93.19; 103.3.11; 125.2; *Serm.* 31.3; *Serm. Guelf.* 28(313E).1; 31(335B).2.

129. *Serm. Guelf.* 31(335B).1–2.

130. J. Patout Burns and Robin Margaret Jensen, *Christianity in Roman Africa: The Development of Its Practices and Beliefs* (Grand Rapids: Eerdmans, 2014), 207. J. N. D. Kelly dates the appearance of this clause in the creed in

the middle of the fourth century, though the doctrine was already common in the second century. Augustine did not treat it as a triumph over the devil and hell, the understanding Kelly suggested might have brought it into the creed. J. N. D. Kelly, *Early Christian Creeds*, 3rd ed. (London: Continuum, 2006), 378–83.

131. *Ep.* 164 is dedicated to the topic.

132. *Psal.* 48.2.5 and *Serm.* 285.2 contain only passing references.

133. *Serm. Morin* 11(53A).13.

134. *Serm.* 373.3.

135. *Serm.* 285.2.

136. *Serm. Liver.* 8(265A).1.

137. *Serm.* 263.2.

138. *Psal.* 56.8.

139. *Serm.* 264.4, 6.

140. *Serm.* 361.18.17; *Psal.* 26.2.8; 102.26.

141. *Serm. Casin.* 2.76(265B).1.

142. *Serm. Mai* 87(242A); *Serm. Casin.* 2.76(265B).2, 5.

143. *Eu. Io.* 12.8–9.

144. *Eu. Io.* 27.4–5; *Serm. Mai* 98(263A).3; *Serm. Casin.* 2.76(265B).2; *Serm.* 294.9.9.

145. These same arguments are made in the works that were not preached: *Agon.* 27; *Maxim.* 2.20.3; *Serm. Arian.* 6; *Eu. Io.* 111.2.

146. *Serm. Mai* 98(263A).2; *Eu. Io.* 12.9. The same text is used to identify Christians with Christ enthroned in heaven. *Serm.* 144.4.5; 362.14.16.

147. *Serm. Mai* 98(263A).3.

148. *Serm.* 91.6.7; 144.4.5; 294.10.10; *Psal.* 122.1; *Eu. Io.* 12.8.

149. *Psal.* 65.1; this argument is also made against the Pelagians in *Pecc. merit.* 1.31.60.

150. *Serm. Mai* 98(263A).1–2; *Serm.* 294.9.9.

151. *Psal.* 122.1.

152. *Serm.* 144.4.5; *Eu. Io.* 12.8.

Chapter Nine

1. *Gen. Man.* 2.4.5–5.6, 14.20–15.22, 18.28–21.31.

2. *Mor. eccl.* 1.19.35.

3. *Lib.* 3.5.14–15, 9.28–10.31, 11.34, 14.39.

4. *Lib.* 3.19.53–20.55.

5. *Lib.* 3.20.56–58, 22.63–64.

6. *Conf.* 8.5.10–12, citing Rom. 7:22–25.

7. *Simpl.* 1.2.17, 20.

8. *Lib.* 3.23.66–67.

9. *Quaest.* 66.5–6; 70; *Rom. prop.* 45–46; 50; *Gal.* 46; 48; *Simpl.* 1.1.10, 11.

10. *Rom. prop.* 44–46; *Gal.* 46.1–5; 47.1–2; *Quaest.* 66.2–3, 5; *Simpl.* 1.1.1.

11. *Quaest.* 66.1; *Rom. prop.* 38; 44; 47; *Simpl.* 1.1.2, 6.

12. The sting of death is sin; the power of sin is the law: *Faust.* 15.8; *Leg.* 2.28; *Mor. eccl.* 1.30.64.

13. *Gal.* 46.6–9; 47.3–5; *Quaest.* 65, 66.5–7; *Rom. prop.* 45–46; *Simpl.* 1.1.13–14.

14. *Mor. eccl.* 1.19.35; *Simpl.* 1.2.16; *Qu. eu* 2.38.3.

15. *Psal.* 147; 103; 80; 146; 102; 57; 66. Anne-Marie La Bonnardière dated them in December 409. "Les Enarrationes in Psalmos Prêchées par Saint Augustin à Carthage en Décembre 409," *Recherches Augustiniennes* 11 (1976): 52–90. Pierre-Marie Hombert has more recently argued for 403. Some of the Dolbeau sermons (2, 5, 12, 21, 23–26) are also placed in December 403 or January 404, others in the months following. See Hombert, *Nouvelles Recherches de Chronologie Augustinienne*, Collection des Études Augustiniennes, Série Antiquité 163 (Paris: Institut d'Études Augustiniennes, 2000), 563–88. François Dolbeau offered evidence for dating other sermons to this period, *Augustin d'Hippone, Vingt-six Sermons au Peuple d'Afrique*, ed. François Dolbeau, Collection des Études Augustiniennes, Série Antiquité 147 (Paris: Institut d'Études Augustiniennes, 2009), 428–30.

16. For dating, see Anne-Marie La Bonnardière, *Recherches de Chronologie Augustinienne*, Collection des Études Augustiniennes, Série Antiquité 23 (Paris: Institut d'Études Augustiniennes, 1965), 19–62; and Suzanne Pogue, "Trois Semaines de Prédication à Hippone en Février-Mars 407," *Recherches Augustiniennes* 7 (1971): 169–87.

17. *Psal.* 47.9.

18. *Serm. Dolb.* 2(359B).7.

19. *Serm. Dolb.* 26(198 augm).32–33, 36.

20. *Psal.* 57.18. He would repeat the analysis and its application in *Psal.* 35.10, 18, at the beginning of the Pelagian controversy.

21. *Serm. Dolb.* 21(159B).11.

22. *Psal.* 84.7; 103.4.6; 146.4.

23. To this was added the analysis of Rom. 7:1–14. *Quaest.* 66.1, 70; *Rom. prop.* 24.3, 37–40, 44, 47; *Simpl.* 1.1.2, 6, 15. See also *Faust.* 15.8; *Leg.* 2.28.

24. *Psal.* 143.5.

25. *Serm.* 361.16.16–17.17; *Serm. Dolb.* 2(359B).7; 26(198 augm).39.

26. *Psal.* 84.7; 102.6; *Serm.* 362.11.11.

27. *Psal.* 84.10.

28. *Psal.* 114.3; 134.11; 141.18–19.

29. *Psal.* 84.7, 10 (400–405; winter 403); 102.6, 17; 114.3; 127.16 (January 407); 143.9 (409); see also *Eu. Io.* 12.11 (February 407). For the dating, see Hombert, *Nouvelles Recherches*, 558n18, 617–19; La Bonnardière, *Recherches de Chronologie Augustinienne*, 19–62; and Marie-François Berrouard, "La Date des Tractatus I–LIV in Iohannis Evangelium de Saint Augustin," *Recherches Augustiniennes* 7 (1971): 107–19.

30. *Serm.* 51.15.25.

31. *Serm. Dolb.* 21(159B).7.

32. *Psal.* 57.19.

33. *Psal.* 101.1.11.

34. *Psal.* 36.3.19; 57.16; 66.4; 75.4–5.

35. *Psal.* 83.10; 84.10; 102.15; 143.6.

36. In the sermons and expositions of this period, he did refer to charity and cite Rom. 5:5, "God's love has been poured into our hearts through the Holy Spirit that has been given to us," in the context of opposing lust and obeying the moral law.

37. *Psal.* 83.7.

38. *Psal.* 36.1.6; 66.4; 75.5; 140.16; 146.6; 147.26; *Serm. Morin* 11(53A).12.

39. *Psal.* 75.5.

40. *Psal.* 84.7.

41. "Tradux mortis, tradux mortis de primo peccato." *Psal.* 103.4.6, CSEL 95/1:192.20–21.

42. *Ep. Io.* 4.11.

43. *Eu. Io.* 3:12; 4.10; 10.11–12; preached between December 406 and February 407.

44. *Eu. Io.* 14.13; see also *Psal.* 101.1.11 (403–8). The sermon was preached in March 407, shortly after *Eu. Io.* 10, just noted.

45. *Psal.* 57.19; 125.5; 140.14–16; 141.17; 146.6; *Serm. Morin* 11(53A).12.

46. *Psal.* 44.7; 57.4; 75.4; 83.9–11; 84.4–6; 147.26.

47. In *Psal.* 83.9–10 and 84.4–6, the text is assigned to Paul speaking for himself. In *Psal.* 36.1.6 and 102.15 it is an expression of the human situation.

48. *Psal.* 75.4; 137.13; 140.15; *Serm.* 351.1.1.

49. *Psal.* 44.7 (9/403); 75.5; 83.9–10 (404); 140.14–16 (404); 146.6 (12/403). For the dating, see Hombert, *Nouvelles Recherches*, 28, 582n78, 344n8, 563–88.

50. *Psal.* 134.12; 140.15; 141.17. This interpretation would become more prominent during the Pelagian controversy.

51. *Psal.* 146.6; 134.12. Augustine would return to this interpretation but would provide a different foundation for it.

52. *Psal.* 36.1.6; 140.16; 146.6; *Serm. Morin* 11(53A).12.

53. *Psal.* 75.5.

54. *Eu. Io.* 12.8–9.

55. *Eu. Io.* 12.10–11.

56. Augustine would use this passage and interpretation to show the necessity of baptism as a means of being joined into Christ in *Pecc. merit.* 1.31.60; *Serm.* 91.6.7; 144.4.5; 294.8.9–10.10; 362.14.16.

57. *Psal.* 57.17–18. Augustine was drawing upon a parallel use of the same text to explain God's allowing sinners to act out their evil intentions, punishing them even with the power to perform miracles. *Quaest.* 79.1.

58. *Psal.* 57.19–20.

59. *Serm. Dolb.* 26(198 augm).33.

60. He next used the idea in *Pecc. merit.* 2.22.36 and *Nat. et grat.* 22.24–23.25.

61. Augustine provided that explanation of the position in *Serm.* 294.1.2–2.2. He had taken a somewhat similar position in *Lib.* 3.23.66–67 but had modified it in *Ep. Io.* 4.11.

62. The sermons were *Serm.* 293, 294, 299 and *Psal.* 50. The treatises were *On the Merits and Remission of Sins and the Baptism of Children*; *On the Spirit and the Letter*; *On Nature*; and *On the Perfection of Human Justice*.

63. *Serm. Dolb.* 30(348A).5. This change took place in a sermon preached in May or June of 416 in Hippo. For expressions on Augustine's continuing hope for his conversion see *Ep.* 176.4; 177.3.

64. Augustine's *Ep.* 175; 176.

65. Augustine's *Ep.* 181–183.

66. He mentioned him by name in only seven of his surviving sermons: *Psal.* 58.1.19; *Serm.* 181.2.2, 5.7; 183.8.12; 278.13.13; 363.2; *Serm. Dolb.* 30(348A augm).6, 7; *Serm. Morin* 10(163A).3.

67. For dating see both, Gert Partoens, "La Datation des Sermons 151–156," and Josef Lössel's "Dating Augustine's Sermons 151–156: Internal Evidence," in *Sermones de Novo Testamento (151–156)*, ed. Gert Partoens, CCSL 41Ba (Turnhout: Brepols, 2008), ix–xxii, xxiii–lv. Marie-François Berrouard, "L'Exégèse Augustinienne de Rom., 7, 7–25," *Recherches Augustiniennes* 16 (1981): 190n405, following Othmar Perler and Jean-Louis Maier, *Les Voyages de Saint Augustin*, Collection des Études Augustiniennes, Série Antiquité 36 (Paris: Institut d'Études Augustiniennes, 1969), 357–59, who had placed them two years later, in October 419, contemporary to the first book of *On Marriage and Concupiscence*.

68. *Serm.* 330.3 (assigned by Hombert to 415–30) links a person's loss of love of God to a turn to goods outside the self—the arousal of carnal lust. *Serm.*

344.1–2 (assigned to 425–30 by Kunzelmann) describes the ordering of love of God, of neighbor, and of material goods. None of the preached expositions of the Psalms are assigned to this period. Augustine devoted more attention to writing than to preaching in the final four years of his life, beginning with the appointment of Eraclius as his future successor. For the dating, see Pierre-Marie Hombert, *Nouvelles Recherches*, 369n13, and Adalbero Kunzelmann, "Die Chronologie der Sermones des hl. Augustinus," *Miscellanea Agostiniana*, ed. Germain Morin and Antonio Casamassa (Rome: Typis Polyglottis Vaticanis, 1930–31), 2:509–10.

69. *Eu. Io.* 3.12.

70. *Serm.* 90.7; *Psal.* 61. All humans were present in Adam because he was the source of their generation. *Serm. Guelf.* 31(335B).1, preached 415–20 according to Hombert, *Nouvelles Recherches*, 223n40. See the earlier parallel in *Pecc. mer.* 3.3.5, 4.7, 7.14.

71. *Serm.* 174.7.8.

72. *Psal.* 70.2.7–9. See also *Psal.* 73.18 and the earlier *Serm. Dolb.* 2 (359B).7.

73. *Serm. Guelf.* 31(335B).1. Augustine had introduced this interpretation a decade earlier in *Psal.* 47.9. Parallel interpretations are found in his treatises in *Pecc. mer.* 2.19.33 and *Gen. litt.* 11.30.39, 31.41.

74. *Serm.* 351.3.3. Another interpretation of those leaves made them a symbol of the itch of lust that Adam's sinning brought upon him. *Serm.* 69.3.4.

75. Because he judged baptism and eucharist necessary for salvation (John 3:3; 6:53), Augustine could not assert that Christ brought salvation to all humans, in a strict parallel to Adam's burdening them with death. Christ did bring bodily immortality to all. See p. 280.

76. *Serm.* 293.8–10. This argument appears to have been introduced in *Ep. Io.* 4.11.

77. *Serm.* 293.11.

78. *Serm.* 293.12.

79. *Eu. Io.* 3.12 in 406; *Serm.* 361.17.16 in 410–411, Adalbero Kunzelmann, "Die Chronologie der Sermones des hl. Augustinus," 463.

80. *Serm.* 90.7 (412–416), Adalbero Kunzelmann, "Die Chronologie der Sermones des hl. Augustinus," 480.

81. He used the same argument in the contemporary *Pecc. merit.* 1.8.8 and 3.11.19.

82. *Psal.* 70.1.2–6; 61.7; 34.2.3; *Serm.* 90.7; 174.6.7–7.8; *Eu. Io.* 43.9. In many instances, however, Adam and Christ are simply paired as opposites. *Serm.* 30.5, 151.5.5.

83. The mediating role of the church, particularly in providing baptism,

had been highlighted by the Donatist controversy. Its influence can be noted in *Eu. Io.* 12.8–9.

84. He admitted this three days later, in *Serm.* 294.2.2. The same point had already been discussed in *Pecc. merit.* 1.20.26, 25.41.

85. He referred to Aurelius's role in the sermons in *Gest. Pel.* 11.25.

86. *Serm.* 294.3.3–4.4.

87. *Serm.* 294.5.5–7.8.

88. *Serm.* 294.7.7. Parallel in *Pecc. merit.* 1.21.29–30. He had preached a whole sermon on the text, *Serm. Dolb.* 21(159B), sometime in 403–4, according to F. Dolbeau in *Augustin d'Hippone, Vingt-six Sermons au Peuple d'Afrique,* ed. François Dolbeau, Collection des Études Augustiniennes, Série Antiquité 147 (Paris: Institut d'Études Augustiniennes, 2009), 272–73.

89. *Serm.* 294.8.9–10.10.

90. *Eu. Io.* 12.8–9. See above, pp. 92, 208–9.

91. He had used it for a similar purpose in *Pecc. merit.* 1.30.58–31.60—but with the inclusion of Gen. 2:24.

92. "Misit enim deus filium suum, non in carne peccati; sed, sicut sequitur qui scripsit, in similitudine carnis peccati; quia non de complexu maritali, sed de utero uirginali. misit in similitudine carnis peccati: utquid hoc? ut de peccato damnaret peccatum in carne (Rom. 8:3): de peccato peccatum, de serpente serpentem. quis enim dubitet nomine serpentis appellari peccatum? ergo de peccato peccatum, de serpente serpentem: sed de similitudine, quia in Christo nullum peccatum, sed sola similitude carnis peccati." *Serm.* 294.11.13, PL 38:1342–43.

93. *Serm.* 294.10.11, 12.13. This presentation of the efficacy of Christ's death was more fully elaborated than it had been in *Eu. Io.* 12.11. For a fuller exposition of this explanation of the redemptive work of Christ, see above, pp. 186–203.

94. Augustine explained in a later sermon that infants were not required to undertake penance before their baptism because they had incurred no personal sin and guilt. Their shared guilt could be forgiven through the confession of their parents or sponsors. *Serm.* 115.4; 351.2.2.

95. *Serm.* 294.11.12. This argument provides a remarkable insight into Augustine's appreciation of the role of the charity operative within the laity in the sanctification of the baptized. See the discussion in the chapter on baptism, pp. 92–93 above.

96. *Serm.* 294.13.14.

97. *Serm.* 294.12.13. In *Eu. Io.* 12.11, mortality had been inherited from Adam and had become the source of individual sins in his offspring.

98. *Serm.* 294.14.15–15.15.

99. Augustine cited 1 Pet. 3:18 that Christ is dead in the flesh and alive in the spirit; he concluded that Christians were decayed in the flesh but justified in the spirit. *Serm.* 294.16.16, 17.17–19.17. A similar argument was made in the contemporary *Serm.* 174.8.9.

100. *Serm.* 299.1. For the dating of the sermon in 413 rather than the traditional 418, see Hombert, *Nouvelles Recherches*, 387–98. He links the discussion of death as a penalty to the contemporary *Pecc. merit.* 1.2.2, 4.4.

101. *Serm.* 299.7–8.

102. The connection to Pelagian teaching is not announced until the end of the sermon, 299.11–12. The issue had been treated, using 2 Cor. 5:2–4 but not 1 Cor. 15:53–56, in *Pecc. merit.* 1.2.2, 4.4.

103. *Serm.* 299.8–9.

104. That interpretation of the sting of death being sin was offered in *Eu. Io.* 12.11; *Psal.* 84.10; 127.16; 143.9; *Serm. Denis* 13(305A).7–8.

105. *Serm.* 299.10.

106. *Serm.* 163.9.9 (417) and 151.7.7. (417/19). For the dating, Adalbero Kunzelmann, "Die Chronologie der Sermones des hl. Augustinus," 475, and p. 332 n. 67 above. He continued, as shall be seen, to use mortality to account for the conflict between flesh and spirit or mind. *Serm.* 131.7; 151.3.3, 8.8; 155.2.2.

107. "Etiam ipsum uinculum mortis cum ipsa iniquitate concretum est. Nemo nascitur nisi trahens poenam, trahens meritum poenae." *Psal.* 50.10, CCSL 38:606.15–17.

108. *Psal.* 50.10. Augustine had used the text of 1 Pet. 3:18 to make the same point in *Serm.* 294.16.16.

109. *Serm. Dolb.* 30(348A augm).2; *Serm.* 30.6.

110. *Psal.* 34.2.3; *Eu. Io.* 43.9; *Serm.* 174.8.9.

111. *Serm.* 294.10.11, 12.13; *Psal.* 50.10; see also *Psal.* 34.2.3; *Eu. Io.* 43.9; *Serm.* 99.6; 174.8.9; and *Serm.* 153.11.14.

112. *Serm. Dolb.* 30(348A augm).5–6, which was preached in May or June 416 in Hippo according to François Dolbeau, "Le Sermon 348A de Saint Augustin contre Pélage: Édition du Texte Intégral," *Recherches Augustiniennes* 28 (1995): 37–63; see p. 41.

113. *Serm. Dolb.* 30(348A augm).8–9, repeated in *Serm.* 26.8.

114. *Serm. Dolb.* 30(348A augm).8. See also *Serm.* 30.1–2.

115. See J. Patout Burns, "Human Agency in Augustine's Doctrine of Predestination and Perseverance," *Augustinian Studies* 48 (2017): 45–71.

116. The metaphysical insight, foundational to the Platonic and Aristotelian systems, was that an adequate cause is always better and more powerful than

the effect it produces. Put more blandly: new realities and improvements of existing realities do not just happen; they are produced by existing, and better, causes.

117. *Serm. Dolb.* 30(348A augm).8 for the Pelagian assertion; *Serm.* 169.11.13; 176.5; *Serm. Guelf.* 18(260D).1.

118. *Serm.* 13.2–3; 169.11.13, 12.15–13.16; 156.5.5.

119. *Serm.* 26.2–3.

120. *Serm.* 170.11.

121. *Serm. Dolb.* 30(348A augm).1–2.

122. The fullest early explanation of the term was offered in *Psal.* 57.18, in an exposition of the meaning of Rom. 1:24 that may have been preached in 403. From the same period see *Psal.* 26.2.7; *Serm. Dolb.* 26(198 augm).33. See also *Quaest.* 79.1; *Nat. et grat.* 22.24; *Serm. Dolb.* 28(20B).6. For dating of *Psal.* 57, see above, p. 330 n. 15.

123. *Ep.* 156 from Hilary was answered in *Ep.* 157. *De natura* was evaluated in *de natura et gratia*.

124. See, for example, explanations of Romans 7 in his commentaries on the Psalms that are dated to 403–4: *Psal.* 42.7; 75.4–5; 84.4; 134.12; 140.16; 146.6. For the dating of *Psal.* 42, see Seraphim M. Zarb, *Chronologia Enarrationum S. Augustini in Psalmos* (Valletta: St. Dominic's Priory, 1948), 63–68, 79–81, 162–63. For the dating of the remainder, see Hombert, *Nouvelles Recherches*, 582n78, 617–19, 633–34, 344n8.

125. *Serm.* 128.6.8.

126. *Psal.* 70.1.2, 6; *Serm.* 125.2, 6; 145.5; 351.1.1; *Serm. Guelf.* 33(77A).2.

127. *Serm.* 128.8.10–9.11, using 1 Cor. 15:53–55 and Gal. 5:17; see also *Serm.* 56.5.8; 299.9; *Serm. Guelf.* 33(77A).2; *Psal.* 51.31; 143.9; *Eu. Io.* 41.13.

128. *Eu. Io.* 41.10; *Serm. Guelf.* 33(77A).2; *Serm.* 152.3; 155.9.9; 351.3.3.

129. *Serm.* 128.6.8, 30.4; 153.5.6, 8.10; 154.6.8.

130. *Serm.* 145.3; *Psal.* 70.1.2.

131. *Eu. Io.* 41.10; *Serm.* 156.13.14. In his earlier Pauline commentaries, he had described it as preparing a person for hearing and responding to the gospel. See above, p. 215.

132. *Eu. Io.* 41.11; *Psal.* 67.11, 24; *Serm.* 128.6.8; see also *Serm.* 154.5.7–6.8.

133. *Serm.* 145.3, 5; *Serm. Dolb.* 15(283 augm).3.

134. *Serm.* 128.2.4.

135. *Serm.* 128.3.5.

136. *Serm.* 128.2.4–7.9.

137. *Serm.* 128.4.6–6.8, 10.12. This is Augustine's first use of the distinction

in Gal. 5:16–17 between having a desire and completing it. The reference to the iniquity in the body is repeated in *Serm.* 30.6.

138. *Eu. Io.* 41.12; *Serm. Guelf.* 33(77A).2–3.

139. *Eu. Io.* 41.12; *Serm.* 128.9.11–10.12.

140. *Serm.* 128.11.13; *Serm. Guelf.* 33(77A).2.

141. *Eu. Io.* 41.11.

142. *Eu. Io.* 41.11–12; *Serm. Guelf.* 33(77A).1, 3.

143. *Serm.* 56.7.11–9.12.

144. *Serm.* 115.3; *Serm. Mai* 17(16B).4.

145. *Serm.* 99.6. Augustine had observed a parallel divine intervention in conversion in *Simpl.* 1.2.14–15.

146. *Serm.* 163.9.9–10.10; 156.1.1.

147. *Psal.* 102.15; 31.2.17; *Serm.* 125.2; 145.5; 351.1.1.

148. *Psal.* 139.11; *Serm.* 193.2; 163.12.12.

149. *Serm.* 152.6; 153.10.13; 154.1.1; 155.4.4; 156.2.2.

150. *Serm.* 145.3; 153.4.5.

151. *Serm.* 151.4.4; 153.5.6; 154.2.2; 155.4.4. He added the theater in *Serm.* 153.8.10.

152. *Serm.* 152.6.

153. *Serm.* 152.5–7; 153.5.6; 155.2.2, 7.7.

154. *Serm.* 152.7; 153.7.9; 154.1.1; 155.2.2.

155. *Serm.* 152.6; 153.5.7.

156. *Serm.* 125.2; 152.5, 7; 153.5.7–7.9, 10.13–11.14; 154.1.1; 156.2.2.

157. *Serm.* 153.7.9. Because he had another role for Paul in this whole section in mind, however, he qualified the interpretation with a "perhaps."

158. *Serm.* 155.2.2, and in conjunction with Rom. 5:20—the law entered so that sin might abound—*Serm.* 151.7.7; 163.10.10–11.11.

159. *Serm.* 156.4.4, 6.6–8.8, 9.10–10.10; 163.10.10.

160. *Serm.* 169, preached in Carthage in 416, probably in September. François Dolbeau, "Le Sermon 348A de Saint Augustin contre Pelage," 37–63. For a more recent dating, see Gert Partoens, "Augustine's *Sermo* 169: Correction of Two Misinterpretations and Proposal of a New Date," in *Ministerium Sermonis: Philological, Historical, and Theological Studies on Augustine's "Sermones ad populum,"* ed. Gert Partoens, Anthony Dupont, and Mathijs Lamberigts, Instrumenta Patristica et Mediaevalia 53 (Turnhout: Brepols, 2009), 69–95.

161. *Serm.* 169.9.11. See also *Serm.* 156.11.12–12.13.

162. *Serm.* 169.6.8; 170.5, 6.

163. *Serm.* 169.7.9; see also *Serm.* 170.7, 10; 163.9.9–10.10; 156.7.7–8.8, 9.10.

164. *Serm.* 169.7.8; 251.7.6.

165. *Serm.* 169.7.9–8.10.

166. *Serm.* 270.4.

167. *Serm.* 169.11.14.

168. *Serm.* 169.8.10; 251.7.6–8.7; 154.7.10.

169. *Serm.* 34; 128.2.4–3.5; 156.5.5, 10.10.

170. *Serm.* 145.3.

171. *Serm.* 169.12.15–13.16.

172. *Serm.* 169.13.16–15.18; 170.7; 154.3.3.

173. *Serm.* 152.3.

174. *Serm.* 158.6.6–8.8.

175. *Eu. Io.* 41.11–12; *Serm. Guelf.* 33(77A).1, 3.

176. *Psal.* 143.6. For the dating of this text, see Hombert, *Nouvelles Recherches*, 558n18, where it is associated with the Songs of Ascent on which Augustine commented in 406–7.

177. *Eu. Io.* 34.10.

178. *Serm.* 163.6.6.

179. *Eu. Io.* 41.12; *Serm.* 128.8.10–9.11; 30.4; 151.8.8.

180. *Eu. Io.* 41.12. His analysis was assisted by the use and contrast, in his Latin translation of the letter, of the terms *facio* and *perficio* ("I do" and "I complete").

181. *Serm.* 145.3; 128.8.10.

182. François Dolbeau assigned *Serm. Dolb.* 30(348A augm).10 to May/June 416. See "Le Sermon 348A de Saint Augustin contre Pélage," 37–63. A parallel application of these texts to a baptized Christian appears in contemporary treatises: *Nat. et grat.* 50.58–54.64; *Perf.* 11.28; *Gest. Pel.* 6.20–7.21. Only in *Ep.* 196.2.5–6, however, is the elimination of carnal desire identified as the good the speaker intends. In *Pelag.* 1.8.13–11.24, Augustine defended the interpretation of Rom. 7:14–25 and its application to every faithful Christian struggling against carnal lust, including Paul.

183. *Serm.* 30.3–5.

184. *Serm.* 151.2.2, 8.8; *Serm. Morin* 4(154A).1–2. On this last sermon, see Volker Drecoll's analysis in "The Exegesis of Romans 7 in *Serm. Morin* 4(154A)," in *Ministerium Sermonis*, 143–56.

185. *Serm.* 151.6.6; 152.1; 154.2.2. Indeed, this was the earlier interpretation that Augustine had used and would continue to use occasionally.

186. *Eu. Io.* 41.10; *Serm.* 151.1.2; 152.1; 154.2.2–3.4, 6.8–7.9, 8.11, 9.13.

187. *Serm.* 151.6.6; *Serm. Morin* 10(163A).3; 4(154A).2.

188. *Serm.* 154.3.3–6.8 shows Augustine struggling to deal with this interpretation. *Serm.* 151.1.1, 6.6 shows him using it as established. The working hypothesis of this essay is that *Serm.* 154 (and its companions 153 and 155) preceded *Serm.* 151 and its companion *Serm.* 152, or that the two sets were preached to significantly different audiences.

189. *Serm.* 154.3.4–5.6. See also *Serm.* 163.8.8.

190. *Serm.* 154.3.3–6.8. In *Serm.* 128.2.4, Augustine had identified that gift as the Holy Spirit.

191. *Serm.* 154.6.8–7.9.

192. *Serm.* 154.9.13; 155.2.2. Yet he insisted that the flesh was Paul's own, just as the mind. When acting under divine grace, the mind had the greater right and power to control the bodily members. When it acted independently of divine guidance, however, it played the role of a tyrant. *Serm.* 155.2.2.

193. *Serm.* 154.7.10. Thus, Paul was not making himself a model for others to follow into sin.

194. *Serm.* 152.5–7. The distinctions between the law of the spirit of life (charity), the law of sin and death (lust), and the law of deeds (Decalogue) are explained in this section, in the exposition of Rom. 7:23, 25, and 8:2. See also *Serm.* 30.4; 128.3.5, 6.8.

195. See above, p. 218.

196. *Serm.* 151.5.5; 154.6.8. It was the only way to attribute the passage to Paul: *Serm.* 154.10.14. The point is repeated in *Serm.* 155.1.1–2.2.

197. *Serm.* 30.4; 154.9.13; *Serm. Morin* 10(163A).3.

198. Igitur ipse ego (ego ipse!) mente seruio legi Dei, carne autem legi peccati. Serm. 154.7.9, *CCSL* 41Ba:89.196–97. See also *Eu. Io.* 41.11.

199. *Serm.* 154.10.15–12.17; 155.14.15.

200. *Serm.* 299.9. See above, p. 232.

201. *Psal.* 75.4; a similar solution was used in his commentaries and even in *Conf.* 8.5.10.

202. *Psal.* 75.5; 140.16, assigned to 404 by Hombert, *Nouvelles Recherches*, 344n8. Augustine continued to blame the problem on mortality. *Serm.* 30.4; 256.2.

203. His interpretation of 1 Cor. 15:56, the sting of death is sin, changed in the refutation of Caelestius. See above, p. 232.

204. *Serm.* 151.5.5.

205. Augustine then began to say that Paul presented the conflict as his own and to assign the lusts to Paul himself. *Serm.* 151.6.6.

206. *Eu. Io.* 41.11–12; *Serm. Guelf.* 33(77A).1, 3.

207. *Serm. Guelf.* 33(77A).2; *Serm.* 154.8.11–9.13; *Serm.* Morin 4(154A).2.

208. *Serm.* 30.6–10; *Serm. Morin* 10(163A).3; *Serm.* 151.7.7; 155.9.9.

209. *Serm.* 152.2; 156.6.6; 170.11.

210. *Serm.* 163.7.7–9.9.

211. *Serm.* 155.9.9.

212. *Serm.* 154.6.8, 12.17; see also *Serm.*155.13.14; 256.2.

213. *Serm.* 155.14.15.

214. *Serm.* 255.7.7–8.7.

215. *Serm.* 154.11.16; see also *Serm.* 128.3.5.

216. *Serm.* 170.9; 158.6.6–9.9; 255.6.6.

217. *Serm.* 156.15.16. This was a constant theme for Augustine; see also *Psal.* 26.2.16.

218. *Serm.* 151.3.3; 152.4; 155.10.11.

219. *Serm.* 151.3.3, 5.5; 152.4.

220. *Serm.* 156.11.11–12.

221. "Occasione autem, inquit, accepta peccatum per mandatum fefellit me et per illud occidit. Sic factum est primo in paradiso." *Serm.* 153.9.11, CCSL 51Ba:67.255–56.

222. *Serm.* 153.9.11. In this sermon, Augustine applied the term *peccatum* to the serpent rather than to the hidden sin of pride that Eve had already committed. See his interpretation *Gen. litt.* 11.5.7; 30.39; 31.41; 35.47.

223. *Serm. Guelf.* 31(335B).1.

224. *Serm. Dolb.* 30(348A augm).2.

225. *Serm.* 30.6.

226. *Serm.* 156.6.6, 8.8.

227. *Serm.* 128.6.8; 151.5.5.

228. *Serm.* 151.5.5; 152.5; 153.11.14; 156.2.2.

229. *Serm.* 153.11.14; 152.5.

230. *Serm.* 30.6; 151.2.2.

231. *Serm.* 151.8.8.

232. *Serm.* 152.5; 155.1.1.

233. *Serm.* 153.4.5.

234. *Serm.* 151.3.3.

235. *Serm.* 163.7.7–9.9. It was an antidote made from the snake's own venom.

236. *Serm.* 294.10.11, 12.13; *Psal.* 50.10; see also *Psal.* 34.2.3, *Eu. Io.* 43.9; *Serm.* 174.8.9.

Chapter Ten

1. Although he did not avoid the term substance to describe the duality. *Serm.* 130.3; 186.1; *Psal.* 67.23; 88.2.3.

2. *Serm.* 67.4.7; 186.1; *Psal.* 34.2.3; 40.2.

3. *Serm.* 67.4.7; *Psal.* 108.23; *Eu. Io.* 49.18; *Serm. Denis* 5(375B).4. See also *Eu. Io.* 82.4; *Trin.* 13.12.17 for similar explanations that were not preached. This explanation may have carried with it the fuller understanding of the divine operating initiative and creaturely dependent cooperation in all good willing and action.

4. *Eu. Io.* 19.15; *Serm.* 186.1.

5. *Serm.* 242.4.6.

6. In his commentary of Romans 7, for example, he insisted that actions performed in both soul and flesh were to be assigned to the same person. *Serm.* 154.7.9; 155.3.3.

7. *Psal.* 70.2.10; 138.2, 8; 142.3.

8. The final phrase, "who is in heaven," was in Augustine's Latin text of the passage and some witnesses to the Vulgate. He considered it genuine.

9. Thus, in *Eu. Io.* 27.4.

10. *Eu. Io.* 12.8, 10 (part of a series preached in 406–7).

11. *Serm.* 294.9.9 (preached in June 413, during the Pelagian controversy). See also *Serm. Casin* 2.76(265B).2, which adds that the Savior was everywhere by his divine powers.

12. *Eu. Io.* 12.8.

13. *Eu. Io.* 27.3–4.

14. *Eu. Io.* 31.9.

15. *Psal.* 44.3; 90.2.5; *Ep. Io.* 1.2.

16. *Psal.* 18.2.10; 30.2.1.4; 34.2.1; 40.1; 55.3; 68.2.1; 71.17; 74.4; 138.2; 140.3; *Serm.* 45.5; 362.14.16; *Serm. Dolb.* 22(341 augm).20; *Eu. Io.* 9.10.

17. *Sponsus* and *Sponsa*: *Ep. Io.* 1.2; *Psal.* 30.2.1.4; 74.4; 101.1.2; *Serm.* 91.7.8; 362.14.16.

18. *Serm. Dolb.* 22(341 augm).19.

19. Augustine explicitly distinguished the Father and Word who were one thing (*unum*) from the Word and flesh who were not one thing and Christ and the church who were one person (*unus*). *Psal.* 101.1.2.

20. See nn. 2 and 3 above for references. Augustine found a parallel to this sort of personal unity in the existence of offspring in their progenitors prior to beginning a separate existence. In such existence, they could become

responsible for sins "committed" in that unity. They carried the guilt and punishment of such sin with them into the separate existence they attained at birth.
See especially the controversy with Julian of Eclanum, and the insistence that
children could not be punished for sins in which they had no personal part.
Iul. imp. 3.57.1–2, 3.63. See also *Psal.* 50.10, preached during the early stages of
the Pelagian controversy, p. 250.

21. The lector for the service had misunderstood the instructions and used
this psalm instead of the one Augustine intended (and was prepared) to explain. The preacher took the apparently innocent error as a divine prompt to
address this text. Perhaps to buy a little time, he began with a review of his
method in interpreting the Psalms. *Psal.* 62.1–2.

22. *Psal.* 44.3; 148.8; *Serm.* 161.1.1; *Serm. Dolb.* 26(198 augm).43; *Ep. Io.* 1.2;
2.2. Augustine could speak of the angels as members of the City of God but
not of the body of Christ. See *Serm.* 23.10; *Serm. Dolb.* 22(341 augm).19; *Ciu.*
11.25; 16.5; 22.29.

23. *Psal.* 62.23; *Serm. Dolb.* 22(341augm).19.

24. E.g., *Psal.* 30.2.1.3–4, 2.2.1, 2.3.5; *Serm.* 261.7.

25. See, in particular, the treatment in the chapter on the redemption, pp.
204–5.

26. *Psal.* 138.2. See the section below on the Savior as exclusive mediator,
pp. 263–66.

27. Below, pp. 268–79. See *Serm.* 71.16.26–27 for divine operation in human
operations.

28. *Psal.* 32.2.1.4; 142.3; *Serm.* 361.14.14.

29. *Psal.* 142.3; *Serm.* 395.1; *Serm. Denis* 8(260A).4.

30. *Psal.* 62.2.

31. See above, pp. 256–58.

32. *Eu. Io.* 12.9; *Psal.* 100.3; 142.3; *Serm.* 144.4.5.

33. *Psal.* 88.1.5.

34. See above, pp. 201–3.

35. *Psal.* 142.3; 138.21.

36. *Psal.* 62.5.

37. *Psal.* 62.17–18.

38. *Psal.* 44.3; 90.2.5; *Ep. Io.* 1.2.

39. *Psal.* 18.2.10; 30.2.1.4; 34.2.1; 40.1; 55.3; 68.2.1; 71.17; 74.4; 138.2; 140.3;
Serm. 45.5; 362.14.16; *Serm. Dolb.* 22(341 augm).20; *Eu. Io.* 9.10.

40. *Serm. Dolb.* 22(341 augm).19.

41. *Serm.* 144.4.5.

42. *Eu. Io.* 49.18.

43. *Psal.* 48.2.3; 62.2.

44. In faith: *Serm.* 362.14.15. In hope: *Psal.* 70.2.10; *Serm.* 395.1; *Serm. Denis* 8(260A).4. In love: *Serm. Mai* 98(263A).1. In spirit: *Serm.* 362.20.23.

45. *Eu. Io.* 14.9; 26.13; 39.5; *Serm. Guelf.* 11(229G).5.

46. *Serm.* 267.4; 268.2.

47. *Eu. Io.* 14.9; 18.4; *Psal.* 131.5.

48. *Eu. Io.* 26.13.

49. See above, pp. 208–9, 257. Except in its identification with the City of God, which, unlike the body of Christ included the faithful angels. See above, p. 346 n. 22.

50. *Psal.* 44.3; 148.8; *Serm.* 161.1.1; *Serm. Dolb.* 26(198 augm).43; *Ep. Io.* 1.2; 2.2.

51. Origen's two homilies on Psalm 15 provide a full exposition of the practice and its foundations. Origen, *Homilies of the Psalms: Codex Monacensis Graecus 314*, trans. Joseph Wilson Trigg (Washington, DC: Catholic University of America Press, 2020), 37–75.

52. *Psal.* 122.1.

53. Divine: *Eu. Io.* 26.19; *Psal.* 29.2.2; 100.3; 103.4.8; 117.22; 142.3; *Serm.* 47.21; 293.7; 361.16.16–17.16; *Serm. Dolb.* 22(341 augm).2, 11–14; 26(198 augm).40, 49. Human: *Psal.* 3.10; 29.2.2–3; *Serm.* 174.2.2; *Serm. Dolb.* 26(198 augm).44, 61.

54. *Serm.* 47.12; *Serm. Dolb.* 26(198 augm).36.

55. *Psal.* 29.2.1; *Serm.* 293.7. As Son, a lower divine being might be imagined as a mediator between humanity and the fully divine Father but not, as the scriptural text states, between God—the Trinity—and humans.

56. *Serm. Dolb.* 22(341 augm).11.

57. *Eu. Io.* 16.7; *Psal.* 104.10; 117.22; *Serm.* 26.7, 12.

58. *Psal.* 103.4.8; *Serm.* 293.7; *Serm. Dolb.* 26(198 augm).49.

59. *Serm.* 81.6; *Serm. Dolb.* 26(198 augm).49; *Psal.* 103.4.8.

60. *Psal.* 134.5; *Serm.* 121.5.

61. *Serm.* 121.5; 240.4; *Serm. Dolb.* 26(198 augm).39.

62. *Eu. Io.* 12.8; see also *Serm.* 91.6.7; 144.4.5; 293.7; 294.10.10; 362.14.16; *Serm. Mai* 98(263A).3; *Psal.* 26.2.8.

63. *Psal.* 134.5; *Eu. Io.* 47.3.

64. *Serm. Dolb.* 26(198 augm).36–39.

65. *Eu. Io.* 41.5; *Psal.* 103.4.8; *Serm. Dolb.* 26(198 augm).36.

66. *Serm. Dolb.* 26(198 augm).39–41; *Serm.* 361.16.16–17.16.

67. *Psal.* 90.2.1; *Serm.* 26.12.

68. *Psal.* 90.2.1; 117.22; *Serm.* 26.12; 156.5.5; *Serm. Dolb.* 26(198 augm).44.

69. Parmenian of Carthage was probably elaborating a claim of Cyprian that the bishop, rather than the martyr, was the true intercessor for Christians

who had failed during the Decian persecution. See Burns and Jensen, Christianity in Roman Africa, 324–28.

70. *Psal.* 19.2.4; 29.2.1; *Serm. Dolb.* 26(198 augm).53–54.

71. *Serm. Dolb.* 26(198 augm).54; see the parallel in *Serm.* 75.1.1–2.3.

72. Rom. 8:34; *Serm. Dolb.* 26(198 augm).55.

73. *Serm. Dolb.* 26(198 augm).49.

74. *Serm. Dolb.* 26(198 augm).53–54.

75. *Serm. Dolb.* 26(198 augm).57. See also *Psal.* 26.2.2 for the relation between Christ and the church.

76. See above, p. 181.

77. *Eu. Io.* 5.6–7; 6.15. These sermons were preached in the winter of 406–7.

78. *Eu. Io.* 19.14–15.

79. *Eu. Io.* 19.15–16. If Christ were to judge only the just, the human engagement would have been unnecessary.

80. *Eu. Io.* 19.16. M.-F. Berrouard dated the set of sermons to which this exposition belongs to the summer of 414. See above, p. 310 n. 48. See Pierre-Marie Hombert, *Nouvelles Recherches de Chronologie Augustinienne*, Collection des Études Augustiniennes, Série Antiquité 163 (Paris: Institut d'Études Augustiniennes, 2000), 385–86.

81. *Psal.* 74.5; *Eu. Io.* 28.6.

82. *Psal.* 74.5; see below, pp. 268–79.

83. For the late dating of this Sermon 71 in the period after 417, see Hombert, *Nouvelles Recherches*, 370n17. The perspective and context are different from that of the discussion of the transferring of the power to baptize in the commentaries on the Gospel of John, which are dated at least a decade earlier, in the winter of 406–7.

84. A literal translation of both the Latin and Greek terms used in Matt. 12:27; Luke 11:19.

85. *Serm.* 71.1.2–3. Although Augustine offered no justification for the interpretation in this sermon, elsewhere, he connected the judging role of these exorcists to that of the disciples judging Israel (Matt. 19:28) in *Adu. Iud.* 11; *Ciu.* 20.5. The interpretation could have been based on the prior mission of the disciples and the prediction that they would be identified, as the Savior was, as demonic. See Matt. 10:8, 25.

86. *Serm.* 71.12.19.

87. *Serm.* 71.12.18–14.24.

88. *Serm.* 71.15.25.

89. *Serm.* 71.16.26–27.

90. *Serm.* 71.17.28–29.

91. *Serm.* 71.20.33. The role of the church will be taken up in the following section.

92. In *Eu. Io.* 19.17, he distinguished the power of Christ as Son of Man over the just and unjust, all of whom would rise and come forth from the tombs, from his power as Son of God over the just, who would come forth to life. See above, pp. 266–67.

93. *Psal.* 32.2.2.29.

94. *Psal.* 47.8; 131.13; 146.9; 147.20, 23, 26.

95. *Eu. Io.* 5–7.

96. *Eu. Io.* 5.5–15. See above, pp. 173–76.

97. *Eu. Io.* 6.7–12, 14–15, 20–21; 7.1–3.

98. *Serm.* 269.2; *Serm. Denis* 8(260A).3–4; *Psal.* 48.2.1.

99. *Eu. Io.* 12.9; *Serm.* 294.10.10.

100. *Serm.* 294.10.11–11.12, 17.17–19.17.

101. *Serm.* 71.19.32–23.37.

102. *Serm.* 294.11.12, 17.17–19.17. See above, pp. 92–93, 230–31.

103. See Cypr., *Unit. eccl.* 4–5; *Ep.* 43.5.2, 4; 57.1.1–2.2.

104. *Serm.* 99.9; 82.4.7; 295.2.2; *Serm. Lamb.* 3. See the discussion of the power of forgiveness, pp. 169–70.

105. *Serm.* 83.1.1, 2.2, 6.7; *Serm. Frang.* 9(114A).2, 5.

106. *Psal.* 103.1.19; 129.3–5; 147.13; *Serm.* 56.10.14; 71.15.25; 114.5.

107. *Serm.* 316.3–4; 317.6.5. The church as a whole prayed for the forgiveness of its members performing the rituals of repentance. *Serm.* 392.3.

108. *Serm.* 71.1.3. The text of Matt. 12:27 refers to the other exorcists as "your children," and Jesus was responding to a charge made by the Pharisees. Yet Augustine interpreted it as a reference to his own disciples, both present and future. This indicated his commitment to the Christians' sharing in the power to forgive. He did the same in *Ep.* 186.31; *Ciu.* 20.5; *Adu. Iud.* 11. See above, p. 344 n. 85.

109. *Serm.* 99.9; 295.2.2; *Psal.* 108.1; 149.7. See above, pp. 165–67.

110. *Serm.* 71.20.33; *Eu. Io.* 18.4; 39.5.

111. *Eu. Io.* 14.9; *Psal.* 132.2; *Serm. Guelf.* 11(229G).5; *Serm.* 71.12.18, 17.28–29, 21.35.

112. *Serm.* 71.11.17, 19.32. Augustine was particularly harsh in his criticism of the congregation's rejection of a convert whose motives they suspected as unworthy. *Serm.* 296.13–15. See above, p. 69.

113. *Eu. Io.* 26.15, 17; *Psal.* 45.9; *Serm.* 71.17.28, 19.32–21.34, 23.37; 271.

114. Or the dove *Serm.* 295.2.2. This term is more regularly used in the treatise *Bapt.* 3.17.22–18.23; 5.21.29; 6.40.78; 7.44.87–45.89, 49.97, 51.99.

115. *Serm.* 71.19.32; *Eu. Io.* 50.12; *Serm. Guelf.* 16(229N).2.

116. A similar consideration would have maintained the unicity or unique-ness of the baptism when administered by a sinful minister inside or outside the visible communion of the church. The one baptism of Christ was conferred and received by both good and evil ministers and candidates, although Augus-tine does not seem to have addressed it in his preaching. See *Bapt.* 7.53.101–2 and the discussion in J. Patout Burns and Robin Margaret Jensen, *Christianity in Roman Africa: The Development of Its Practices and Beliefs* (Grand Rapids: Eerdmans, 2014), 213–14.

117. The minister of baptism, in Augustine's theory, could claim no contri-bution to the efficacy of the ritual; only the intention to baptize was necessary. To participate in the divine power to forgive (and to be forgiven their own sins), Christians had to forgive the offenses committed against them and, if necessary, to take the initiative in the process of reconciliation.

118. *Serm.* 211.4; 386.1–2. See above, p. 63.

119. These sermons are relatively brief and seem to have been delivered during the eucharistic ritual itself, after the unbaptized had been dismissed.

120. *Serm.* 161.1.1–2.2. For a fuller discussion, see above, pp. 105–6, 131.

121. *Serm.* 227; *Serm. Guelf.* 7(229A).1; *Eu. Io.* 26.13–14.

122. *Serm.* 272.

123. *Serm. Guelf.* 7(229A).1. Augustine quoted the text with its introductory "because" only twice in his corpus: *Eu. Io.* 26.14 and *Ep.* 185.11.50. In every other citation, he made the shared bread a symbol of the one body of Christ. See also *Ciu.* 21.25, CCSL 48:794.30–31.

124. *Eu. Io.* 26.18; 27.1, 6.

125. *Eu. Io.* 26.15–18. Augustine here explained that the saints were the pre-destined (Rom. 8:30). They had been converted, joined to Christ, were living as his members, and would be preserved from failure, so that they reached salvation, see also *Psal.* 131.13; 146.9; 147.20, 23, 26. In the parallel statements in *Bapt.* 3.17.22–18.23, 19.26, and 6.3.5–5.7, his language was more ambiguous.

126. *Eu. Io.* 27.6; 26.17.

127. *Serm.* 161.1.1–2.2.

128. *Serm.* 272. Augustine offered the monks and nuns as contemporary examples of the attempt to realize a single person as a community through the sharing of property: one heart and one soul in many bodies. *Psal.* 132.6; *Serm. Dolb.* 26(198 augm).48. The giving of alms to the poor was a way in which families could participate in this practice. *Serm.* 41.6–7; 389.6.

129. *Serm. Dolb.* 26(198 augm).49, 53–54; *Psal.* 36.2.20.

130. *Psal.* 42.5; 130.4; *Eu. Io.* 17.11.

131. *Serm. Dolb.* 26(198 augm).57.

132. *Psal.* 26.2.2; *Serm. Dolb.* 26(198 augm).49–51, 53, 57.

133. *Serm. Dolb.* 26(198 augm).49.

134. Augustine vigorously rejected the Donatist claim that the Christian bishop served as a mediator between God and the congregation. *Serm. Dolb.* 26(198 augm).36–63.

135. See above, pp. 175–76.

136. *Psal.* 42.6–7; 87.3; 93.19; 142.9; *Eu. Io.* 52.1.

137. *Psal.* 93.19; 63.18; 31.2.26; *Serm.* 31.3; 40.6; *Eu. Io.* 52.2.

138. *Psal.* 31.2.26; 63.18; 87.3; 93.19; 103.3.11; 140.4; 142.9; *Serm.* 31.3; 40.6; 305.2–4; *Eu. Io.* 52.3.

139. *Eu. Io.* 52.1–3.

140. *Psal.* 37.27; 43.2; 140.5–7.

141. *Psal.* 21.1.1; 37.27; 58.1.2; 62.2; 68.2.11; 70.1.12; 140.5.

142. *Psal.* 70.1.11; *Serm.* 336.5; *Serm. Guelf.* 4(223B).1; *Serm. frg. Verbr.* 29(228A).

143. *Eu. Io.* 19.14–16. See above, pp. 266–67.

144. *Psal.* 74.5; see also *Psal.* 85.22; *Eu. Io.* 28.6.

145. *Serm.* 351.4.8; *Psal.* 149.10; 86.4; 90.1.9.

146. *Psal.* 49.8; 90.1.9; *Serm.* 351.4.8.

147. *Psal.* 93.18; *Eu. Io.* 28.6.

148. *Psal.* 100.10. Augustine's Latin text read "will sit" from the Greek Septuagint rather than "will dwell" from the Hebrew.

149. *Psal.* 49.10; 90.1.9; 100.10; *Eu. Io.* 28.6. He qualified this as applying only to the judgment of the evil angels; the saints would be equals and not the judges of the good angels who accompanied Christ. *Serm. Cail.* 2.11(112A).13.

150. *Serm.* 188.3.4; *Serm. Dolb.* 22(341 augm).12; *Psal.* 90.2.9; 147.10; *Eu. Io.* 13.12.

151. *Eu. Io.* 9.2.

152. *Psal.* 145.18.

153. They were joined to the celibates in charity. *Psal.* 121.10.

154. See above, p. 270 n. 100 and pp. 92–93.

155. *Serm.* 51.13.22; *Serm. Dolb.* 12(354A).7–9.

156. In his surviving sermons, he did not make the attempts to explain the relations of the personal unions and the natures in ways that approached what he attempted for the Trinitarian persons or single nature in *Serm.* 52; 117; 118; *Serm. Denis* 2(223A) or the shared external operations in *Serm.* 71.

157. *Serm.* 161.1.1–2.2.

158. *Psal.* 148.8.

159. *Psal.* 44.3.

160. *Serm. Dolb.* 26(198 augm).43; *Ep. Io.* 1.2.

161. *Eu. Io.* 2.2.

162. See above, pp. 198–203.

163. See above, pp. 130, 217.

164. *Eu. Io.* 19.14–16; 28.6; *Psal.* 74.5.

165. *Serm.* 161.1.1–2.2.

166. *Eu. Io.* 26.13 had used the principle that a human soul can animate only its own body to discount the life-giving power of the presence and reception of the humanity of Christ in the eucharist. See above, pp. 116–17, 130.

167. *Eu. Io.* 14.9; 18.4; 39.5; 26.13; *Serm.* 71.21.35; *Serm. Guelf.* 11(229G).5.

168. *Serm.* 267.4; 268.2; *Psal.* 122.1.

169. *Eu. Io.* 14.9; 18.4; 39.5; *Serm. Guelf.* 11(229G).2.

170. *Serm.* 71.21.35; *Eu. Io.* 39.5.

171. *Eu. Io.* 26.13; 39.5.

172. *Eu. Io.* 14.9; 18.4; *Serm. Guelf.* 11(229G).5.

173. In *Serm.* 169.12.15–13.16, he contrasted God to an unwelcome and overbearing houseguest whose family and retainers push a family out of its own dwelling. In *Serm.* 71.16.26–27, he illustrated the complementarity of divine and human operation in the Savior's walking on the sea.

174. *Serm.* 272; a parallel in forming the Christians into a holy temple, *Psal.* 131.5.

175. See above, pp. 129–30.

176. *Eu. Io.* 3.12; *Serm.* 293.12; 294.14.15–15.15.

177. *Serm. Guelf.* 31(335B).1. During the prior period, he had appealed to this unity in *Psal.* 84.7.

178. *Serm.* 165.5.6–7.9.

179. *Serm.* 174.8.9; 294.16.16, 17.17–19.17; *Psal.* 50.10; see esp. *Serm.* 154.7.10.

180. *Serm.* 128.3.5; 154.11.16.

181. This Adamic identity may have been initially proposed in *Serm.* 294.14.15–15.15, preached in Carthage in June 413.

182. See above, p. 11.

A NOTE FOR INSTRUCTORS ON FURTHER READING

I F YOU WISH TO ASSIGN RELATED READING in English translations of the primary texts, or to read such translations for yourself, the good news is that, with some few exceptions, translations of all texts studied here are available. In particular, all of Augustine's preached works have been published in the third part of The Works of Saint Augustine: A Translation for the 21st Century by New City Press. The bad news is that these works are published in twenty volumes, only some of which are available in paperback. Many college and university libraries subscribe to and own the full set. In addition, these same libraries may have an electronic version accessible in the Past Masters database.

New City Press has also published three volumes of selected letters, sermons, and expositions of the Psalms in paperback. *Essential Sermons* includes about 30 percent of the texts to which this study refers. *Essential Expositions of the Psalms* includes about 16 percent of the texts. The homilies on the Gospel and First Letter of John are published complete in three paperback volumes.

Below are provided suggestions of texts that might prove particularly useful for reading with each chapter of this study. These would be available in the full series publication and database. Recommended sermons that are found in the *Essential* volumes are indicated by italics.

1. Interpreting the Scripture
Psal. 85 WSA 3/18:220–45

2. Riches and Poverty
Serm. 61 WSA 3/3:142–49
Psal. 72 WSA 3/17:470–92
Serm. 38 WSA 3/2:208–15

3. Sin and Forgiveness
Serm. 98 WSA 3/4:43–48
Serm. 82 WSA 3/3:369–78

4. Baptism
Serm. 99 WSA3/4:50–58
Serm. 266 WSA 3/7:283–86

5. Eucharist
Serm. 229 WSA 3/6:265–67
Serm. 272 WSA 3/7:300–301
Tractates on John 26 WSA 3/12:449–65

6. Marriage
Serm. 392 WSA 3/10:421–24
Serm. 51 WSA 3/3:33–36

7. The Ministry of the Clergy
Serm. Dolb. 26.49–63 WSA 3/11:218–28

8. The Saving Work of Christ
Psal. 21.2 WSA 3/15:227–43
Serm. 134 WSA 3/4:341–44
Serm. 152 WSA 3/5:48–55

9. The Human Situation
Serm. Dolb. 26.25–33 WSA 3/11:25–33
Serm 294 WSA 3/8: 108–95
Serm 128 WSA 3/4:293–301
Serm 169 3/5:222–35

10. Christ and the Church
Psal. 140.1–8 WSA 3/20:301–8
Serm. 267 WSA 3/7:274–76
Serm. 71 WSA 3/3:246–70

Bibliography of Secondary Sources Cited

Babcock, William S., translator. *Tyconius: The Book of Rules*. Atlanta: Scholars Press, 1989.

Barja de Quiroga, Pedro López. "Patronage and Slavery in the Roman World: The Circle of Power." In *The Oxford Handbook of Greek and Roman Slaveries*, edited by Stephen Hodkinson, Marc Kleijweft, and Kostas Vlassopoulos. New York: Oxford University Press, 2020. https://doi.org /10.1093/oxfordhb/9780199575251.013.31.

Berrouard, Marie-François. *Introduction aux Homélies de Saint Augustin sur l'Évangile de Saint Jean*. Collection des Études Augustiniennes, Série Antiquité 170. Paris: Institut d'Études Augustiniennes, 2004.

———. "La Date des Tractatus I–LIV in Iohannis Evangelium de Saint Augustin." *Recherches Augustiniennes* 7 (1971): 107–19.

———. "L'Exégèse Augustinienne de Rom., 7, 7–25." *Recherches Augustiniennes* 16 (1981): 101–95.

Brown, Peter. *Through the Eye of a Needle: Wealth, the Fall of Rome, and the Making of Christianity in the West, 350–550 AD*. Princeton: Princeton University Press, 2012.

Bruyn, Theodore S. de, Stephen A. Cooper, and David G. Hunter. Introduction to *Ambrosiaster's Commentary on the Pauline Epistles: Romans*, edited by Theodore S. de Bruyn, xxiii–cxxx. Writings from the Greco-Roman World 41. Atlanta: SBL Press, 2017.

Burns, J. Patout. "How Christ Saves: Augustine's Multiple Explanations." In *Tradition and the Rule of Faith in the Early Church*, edited by Ronnie J. Rombs and Alexander Y. Hwang, 193–210. Washington, DC: Catholic University of America Press, 2010.

———. "Marital Fidelity as a *remedium concupiscentiae*: An Augustinian Proposal." *Augustinian Studies* 44 (2013): 1–35.

———. "Situating and Studying Augustine's Sermons." *Journal of Early Christian Studies* 26 (2018): 307–22.

Burns, J. Patout, and Robin Margaret Jensen. *Christianity in Roman Africa: The Development of Its Practices and Beliefs.* Grand Rapids: Eerdmans, 2014.

Cameron, Michael. *Christ Meets Me Everywhere: Augustine's Early Figurative Exegesis.* Oxford Studies in Historical Theology. New York: Oxford University Press, 2012.

———. "Enarrationes in Psalmos." In Fitzgerald, *Augustine through the Ages*, 290–96.

Dolbeau, François. "Le Sermon 348A de Saint Augustin contre Pélage: Édition du Texte Intégral." *Recherches Augustiniennes* 28 (1995): 37–63.

Dolbeau, François, ed. *Augustin d'Hippone, Vingt-six Sermons au Peuple d'Afrique.* Collection des Études Augustiniennes, Série Antiquité 147. Paris: Institut d'Études Augustiniennes, 2009.

Drecoll, Volker. "The Exegesis of Romans 7 in *Serm. Morin* 4(154A)." In Partoens, Dupont, and Lamberigts, *Ministerium Sermonis*, 143–56.

Drobner, Hubertus R. *Augustinus von Hippo: Sermones ad Populum.* New York: Lang, 2010.

Dupont, Anthony. *Gratia in Augustine's* Sermones Ad Populum *during the Pelagian Controversy: Do Different Contexts Furnish Different Insights?* Brill's Series in Church History 59. Leiden: Brill, 2013.

Fiedrowicz, Michael. Introduction to *Expositions of the Psalms, 1–32*, edited by John E. Rotelle, 13–66. WSA III/15. Hyde Park, NY: New City Press, 2000.

Fitzgerald, Allan D. "In Johannis Evangelium Tractatus." In Fitzgerald, *Augustine through the Ages*, 474–75.

———. Introduction to *Homilies on the Gospel of John*, edited by John E. Rotelle, 13–38. WSA III/12. Hyde Park, NY: New City Press, 2009.

Fitzgerald, Allan D., ed. *Augustine through the Ages: An Encyclopedia.* Grand Rapids: Eerdmans, 1999.

Grubbs, Judith Evans. *Women and the Law in the Roman Empire: A Sourcebook on Marriage, Divorce, and Widowhood.* London: Routledge, 2002.

Harmless, William. *Augustine and the Catechumenate.* Collegeville, MN: Liturgical Press, 1995.

Hombert, Pierre-Marie. *Nouvelles Recherches de Chronologie Augustinienne.* Collection des Études Augustiniennes, Série Antiquité 163. Paris: Institut d'Études Augustiniennes, 2000.

Houghton, H. A. G. "Scripture and Latin Christian Manuscripts from North Africa." In *The Bible in Christian North Africa*, Part 1: *Commencement to the Confessions of Augustine*, edited by Jonathan P. Yates and Anthony Dupont, 15–49. Berlin: de Gruyter, 2020.

Hunter, David G. "Augustine, Sermon 354A*: Its Place in His Thought on Marriage and Sexuality." *Augustinian Studies* 33, no. 1 (2002): 39–60.

Jensen, Robin Margaret. "Recovering Ancient Ecclesiology: The Place of the Altar and the Orientation of Prayer in the Early Latin Church." *Worship* 89 (March 2015): 99–124.

Kelly, J. N. D. *Early Christian Creeds*. 3rd ed. London: Continuum, 2006.

Kunzelmann, Adalbero. "Die Chronologie der Sermones des hl. Augustinus." In *Miscellanea Agostiniana*, ed. Germain Morin and Antonio Casamassa, 2:417–520. Rome: Typis Polyglottis Vaticanis, 1930–31.

La Bonnardière, Anne-Marie. *Biblia Augustiniana: A. T.: Le Livre de la Sagesse*. Collection des Études Augustiniennes, Série Antiquité 42. Paris: Institut d'Études Augustiniennes, 1970.

——. "Les Enarrationes in Psalmos Prêchées par Saint Augustin à Carthage en Décembre 409." *Recherches Augustiniennes* 11 (1976): 52–90.

——. *Recherches de Chronologie Augustinienne*. Collection des Études Augustiniennes, Série Antiquité 23. Paris: Institut d'Études Augustiniennes, 1965.

Lössel, Josef. "Dating Augustine's Sermons 151–156: Internal Evidence." In Partoens, *Sermones de Novo Testamento (151–156)*, xxiii–lv.

Mayer, Cornelius Petrus, ed. *Corpus Augustinianum Gissense*. Basel: Schwabe, 2013.

O'Connell, Robert J. *The Origin of the Soul in St. Augustine's Later Works*. New York: Fordham University Press, 1987.

——. *St. Augustine's Early Theory of Man, A.D. 386–391*. Cambridge, MA: Harvard University Press, 1968.

Partoens, Gert. "Augustine's *Sermo* 169: Correction of Two Misinterpretations and Proposal of a New Date." In Partoens, Dupont, and Lamberigts, *Ministerium Sermonis*, 69–95.

——. "La Datation des Sermons 151–156." In Partoens, *Sermones de Novo Testamento (151–156)*, ix–xxii.

Partoens, Gert, ed. *Sermones de Novo Testamento (151–156)*. CCSL 41Ba. Turnhout: Brepols, 2008.

Partoens, Gert, Anthony Dupont, and Mathijs Lamberigts, eds. *Ministerium Sermonis: Philological, Historical, and Theological Studies on Augustine's*

"Sermones ad Populum." Instrumenta Patristica et Mediaevalia 53. Turnhout: Brepols, 2009.

Pellegrino, Michele. Introduction to *Sermons, 1–19*, edited by John E. Rotelle, 13–83. WSA III/1. Hyde Park, NY: New City Press, 1990.

Perler, Othmar, and Jean-Louis Maier. *Les Voyages de Saint Augustin*. Collection des Études Augustiniennes, Série Antiquité 36. Paris: Institut d'Études Augustiniennes, 1969.

Pogue, Suzanne. "Trois Semaines de Prédication à Hippone en Février-Mars 407." *Recherches Augustiniennes* 7 (1971): 169–87.

Rebillard, Éric. "Sermones." In Fitzgerald, *Augustine through the Ages*, 773–92.

Rondeau, Marie-Josèph. *Les Commentaires Patristiques du Psautier*. Orientalia Christiana Analecta 219–20. Rome: Pontificale Institutum Studiorum Orientalium, 1982.

Savon, Hervé. *Saint Ambroise devant l'Exégèse de Philon le Juif*. Collection des Études Augustiniennes, Série Antiquité 72–73. Paris: Institut d'Études Augustiniennes, 1977.

Trigg, Joseph Wilson, trans. Origen, *Homilies of the Psalms: Codex Monacensis Graecus 314*. Washington, DC: Catholic University of America Press, 2020.

Verbraken, Pierre-Patrick. "Le Sermon 57 de Saint Augustin pour la Tradition de l'Oraison Dominicale." In *Homo Spiritualis: Festgabe für Luc Verheijen zu seinem 70. Geburtstag*, edited by Cornelius Petrus Mayer and Karl Heinz Chelius, 411–24. Würzburg: Augustinus Verlag, 1987.

Vössing, Konrad. "Saint Augustin et l'Ecole Antique: Traditions et Ruptures." In *Saint Augustin: Africanité et Universalité: Actes du Colloque International*, edited by Pierre-Yves Fux, Jean-Michel Roessli, and Otto Wermelinger, 1:153–66. Fribourg: Éditions Universitaires, 2003.

Wright, David. "The Manuscripts of St. Augustine's *Tractatus in Euangelium Iohannis*: A Preliminary Survey and Checklist." *Recherches Augustiniennes* 8 (1972): 55–143.

Zarb, Seraphim M. *Chronologia Enarrationum S. Augustini in Psalmos*. Valletta: St. Dominic's Priory, 1948.

INDEX OF AUTHORS

INDEX OF SUBJECTS

Jacob, 96, 140, 198; and Esau, 61, 282

Jerusalem, 30, 32, 88, 160, 190, 224, 274, 278, 281

Job, 25, 58

John the Baptist, 21, 31, 74, 94, 161–62, 228–29, 270

Jonah, 55, 56

Joseph, 154, 227

Joshua, 227

Judas, 62; participation in eucharist, 127, 129, 162; represents evil in church, 115, 168; role in redemption, 191, 196, 201

judgment by God, 54

judgment of Christ: Christians participating, 53, 277; delayed, 52, 56; evading, 53–54

justice of God, 67

justification, 240; of elect, 120; human righteousness, 240–41; partial, 237–38

keys, power of, 71–72, 165–67; belongs to whole church, 72; exercised by intercession, 72; Peter's reception of, 72,

kingdom of God, 52–53; charity necessary for, 52; salvation broader than, 52–53, 91–93, 229

Last Supper, 115

law, Israelite sacrificial, 56. *See also* Mosaic law: sacrificial practices

law, moral; fulfilled only with grace, 239; intended to manifest sin, 56, 239, 249; power of sin, 239–40; provoked resistance, 240; recognized as good, 239; transgression added, 240. *See also* Mosaic law

law of sin. *See* sin, law of

Lazarus, beggar, 25, 74

Lazarus of Bethany, 57, 68–69, 71, 81, 82, 164

literal interpretation of scripture, 13, 21

Lord's Prayer, forgiveness, 58–60, 67, 74, 79, 145, 271

love: of God and commanded good, 220–21, 236; law of, 9, 236–37; necessary for good action, 236. *See also* charity

lust, 227, 333n74; in marriage, 140; and original sin, 215, 218–19. *See also* concupiscence

manna: eucharistic, 86, 114, 116

marriage: bond, 147–48; concession of a lesser good, 143; contract (Roman), 141, 157; divorce for wife's adultery, 148; forgiveness within, 65, 278; for wealth, 149. *See also* family

marriage, sexual practice, 140–47; abstinence (temporary), 142; clerical, 145; concession of excessive, 142–43, 146; consequences of sin, 140; continence, 142, 145–47, 154; for generation alone, 141–43, 147; lust as punishment for sin, 140; managing lust, 143–45, 154; mortality and generation, 140; patriarchs as models, 140, 145

marriage of Christ and church, 145, 150–55, 278; and body of Christ, 151; Christian participation in, 154–56; Christ leaving synagogue, 153; continent marriage, 151; Eve drawn from side and "One Flesh," 152–54; for generation, 156; and marriage

Index of Scripture References